The CORBA Reference Guide

Understanding the Common Object Request Broker Architecture

Alan Pope

ADDISON-WESLEY

An imprint of Addison Wesley Longman, Inc.

Reading, Massachusetts • Harlow, England • Menlo Park, California

Berkeley, California • Don Mills, Ontario • Sydney

Bonn • Amsterdam • Tokyo • Mexico City

Many of the designations used by manufacturers and sellers to distinguish their products are claimed as trademarks. Where those designations appear in this book and Addison-Wesley was aware of a trademark claim, the designations have been printed in initial caps or all caps.

The author and publishers have taken care in the preparation of this book, but make no expressed or implied warranty of any kind and assume no responsibility for errors or omissions. No liability is assumed for incidental or consequential damages in connection with or arising out of the use of the information or programs contained herein.

The publisher offers discounts on this book when ordered in quantity for special sales. For more information, please contact:

Corporate & Professional Publishing Group
Addison Wesley Longman, Inc.
One Jacob Way
Reading, Massachusetts 01867

Library of Congress Cataloging-in-Publication Data

Pope, Alan, 1954–
    The CORBA reference guide : understanding the common object
request broker architecture / Alan Pope
      p.   cm.
    Includes bibliographical references and index.
    ISBN 0-201-63386-8 (alk. paper)
    1. CORBA (Computer architecture)   2. Object-oriented programming
(Computer science) I. Title
QA76.64.P66   1997
005.2'73'0218--dc21   97-38067
                                             CIP

ISBN 0-201-63386-8

Text printed on recycled and acid-free paper.

1 2 3 4 5 6 7 8 9 10 –MA– 01 00 99 98 97

First printing, *December 1997*

The CORBA
Reference Guide

I dedicate this book, with love, to my foundation and inspiration,
Fern and LaMont Pope,
Opal and Lorenzo Hugh Shepherd,
and Ashley Collette Pope.

Contents

Foreword

The poet in Alan Pope begins this book with a quote from de Unamuno: "The noblest function of an object is to be contemplated." Sartre would be proud. More important, the average software engineer would be pleased to find the play on not only the word *object* but also the word *function*. I suppose there's a method in this madness! Clever literary parallels aside, I must disagree with the characterization. In fact, the noblest function of an object is to be composed. The power of object systems, especially in the heterogeneous, distributed world in which we live, is found in the reduction of complexity that comes from well-described interfaces and ways to compose those structures. But, of course, Alan is well aware of this fact.

Having participated in the birth of the Common Object Request Broker Architecture from 1989 to 1991, the author knows the decisions and compromises that went into that design. As anyone who follows politics knows, consensus-building is hard; consensus-building of a technical foundation is even harder. For eight years now, the Object Management Group has fostered that consensus-building, and the central products of that process are the CORBA architecture itself and the surrounding services that this book describes. And in what detail! This book blazes the path as a reference guide.

Building on an account of the original development of OMG and CORBA, we see here in extreme detail not only structure, but the reasons for that structure; interfaces and complete descriptions of those interfaces; and clear definitions of why the parts make up the whole. Distributed systems with secure interoperability and transaction semantics are difficult to understand—this book makes them reachable targets.

Leafing through this book gives one a feel for the monumental efforts made by worldwide organizations, such as CNN, Her Majesty's Customs and Immigration Service, Hong Kong Telecom, and others, in putting CORBA-based systems in place before the current flood of books on the topic. Fortunately, the reader need not go through that painful process, as he or she has an encyclopedic reference in hand.

The Object Management Group continues to operate; in fact, it is busier than ever before. Besides the need to correct errors and expand the basic infrastructure this book covers, the OMG is actively engaged in leveraging that infrastructure to define portable and interoperable standards for vertical market IT support interfaces; areas include telecommunications systems, health-care and patient records, intermodal transportation systems, financial and insurance instruments, public utility systems, and so forth.

As Alan points out here, this is a never-ending process and any single-point attempt to capture that activity is doomed to failure (personally, I blame Mr. Nyquist). Nevertheless, this reference guide provides a strong foundation for building enterprise distributed systems.

Richard Mark Soley, Ph.D.
Object Management Group, Inc.

Preface

The motivation to write this book came from a desire to help people understand CORBA and its basis. A great deal of misunderstanding arose in the first few years after CORBA appeared. In the time it took to write this book, however, many people became aware of and well informed about CORBA. The misstatements heard today are not nearly as prevalent as they once were. Still, I believe the need for a book such as this has not gone away.

Today people have a number of requests for features they want to see become part of CORBA. Occasionally these features have been given a great deal of consideration before being discarded or shelved. This book tries to record some of the thoughts behind the discarding of several ideas. It does not attempt to examine all of them because that would be an immense task. Rather, the most fundamental appear here.

This book is for system architects, designers, and programmers, specifically those working in information systems. It is not a programming guide. Instead, it provides a general background and reference to the architecture and various services. I suspect programmers will find this background material useful but not very meaty. The intent is to present CORBA with enough detail and background to help people fully understand and properly utilize its features.

This book started out as an explication for system managers and architects, but then several such books came onto the market. A more in-depth reference instead of a cursory explanation became more interesting. As more and more people began committing substantial resources to constructing systems using this technology, it became obvious that someone was appropriately informing management.

The Object Management Group (OMG) submission adoptions include details for both application builders and those implementing Object Request Brokers (ORBs). Frequently the bias is more toward ORB implementers. I attempt to remove most of this unless it is important for a good understanding. In some cases, I may have included too little or too much of this auxiliary information.

A separate book that gives good application examples is desirable. Documenting all aspects of the architecture and providing coding examples for each would be an extremely large and complex task. Either the examples or the descriptive content would suffer. In the future, it is more likely we will see books that either focus primarily on examples, or books that select some subset of the entire architecture, each concentrating on a different area of emphasis and focus.

A number of factors made this book hard to write. For one thing, the rate of adoption of proposals and their complexity is rapidly increasing. It is much harder to stay completely on top of every topic with so many different groups of people working in parallel. It also is impossible to capture in a single book every up-to-the-minute adoption because the production time leaves a window open for new technology that cannot be included. For the short term, anyway, this is a losing battle. The most current source of information is always at the OMG, within the submissions themselves.[1]

A second factor, for me, was unexpectedly becoming a single parent to my two-year-old daughter. With a full-time job at Quantitative Data Systems, Inc., the book was already a second full-time job. Finding myself suddenly with a third full-time job, priorities being what they are, the book became the lowest priority of the three. Had I known what would occur over the last two years, I most likely would have had the sense not to sign up to write a book, which is immensely time-consuming.

I am responsible for all errors that appear. Although some very astute people in this field gave me very sound advice, I may have totally misinterpreted or entirely missed their points. The people I name are not accountable for any of the book's content. They made their best attempt at making sure I understood things clearly. I made my best attempt to listen and incorporate their advice.

In some sense, I had the pleasure of building two ORBs while I was in the employ of Sun Microsystems. The first ORB was built in eight weeks by about sixteen engineers.[2] This is the original HP/Sun ORB that became

---

1. The OMG has a lot of publicly accessible papers available at http://www.omg.org

2. A lot of the groundwork, such as the IDL syntax and the products on which this ORB was based, have a much longer history (many years).

CORBA with the incorporation of the DII (from the DEC and Hyperdesk submission). This incorporation was the first submission merger and its revision was to appear in 90 days. Construction of this second ORB took much longer and involved quite a few more people.

Specifically, from the original eight-week stretch, I want to thank: Sally Ahnger, Dave Brownell, Steve Byrne, Alain Demour, Jacob Levy, Joe Pallas, Michael Powell, Sami Shaio, and Bart Smaalders. Unfortunately, there are several dozen others from my ORB-building period as well as from the time I was at Sun but both space and memory conspire against me, so this list is artificially short.

A number of people managed to read through my rough manuscript, something I still find quite astonishing. I can only thank and account for those that I know: Dr. Daniel R. Edelson, Bret Hartman, Jishnu Mukerji, Dr. Richard Mark Soley, Mark G. Wales, and Andreas Vogel.

Some folks also have no idea that they were contributing to anything. They require thanks, though, because they did. The following list of people either said something to cause an epiphany or clarified some aspect that had not previously been so clear (although the new clarity sometimes was 180 degrees from the original intent). They are Rick Catell, Ralph Johnson, Douglas Lea, Jeff Michinsky, Alan Snyder, Drew Wade, and Jim Waldo.

Certainly not least are the staff of Addison Wesley Longman who patiently waited for me to exhibit signs of life and made extremely valuable suggestions. Among them, certainly John Wait, Mike Hendrickson, Marina Lang, Katie Duffy, and Sarah Weaver deserve several rounds of applause. Both Marilyn Rash and Ann Hall deserve special thanks for helping to get this book in useful form.

My current employer, Quantitative Data Systems, Inc., probably deserves some award, specifically Jerry Conrad and Robert Morse, because writing this book sometimes took priority over my real job.

In addition, for helping me survive I'd like to give a special thanks to Lisa Walker, Louise Allen, and Charlotte Einar. Without the help they gave me I would never have been able to finish this book.

Last but never least, although she had little or no choice in the matter, I would like to thank Ashley, who got short shrift and not nearly as much attention as she deserves but loves me anyway.

List of Figures

List of Tables

CHAPTER 1 *Introduction*

> *By abstraction we mean the act of singling*
> *out a few properties of an object for further*
> *use or study, omitting from consideration*
> *other properties that don't concern us for the*
> *moment. The main property that we single out . . .*
> *is what it does; the main property that we omit*
> *from consideration is how it does it.*
> —David Gries

> *Tell me, did you invent this distinction yourself,*
> *which separates abstract ideas from the*
> *things which partake of them?*
> —Plato from *Dialogues, Parmenides*
> (c. 428–348 BC)

This chapter contains general background on distributed computing and it also includes short pieces on client-server computing, objects, and object-orientation (OO), and some general background on communication.

Many more detailed books have been written on each of these topics. If you want to learn about Common Object Request Broker Architecture (CORBA), this book provides a fairly quick way to digest some of the background and establish the necessary ideas. If nothing else, the introduction provides a list of topics that should be studied for a full understanding of distributed objects. Readers already familiar with these topics should immediately skip to Chapter 2.

1.1 COMPUTING PARADIGMS FOR THE NEXT CENTURY

Information technology (IT) has undergone many rapid changes over the last several decades. Manual systems gave way to automated computer systems, and information processing became batch systems. When CPUs became more powerful, information processing converted to on-line systems. As CPUs became less expensive, personal systems began performing computations. This last change left many islands of information spread all over organizations. These islands were not immediately interactive or accessible. The trend then moved on to integration and the appearance of distributed systems. Figure 1-1 depicts this progression.

Information technology has rapidly evolved over the decades.

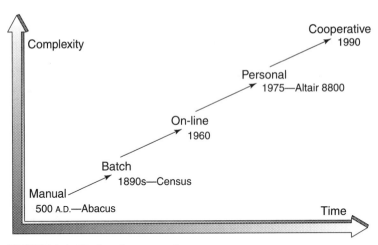

FIGURE 1-1. Modes of computation

Hardware expands capacity and software attempts to manage complexity.

Many changes in information-processing methods occur as a result of progress in hardware.[1] Hardware is only a part of the evolutionary impetus, however. Software evolves to use the new environment, leveraging hardware advances. Software also evolves of its own accord in ways not solely due to advances in hardware. Software history moves from plug boards to machine code, to assembler, toward more descriptive programming languages. Software's ever-increasing shift (besides taking full advantage of the ever-increasing power of the hardware) finds motivation in a requirement to manage complexity.

Complexity and technology advance in seeming lockstep.

The complexities of the plug boards or machine language binary numbers make them difficult for a human to comprehend and use. The difficulty is apparent even if their only use is for very simple programs such as adding two numbers. The mnemonic representation of machine instructions by assembly language is much easier to cope with for the human mind (Figure 1-2).

Software grows to consume additional hardware capacity.

It is a well-known maxim that when hardware capacity increases, applications grow to consume that capacity. With each increase in capability, complexity increases. Programming languages evolve to aid in solving the increasing challenges. Hardware expands to provide ever-increasing capabilities and the organization of software changes from instruction lists to procedural groups, to functional groups, to abstract data types and objects. The operational mode also changes from batch, to on-line, to each person as a distinct user, to consortiums of individuals all working interactively in collaboration.

Complexity motivates language change.

Much of the change, however, comes from the need for better control of complexity. The late '70s and early '80s saw the paradigm move into func-

---

1. An interesting aside is the comment from one of the inventors of the IBM-Harvard Mark I computer. He is said to have cautioned his compatriots with the statement that America could not have use for more than about five of his machines [Macrae-1992].

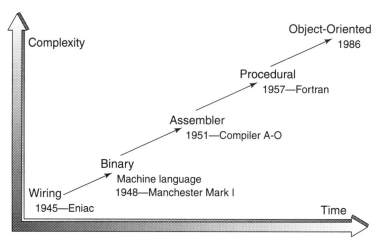

FIGURE 1-2. **Conquering complexity**

tions.[2] Older languages became more vital by adopting such newer facilities to manage their ever-increasing complexity.

Each major shift in information processing technology motivates changes in the way we conduct business. Manual business systems and their transactions change to batch operations. We change procedurally and sometimes organizationally and conduct our business in a batch mode. Later, these systems became more interactive, with on-line transactions and the time-share environment. Business processes also became more interactive but under central control.

Business and information influence each other's capabilities.

Personal computers move some business interactions into a still greater interactive approach with operations outside the hierarchy of a central authority. However, the validity of such information is questionable while it remains outside the control of the central system. Personal, here, is virtually synonymous with private (leaning heavily toward unreliable). At this phase the real information processing work still occurs in the on-line or batch system.

Information and business diffuse.

Real information is the valid information that is accessible and usable by everyone who needs it. We trust its accuracy. By extension, *unreal information* is that which is unverifiable by anyone else and may only approximate real information—its integrity is in question because the information is not in synchronization or otherwise under control.

The validity of uncontrolled information is questionable.

Through decentralization some work migrates (off-loads) from the mainframes. The structuring, control, and automation of this decentralization process

---

2. I do not imply functions were born here, just that they started to become more widely manifest and gained more presence as a standard information technology tool. This also is not meant to be the date functional organization was invented, but the date at which it found more widespread use in the corporate IS infrastructure.

gives birth to the distribution of processing, where information integrity is ensured. The business process and structure undergo a similar decentralization.[3]

Function calls become useful to hide cross-machine boundaries.

For programmers, it is easier to use the same model of programming with which they are familiar. Function calls came into wide use as a practical model for computation in distributed environments. The remote procedure call (RPC) became more apparent in corporate development starting in the late '80s.[4]

Resource specialization starts client-server.

The client-server model for processing information got its start through the specialization of software for specific resources. This diffusion of the workload promotes a theme of "downsizing" or "rightsizing." Note that these three terms—client-server, downsizing, and rightsizing—have similarities but mean distinctly different things.

Objects began appearing in the IS landscape in the 1980s.

Objects began arriving on the information systems frontier as a means of reducing complexity during the last years of the 1980s, although they had already been around for the previous decade. They did not become regular features in information technology until the early to mid 1990s.

The current shift is to distributed objects.

We are now undergoing another major shift in software, one that ultimately changes the landscape in similarly remarkable ways. One blueprint for this landscape comes from the Object Management Group (OMG). It is crucial to correctly understand this new landscape.

1.2 CLIENT-SERVER GOALS

Some reasons for leveraging client-server technology are invalid.

The rationales for moving IT into a client-server configuration are nearly as numerous as the number of books available about the topic. Several often-heard reasons for adopting client-server are not valid. Rather, they sometimes occur as the motivating rationale with slightly unreasonable justification. This book makes no attempt to provide a rationale for a such a conversion. There are many books that focus strictly on client-server and cover the topic in some detail. Some of the goals that client-server provides point in interesting directions.

Client-server derives from supply and demand.

Client-server technology, in a rudimentary definition, is an economic transaction. Someone over here (a consumer) wants something that someone over there (a producer) can provide. The producer's (server's) ability to produce something (typically called a service) and the consumer's (client's) requirement or demand (request) are what determine the nature of this relationship. Producers have ready access to some resource that they use in satisfying requests. Consumers may be anywhere, but they require some form of access to the producer.

---

3. Thirty years ago, M.E. Conway stated: "Organizations which design systems are constrained to produce systems which are copies of the communication structures of these organizations" [Brooks-1975].

4. There is some additional detail about the history of RPC that accompanies its contrast with CORBA in Chapter 4.

Although there generally is a many-to-one relation for clients to server, on occasion, clients want more than a single server. Contrast this with the architecture of the central system, which is a monopolistic provider. If you want something, there is only one place where you can obtain it.

Centralized systems are monopolistic.

Sometimes a single source, focusing solely on a specific kind of production, is beneficial. At other times it can be expensive because of price inflation, the risk of central outage (single-failure point), too little specialization (resource utilization may not be optimal), long queues for goods or services, large distances over which products ship to the consumers, and so forth.

In the centralized system dumb terminals (DT) do no computation except rudimentary display control (Figures 1-3 and 1-4). This requires the central system (mainframe) to handle the entire computational load. Multiply this by the number of consumers currently making requests and you have a potentially serious bottleneck.

Dumb terminals require centralized processing.

The client-server approach moves production out to specialists by distributing the production facilities. Correct deployment reduces costs, risks, and queues; provides resource specialization (optimal resource usage); and moves the product to within easy access of the consumer.

Client-server moves production near resources.

New solutions always introduce new problems, however. Client-server is not a "silver bullet."[5] The decision to convert facilities requires a thorough cost and benefits analysis before conversion. It is extremely important to understand both the good and the bad. Careful planning requires that you

Client-server is not magic; careful planning is mandatory.

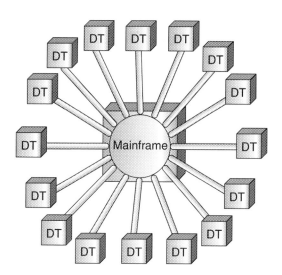

DT = Dumb Terminal

FIGURE 1-3. **Centralized system architecture**

---

5. [Brooks-1987].

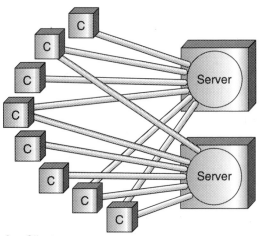

C = Client

FIGURE 1-4. Client-server architecture

understand all the risks and ramifications of changes and how to avoid or deflect problems and then move on when (and if) something goes wrong.

Costs of network support and development differences should not be overlooked.

For instance, the cost of *big iron* (mainframes) may go down on conversion to client-server, but communication costs may rise. The cost recovery may disappear into the network, its maintenance, and support. This is not always the case but frequently the difference in maintenance and support costs is overlooked or underestimated. Development costs may rise as well; specifically, distribution introduces more difficult problems into an enterprise's system-building equation. The logistics of coordinating multiple sites is difficult.

Distribution has problems such as latency, scalability, and data integrity.

Network *latency* and *scalability* are two serious problems that are difficult to determine before complete deployment. Replication or distribution of bad information (data that has a poor design, that has lost integrity, or is inappropriate) is another significant cost driver. Having one copy of bad information is unfortunate. Multiply that by a hundred or a thousand and you have a catastrophe.

Shortcuts are almost never effective for a long-term strategy.

Many guidelines and tactics are available on how to avoid or work around problems in these areas. Even though a bypass here and a shortcut there are expeditious, they are seldom effective in the longer view of cost.

Difficulties are best thwarted through careful planning.

Although there are more difficulties in distributing applications and data than in centralizing it, most of these difficulties have fairly well-known or easily located solutions. The solutions are not usually hard but they may be unfamiliar. The problems are surmountable with careful forethought, preparation, and planning.

1.3   OBJECT-ORIENTATION

Once upon a time, data living in some location was manipulated by a set of sequential instructions from one or more other locations. Data lived in the data space; instructions lived in instruction space. In the object-oriented world, both data and instructions live together in a bundle. This bundle is an abstraction known as an object.

Instructions and data combine, and programs become less obviously sequential.

The data of an object is only visible in the sense that it helps describe an object's behavior. Programs once read sequentially as a story might be visible in this sense. They now read more like a play with various actors (the objects), each having specific lines to read as they interact with other actors on their stage.

Both business and computing systems share a common organization. The Adam Smith specializing organization grows to resemble a pyramid. This is commonly known as the *division of labor* or *specialization of function.*

New models of organization

Although this arrangement adequately minimizes communication problems, the view from any individual position is of only the immediate and narrow scope of some business aspect.[6] That aspect may or may not have direct involvement with the fundamental business process. The procedures of the business generally flow through multiple departments (organizational units) before affecting a customer. No single individual with direct involvement in

Hierarchic organization can lead to problems as a process enters and leaves units.

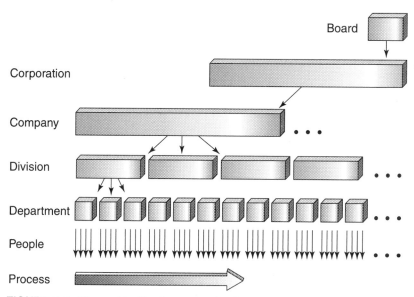

FIGURE 1-5. **Hierarchical business organization**

---

6. Among n people there exists a possible $(n^2 - n) / 2$ communication paths.

the process owns the whole. Each individual with direct involvement owns it for only a short fraction of its life; the business process enters his or her realm and then leaves. The process passes through one sphere of ready communication and enters another.

Information system applications acquire this structure. It is as if Adam Smith influenced the making of all things with his specialization by divisions of labor. An application that makes something is a composite of individual statements (akin to the operations of people in the organization). These are inside procedures (departments). In turn, they collectively organize into modules, packages, name spaces, and libraries (divisions) that together form the applications (companies) and run as a process (corporation) overseen by the executive (board).

Procedural code is often a hierarchic organization.

The command hierarchy of traditional business organizations is uncannily similar to the call hierarchy in a typical application. Whether single-threaded or not, control flows from the top. Starting with the executive, control trickles down through the application to individual lines of code that perform the actual work—making something.

This model, depicted in Figure 1-6, epitomizes structured design and code in its fullest sense. Data enters, travels about, and then finally goes out on the other side of the hierarchy. Meanwhile, data is exposed to hundreds of statements (lines of code), all doing approximately similar things (since the number of useful things you can do with a piece of data is finite).

Hierarchies are often brittle—hard to change or rearrange.

The problem-solving capability of any single procedure is immediately dependent on its predecessor's result. Because of this tight coupling, the software only produces the expected result when the flow always occurs in the

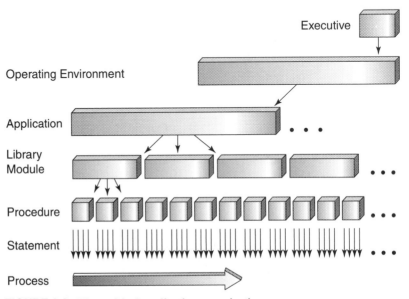

FIGURE 1-6. Hierarchical application organization

same way and in the same order. This organization is not easy to rearrange (it is brittle), nor can we remove or extend portions easily.

Specializing (hierarchical) organizations of software are pervasive. Alternate approaches exist, from research, in examination, and implementation. The usefulness of such approaches is apparent through their increasing acceptance over the last two decades. More and more developers are replacing hierarchical systems with object systems.

Business process reengineering (BPR) often takes an object-oriented approach to business and its organization. In BPR the focus is on the process, that unit of work expressing the life cycle of some product. The product is not necessarily for an external customer; it may be specifically for someone elsewhere within the same organization. The scope of BPR's focus is the entire business entity. The business undergoes radical change in the way its process occurs. The people and procedures that are responsible for a product are with that product throughout its entire life cycle in the company.

The result of business process reengineering keeps procedure and product together.

1.4 OBJECTS: THE GENERAL ABSTRACTION

An object-oriented approach to systems building is similar. Analysis of the process creates an abstraction, bundling together all *operations* (the process steps or *methods*) and corresponding *attributes* (the product—those things that the process operates upon). They stay together for the entire life cycle of the object.

The operations that are intrinsic to the process transform through analysis to an object abstraction. Intrinsic means those operations that embody the process directly. Such operations collectively form an object's *behavior*. Objects combine in *interesting* ways to provide the *essential building blocks* from which one composes *useful constructs*. Like a business process, an object is an interesting unit of work.

What, after all, is an object? Different schools of thought have different answers to this question. In one sense, there is no one-size-fits-all definition. A CORBA object is not identical to a C++ object or to an Objective-C object. It is not the same as a Self object. It is not quite like a Simula object . . . and the list continues. They generally share characteristics even though the intersect is not even the same for all sets of objects.

A CORBA object is not quite the same as an object in a programming language.

An object combines operations and state through encapsulation. An object is the instance of an abstraction that exhibits specific behavior. The behavior of an object is known by the requests that object can satisfy. An object has methods (operations) that are the venue through which one makes requests (or passes messages). It encapsulates state (contains attributes).

An object has methods, state, and a characteristic behavior.

An object is an instance of some *class*. Instance generally indicates physical presence in the runtime, whereas class is more of an idea. In other words, an object's class is a description of its behavioral characteristics. The term *class* derives specifically from its form as a classifier.

Objects are a physical manifestation of some class.

Such concepts (of type theory) have been around a long time.

For philosophers, a class is akin to the notion of a Platonic absolute.[7] The absolute is a template of shared characteristics by which we are able to recognize its members. A chair is recognizable as a chair (and not an ostrich) because of the degree to which its characteristics adhere to its absolute, its "chairness."

1.5   OBJECT-ORIENTATION AND BENEFITS

Objects are conceptually simpler.

Many of the publications about object-orientation that explain why objects are good frequently pass over one of its more important benefits. An object is simpler to conceptualize than procedural code. The major benefit is that more objects can be conceptually and abstractly held in a person's mind. This typically means that the person can better grasp and manipulate more intricacies.

The immediate apprehension of things occurs in "chunks."

The Scottish philosopher Sir William Hamilton (1788–1856) noted that "If you throw a handful of marbles on the floor, you will find it difficult to view at once more than six, or seven at most, without confusion."[8] William Stanley Jevons (1835–1882) threw beans in a box in a confirming experiment. These results are in "The Magic Number Seven, Plus or Minus Two," a seminal paper (1956) from the American psychologist George Miller about "chunking." Though this deals with visual apprehension, it has a bearing on other modes of apprehension.

A rough rule of thumb for complexity

Obviously this is a generalization because not everyone has the same emotional capacity for apprehension. Also obvious is that apprehension is different from conceptualization. However, this "magic number seven" is a useful rule of thumb when it is hard to predict who shall maintain systems.

Design and code reuse and reduced complexity are benefits.

This is not to say that all the other benefits are unimportant, even if some are side-effects. Design and code reuse may effectively reduce costs. Encapsulation hides complexities from the overall view. Another potential benefit for reuse comes from inheritance.

While objects are a good thing, they also are not a cure-all. Virtually anything is capable of abuse given the appropriate lack of knowledge.

1.6   OBJECTS: MORE FORMALLY

Abstract data types

Abstraction is a useful tool to reduce complexity. As software becomes more complex, the ability to work with abstractions becomes more important. One interesting and useful abstraction from research in the '70s is the *abstract data type* (ADT). An ADT is an encapsulation of a data structure along with the procedures (operations) that manipulate that data. It is encapsulated when

---

7. That probably should be the neoplatonist absolute. Plato's doctrine of forms [Coppleston-1946] as occurs in *The Sophist* appears most like the notion of object classes but, depending on whom one reads, one may come away with totally different interpretations.
8. [Gregory-1978].

its state is implied, meaning that the data structure is only visible and accessible through its procedures. Languages that implement ADTs are Modula2 and Ada.

The utility of ADTs has seen further evolution, transforming into languages said to be object-oriented. Such languages express their ADTs as objects. Expressing an ADT as an object requires additional features that ADTs do not possess.

Besides the traits of an ADT, an object also possesses the means to manage its life cycle. In other words, it is an operation or method to dynamically create new copies, such as constructors or factories, and possibly destructors. Objects are grouped and categorized by their common attributes and behavior. Such a grouping (often referred to as its class) administers the entire set of its members. Further, objects require a means through which they may be generalized and specialized.

Objects manage their life cycle.

Encapsulation hides the inner workings of an object from external view. For example, it hides attributes from public view (external to the object). An object's hidden attributes may be deducible by observing the operations available. This does not make those attributes a requirement and only points out a potential solution to an operation. The inner *stuff* within the object, which satisfies an operation, is its *implementation*. The implementation may contain, borrow, or compute attributes.

Objects also have encapsulation.

An object's attributes may be atomic (indivisible).[9] They may be compositions of one or more objects. An example might be a person object (a composition, in this example) that has a date object (atomic) signifying its date of birth as one of its attributes.

Attributes may be compositions.

An object, then, is a basic computational unit consisting of a defined behavior and perhaps some attribute(s) (see Figure 1-7). The attributes retain the effect of behavior. Requests made on an object are *messages* (or *methods*). Objects may support more than one method.

Messages defined

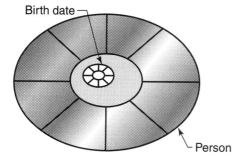

Birth date

Person

FIGURE 1-7. **A simple compound object**

---

9. This was believed in the pre-Socratic world by the Atomists, and proposed by Leucippus and Democritus.

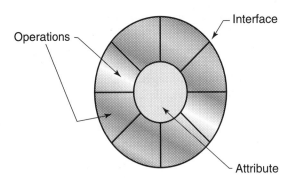

FIGURE 1-8. Interface, operations, and attributes

Interface as part of an object

As Figure 1-8 shows, the visible portion of an object is its *interface.* An interface to an object is the combined sum of the messaging protocols used to request services. An object interface consists of an object name and its set of valid methods.

Methods have two parts.

Methods consist of two parts: a signature and an implementation. A signature consists of a method (operation) name, its parameter names and types, along with return values and exceptions. A method's implementation is the code that executes to produce the desired operation.

Interface and type are distinct.

An object's interface describes its behavior. All too frequently, interface is synonymous with an object's type, which it is not. *Type* is really a protection device used to ascertain the validity of its underlying properties. Checking type validity at compile time is static typing. Checking type validity at runtime is dynamic typing.

Class has intensional and extensional parts.

Class, which is an instance of a type, consists of intensional and extensional parts. The intensional part defines the common characteristics and structural qualities of the class. The extensional part includes an extent and a constructor. The *extent* of a class is all the object instances belonging to the class that exist (are not yet destroyed).

Behavior and contracts

The behavior of an object is the contract that it offers publicly. An object's *contract* is a guarantee that invoking one of its methods using the specified signature produces either the result or the exceptions specified. A contract consists of a signature and the necessary preconditions, invariants, and postconditions.

Preconditions, postconditions, and invariants

Preconditions are those qualities that must exist before a contract executes to ensure its validity. *Postconditions* are those qualities that will exist after the contract's execution successfully concludes. *Invariants* are those aspects that never change throughout the life of the contract. The contract is the object's guarantee and is axiomatic.

Service and client objects

The provider of a contract is a *server.* The beneficiary of a contract, also known as a service requester, is the *client.* A client requests a service; a requester invokes a method on a provider. Another way of thinking about this is to say that the client sends a message to a server. That message must observe the protocol of the object.

As already mentioned, inheritance enables a variation of reuse by establishing families of objects with similar (inherited) traits.[10] An object that inherits from another derives from the other. The object it derives from is a *base object*. General OO calls a base object's type a supertype and the derived object's type a subtype. The derived object inherits all the base object's behavior. All objects deriving from a common base are a family.

Inheritance reuses family traits.

A *derived class* is a specialization of the base class. Specialization is frequently an extension. Objects that allow multiple base classes (called *multiple inheritance*) may specialize by deriving from multiple parents to *mix in* the functionality from two or more parent classes. A specialized class is narrower than the class from which it derives. The class from which it derives is wider, more general (having less specialization).

Two kinds of specialization: by extension and by mix-in

Polymorphism is the ability to use an object correctly even if one knows only the family to which that object belongs. More specifically, polymorphism makes certain that a request goes to the appropriate object. Your ability to use an elevator you have never seen before is an example.

Polymorphism directs a command to the appropriate family member.

The capabilities of an object family closely relates to the idea of substitutability. This states that anywhere a base object finds use, any one of its derivations will also work. This is because the derivation has all the wider object's capabilities in addition to its own. This is the principle of substitutability.[11]

A derived object may be used anywhere its base may be used.

Among the traits that a family may share are common names for requests that may do different things depending on which family member receives them. When such requests are available by the same name from multiple members of the family, each member object may give them different semantics and implement them differently, according to their specific needs. A name is *overloaded* when the same name applies to operations on different members in such a family.

Operations with the same name in a different family may "overload" an operation.

For example, a rectangle and a square may each have an operation named draw. Assume that the square, having equal sides, inherits from the rectangle as a specialization. The name "draw" indicates that the behavior is similar (assuming the naming scheme is any good). However, the drawing of a rectangle and the drawing of a square may occur differently and may have different implementations. This is an example of overloading. Their semantics may differ in that they require different parameters. For example, the square may take a corner location and a length, whereas a rectangle may take a corner and a horizontal length and a vertical length as its parameters.

Overriding is a special case of overloading. The operation appears identical in each object and only the implementation varies. Overriding also applies to internal variables (*instance variables*), which are not publicly visible due to

Operations sometimes "override" the name.

---

10. At least this may be true when one fully understands the differences and possible ramifications of using inheritance and how it compares to composition.

11. [Liskov-1988].

their encapsulation but are still a part of the implementation. Overriding a method hides an identical method in a parent class.

An example of overriding might be an interface, A, that has an operation, op. If B inherits from A, introducing a new operation (also op) with the same signature but differing in implementation, the op in B overrides that of A. When it occurs within a type family, the derived operation is said to override those in the base.

1.7 DISTRIBUTED OBJECTS

Distributed objects have slight differences from either OO or C/S alone.

As envisioned by the CORBA, distributed objects (DO) are the melding of concepts from two paradigms—client-server (or, more precisely, distributed computing) and OO, with some explicit differences:

- A client knows an object by its interface.
- Objects are not always local with respect to their clients.
- Dynamic composition may compose objects into new applications.
- Objects hide many of the underlying differences in architecture through encapsulation.

Although CORBA does not hide the operating system or make everything an object, it gives every indication that a completely object-oriented environment has merit. If the operating system and everything else in the environment is an object, creating the system implementation is easier.

1.7.1 An ORB as Middleware

As object systems become more pervasive, the scale of their constructs expands from individual processes or run-times to operating systems to distributed operating systems. One scaling mechanism is an object request broker (ORB). From the application viewpoint it acts as a platform for distributed objects. An ORB may run on top of operating systems that are not object-oriented. In such a case, the ORB encapsulates some aspects of the underlying OS and networking layers just as an object encapsulates its attributes. In this capacity it is middleware. It hides as much of the underlying platform as possible under its object abstraction (see Figure 1-9).

Middleware makes it easier to get software to market or into production.

Middleware hides the underlying details from the application. It does this by providing a common set of services across all the platforms on which it lives. This means that an independent software vendor (ISV) is able to write to one set of application program interfaces (APIs), making the code that much more portable. The APIs are the interfaces to the middleware.

Common APIs can attract software written for various systems.

To a system vendor, offering a combined base of software platforms is a way to attract developers. The platforms are not identical, but support for standard APIs decreases the amount of platform-specific code. The more applications that are available, the happier we are as customers. Although the perception is that middleware is an equalizer, system vendors still distinguish

Interesting Units of Work

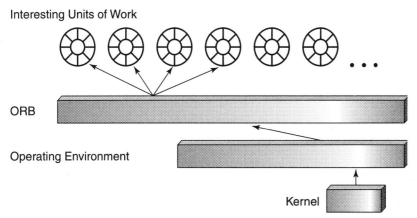

ORB

Operating Environment

Kernel

FIGURE 1-9. ORB as a layer above OS and network

their platforms through price and performance, and by offering additional options such as ease of administration, quality of service, or specialty facilities and resources.

The combination of client-server with objects gives us their best features: the ability to distribute risk, rightsizing system development with small composable subtasks, and having looser coupling with well-defined integration. The advantage we achieve also has a much more complicated topology than that typically found in client-server.

Distributed objects offer the best of OO and C/S.

The use of client and server in distributed objects is relative to an interface among objects. Clients make requests on the server offering the interface. Virtually all servers are clients of other interfaces. As Figure 1-10 shows, when everything is an object, we potentially have what appears to be a random mix of clients and servers. The topology is extravagant.

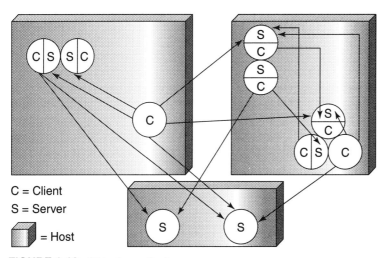

C = Client
S = Server
= Host

FIGURE 1-10. Objects as client-server

1.8   BASIC COMMUNICATIONS AND RELIABILITY

The construction of communicating systems or applications is highly dependent on the available communication facility. It is important to have a strong foundation when dealing with the complexities of such systems.

This section looks into the protocol and covers the basics of message synchronization, reliability, and indeterminacy. These elements are important for builders of communicating systems, whether client-server or distributed objects. The section also provides useful background for answering some complaints about CORBA.

Information flows from producer to consumer.

Communication in its simplest form is the passing of messages, or the exchange of information between two entities. The information is of arbitrary form (untyped).[12] The flow of information is unidirectional from producer to consumer.

1.8.1   Message Synchronization

If the entities are in different threads of control, they are *asynchronous* with regard to each other. They synchronize at the moment that they exchange a message. *Synchronization* means that they are at the same place at the same time when the message exchange takes place. The exchange is akin to runners handing off a baton in a relay race; it requires both entities to be at the same place at the same time.

The system depicted in Figure 1-11 appears to transfer the message directly between processes (an apparent channel) but in reality the message transfers several times through the network system. The producer constructs the message and issues a Send. The network (or communication) system transfers the message to the location where the consumer is issuing a Receive.

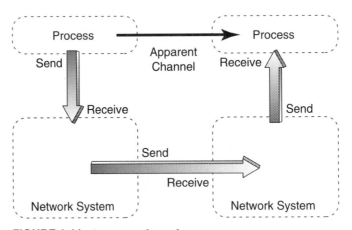

FIGURE 1-11.   Apparent channel

---

12. If the form were not arbitrary, it could be checked for validity and would be "typed."

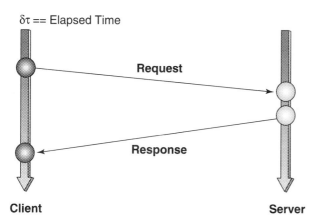

FIGURE 1-12. **Bidirectional communication via Request–Response**

Adding just a touch of sophistication to this primitive message passing, we get a bidirectional exchange during the hand-off. Such a synchronization is a *rendezvous*. Two-way communication is symmetric in that a sender must also have Receive capability. Sending a message in both directions requires the producer and the consumer of the message to be available simultaneously. A simplified request–response interaction appears in Figure 1-12.

A rendezvous is a bidirectional exchange.

1.8.1.1   Blocking

Let us briefly look at more of the details and consider the various forms of blocking for contrast. A request and response with blocking appears in Figure 1-12.

The receiver has a window between the Receive call's return and sending the result when it performs the actions for the request. The requester blocks until the response arrives. In Figure 1-13, the server arrives at the rendezvous first, so the client is able to send immediately. Figure 1-14 illustrates the reverse, when the client arrives at the rendezvous first and waits to send.

Blocking indicates one party waits to synchronize with the other.

In neither case does the server block on sending the result because the client is already blocked awaiting the result. The client's presence allows the server's immediate send. Table 1-1 lists the various forms of blocking.

TABLE 1-1. **Blocking modes**

Send	Receive
Blocking	Blocking
Nonblocking	Blocking
Nonblocking	Nonblocking

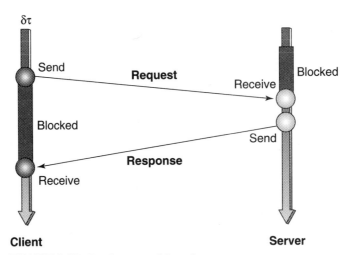

FIGURE 1-13. Rendezvous with early server

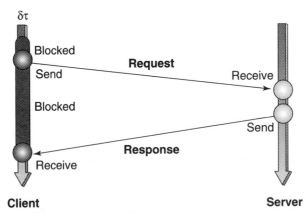

FIGURE 1-14. Rendezvous with early client

Figures 1-12 and 1-13 show the first form, where both sender and receiver block (see also Figure 1-14). Both of these forms refer to message exchange without buffering. These are synchronous communication methods because the producer and consumer synchronize to perform the exchange. Buffering introduces new considerations.

1.8.1.2   *Asynchronous Messaging*

Asynchrony, or no-wait send, uses a buffer as intermediary.

The most important factor in the introduction of a buffer for message exchange is whether its size has limits (whether it is bounded or unbounded). An unbounded buffer never requires the producer (sender) to wait. In other words, a buffer that is bound may fill up so that some new message may not fit, requiring the sender to wait until the full buffer drains to the point where there is room for the message. This *no-wait send* is the basis of an asynchronous messaging or message-passing system.

The distinction between the two no-wait send diagrams (a and b in Figure 1-15) is on receipt of the response. In (a) the client did a Receive before the server was ready to send the response, so the client blocked, awaiting the result. In (b), the server sent the response before the client attempted to receive, so the client did not block. In each case the server blocked during request on the Receive, since it was listening for the next request.

Buffer creation is an initialization requirement for such protocols. Part of the initialization creates a *port* or *mailbox*. The producer sends the message to the port (or places it in the mailbox) where it sits until the consumer retrieves it.

A port or mailbox is a no-wait send buffer.

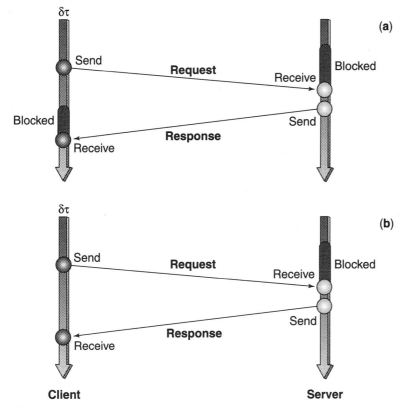

FIGURE 1-15. Blocked and unblocked Receive response

1.8.2   Message Reliability

If we look at messages as unreliable versus reliable transport, we get inter-action diagrams similar to Figures 1-16 and 1-17. Adding an acknowledge makes a transmission reliable.

A three-packet reliable message degrades under loading.

This Request–Response with acknowledge (Figure 1-17, three-packet form) has poor characteristics when loading occurs. A reliable Request–Response that does not degrade under loading occurs with a reliable receive. A reliable receive does an immediate acknowledge. The server sends an immediate acknowledge on receipt of the request and the client sends an immediate acknowledge on receipt of the response.

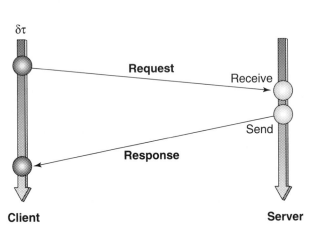

Client   **Server**

FIGURE 1-16. **Unreliable primitives**

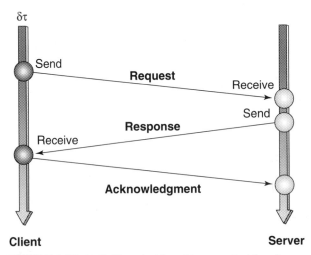

Client   **Server**

FIGURE 1-17. **Reliable primitives (three-packet form)**

1.8.2.1   At-Least-Once Semantics

Three- and four-packet reliable messages have *at-least-once* semantics (see Figures 1-18 and 1-19).

    Figure 1-19 shows what occurs in the event of a send failure and a receive failure. If the failure occurs during the acknowledge and the server forgets executing the request, it can execute it again on rebooting.

Three- and four-packet messages have at-least-once semantics.

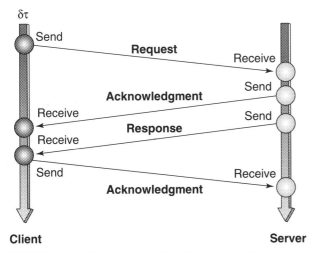

FIGURE 1-18. **Reliable primitives (four-packet form)**

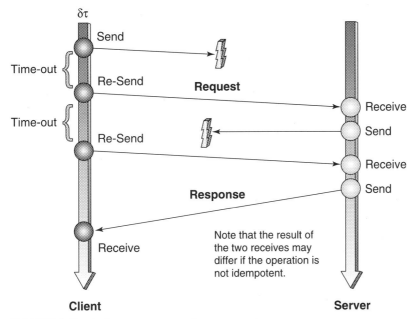

FIGURE 1-19. **At-least-once semantics**

At-least-once semantics are good for idempotent operations.

At-least-once semantics may be sufficient, depending on what operation the client is requesting. For example, most operations on a file are *idempotent* (executing these operations more than once produces the same result). Both read and write are idempotent. Both create and delete operations are almost idempotent. If either of these latter occur twice, the second occurrence receives an error (saying the file already exists or no such file exists). Unfortunately, however, append is a nonidempotent operation. Doing multiple appends produces different results because the second occurrence will append the data again.

1.8.2.2   *Exactly Once and At-Most-Once Semantics*

Exactly once semantics are desirable, not always achievable, and expensive.

The most desirable semantic is that of *exactly once*. In a distributed system where an *amnesia crash* (the crashing server forgets what operations it previously executed) can occur, exactly once is not possible to achieve. The best one can do is obtain *at-most-once* semantics. To achieve the at-most-once semantic (Figure 1-20), the server records state in stable store. This makes the protocol very expensive, especially considering that such a failure of a node is fairly rare.

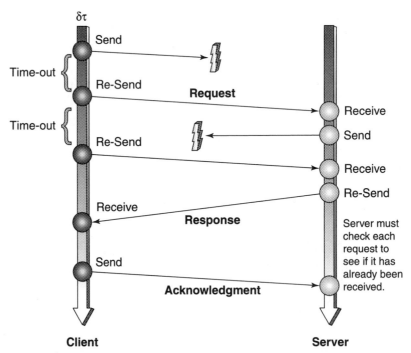

FIGURE 1-20. At-most-once semantics

1.8.2.3   Reliable Transport and Unreliable Messaging

In a protocol such as TCP/IP, which is a reliable transport, the acknowledgments occur in the Host-to-Host (TCP) layer. In some senses the response is an application-level acknowledgment. The application is the only place where the importance of the message is understood. The network system has no idea whether it should retry indefinitely or if the message is not that important. If a response never gets to the application, even though the protocol is reliable, the messaging is unreliable (see Figure 1-21).

TCP/IP is a reliable transport.

  The client never knows whether the request occurs in Figure 1-22. The client is unable to distinguish a very slow server from one that is dead.

1.8.3   Indeterminacy

Indeterminacy, depicted in Figure 1-23, enters into the picture during a system fault, network partition, or when systems or network are exceedingly slow. Under at-least-once semantics, one may enter a state in which the outcome from a request is uncertain—did it occur or not?

Indeterminacy introduces uncertainty about completion.

  Applications are the usual arbiters of such indeterminacy. They decide whether to continue, retry, or allow the request to potentially drop on the floor. The application programmer in a distributed environment needs to be aware of such indeterminacy in the environment and code in the appropriate failure semantics.

  Although the programmer is responsible, in some cases, for dealing with the indeterminacy of a request, some application development environments attempt to make the determination and frequently set defaults. These defaults may be adequate in certain cases, but it may take programmer intervention to make a best determination in all cases. Programmers constructing such applications with fourth- or fifth-generation tools ought to be aware that the requests they are constructing occur indeterminately.

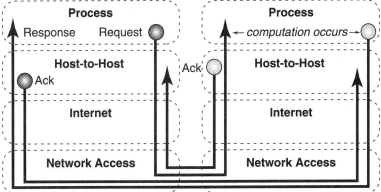

FIGURE 1-21. An unacknowledged message on a reliable transport is still unreliable

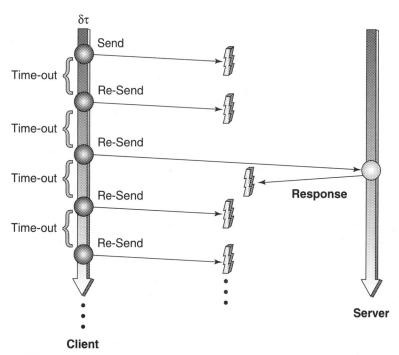

FIGURE 1-22.   **The inability to distinguish a slow server from a dead server**

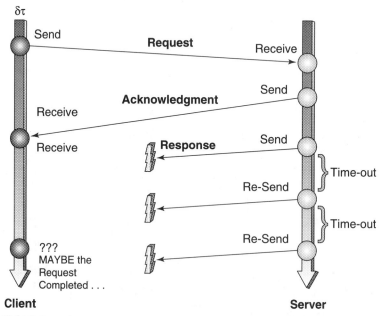

FIGURE 1-23.   **Indeterminate Request outcome**

CHAPTER 2   *Enter the OMG*

*The Beautiful arises from the perceived harmony
of an object . . . with the inborn and constitutive
rules of the judgment and imagination:
and it is always intuitive.*
—Samuel Taylor Coleridge from *On the
Principles of Genial Criticism* (1814)

The Object Management Group (OMG) was formed in 1989. On start-up there were just short of a dozen corporate members in the consortium. Their vision was that the computing superstructure was about to change and that such a change would prove the most radical yet. They formed in anticipation of the gigantic mess that could ensue without such a mediating organization. The vision, in part, was to organize the various system vendors and software developers into a consortium in which consensus came easily. They wanted to marshal global support without imposing obstacles or selecting blue sky technology.

OMG anticipates the trend.

One of their founding principles is that the proposals they adopt are for existing implementations. They select proven technologies and prefer that everyone reach consensus on using a common, existing, and, therefore, achievable technology. Customers want industry consensus and they want it as soon as possible. Although it is up to the members to reach a consensus, the OMG provides an environment in which members can discuss their goals and options to seek common ground in a nonhostile and nonthreatening environment (which is mostly the case but not always!). To date they have admirably achieved those goals.

Attempting to avoid blue sky, they select extant implementation.

There is still much fighting about who is going to win major market shares; only the battlegrounds have changed. Customers are insistent: they want open systems, more software choices, and adherence to standards, and they want needless proprietary and nonextensible systems to disappear.

OMG solved all problems? Hardly.

The vendors listened. They have learned that collaboration is productive. OMG has given them some common ground without imposing too many constraints. The OMG's efforts have not gone unrecognized. Nearly 800 members are in the OMG today and it is still growing.

The concern is not just one for system vendors, but for application developers and end users as well. Many have concerns about the management of the distributed objects that they will require over the next several years.

System vendors, application vendors, and users all drive OMG.

Everyone wants to either keep up on all the latest accepted proposals or to have a say in the adoption of his or her favorite proposals.

Some problems come from an embarrassment of bright ideas.

Are there problems? You bet. Any time you get several hundred very bright and competent people together for discussions about technical merits, there is disagreement. Everyone has exceptionally good reasons why his or her particular brand or flavor of technology is the best of all those available. Bright people cannot help coming up with bright ideas. A bright idea is just that. So it becomes very difficult to sift through all of these very good ideas about technology and select the subset that makes the most sense.

The general principles of the architecture were nailed first.

The OMG members did the correct thing: first off they wrote a guideline about how to select the best of the good ideas and technological innovations. They did this by writing an architecture describing the details of what distributed-object management requires and what foundations provide the best base for moving forward. They achieve this by culling both fields of distributed computing and objects to arrive at some *first principles*, or *guidelines*. The OMG members wrote the object management architecture. They also recognize that their is not an ultimate end. They explicitly state that their model is just one approach and not necessarily the best approach.

2.1   THE OMG PROCESS AND STANDARDS

OMG has its nay-sayers.

Strictly speaking, this section is rhetorical. It primarily discusses issues about the OMG that seem to crop up frequently. The OMG has detractors, too. The following is a list of the general complaints about the OMG that will be discussed in the rest of this section:

- The OMG is specifying standards prematurely.
- The OMG cannot decide if it is a technical or a marketing consortium.
- OMG standards are solely for system manufacturers.
- The OMG is moving too fast.
- The OMG is not moving fast enough.
- OMG standards allow too many issues to remain unresolved.

These statements are not totally without credibility or justification, but they are also false.

2.1.1   What Is the OMG?

The first set of complaints comes from a lack of understanding about what OMG represents and its charter.

2.1.1.1   Not a Standards Body

The OMG is not an official standards body.

First, the OMG is not a standards body or part of any officially established standards body. It is not part of the International Standards Organization (ISO) or the American National Standards Institute (ANSI). It is often the first to point out the differences between its operation and the official standards bodies. However, it is making every effort to collaborate with those bodies. It appears that official standards bodies also are cooperating in the OMG effort.

2.1.1.2   Hype Versus Significant

Another frequent accusation is that the OMG is more hype than it is of any practical significance. Rather than attempting to prove otherwise here in a short paragraph, we defer to the reader. Hopefully the content of this book makes the practical significance obvious.

2.1.2   Complaints About OMG

Other complaints appear to come from hearsay. These nay-sayers appear to not have any direct contact with the OMG.

2.1.2.1   Premature Standards

The OMG does not issue or set standards. It is a body providing a framework for technology selection. Members are not just system vendors but real, live end-users. It provides a structure under which members may discuss options, exchange ideas, provide constructive criticism, and, hopefully, achieve results.

OMG selections are frequently consensual.

The OMG does not specify or mandate anything because it has no official standing. Through its process members select technology. Its selection frequently comes prior to widespread distribution of the technology, so it is premature in comparison to many *de facto standards* of our experience. However, it is not selection based on *blue-sky* proposals but on actual working implementations. In other words, any submission in response to an OMG request for proposal (RFP) is about an existing implementation. The OMG does not adopt technology that exists only on paper.[1]

OMG adopts proposals for systems that exist.

When conflicting submissions come in, typically, the submitting groups decide to merge their proposals into a single, combined proposal.[2] While this sounds dangerously like design by committee it is not quite as ugly. First, the design usually is by one or two people (or companies). During review, other companies may sign on or ask to make a few changes before signing on. If two groups decide to merge their submissions, usually just a few people sit down and hammer out the details. It is usually only a two-party compromise if it occurs, not a be-all and end-all for every stratagem that is potentially of

OMG members cooperate.

1. This is true in theory but not exactly in practice. Submissions are supposed to be based on working implementations but in the event they are revised in accordance with technical committee advice or in the event that multiple submitters decide to merge their proposals, what actually is adopted is often at variance with the original submission, which is based on an implementation.
2. This is typical, but not always the case. After the initial presentation, the submitters have a number of days in which to revise their submissions and incorporate comments. During this time, the submitters sometimes collaborate on merging their proposals. Sometimes this is successful and sometimes not. At other times, they see no grounds for collaboration and continue to pursue their independent proposals.

interest. So far, no one has designed a camel when his or her intent was to design a horse.[3]

2.1.2.2   Technical or Market-Driven?

OMG is technical- and market-oriented.

The discussion about whether the OMG is either a technical or a marketing consortium seems moot. Most high-tech companies are both—they make technical decisions about products and then market those products. The OMG markets itself to solicit more members, thereby attaining a wider consensus. It markets the adoptions, stating that such selection is a good thing. Otherwise it becomes the proverbial party to which no one comes; adopting a technology that no one uses is not terribly useful.

The Architecture Board acts as oversight to the technical committees.

The OMG also has an Architecture Board of technical members that deal with and coordinate the technical aspects of the arena from which technology selections occur. There exists a very complete and well-defined process for making these selections of technology. Two technical committees report to the Architecture Board: a Platform Technical Committee (dealing with the underlying platform architecture) and a Domain Technical Committee (dealing with domain-specific areas of concern).

Nine task forces report to the two technical committees.

A task force seeks advice and makes a recommendation on a proposal before it goes before its technical committee for a vote. The Platform Technical Committee has three task forces: Object Analysis and Design, CORBAservices, and CORBAfacilities. The Domain Task Force consists of six task forces to date: Business Objects, Electronic Commerce, Finance, Manufacturing, Medical (as health-care), and Telecommunications. The task force issues requests for information (RFIs) and RFPs for matters requiring a solution, as the technical foundations for what came afterward.[4]

Members' votes are motivated by technical and marketing concerns.

Any given member, including end-users, may vote in accordance with technical or marketing principles, depending on his or her overall company or personal strategy, or strategy that specifically applies to the consortium. A company usually follows one orientation or the other regardless of its foundation. Technology drives some companies, marketing drives others, and still others have strategies that vary by issue between these two. An individual generally is a member of the representative market and wants a competent technical solution.

2.1.2.3   System Manufacturer Standards

Those making submissions are those doing the implementations, since they must have an implementation to submit a proposal. Frequently, submissions

---

3. Actually, there is one instance of a camel, which I will mention later. However, compared to the scope of adoptions, one camel may be forgivable.
4. This is not to say that proposals are always adopted in the correct order, although they can be pretty close. The fundamental issues are generally in solution prior to their dependents.

are somewhat driven by marketing issues since there is not much call to create something for which there is no demand. So the selections that the OMG's voting members adopt are usually submissions from system manufacturers, if we can call each implementation a system. The OMG is not a technical body selecting technically correct pieces of technology that no one is able to implement.

2.1.2.4   Moving Too Fast?

The OMG is making selections and achieving consensus at a rapid rate. Even if we discover that some consensus is premature, the OMG should still be congratulated on its ability to move quickly despite having so many members. Obtaining consensus from this many competitive vendors and potential customers is amazing. Too fast is relative and highly subjective.

For a body of its type, OMG is making rapid progress.

If some adoption truly is premature, the OMG has a mechanism for amendments. This process was not in its original charter during the original round of RFPs for CORBA 1.0 and the subsequent adoptions. Amendments and changes have come about, however, and the process appears to work well.

Omissions occur and corrections follow.

2.1.2.5   Moving Too Slow?

The detractors that say the OMG is moving too slowly are typically waiting for some specific piece of the architectural puzzle as it assembles. An RFP may not yet exist. They do not like waiting. Unfortunately, this happens for every piece of the puzzle regardless of who is waiting. The alternative is to make do since it cannot happen before it can happen.

The adoption process requires time to select and validate submissions.

Many pieces are necessary to put together distributed systems and many people are involved in this process. The process has seven specific steps that occur for various stages:

1. n number of days to write an RFI
2. n number of days in which to respond to an RFI
3. n number of days to evaluate RFI responses
4. n number of days to write an RFP
5. n number of days in which to respond to an RFP
6. n number of days to evaluate RFP responses
7. n number of days for a vote

These details take time. Resources are also finite. Some companies may have several people working on issues while others may have only one. It takes time and resources to build implementations. It then takes more time to draft RFPs and responses. Not all the difficult problems in distributed computing systems of this sort can be solved simultaneously because some issues depend on the outcome of other issues, and so on. So, no, not all problems can be solved overnight. On top of all this, an implementation is built if one does not already exist. Too slow? That is extremely subjective.

Resources are limited.

Stepping up the pace may thoroughly swamp the Technical Committee.

Historically, the bottleneck has been the Technical Committee. No single body can digest and assimilate all possible additions simultaneously. In early 1996 the OMG adopted a new organizational structure geared toward handling a higher volume of ongoing work. Some of the new volume will come from domain task forces that were formerly Special Interest Groups (SIGs). In their previous incarnation, SIGs could only lobby ideas to groups such as the CORBAfacilities Task Force. Now, if they have the appropriate charter, they can begin producing their own RFIs and RFPs.

2.1.2.6   Unresolved Issues

Not everything can be selected simultaneously.

During the process it sometimes becomes apparent that dependencies exist that must remain unresolved until they are incorporated into the schedule. So, some issues remain. However, those issues usually enter into an agenda somewhere. If they are not on an agenda, it is likely that no one brought the issue to the attention of the group that is responsible. The groups meet regularly every six to eight weeks.

2.1.3   When Is It Complete?

The entire process may take years.

The next question, although not mentioned in the list of complaints by detractors, is probably: When is it complete; when do they finish? That is a hard question. What does complete or finished mean? Is it the point at which there are no more services, facilities, or basic features left to adopt? I would answer that question with "whenever distributed objects become noninteresting."

To paraphrase, as long as there is interest in distributed objects (or multiple producers of such beasts) then there is a requirement to help achieve consensus. All too frequently, old technologies never die—they just reincarnate forever.

If no one can achieve any further consensus, it could also end.

Another answer might be, whenever no one can achieve or still desires to achieve consensus on issues. This latter could potentially happen before the former. However, there is such momentum built up by the adoptions so far, that were any single vendor to drop out he or she would likely forfeit some fairly large potential markets. This assumes that the customers are also successful in applying the technology. Technology, no matter how exciting, is not terribly interesting if no one wants to use it.

Vendor consensus does not a market make. Someone must actually buy the product.

So, if there are no customers, all the consensus in the world will not sell a product. If there are no more customers, then no one will care if the process stops. However, there appears to be a lot of interest by end users, judging by the number of OMG members that are not system vendors. Some very substantial investments also are being made by end users who are staking their information systems or long-term product strategies on this technology, and, by extension, the future of their companies. Business is making vast inroads and it appears that there is little that may slow it, let alone stop it from occurring.

The OMG documents its formal adoption process in their book *Object Management Architecture Guide.* Anyone who desires to participate should read about their process.

For years, system users have known the plague of trying to interconnect a myriad of incompatible systems. They continue to state that this is what they require. Certain customers prefer system selection that they can optimize for the task at hand. Both desires are perfectly valid. Middleware hides some incompatibility.

Middleware as an answer to reduce development time

However, like all panaceas in the information age, each frequently receives far more hype than it deserves. Were relational databases the panacea for clearing the application backlog? Was C totally portable across all platforms and without various headaches? Did UNIX speed up system development times? Have PCs cut the cost of mainframe-based IS shops? Has OO radically cut development costs? Has the network computer massively decreased system or administration expense?

The answers are all "no." There is no panacea. There is no free lunch.[5] There are no silver bullets. The road to wherever is paved with best intentions, and so on. However, no one should say that things have not improved. The application backlog still exists but how large would the backlog be if we were still using 1960s or 1970s technology? What was a tar pit in Brooks' telling of *The Mythical Man Month* in 1972 has not only not gone away during the intervening 25 years but has grown larger and radically more complex. How much more have we been able to accomplish? On the other hand it may not have grown as much over the years if the technology did not allow it to grow. Work increases to capacity. So we may never know. CORBA is not a panacea. It will not make all of our problems go away.

Middleware is not a panacea. Organizational problems can only be hidden by technology.

The correct use of these technologies does help. Matters may have been far worse than they are now. Technological strides make it possible to continue to manage the ever-increasing complexity. CORBA and its surrounding infrastructure are one more stride. Both client-server and objects also move us toward better complexity-management.

Two worst-case scenarios could occur:

Vendors give up or innovation stagnates.

- The members could reach an impasse and never reconcile their differences, fragmenting the possibility of achieving complete interoperability. (in the sense of like interfaces[6]) between the variant implementations
- The technology could catch on, everyone could start to use it, and we would never develop anything better.

---

5. "There is no such thing as a free lunch." Attributed to Milton Friedman.

6. Interoperability in the sense of a communication protocol is a hurdle that they have already passed. I mean in the larger sense of not making objects available or only those that vary so widely that they are not useful across domains.

The second is bad in that the stifling of inventiveness becomes a millstone or an albatross around our necks. In other words, we could stagnate. (Is retarded technology an oxymoron?)

Basically, none of these worst-case predictions is likely to occur.

I believe that the first of these worst-case scenarios leaves us exactly where we were pre-OMG, except that we now have a large degree of commonality through the existing body of adoptions. Only some specific area of concern may suffer such a fate.

Compatibility for ORBs was formulated in such a way as to specify a core set of functions (known as the Core 92 Model, from 1992) that must be present to consider an implementation as conforming. All the additional adoptions or technology are extensions to the core. The core plus some set of extensions is known as a *profile*. Profiles allow product differentiation. Most companies offering ORBs have either the core set of functionality already or are very close. Several now offer some variant profiles. So we possess the core technology to do meaningful and useful work.

Technological ruts are also hard to achieve in such a competitive economy.

The second worst-case seems doubtful. We have not become stuck in any other technological ruts over the last 40 or 50 years except for those we specifically chose. For instance, a hardware architecture may haunt us for years in a multitude of incarnations. Traditionally known as upward compatibility, this is frequently something that is sought after as a means of minimizing risk. It is ultimately a customer choice that is made to avoid the risks of porting or writing new applications.

Someone out there will always be building something new if someone else is willing to try it or thinks he or she can afford it—considering cost or risk. The ORB itself cannot totally stagnate because vendors constantly try to outdo one another by providing features that they feel differentiate them in the market. Somehow the technology does not seem as decadent as that of laundry detergent where it seems every other week there is a "new and improved" version that is indistinguishable from the last "new and improved" version. At the point when the biggest changes are in packaging, we may have real cause for concerns about stagnating. At least some of these differences ought to be technical innovations.

Although the OMG is dominant in this arena, there are several alternatives.

Is the OMG adoption the only one of its kind and, therefore, the only game in town? Definitely not. Others were first. A system freely available from Xerox Research Parc called ILU (Inter-Language Unification)[7] already has many of the same features and has adopted technology in part. It also offers features not currently found in CORBA.

Bolt Beraneck and Newman Consulting (BBN) had a similar system called Cronus. While it was not truly object-oriented, it had much of the same capabilities. Note that BBN has since come out with a CORBA-compliant product called Corbus.[8]

---

7. ILU information is available through: ftp://ftp.parc.xerox.com/pub/ilu/ilu.html
8. BBN's Corbus home page: http://www.bbn.com/products/dpom/corbus.htm

GTE Laboratories developed a system that was similar to CORBA (called DOM[9]) as a research project, but were using it internally for production in some divisions. There also are many other systems.[10]

Microsoft has not been standing around idly watching; it has had some similar services available for some time in a nondistributed version. It has been talking up its new distributed version, which is now available. The product has undergone several name changes: Cairo, Distributed OLE, and currently Distributed COM (DCOM for short). Meanwhile, several ORB vendors have a means to interoperate with COM and OLE that is based on an OMG technology selection. The details on this are in Chapter 11.

Microsoft offers an independent solution.

The biggest problem with the single-source (nonconsortium) alternatives is that they are single. Single-vendor solutions are sometimes a bottleneck and sometimes not ideal technically. Adopting any such foundation for development is generally a commitment to a long-term direction, so you need to be certain you head towards where you want to go.

---

9. DOM information is available via: F. Manola, S. Heiler, D. Georgakopoulos, M. Hornick, and M. Brodie, "Distributed Object Management," *International Journal of Intelligent and Cooperative Information Systems*, April 1992. There was also a WWW page, now well out of date, because the DOM project is no longer. The URL is: http://info.gte.com/ftp/doc/doc.html

10. In fact, the list is so long that I must apologize for constraining it to so few. Many vendors had previous systems that are (or were) similar. However, most are adopting CORBA and the related services in order to leverage the power of the consensus.

CHAPTER 3   *The Object Management Architecture*

> *The generality is that each layer of the model*
> *and its internal modules provides services by*
> *defining a set of objects which can only be accessed*
> *through well-defined interfaces.*
> —Richard W. Watson [Lampson-1988]

This chapter extends the formal taxonomy of terms. The terminology already appearing is in fairly wide consensual use. Those that follow are specific to this object model and, therefore, may exhibit small variance or specialization from the general terminology. In fact, the Object Management Group's (OMG) rewrite of its architecture has become even more precise and less ambiguous.

We need a reliable vocabulary to make certain we understand what others say.

One reason to become formal about the terminology is that the OMG is attempting to be precise. Part of this is for clarity. Part of it is to make certain everyone truly understands to what he or she is agreeing. Consensus is, in essence, an agreement of terms.

The OMG is concise and its consensus-building is a consensus on terms.

Let us assume you have the general idea about an object[1] and begin with the definition of a CORBA object. (We are leading up to the definition of what it means to manage objects, in OMG terms.)

A CORBA object is an instance of a class encapsulating operations, attributes, and exceptions. CORBA also admits the possibility of types that are not objects and types that the OMG documents call pseudo-objects (more about these later).

A CORBA object has operations, attributes, and exceptions.

The object management architecture (OMA) initially left out the possibility of exceptions (making them exceptional). The current redraft, however, admits them as a part of the Core 92 Model, which also provides much clearer and stronger definitions of the underlying object model.

What is a managed object? It is an object that is subject to systemwide administration and control; management is an indication of scale. A managed object is a client of system services, such as activation, installation, or dynamic behavior (also known as *dynamic control service*). These managed

Three categories of objects use CORBA.

---

1. A brief definition appears at the beginning of this book, but for an easy-to-understand explanation of an object, one of the best is Taylor 90. Alternately, I might recommend Guttman 95, which also goes into some depth about ORBs for nontechnical types.

objects are manifest as one of the following three basic forms (discussed in more detail in subsequent chapters):

- An application object
- An object facility
- An object service

A managed object is not an object request broker (CORBA) and we shall see why.

These objects interact as a framework of managed objects.

Although I will skip over the three forms a managed object may take for the moment, they are the primary building blocks of the OMA. These building blocks may layer, as shown in Figure 3-1. If you like Venn diagrams, they tend to participate somewhat like that shown in Figure 3-2. The original canonical diagram from OMG appears in Figure 3-3.

These are the fundamental, externally visible components of the OMG object model. A part of the objective is for all objects to have common semantics (to behave the same) and to do so regardless of their implementation (in an implementation-independent manner).

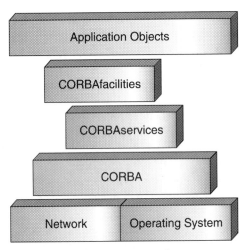

FIGURE 3-1.   Object model as layers

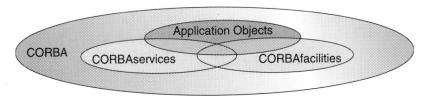

FIGURE 3-2.   Original model as Venn diagram

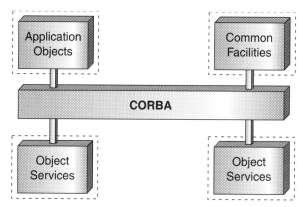

FIGURE 3-3. Original object model diagram

The original model saw changes when members began to see a greater requirement for application domain-specific interfaces. Although not part of the original model, their incorporation was formal in early 1996. Where common facilities find use across application domains, some vertical pieces that are specific to a domain are obvious. These domain interfaces are an area that will start to see interface specification and adoption. There are still application-specific interfaces that are probably too narrowly focused to formally specify (see Figure 3-4).

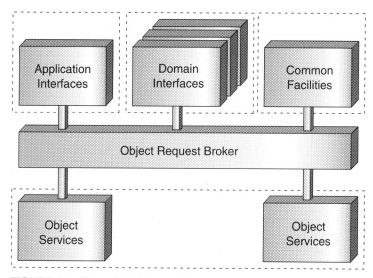

FIGURE 3-4. Extended object model

3.1   BENEFITS OF AN OMA

These are four general benefits of an object management architecture.

The OMA Guide tells us why we want an OMA and lists its many benefits. This information does not appear in the redraft but I think it is important not only for its historical content, but because it describes some of the original rationale. There are the following four major sections:

1. A list of technical objectives that satisfy the architecture
2. An object model, which is a definition of managed objects
3. A reference model, which explains how major parts work together in an ORB
4. A guide to how the OMG process works

The fourth is a metaissue.

The first three are of interest here. The technical objectives are useful as a measure to see if the OMG has accomplished its objectives, and to give some idea of the original proposal; thus, we start with them.

3.1.1   Technical Objectives

OMG is based on a list of basic tenets.

The OMG proposes a series of tenets that are the technical criteria for their objects. This is a set of the high-level original objectives that were the guide to the design and selection of technology for the architecture. The list appears here in the same order as it does in the OMA Guide:

- Conformance
- Distribution transparency
- Performance for both local and remote operations
- Extensible and dynamic behavior
- Provide a naming system architecture
- Queries based on names, attributes, and relationships
- Discretionary control
- Concurrency control
- Transactions to commit results or sequences of operations as atomic actions
- Robust operation and high availability
- Versioning
- Notification of events
- Provide relationship semantics between objects
- Provide a C API for all operations
- Minimal administration and ease management functions
- Internationalization
- Conform to pertinent industry standards

That seems a fair list. We will go on to explain these categories.

3.1.1.1   Conformance

The OMG stipulates that technology should conform to the object model, specifically in four areas:

Objects must conform in interface, implementation, program, and object.

- Interface inheritance (type conformance for interfaces)
- Implementation inheritance (a secondary concern)
- Program conformance—a program (or process) should be able to define and execute at least one method
- Object conformance—the definition and execution of an object's methods may occur in one or more processes

Explaining these conformance criteria is difficult without establishing a few more definitions, so we will jump ahead of ourselves for a moment to add some illumination to these goals. Since this is a book about CORBA, I will use examples from that to illustrate these terms. However, that is somewhat backwards, since the OMA describes a generality that the CORBA makes concrete. The OMA serves as a type, and CORBA is an instance of that type.

In the creation of an ORB, the OMG decided that objects are their interface (and hence they propose an Interface Definition Language). OMG IDL's[2] definition borrows heavily from C++. In fact, its lexical rules are currently in conformance with C++.[3] IDL is not a complete programming language: to be so, it would require flow control and it has none. IDL only describes the interface to operations and exceptions. The state or attributes of an IDL object are seen only as operation descriptions (their signatures), so the definition is indirectly observable by the trace that they leave.

OMG IDL is a language that describes a CORBA object's interface.

An IDL definition resembles a C++ class definition. A *class* is the description of an abstract data type; in other words, a pattern or template to which an object adheres if it is a member of that type family. Inheritance is a way of creating new classes with similarities to an existing one, but it may add something new (specialization). A class of this type is a derived class. A class that inherits from another obtains that other class's traits through inheritance.

IDL is a kissing cousin of C++.

Interface Inheritance

IDL (or the first type of conformance listed above) indicates that type families inherit interfaces (hold them in common). A derived type has at least the same interface as its parent and it may have additional methods (or operations) to which it will respond.

Families of the same IDL type inherit interfaces.

---

2. Throughout this book all references to IDL are OMG's IDL except for explicit exceptions.
3. Working Paper for Draft Proposed International Standard for Information Systems—Programming Language C++, Document Number ANSI X3J16/96—0108, ISO WG21/N0926, 28 May 1996.

Implementation Inheritance

Families of the same IDL type should inherit implementation.

Implementation Inheritance is another area where objects may conform, although it is a less important characteristic. It may sound confusing to say that this is a set of minimal conformance and then wave away part of that set. This means that if objects also conform in the secondary area, it is beneficial. It is not necessary and is not a requirement, but when it occurs it is good.

Implementation inheritance defined

Implementation inheritance means that an operation request to a derived object causes the code in the parent to execute. In effect, they share the same code, which executes whenever an inherited operation is invoked.

Inheritance of implementation tends to polarize people.

As we go along, I will try to point out bones of contention between members. Generally these questions engender debates between the opposing camps—sometimes so much so that it begins to resemble zealous behavior and is aptly termed a techno-religious war. One such debate is interface versus implementation inheritance. The two sides take the following positions:

1. You get more code reuse with implementation inheritance because the whole type family can use the same code.
2. You get less potential conflict in languages that do not share code well with interface inheritance.

Sharing implementation virtually guarantees that you always get the same behavior.

OMG widely allows the contested inheritance but does not require it.

In some type families this is not always desirable because the derived class (considered to be a more specific class) may require more specific behavior. OMG diplomatically allows both requirements in the minimal set for conforming to the objectives but it states that if you must give up one, then implementation is the one to let go.

Implementation inheritance is an implementation detail.

The final part to this point is that the OMA is about interface and not about implementation. Since only interfaces are up for adoption it does not make much sense to require implementation conformance, and implementation inheritance to a large degree is an implementation issue.

Program or Process Conformance

Minimally, a program (or process) must perform some computation.

The requirement for a program or a process to conform to OMG objectives is that it must define and execute at least one method. Note that this does not say if the method that it defines and executes is even in the process that defines it. If it, too, conforms, it must do both: define and execute.

Object Conformance

An object must also perform some computation.

For an object to be considered conforming it may have its methods defined and executed in one or more programs and processes. Note that this implies a single object may exist across multiple processes or even have different method definitions and executions in different processes. This makes for some peculiar-looking multiprocess objects.

3.1.1.2   Distribution Transparency

Transparency of distribution appears in 11 areas, as seen by the client of the object:

Transparency occurs in 11 cases.

1. Location
2. Access
3. Relocation
4. Representation
5. Communication mechanism
6. Invocation mechanism
7. Storage mechanism
8. Machine type
9. Operating system
10. Programming language
11. Security mechanism

The primary purpose of this is to make it easier to configure and move services, and to provide portability and interoperability for the clients of managed objects. Changes in any of these items should not require a client's recompilation or modification. Such changes should be transparent to the client.

This transparency makes an application developer's life easier.

Location Transparency

The client has no dependency on the physical location of an object, its operations, or attributes. Knowledge of an object's location is not interesting.

Oblivious to location

Access Transparency

The client has no dependency on the path to the object. The communication method or network protocol through which the object is accessible is not interesting to the client.

Oblivious to access path

Relocation Transparency

The client has no dependency or requirement to know if an object (its operations or attributes) relocates. Object relocation is secondary, but when it occurs, a client should not require any modification to obtain service after it relocates. The client not only does not want to know where an object is, it does not want to know if it moves. In other words, the client should work regardless of these types of changes.

Oblivious to issues such as the object has moved

Representation Transparency

The client could care less how attributes and methods affect an object (this includes persistence and computation). An object's internal representation is free to change without affecting its client.

Oblivious to how an object does what it does

Communication Mechanism Transparency

Oblivious of how it gets a request

The client does not see the transport and has no concerns about that underlying transport, whether local or remote.[4] The communication mechanism is transparent in that the client is unaffected regardless of how it must communicate.

Invocation Mechanism Transparency

Oblivious to how an object is invoked

An object requires no knowledge about the way in which invocations occur: invocation in the client may occur through the static or dynamic interfaces. Additionally, the client does not require any knowledge of how the delivery of a request to an object occurs: delivery to the implementation may be through static or dynamic interfaces.

Storage Mechanism Transparency

Oblivious to how an object survives

Persistence (the storage mechanism) is another area that is a system implementation detail of which the client is unaware.

Machine Type, Operating System, and Programming Language Transparency

Oblivious to environment

These items also should not affect the client. This is inherent as a definition of middleware, whose purpose is to hide or minimize these very aspects of the computation environment.

Security Mechanism Transparency

Oblivious to security issues

The client need not be aware of the security mechanism and its implementation. This is true up to the point where the client wants to make decisions about security.

3.1.1.3 *Performance for Both Local and Remote Operations*

Six technical objectives are cited as evaluation criteria in the OMA for performance. They will be discussed in the following sections.

Scalability

The infrastructure must be scalable.

Specifically, scalability applies to request-processing time as the number of client-reachable objects and requests increase. The system requires acceptable operation performance in domains with either a high volume of requests, a large number of objects, or both.

---

4. There is a slight problem with this wording in that the outcomes of all operations are not equal. They are primarily different when the thread of control is within a single process as opposed to crossing process boundaries. A thread of control that crosses such bounds may fail with the outcome uncertain, thus allowing three states—success, failure, and maybe. There is more detail on this in Chapter 4.

Method Invocation Time

This includes the performance associated with both the first and all subsequent requests to local and remote objects and the subsequent responses.[5] If the system is not responsive and imposes much in the way of penalty, it is not nearly as useful.

Objects must be responsive.

Storage Overhead, and Resource Consumption

The storage overhead and resource consumption in the runtime use and performance of an object is not a concern. The object should not concern itself with environmental constraints. On a single machine the operating systems of today tend to optimize away these types of constraints. In a distributed environment, an ORB ought to serve a similar function (perhaps by orchestrating such operating systems) so that these types of issues are of less concern to application programmers.

Oblivious to environmental constraints

Parallelism

Parallelism is the degree to which concurrency finds support. Clients need do nothing special in support of concurrency. Again, operating systems traditionally perform this for applications. An ORB should help to hide these concerns from objects.

Oblivious to how concurrency occurs

Throughput

The capacity with which an object can handle significant numbers of simultaneous requests and responses is known as throughput. Object implementations using an ORB should handle high throughput nearly as well as implementations that do not use ORBs.

Oblivious to throughput constraints

Extensible and Dynamic Nature

The OMA specifically states "it should be possible" to dynamically make changes to the implementation of objects without affecting other objects whether or not they are clients. I specifically quote the "*should be*" because without that loophole this might prove to be a nearly impossible level of conformance. The OMA specifically cites the following types of changes, and states that it does not require client objects to recompile, relink, reload, or shut down the environment. The sense indicates a switch of one implementation

Oblivious to objects that change on the fly

---

5. The distinction between first and subsequent requests is primarily because additional overhead may accompany a "first" call as opposed to those that follow. If an object is inactive, the first call may activate it. If the object is run in a process, the first call may also have to awaken (or set up) that process. If the object is persistent, the first call may cause the persistent form to return to memory. The first call may also have to make a determination of an object's location or its new location (if it relocated), which may disappear through optimization for subsequent calls. Some security issues may require a decision on a first call. So in a best-case implementation and a worst-case first call there may exist significant differences between the first operation request and all subsequent requests.

for another and not modifying an implementation's code while it is running (until we get to item 4 below). The changes are specific:

Changes that should not affect objects

1. Adding new implementations should not affect existing objects.
2. Replacing implementations should not require interface change. The following also should not affect other objects:

   - The addition, deletion, or replacement of methods or attributes
   - Changing the type of an attribute or method
   - Renaming classes, attributes, or methods
   - Changing the class relationship (inheritance graph)

Replacing an implementation

3. Replacing the implementations where changes to the interface occur is a secondary concern. The nature of change is specifically to occur through versioning or through some dynamic facility for upgrade.

   - In the case of versioning, it must accommodate the older versions of the interface.
   - For instance, consider the deletion of a method. If an older client makes a request on an implementation by way of a method that is no longer present, the implementation should have a mechanism to handle this gracefully. Ideally, the request routes to a previous version still supporting that method but the *should be* caveat does allow a graceful failure.

Changing objects

4. Dynamic changes should be possible without changing the location of implementations (secondary). This allows the possibility of maintaining an interface at the original location while the implementation changes. Any part of the physical implementation can change, for example, methods, attributes, or relationships to other objects. Changes that are not dynamic are supportable, especially when they provide tangible benefits in performance or resource utilization.

3.1.1.4   *Provide a Naming System Architecture*

Various naming facilities need support.

It "should be possible" to support alternative naming conventions or systems and policies. Specifically, the naming system must support *names* mapped within a *context* to an *object*. This provides:

1. Name spaces (presumably scoped contexts) in which unambiguous object naming occurs. Objects may have more than one name or change names. So names are attributes and objects are values, and either attributes or values may change.
2. Object handles are a unique reference to an object regardless of other names. This "handle" uniquely identifies an object.[6]

---

6. There are a large number of caveats that ought to accompany this particular objective. Several terms really require further definition: what does it mean to "uniquely identify an object"? This may be easy or hard depending on how intimately "identify" is defined and whether the object is local or remote, or whether this means that identification by handle is only valid for implementations and not for clients, or if "unique" applies to a class as opposed to an instance.

CHAPTER 4 *Common Object Request Broker Architecture*

Not ideas about the thing but the thing itself.
—Wallace Stevens

Common Object Request Broker Architecture (CORBA) is a communication facility specifically for objects. Below it lies the transport, which the ORB uses according to the vendor's desire. Above it are all the OMA-compliant objects, services, and facilities. Also above it is whatever application you have chosen to create or buy, which understands and knows how to communicate using CORBA.

The CORBA interface describes its contract with OMA-compliant objects that use it.

CORBA is a layer of abstraction that hides, or papers over, the differences in a heterogeneous environment. As middleware it sits in the middle, between the application and the network operating system. CORBA layers over the network and OS in a heterogeneous environment. It does not hide the network and OS so much as it allows developers to hide them. If application programmers really need to make a direct OS or network service call, they may. However, CORBA abstracts many network and OS services, making them appear as objects within the ORB. CORBA objects may also wrap the non-ORB requests that may occur. These inherently non-ORB services then become the implementations of some CORBA object.

What CORBA does not hide directly may hide behind object interfaces.

Non-CORBA applications may coexist with applications that are written using CORBA. It is not necessary that all applications use CORBA once one CORBA application is installed. CORBA is not externally apparent outside of its applications, except in some minimal administrative ways, such as installing and running an ORB daemon if there is one for the given implementation. CORBA, as a messaging system, bridges (or acts as a message conduit) between clients and implementations. When both exist within a single process or runtime, the bridging occurs all within that single process. Message bridges within a single process are known by their style of invocation: intraprocess.

CORBA has three invocation styles: intraprocess, interprocess, and intermachine.

When a client and implementation are in different processes on the same machine, CORBA messages between the two. This invocation style is interprocess.

Note: Poem line from a poem of the same title in *The Palm at the End of the Mind: Selected Poems and a Play* by Wallace Stevens, edited by Holly Stevens. Copyright © 1967, 1969, 1971 by Holly Stevens. Used with permission of Vintage Books, a division of Random House, Inc., New York.

A third form of invocation style is intermachine. In this, requests from a client to an implementation cross machine boundaries. The client resides in a process of one machine while an implementation that the client uses lives in a process on another machine.

All three styles of invocation are virtually identical to the client. The differences are pointed out in Section 4.7.4, Location Transparency. The client makes all three styles as a local (intraprocess) invocation.

CORBA is not just a single entity. It trivially consists of four primary components: (1) the ORB, (2) the stub, (3) the skeleton, and (4) the object adapter (OA). Frequently such a description includes four other primary components: (5) the dynamic invocation interface (DII), (6) the dynamic server interface (DSI), (7) the interface repository, and (8) the implementation repository.

Let us look at the surface of CORBA so that we can understand it by seeing its features.

4.1   OBJECT INTERFACES

An interface definition language specifies a CORBA object's contract with the system.

For practical purposes we are going to discuss a CORBA object every time we discuss objects unless we indicate otherwise. The CORBA object is an interface definition in Interface Definition Language (IDL).[1] IDL will be discussed further in Section 4.4. An IDL interface is a contract by an object to perform in certain ways. A well-specified interface is a contract that guarantees an object's behavior.

An IDL contract does not support certain issues.

There may be trade-offs that are desirable for a client, just as there are trade-offs in implementations. A variety of reasons motivate trade-offs, including:

- Faster operation
- Greater accuracy
- Minimization of valuable resource usage
- No interruptions of other services
- No interruptions by other services

IDL does not make quality-of-service guarantees.

These reasons often go by the name *quality-of-service* (QOS). IDL does not currently specify any QOS issues in the contract. If implementation detail was a part of IDL, then certain contracts might be able to tell us something more specific about the QOS issues. However, while the OMA Guide lists implementation inheritance as a secondary technical objective it would like to see achieved, there is no way at the moment that this occurs.[2]

Some QOS may be available at runtime by way of a broker, a trader, or just a service directory lookup. These may be able to tell you the additional information you need to know before accepting a contract for a particular service.

---

1. There is a potential for this one-to-one correspondence between object and interface to change. Objects that offer multiple interfaces are under discussion at the moment but it is a little early yet to predict the outcome.

2. Although, as always, it is under consideration and has been the center of frequent discussions. Some QOS issues are bound to be solved in the very near future.

4.2   CORBA INTERFACES

As was mentioned earlier, CORBA interface is a collection of three things: operations, attributes, and exceptions.

> *A CORBA interface is operations, attributes, and exceptions.*

An operation is similar to a function call, process call, or method invocation. It passes a message to an object to perform some request.

An attribute is some visible information (state or data) that an object possesses. As it happens, there are read-write and read-only attributes (in the IDL language). The actual access to an attribute is through an operation. Attributes are really *accessor* (a get operation) and *mutator* (a set operation). A read-only attribute has only the accessor.

Finally, an interface may have one or more exceptional conditions associated with it. These are the possible failure conditions that one may generate when some unexpected condition occurs. Exceptional conditions notify a client of a fault occurring. An operation error is user or programmer error. A fault is a system failure of some sort.

On the other hand, the interface itself does not raise exceptions; the methods within that interface raise exceptions. The exception is a part of an operation definition. So the interface is only a collection of operations. Exceptions are singled out partially because they are exceptional. Attributes are singled out because they are operations that have very little (some would say no) interesting behavior and appear visually distinct in an interface.

> *Exceptions are bound to operations.*

An object with zero operations is not interesting, except as a name-space qualifier. If it has no operations, it cannot send or receive messages. Messages are the crux of CORBA.

> *An interface without operations is a name-space qualifier.*

Because CORBA does not distinguish between local and remote objects to the client, the operation is similar to an RPC, which many people use today to build client-server systems. If an operation in CORBA is the same as an RPC, why was all this work necessary, and why all the fuss over an OO version of an RPC? CORBA is also unlike an RPC, as we shall see.

4.2.1   Function Call Versus Method Semantics

A function call is procedural code. It is not explicitly local to data (in the way an object encapsulates and provides access through the method invocation). It primarily affects data that appears as a parameter or that it constructs and returns, or that is generally visible to it (visible globally). The ORB would lose some object orientation.

> *Function calls frequently expose their state as parameters.*

Coupled with the semantics is the idea of an interface as a first-class type that appears in CORBA. An operation belongs to an object, and that target is implicit in the signature, acting as a *controlling parameter.* A procedure or function call has none.

> *Function calls have no controlling parameter.*

A function call does not have a notion of interface, or encapsulation. Function calls do have a signature. A function call has no attributes—other than its parameter(s) and result.

> *Functions have no interface or attributes but do have signatures.*

Interfaces are natural groups for managing sets of like things.

Objects are interfaces, and interfaces are an important method by which one may find interesting services at runtime. To facilitate this type of discovery, the CORBA comes with an interface repository. This is a place to investigate available interfaces. For function calls to offer similar facilities they would need artificial grouping (perhaps even replicated by group by data type, if they operate across multiple types).

Objects require activation.

Objects also require activation. If they are in a separate (server) process, this process may require starting (function calls as RPCs generally can do that now with some auxiliary support).[3] However, the server (for instance a spreadsheet program) may also require information about the specific object (a spreadsheet cell) to activate it as well as the process. This information includes where it is stored (if it is persistent), who has write-access to it, and what sort of services are available with the object. CORBA has the notion of activation for objects. Function calls have no such notion.

4.3 OBJECT IDENTIFIERS

Object identifiers are handles to objects.

The OMA specifies that objects have handles by which we may reference them. These handles are object identifiers (OIDs). The OID is a first-class representative for an object because the OID is also an object, at least when the IDL maps into an OO language. This OID is a handle for the object that is currently in use.

In most cases passing the handle over the wire can be cheaper than passing the object.

Instead of passing the object over the wire as a parameter, we pass its handle instead. This makes sense because handles are only identifiers and usually are much smaller than the object. Passing the handle to an object saves bandwidth.[4]

Because this handle is a first-class representation for the object, you can make operation requests right on the handle as you would if you had the object it represents. This handle forwards the request to the actual object so you do not need to know any location information, thus providing location transparency.

Object reference invocation automatically routes requests to the object through CORBA.

In CORBA the OID exists as an object reference (objref for short). In both the C and C++ language mappings the objref is the only part of an object that the client sees. It behaves as if it were the object. The client makes requests on the objref, and the request routes (under the covers of the CORBA) to the real object. This occurs whether it is local (intraprocess) in the same runtime, in a different process (interprocess), or on another machine (intermachine) entirely.

3. A section contrasting CORBA and RPCs can be found in Chapter 6.
4. There are cases where a multiple request on an object reference is more expensive than copying the entire object locally once. Such things happen frequently when over-the-wire occurs on a wide-area network (WAN).

The drawback to this is that sometimes it seems necessary to transfer an actual object to the operation. CORBA more or less disallows this because of the nature of its objects. There are ongoing discussions about adding objects that may occur as a parameter or result, perhaps by adding a new keyword to IDL. Such transferable objects sometimes go by the name of *server-less objects* or *pass-by-value*.

Parameters and results are never CORBA objects, only object references.

Early on it becomes apparent that it is useful to define almost all objects in IDL, even those that are not going to be first-class CORBA objects. These objects have IDL definitions but are always created in some target language without using IDL. Such objects are pseudo-objects (to distinguish them from CORBA objects and from OMA nonobjects). They appear in IDL for consistency, but the ORB implementer creates them directly. The primary pseudo-objects are: BOA, Context, Environment, NVList, ORB, Principal, Request, and TypeCode. Each is covered separately later in this book.

Pseudo-objects have IDL definitions but are not implemented via IDL.

The objref is a construct of the IDL compiler, which generates the specific language mapping.[5] It is a type relation to the interface (there will be more detail in Section 4.4). In C++ it is an object (or a reference to an object) that references the real object. In the C language it is likely a collection of function calls that are stand-ins for the object operations. The C language does not have a natural object representation. You do it figuratively as if you were manipulating an object by way of methods. While C has no object type, it still has complete access to CORBA objects. The C mapping was the first language-mapping standard from OMG. It was critical to offer C language support to those shops still using much C code or having Legacy systems written in C.

IDL even supports non-OO languages.

4.4 CORBA IDL

OMG IDL is one of the founding principles of CORBA and all of the OMG adoptions to date. IDL is CORBA's object contract language. IDL is not a complete programming language. It has no iterators or flow control. It is primarily a language in which one can express complex types called interfaces. It does not provide implementations for interfaces. The IDL language supports data types, a few (very few) conventions that allow some preprocessing work, and things like name scoping.

IDL is an object contract language.

Figuratively, the IDL compiler can be thought of as being composed of two parts: a front end (FE or IDL Compiler) and the back end (BE or IDL BE). While this two-stage implementation is not a requirement, it makes discussion easier by separating functionality into two logical parts. The IDL FE understands IDL and may do some of the preprocessing (assuming it does not happen through a preprocessor before reaching the real IDL FE). The BE

The IDL compiler translates IDL into a target language.

---

5. Technically, the IDL compiler is really an IDL translator. It does not compile anything, but it does translate IDL into some programming language according to how its mapping is specified.

takes information from the FE and produces the translation (or mapping). The BE is target-language specific. In other words, it understands the target language mapping and creates source code (for C, C++, Smalltalk, Ada, Java, Rexx, COBOL, or whatever—each target may be a separate BE).

IDL is similar to tools used for creating RPC code.

The BE for C and C++ generates stubs for the client side of the interface and skeletons for the implementation side of the interface. If you have used an RPC language translator then you are probably familiar with the concept. Sun's RPCGEN and DCE IDL are very similar to an OMG IDL stub and skeleton mapping. RPCs generally produce a client-side and a server-side set of stubs.

C and C++ code interoperability constrains the C++ mapping.

However, C code generated by IDL has some constraints due to C's lack of objects (as do all nonobject language mappings). The CORBA designers also wanted to make the C and C++ mapping interoperable. This constrained the C++ mapping because some C++ things cannot be done in any reasonable manner from C. An example is passing a C++ class instance into a C program for method invocation. Receiving it back again intact could cause considerable aggravation. Because C only understands things at a function call level, one must pass pointers only to method calls. C also has no understanding of C++ references, which do not translate well (they translate to pointers in C) although they might in Pascal, where pointers would not work well.

4.4.1   Object Description

IDL allows type declaration and type definition.

The primary thing to create in a language for interfaces is an interface. In IDL the word *interface* is a keyword and means something quite specific. IDL allows type declarations (the act of declaring that something is of some type) and type definitions (where a type is a composition of types that IDL understands).

The composition of a simple interface in IDL would appear as shown in Example 4-1. This IDL defines a CORBA object with the name box. It has one attribute, which is a content, that has the type short (short integer, as in C or C++).[6]

EXAMPLE 4-1. Trivial interface

```
interface    Box
{
    attribute    short    content;
};
```

---

6. Strictly speaking, an IDL short-maps to an integer within a specific range, independent from potential target implementation languages. It then maps into an appropriate target-language type satisfying the range requirement.

Attribute is a convention that makes it appear you are defining some state with the name `content` in the interface but the mapping generates operations. In both C and C++ this maps into two separate operations. One applies (sets or mutates) the state (`content`) while the other retrieves (gets or accesses) the state. The attribute keyword is shorthand notation for operations that occur frequently in objects: get and set operations.

Attribute is a short form for declaring get and set operations for some state.

4.4.2 Signatures

The IDL definition here of a window interface illustrates signatures as shown in Example 4-2. This interface has two operations: one called `open( )`, the other `close( )`. Neither of the two signatures accepts parameters, and both indicate a `boolean` (true or false) result.

Instead of the operations returning a state, their signatures indicate they may raise an exception of failure or do nothing on success (see Example 4-3).

An object definition of the second form is a totally different object than the one shown in Example 4-2. The signatures of the operations are different. Although they may accomplish the same result, they have different signatures and, therefore, offer totally distinct and separate contracts. Their behavior is different.

Operations may have the same name but their signatures may differ.

Object identities in CORBA are their interfaces. If any signature or attribute declaration changes, the types are different and cannot be the same object. This makes the two interfaces just presented very different even though they are both called Window.

Interfaces express the identity of CORBA objects.

An additional component of the signature that we should mention is its mode; more formally, the operation mode. If there is no mode declaration, then Normal mode is the default. Currently, the only operation mode that one can declare is `oneway`. We will tell you more about this mode later.

EXAMPLE 4-2. Signature

```
interface    Window
{
    boolean    open( );
    boolean    close( );
};
```

EXAMPLE 4-3. Variant signature

```
interface    Window
{
    void    open( ) raises (Failed);
    void    close( ) raises (Failed);
};
```

4.4.3   Parameter Passing Modes

Another interesting part of the signature is a part of the parameter that tells its passing mode. Passing modes have the following types:

- In
- Out
- InOut

Parameter modes add direction to information flowing through an operation.

These instruct the compiler about the direction that information travels through a method. Consider the interface shown in Example 4-4.

EXAMPLE 4-4. Signature with parameter modes

```
interface   Account
{
    void    debit( in money amount, out money balance );
    void    credit( in money amount, out money balance );
    void    adjustment( inout money amount );
};
```

An Account interface here shows three operations: (1) debit, (2) credit, and (3) adjustment. The debit operation has two parameters (as does credit): (1) in amount and (2) out balance, indicating that on invocation, amount will carry information in to the operation and balance will carry information out from the operation on its completion.

The adjustment operation, however, has a single parameter: *InOut amount.* This amount carries information into the operation as well as out.

Parameter modes also indicate ownership.

In addition to the direction information travels to and from the operation, this indicates to the compiler the ownership of the parameter. This is not very interesting in the case of simple types, but it is for more complex types. Ownership is an important distinction for things such as memory management.

Ownership is important for memory-management issues.

For instance, assume the money type is a constructed type, as in Example 4-5. Someone owns the allocation and construction of such a type (someone here may include the language runtime if such allocation and construction are implicit).

EXAMPLE 4-5. Constructed type

```
structure money
{
    long        units;
    short       fractions;
    currency    currency_type;
};
```

In the case of the deposit operation, the caller owns the amount parameter; whereas, something that is called owns the balance parameter. In the adjustment operation, the caller owns the amount parameter but something that is called may alter or change it.

4.4.4   Types

Before giving more examples of interfaces in IDL we need a quick run through the IDL types. What these map into for C or C++ (an IDL target language) is the subject of another book. However, it is useful to have some cursory understanding of what the types map into for illustrative purposes. The IDL types are:

char	unsigned long	union
boolean	long long	string
octet	unsigned long long	wide string
enum	float	array
wide char	double	sequence
short	long double	any
unsigned short	struct	object
long		

The example mappings shown in Tables 4-1, 4-2, and 4-3 are relatively close to the real C mapping. The C++ mapping, however, is much more complicated than C. A quick look at the union mapping provides a taste of the complexity. In C++ object references have two forms: by value and by reference. That means an IDL BE generates virtually twice as much for objects in C++.

TABLE 4-1. **Simple IDL Type Mappings**

IDL Type	C mapping of type	C++ mapping of type
char	signed char	signed char
octet	unsigned char	unsigned char
short	short	short
unsigned short	unsigned short	unsigned short
long	long	long
unsigned long	unsigned long	unsigned long
float	float	float
double	double	double
long double	twice a double	twice a double
boolean	unsigned char	unsigned char
enum	enum	enum

any	`typedef struct any {`
	`    TypeCode _type;`
	`    void *_value;`
	`} any;`
		`class Any {`
		`    ...;`
		`};`

TABLE 4-2. Constructed IDL Type Mappings

IDL type	C mapping of type	C++ mapping of type
struct	struct	struct

union name switch (long) {
case 1: type1 name1;
case 2: type2 name2;
default: type3 name3;
};
	typedef struct {
	long _d;
	union {
	    type1 name1;
	    type2 name2;
	    type3 name3;
	} _u;
	} name;
		class name
		{
		public:
		name();
		name(const &name);
		~name();
		name &operator=(const name&);
		void _d(long);
		long _d() const;
		void name1(type1);
		type1 name1() const;
		void name2(type2);
		type2 name2() const;
		void name3(type3);
		type3 name3() const;
		};

<type>array_name[<length>];	<type>array_name[<length>];	<type> array_name[<length>];

TABLE 4-3. Parameterized IDL Type Mappings

IDL type	C mapping of type	C++ mapping of type
string<length> name;	char *name = buffer[length];	char *

sequence<type,
count> name;
	typedef struct {
	  unsigned long
	_maximum;
	  unsigned long
	_length;
	  type *_buffer;
	} name;
		class name
		{
		 public:
		 name();
		 name(ulong max);
		 name(ulong max, ulong length, type *data,
		boolean release=FALSE);
		 name(const &name);
		 ~name();
		 name &operator=(const name&);
		 ulong maximum() const;
		 void length (ulong);
		 ulong length() const;
		 type &operator[](ulong index);
		 const type &operator[] (ulong index) const;
		};

Additionally, there are variant mappings for the bound versions of string and sequence (we show only the unbounded version). The Any type mapping for C++ allows insertion and extraction via assignment operators (`<<=` and `>>=`). As a result, that class is quite large and complicated because separate operations appear for each of the types.

However, the preceding tables contain enough of the mapping flavor to make light discussions on language mapping and its aspects comprehensible.

As was mentioned earlier, the IDL compiler may have a front end, which understands the IDL syntax. It may also have a back end, which understands how to convert to the compiler's internal representation of IDL into some target language. It is possible to build a lighter-weight compiler that is one piece (one stage). Such a compiler knows how to map into the target language without first constructing an internal representation, as happens in a FE/BE (two-stage) compiler.

The IDL compiler translates from IDL into a target language mapping.

An alternative might be a programming environment that populates its runtime with objects constructed by an IDL specification and then is supplemented with implementation detail by interpreting dynamic code. Another alternative is a mix of IDL compiler supplemented by the Dynamic Invocation interface (see Chapter 5), which operates on the IDL-specified objects. A variety of different implementation styles are available.

Languages that have standard mappings are C, C++, Ada '95, and Smalltalk. The first three are static, or statically bound, languages. A static language is one in which all object definitions (they are bound to their names) occur at compile time; in other words, before runtime. The Smalltalk language is dynamic and is not statically typed or bound.[7]

Several IDL mappings are now available.

The C mapping is in all specifications since the original CORBA Version 1.1 specification. The C++ mapping is part of the CORBA 2.0 specification. The two mappings are able to interoperate from the very first. Partly, this occurs because C and C++ have common ancestry in that C++ is compliant with some aspects of C. The C++ mapping also has constraints due to C's limitations. Although avoiding some of the technical difficulties in a dual mapping (some would say while sacrificing C++ capabilities), the C++ writer must observe certain restrictions as policy because of this desire to achieve interoperable code.

We will now touch on some C and C++ interoperability considerations. One common mechanism by which the two languages achieve interoperability is to provide a C wrapper around a C++ implementation. This is not the only implementation for providing this capability but it provides a fairly understandable example. In a "wrapper" implementation, the implementation may be in C++ with C interfaces wrapping the C++ internal portion. Such a

C and C++ are interoperable target mappings.

---

7. Note that in static and dynamic typing, types are checked (before or during runtime). In static or dynamic binding, names are bound to types. Static and dynamic linking is when (or how) names are linked (assigned) to addresses (in memory offsets). A C++ object is statically typed and statically bound but may be either statically or dynamically linked.

wrapper may be a *thin wrapper,* in which not much occurs except passing the invocations directly through to C++. The wrapper may also be a *thick wrapper.* In these wrappers, a part of each operation or some housekeeping details, such as instance management, may occur before invoking or after receiving the result from the C++ internals.

An alternate implementation is to write the ORB in C (rather than C++) and essentially place C++ objects as wrappers around such a C kernel. Writing a C API directly into an ORB kernel imposes a small penalty at runtime for using the C++ interface. In this scenario, however, when C++ is in use, the ORB would have to flatten (deflate) and inflate C++ objects on entry and exit to the ORB proper.[8] (See Figure 4-1.)

Dynamic languages may choose a different approach.

The Smalltalk implementation, however, approaches the issue from still another front: that of a dynamic environment. For a good explanation of Smalltalk, I would recommend Ben-Natan's CORBA guide.[9] It covers a fair amount of detail about Hewlett-Packard's DST (Distributed Smalltalk) implementation,[10] which is a product distinct from the company's C++ ORB (ORB Plus).

4.4.5 Stubs

On coming across an interface definition, the IDL compiler produces two items of primary import: a client stub (the implementation of the objref) and an implementation skeleton.

The stub is the object reference implementation for a real object.

The stub is the local object through which the client makes requests. A stub is an object that the IDL compiler generates and whose method calls are complete implementations. There is nothing for an engineer to implement in the stub. The compiler makes sure that the interface maps onto the correct

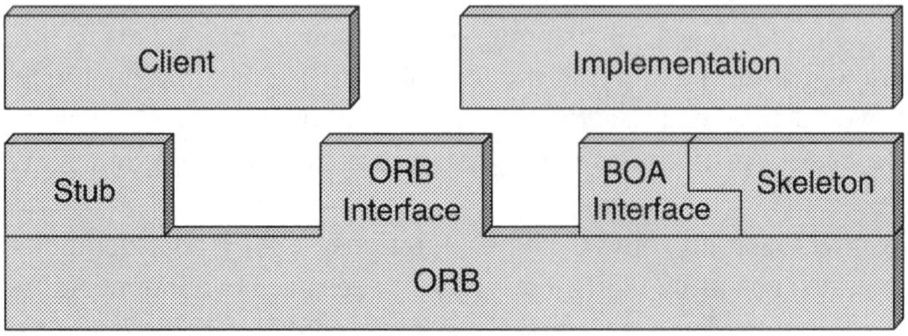

FIGURE 4-1. CORBA with static binding components

8. It may be that neither of these two mechanisms is in use. They are here primarily to demonstrate some of the surrounding complexity and to partially explain why things such as memory management are somewhat less than natural for C++.

9. [Ben-Natan-1995].

10. DST changed hands since his book was written. ParcPlace-Digitalk purchased it. It was originally based on the ParcPlace product and fits right into their product strategy.

target language. It also generates the correct code to locate the skeleton and the marshaling code necessary to encode parameters (place the bytes into the correct order) if they need to go over the wire. The stub code the compiler produces also handles all the transport-specific details that require handling.

How this occurs is partially implementation specific. It does not matter how, as long as access to the stub adheres to the adopted language mapping.

Because the skeleton is the "real" object (a skeleton of the implementation), the stubs frequently get the moniker of *proxy*. This proxy is the object reference's implementation (the stub).

The stub is the "real" object's local (client-side) proxy.

4.4.6   Skeletons

The *skeleton* is the implementation-side equivalent of the stub. The compiler provides the correct language mapping for invocation to the object. The compiler also takes care of the unmarshaling code if the call is coming over the wire. Skeletons are skeletons because they are method calls with no implementation detail. The software engineer constructing the object must fill in the implementation detail for the object by adding code in the empty method calls.

The skeleton is a framework for constructing the object's actual implementation.

The skeleton is also different from the stub in that it coordinates invocation with an object adapter. While the stub and skeleton represent the object's formal type, the object adapter represents the style of the object's implementation. The methods in the skeleton must interact with the object adapter to start the implementation server and activate the object, if required.

Skeletons participate with an object adapter for things such as activation.

This requires that methods be accessible to the object adapter so that the adapter and skeleton can readily cooperate. This requires that the object must make its methods available to the adapter so that the thread of control can pass to the object after (or while) activation occurs. Objects make themselves available to the BOA through something named an implementation definition. Unfortunately, the implementation definition has no definition. It is one of the open issues that are yet to be resolved.

Object adapters access the object's methods by using an implementation definition object.

While not a requirement, one way to implement such a mechanism that provides this type of facility is through an execution procedure vector (EPV). This is a table in which each entry may contain a method reference. Accessing the table through an operation offset, such as by the third method in the object, accesses that method in the implementation object. The methods register at runtime and this allows the object adapter to access them when necessary. Information about object adapters appears in Chapters 7 and 8.

4.5   OBJECT REFERENCE

The object reference is a runtime instance of an OID. It lives in a process. An objref is the client's view of a CORBA object. An objref is a handle through which one requests operations on the object. The client may use it when it is local to the client. To the client the object reference, or proxy, is indistinguishable from the real object because it has the same interface as the object.

An object reference is an instance of a stub.

*Object references may be
made persistent.*

One of the requirements for an objref is that it has a persistent form that should be at least readable enough for a human to transcribe. This allows transfer in e-mail (electronic or otherwise), printing it onto a piece of paper, or keeping it in a file. The persistent form of an objref may not make much sense (comprehensible information may not be apparent) but it requires readability.

*Persistent object references
are translated to printable
strings.*

The persistent form of an objref is a string form. An object reference also needs some method to take it from its string form and turn it back into a valid runtime entity. Valid here may mean that the system fails gracefully if the reconstituted objref is no longer functional for some reason. In most cases the invocation should continue normally and an operation request occurs on the reconstructed object reference.

*Allowing persistent refer-
ences causes architectural
difficulties.*

Having references that are persistent creates a number of problems:

- They may survive for a very long time.
- The object may move one or more times since the object reference's last use.
- The object it references may have been put out of its misery after a long and fruitful life.
- There is no easy way to update or modify the persistent form.
- There is no garbage collection for the persistent form.

*An ORB is the extent of its
object references.*

Additionally, there may exist multiple instances of such ORBs. Any single ORB is known by the scope of its objrefs. In other words, an ORB extent covers the area where its object references are meaningful. References to such extents are domains. An ORB domain's extent is partially an administrative function.

For example, installing applications for an organization requires that they be set up within some domain. If that organization or company has offices in different locations, it may or may not make sense to create separate domains for each office. From an administrative standpoint it may be simpler to have a single domain. From a scaling standpoint, it may be best to have multiple domains.

*A client may participate in
any number of ORBs with-
out realizing it.*

A client may use objrefs that belong to different ORBs. An operation request via objref is managed by the ORB to which that objref belongs. A client is perfectly capable of participating in multiple ORBs by having objrefs belonging to each. The client has no need to know that it is making requests through different ORBs. This is transparent from the client's viewpoint.

Much of this multiple ORB and domain discussion assumes that each ORB domain is an instance of the same implementation (by a single vendor). Different specializations of ORBs (perhaps by different vendors) can have conflicting implementations. In such cases, varying degrees of interoperability are available. These enter the discussion in Chapter 10 on interoperability.

*Object references derive
from the object interface.*

All CORBA objects derive from the object interface; to paraphrase, the object interface is the base type for all objects. Any time an object reference is present, the client has access to all operations in the object interface (Example 4-6).

EXAMPLE 4-6. **Object interface**

```
module  CORBA
{
    interface Object
    {
        ImplementationDef get_implementation();

        InterfaceDef get_interface();

        boolean is_nil();

        Object duplicate();
        void release();

        boolean is_a (in string logical_type_id)();
        boolean non_existent();

        boolean is_equivalent(in Object other_object);
        unsigned long hash(in unsigned long maximum);

        Status create_request(
                    in Context          ctx,
                    in Identifier       operation,
                    in NVList           arg_list,
                    inout NamedValue    result,
                    out Request         request,
                    in Flags            req_flags);

        Policy  get_policy(in PolicyType policy_type);

        sequence<DomainManager> get_domain_managers();
    };
};
```

This object interface has 12 operations:

1. Get Implementation
2. Get Interface
3. Is Nil
4. Duplicate
5. Release
6. Is A
7. Nonexistent
8. Is Equivalent
9. Hash
10. Create Request (see Chapter 5)
11. Get Policy (see Chapter 12)
12. Get Domain Managers (see Chapter 12)

The first nine we will discuss here. Create Request is essential to the DII, so its description is in Chapter 5 on dynamic invocation. The last two are part of the security level two operations (Get Policy and Get Domain Managers) and are in Chapter 12 on security.

4.5.1   Get Implementation

The Get Implementation operation takes no parameters and returns an implementation definition. While an implementation definition has operations in Pseudo-IDL or PIDL (see Chapter 9), it has no standard implementation at this time.[11]

We do know that it is a description of the implementation, that the BOA makes use of it, and that an implementation repository exists. One possible implementation technique for an implementation definition appears at the end of Section 4.4.6 on the skeleton.

4.5.2   Get Interface

The Get Interface operation takes no parameters and returns an interface definition (see Chapter 9). The interface definition is a complete, detailed description of the entire interface (see Chapter 9).

4.5.3   Is Nil

The Is Nil operation is a built-in assertion about whether a particular object reference exists or not. The operation appears on the object interface but does not use the object's implementation, meaning that it is relatively inexpensive and has no requirement to go over the wire.

This operation takes no parameters and returns a Boolean, however, its value is `OBJECT_NIL` (in C) when it is true.

4.5.4   Duplicate

The Duplicate operation allows a client to make a copy of an object reference, essentially a duplicate. This is a requirement because an object reference is an opaque construct that differs from ORB to ORB. The implementation is not necessary for duplicate or release. Duplicate takes no parameters and returns an object.

The fact that the implementation knows nothing about duplication and release also means that it is unable to distinguish whether a request comes from an original or duplicate. Requests on either are intentionally identical. Further, Duplicate is a request to duplicate the reference and not the implementation. If the intent is to make a duplicate implementation, then the implementation must participate in a service like that in Chapter 18.

---

11. PIDL is meant to indicate a pseudo-object—one expressed in IDL but not implemented in IDL.

4.5.5   Release

The Release operation takes no parameter and has no result. This operation allows storage reclamation to take place when the use of the reference is complete. The operation applies only to the reference and not the object implementation. Calling release on a reference affects no other references even if it is the original reference of that type in the runtime. If the intent is to delete an instance of the implementation, then the implementation must participate in a service such as that in Chapter 18.

4.5.6   Is A

The Is A operation returns a Boolean and takes one parameter: a Logical Type ID, which is a string that denotes a Repository ID (see Chapter 9).

The operation returns true if the object is or derives from the type given by the ID. This is without regard to the type the object is currently assuming. The ORB requires this information already to offer type-safe narrow.[12]

4.5.7   Nonexistent

The Nonexistent operation is to the implementation what Is Nil is to the reference—almost.

This operation takes no parameters and returns a Boolean. It returns true when the ORB unequivocally knows that the implementation no longer exists. Otherwise, it returns a false, meaning that if there is some equivocation then a request may still raise an Object Not Exist exception.

The caveat is that it makes this determination without invoking an application-level operation. This does not go quite so far as to say that the implementation does not participate in this determination, but it does say that if it does, it does so through some private means. Because the specification uses these weasel words,[13] this operation is moderately inexpensive, meaning that it may cache this information or make the determination as a side effect of some earlier operation.[14]

---

12. In several OO languages there is no safe way to narrow a derived type that is currently wider than at its creation because the narrower type information is not available. An object reference is capable of narrowing in a type-safe way because all type information is available.

13. The fact that Nonexistent is a useful and necessary operation ought to be clearer in the specification.

14. The least expensive implementation is one always returning false. Fortunately there is text that states an implementation that always returns a false is not compliant with CORBA. Such words do appear in the Object Identity Service (part of the CORBAservices Object Relationship Service). Similarly, though more explicit, the ramifications of Is Equivalent and Hash require study because an easy assumption is that the operations imply something they do not.

4.5.8   Is Equivalent

The Is Equivalent operation returns a Boolean and takes one parameter: an object. The comparison checks the operation's object reference against the parameter object reference to determine equivalence. Two references that are identical are equivalent. The ORB is not required to ascertain if two distinct references refer to the same object, although there is nothing prohibiting an implementation from making that determination.

4.5.9   Hash

The Hash operation returns an unsigned long and has one parameter: an Unsigned Long. The parameter is the maximum or upper bound on the hash value that the ORB returns. The lower bound is always zero.

Object references contain (or have available) some ORB-specific internal information that consists of enough information for an ORB to aid in the routing of requests. Since the implementation is not part of the specification, this internal information may be anything from a globally unique identifier to a lookup service and key where the ORB goes to determine what to do with requests.

Whatever the identifier consists of, the specification states that the value of the identifier never changes throughout an object's lifetime. This being the case, that information always produces the same hash value (assuming the same function applies).

Hashing provides a relatively inexpensive test (less expensive than the pair-wise tests of Is Equivalent). When two distinctly different hashes result, you definitely have two distinct references.

If an application requires a stronger notion of identity or equality, an implementer may use IDL to define the operation in the public interface. The idea is to not make a relatively expensive operation available for free.

4.6   VERSIONING

To reduce the problems caused by allowing persistent objrefs (allowing them to stay around virtually forever), interfaces must necessarily stay around forever (or at least some remnant). To allow object references to continue working much as expected and still provide for regular maintenance (fixes to errors) and upgrades (revisions), there is a requirement for some form of versioning for interfaces.

A specification for versioning is not yet in adoption.

Annotation of the object with some type of version ID (or version number) is one way to distinguish different renditions of an object during its production life cycle. Such a tag may appear in the IDL source and subsequent revisions require a means through which the version ID or version number marks that revision. So, in some sense, versions become another important aspect of an object's interface. However, versioning is currently under discussion and so remains implementation-specific for the short term.

In addition, it is now policy that object references are not truly ageless even though their string forms may stay around for years. On making a request on an objref, the policy is that the ORB attempts "best-effort" to access that object. The discovery of some fossilized objref during an expedition need not make it to a still-valid object. The ORB need only make its best effort to deliver the request but it may still fail to do so.

4.7 COMMUNICATION ISSUES

A number of communication issues come up continually in discussions about CORBA. Their frequency is one of the primary reasons for discussing them in this book. This section provides some background and, hopefully, some illumination about the following issues:

- Asynchronous messaging
- Relation to RPC
- Latency
- Location transparency

4.7.1 Connections, Asynchrony, and Blocking

Frequent complaints arise about CORBA's lack of asynchrony. Unfortunately, this problem muddles at least three classes of similar-sounding concepts: connect-oriented and connectionless, blocking and nonblocking, and synchrony and asynchrony.

Asynchrony and nonblocking can cause confusion.

Connection-oriented services establish a channel between receiver and transmitter, then use and release it. They attempt to provide error-free information transfer. *Connectionless* services treat individual frames as self-contained entities. Information transfer occurs by way of a "best-try" approach. If errors occur, the protocol discards the frame. A *blocking* request is one that waits for a response after sending a request. In a *nonblocking* request, the thread of control continues after a request occurs without waiting. A *synchronous* request (one exhibiting synchrony) is deterministic in that it completes within bounded time. If excess time occurs, the request is invalid, constituting an error. An *asynchronous* request (one exhibiting asynchrony), subsequently, has two characteristics: no bound on the speed of the request and no bound on its delay.

Let us enjoy a little controversy and destroy one myth immediately, namely that *all systems are asynchronous*. Even systems that synchronize every step fit the definition of an asynchronous system. So, complaining about the lack of asynchrony is not valid. Let us examine the known attributes of these systems and see if we can draw some useful conclusions.

All software systems are asynchronous.

Services and protocols are two distinct things. A *protocol* is an agreement or contract between entities about how they will proceed to exchange information. A *service* is something that one protocol layer offers to another layer.

Services and protocols are distinct.

Two types of data transport services are available: connection-oriented and connectionless.

TCP establishes a channel. UDP uses frames.

Connection-oriented service is often called a virtual connection or circuit, whereas connectionless is a datagram service. Some confusion occurs because Transmission Control Protocol (TCP) is a virtual connection protocol (connection-oriented) that is also reliable. User Datagram Protocol (UDP) is a datagram protocol (connectionless) that is also unreliable. An unreliable message is one sent without acknowledgment or retries. Conversely, constructing a reliable transport usually occurs by acknowledging the message.

Acknowledgments make communication reliable.

A reliable protocol can be implemented using a connectionless service by adding acknowledgments. Further, while a connection-oriented protocol utilizes a virtual connection, a connectionless service may create virtual circuits. Essentially, the connection service is a transport layer service and a virtual circuit or datagram occurs in the network layer. Either type of transport-layer service may be implemented with either type of network-layer service.

Blocking and nonblocking send and receive

Now, down to the finale, namely the three forms of messaging listed in Table 4-4 that we mentioned earlier: The first form, where both block, is a synchronous form (sender and receiver synchronize). The other two are asynchronous forms. In the case of the DII, requesting Invoke is the first form: synchronous.

The second form, with blocking Receive, is available with Send and Get Reply (synchronization defers to receive). The third form is available indirectly for both normal and one-way operations by setting flags as `CORBA::RESP_NO_WAIT` (previously described under Request). However, the third form may require more overhead if cycles are spent periodically checking back (polling) to see if a reply is waiting. Continuous checking is spinning.

One way is a nonblocking send.

In the case where a stub makes the request (and the client is not using the DII), however, all calls are blocking, except when the operation mode declaration is One Way (an IDL keyword). In IDL, operations have two modes, called operation attributes: One Way and Normal. Normal mode occurs any time One Way does not appear in the source.

Instructing the ORB to discard replies means the message is not reliable.

Essentially, One Way indicates to CORBA that there is no reply, which means the call occurs and immediately returns. The client continues and never knows precisely if there is a delivery of the request. An indication of `CORBA::INV_NO_WAIT` essentially states that if there is a reply, the ORB

TABLE 4-4. **Three Forms of Message Blocking**

Send:	Receive:
Blocking	Blocking
Nonblocking	Blocking
Nonblocking	Nonblocking

may feel free to discard and never transmit it. However, it is not an indication that an unreliable transport is in use.

It is also a fact that one may write asynchronous software on top of synchronous software, and synchronous software on top of asynchronous software. One may receive an acknowledgment back to a One Way operation by having the server call-back to the client. The timing is a bit more awkward but that is a given in asynchrony; the speed of request or its delay are unbounded.

Call-backs may help attain reliability at some cost.

Threads are the other factor that enters into the picture. Most operating systems have threads. With them, one may block (on Send or Receive) while other threads continue to operate. Using threads to attain asynchrony is recommended, since the application is the only thing that knows the semantics of the request.

Threading allows continuous activity while retaining reliability.

4.7.2   Relation to RPC

A second issue that comes up frequently is the relation of RPC to CORBA. People say they want interoperability. They sometimes wonder why the ORB is not built directly on top of an RPC.

Let us start with RPC. Three flavors of RPC are in frequent use; most of the others are proprietary or research systems. The first, Courier, came from Xerox Research Parc and was born around 1979 as part of Xerox Network Services (XNS). It is still in prevalent use inside Novell's Netware, which uses the Courier model.

RPC came from Xerox Research Parc.

In the mid 1980s Sun Microsystems wrote a second variation of RPC, which it used underneath the Network File System (NFS). Because NFS became popular, Sun's RPC became more widely used on all sorts of platforms. Sun's RPC came with something called eXternal Data Representation (XDR), which mapped the data from its native form into an external form and then to the native form of the receiver of the RPC call.

Sun Microsystems' RPC came along in the mid 1980s.

A third form of RPC came in the late 1980s. This later became the Distributed Computing Environment (DCE). DCE came from the Network Computing System (NCS) around 1986 and the Network Interface Definition Language (NIDL) work of Apollo computers—a workstation company that had many forward-thinking ideas and eventually became part of Hewlett-Packard. NIDL mapped data to alternate types using a principle of the name "receiver-makes-right," which means that it is the receiver's responsibility to map the data to the local architecture if the sender's data was different.

DCE arrived in the late 1980s.

NCS became DCE after HP, Digital Equipment Corporation (DEC), and IBM started a consortium when it looked like Sun and AT&T were ganging up on them back in the late 1980s. NCS wanted to present a common UNIX (look-alike) front of its own without being required to pay AT&T license fees and having all its OS requirements come from a competitor. The consortium it founded was the Open Software Foundation (OSF). Each of the founding companies brought technology to the new organization. OSF did much work on that technology since then. The primary results of that work were DCE and the OSF kernel. That's enough history.

Companies protect their investments.

RPC comes in these three flavors, although not all vendors support more than a single variant. Right off the bat there are compatibility problems. Next, each company has a large software base of networking products in its preferred variant protocol. Switching all of that code from one variant into another takes much work, time, and money, and raises many support issues.

CORBA could exist on top of an RPC.

As CORBA exists in specification, it is buildable on top of an RPC, so much of the base software might not require rewriting. One of the reasons that I believe several of the original OMG-member companies agreed to participate initially is because CORBA offered some neutral ground on which to meet. Neutral ground, however, did not interoperate. At least it did not without a performance penalty.

If people implementing an ORB want to base their ORB on RPC, they may. Vendors who use DCE might opt for DCE. Those who mainly use Sun's RPC/XDR would probably elect that as their base. Still others would opt for their own flavors. This sort of snafu is not much different from the pre-ORB world. Some vendors may create gateways if enough customers made such demands.

Getting interoperability by way of IIOP was a bloody battle.

One of the more challenging (and verbally bloodiest) adoptions over the last couple of years came from an RFP for interoperability. A consortium of vendors answered this RFP with a proposal for a Universal Network Object, their version of an interoperable protocol. On its final submission, it reverts to a layer below RPC, to TCP/IP.[15] This basic transport is vendor-neutral in the sense it avoids anyone's favorite RPC. It also provides ways in which multiple protocols exist as extensions to the proposal. The adoption includes a specific extension for DCE to support those customers who have already invested a great deal in DCE development. It may end up with other extensions based upon RPCs or other protocols.

RPCs are not very CORBA-oriented because of several problems:

- RPC primarily supports function call semantics, not method semantics.
- RPC is not transparent as defined by the technical objectives of the OMA.
- RPC comes with a notion of server activation but does not include object activation.

An ORB is not an OO RPC.

There appears to be much confusion about the relation of an ORB to a remote procedure call. An ORB and RPC are two different things. The ORB is not an OO RPC. Existing RPC applications cannot use an ORB directly, nor may ORB objects directly access RPC applications through the ORB. RPC and CORBA are semantically distinct. An RPC and an ORB share some things. Let us look at some of the differences and common points.

RPC is seldom used within a single process.

An RPC is for remote procedure invocation, while an ORB provides intraprocess, interprocess, and intermachine invocation. An RPC is primarily

---

15. This adoption is for IIOP—Internet Inter-ORB Protocol—explained in Chapter 10.

optimized for intermachine invocation, although implementations exist for interprocess. Virtually no one uses them intraprocess.

An RPC may use a service to start up the process (program or server) that it is calling if it is not active. An ORB has a finer granularity of activation. An ORB may make a process active and also may make individual objects or groups of objects active within that process.

RPCs and ORBs differ in the granularity of their activation.

An RPC is literally procedural and has no notion of objects. A set of RPC calls in collection may emulate a set of methods on an object, but there is no built-in concept for such a set. Nor is there a concept of attributes or of class. All of these require extensions to an RPC so it may resemble objects.

An RPC is procedural.

An RPC requires the location of the service it calls; ORBs are location-transparent. An RPC session requires connection and disconnection explicitly with some known service. An ORB client has no need to know what service it is talking to or the location of that service. It makes an invocation on an object reference and the request forwards correctly: across the runtime, across processes, or across machines.

An RPC is not location-transparent.

An RPC address gets to a program on a host. A CORBA address gets to an object in a program on a host.

Portmappers do not forward requests, although a BOA might. This might be interesting when objects move or otherwise migrate.

An RPC has no built-in notion of server activation styles. An ORB has four notions of server activation style (see Chapter 7).

An RPC generally knows only one activation style.

The RPC portmapper, which is partially similar to an object adapter, has no notion or support for various styles of applications. Object adapters, however, are in existence primarily to support multiple styles of applications.

An RPC does not have dynamic extensibility built in. The ORB has notions of both interface and implementation inheritance that provide different degrees of reuse. Some RPCs provide both a notion of static and dynamic invocation styles, although this is rare. Still rarer is an RPC client's ability to discover an RPC at runtime and make use of it. All of these are fundamental to an ORB.

An RPC is not dynamically extensible.

The typical RPC connection sequence is as follows and is shown in Figure 4-2:

1. The server registers with the portmapper.
2. The server reads (blocks on) its port.
3. The client asks for server port.
4. The client receives server's port number.
5. The client makes a request on the port.
6. The server unblocks (satisfying the read).
7. The client receives the result or exception.

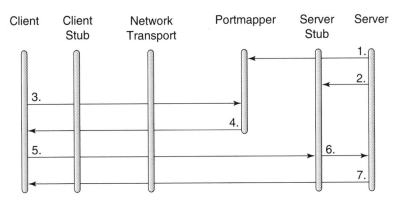

FIGURE 4-2. Typical RPC interaction diagram

An ORB, on the other hand, has the following interaction as shown in Figure 4-3. A typical CORBA object invocation path is seen in Figure 4-4.

1. The client calls through stub.
2. The ORB hands the call to the BOA, which activates the implementation.
3. The implementation registers and declares itself "ready."
4. The BOA passes invocation through skeleton.
5. The result or exception returns.

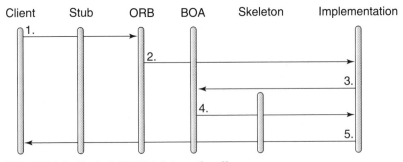

FIGURE 4-3. Typical CORBA interaction diagram

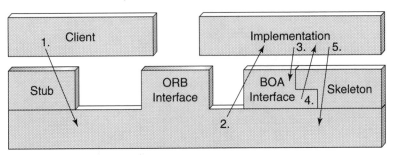

FIGURE 4-4. CORBA object invocation path

That is not to say that an ORB could not have an implementation based on RPC. That is quite possible, although it requires much additional infrastructure, which also means additional overhead. An ORB may derive from an RPC. However, there is nothing that requires an ORB to use an RPC. It might use several different RPCs. An ORB might use none.

4.7.2.1   A Possible ORB Implementation

One possible implementation is shown in the Figures 4-5, 4-6, 4-7, and 4-8. A client makes an invocation to another machine via a TCP socket to a daemon that is listening on a well-known port.

If this imaginary implementation were on UNIX , the daemon forks and executes the implementation's server process. When the process is started it calls the BOA's `impl_is_ready()`. Or for an unshared server (activation policy), it calls the BOA's `obj_is_ready()`. The BOA then passes the method invocation in to the object instance.

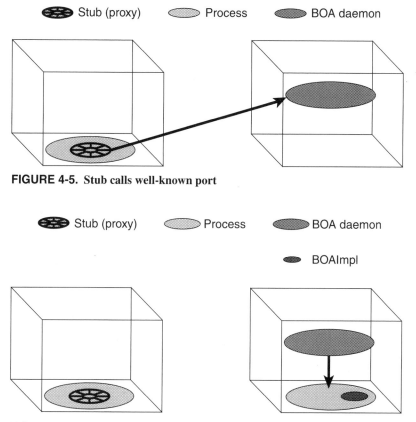

FIGURE 4-5. **Stub calls well-known port**

FIGURE 4-6. **Daemon executes process**

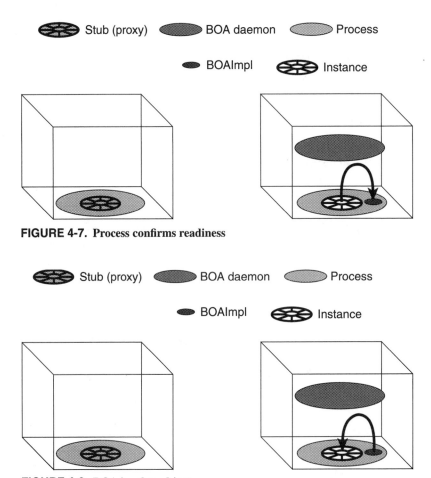

FIGURE 4-7. **Process confirms readiness**

FIGURE 4-8. **BOA invokes object**

The object services the request and returns the result to the client (see Figure 4-9). Notice that this example splits the BOA across the daemon and implementation. After the object is active, additional requests during this session are made directly to the implementation, bypassing the server.

4.7.3 Latency

Latency is round-trip message time minus the application processing time.

Latency, shown in Figure 4-10, is the amount of time necessary for a round-trip message. Latency is the amount of time it takes to go from Send Request to Receive Result. In use it generally refers only to the transit times and not to any processing time that is attributable to the application.

ORB latency approaches native call latency.

In an invocation in which both client and implementation exist in the same process, ORB latency should be close to that of a normal procedure call.

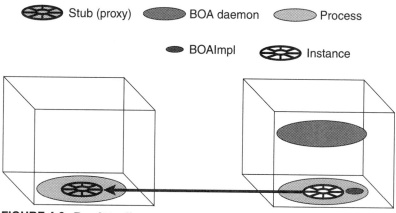

FIGURE 4-9. Result to client

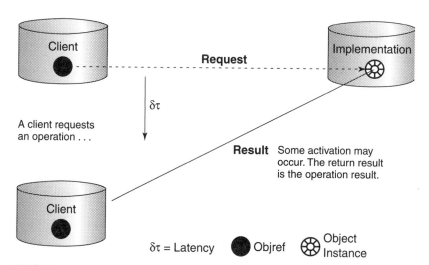

FIGURE 4-10. Latency

It is possible to write an ORB that adds only a slight overhead above that of a typical procedure call.

Latency between two processes on the same machine is the next most expensive invocation in terms of latency. The best case in most single CPU systems requires a context switch for the processor along with the overhead occurring with a same process call.

Cross-process calls exhibit medium latency.

Latency across machines is the most expensive.[16] The time involved for a cross-machine invocation introduces any delays imposed by the communica-

Cross-machine calls exhibit the most latency.

---

16. This is not always true if the context switch for intramachine interprocess communication is higher than that for intermachine, which may not do a context switch.

tion path. In addition, at least one system call is required of the sender, to start the message on its journey.

More unexpected costs arise from unforeseen network expenditures.

This last point also introduces one area that sometimes becomes an unexpected cost increase to organizations that are downsizing or rightsizing. Typically, network costs go up as machine costs go down in a rightsizing effort. They go up as a function of the increase in physical systems (hardware, cable, controller cards, software) but also up in costs associated with maintenance and operation. Sometimes an unexpected cost occurs in rightsizing because mainframes are traditionally very I/O intensive and can provide more I/O bandwidth for less money than can smaller systems. The expenditure in smaller systems to achieve the same bandwidth sometimes costs more than with a mainframe.

However, rightsizing still makes sense under full analysis when one considers that the CPU expenses are much more cost-effective for small systems than for mainframes. Typically, it costs far less to provide the same computation horsepower with small systems than it does with large systems.

A WAN generally exhibits the highest latency.

Latency increases, depending on the speed and bandwidth capabilities of the media and protocol. If the round-trip occurs over a WAN, the latency can increase startlingly.

4.7.4   Location Transparency

Location transparency has come up a couple of times without much examination. This seems like a good place to look at it more closely because we are discussing some of the general functionality of an ORB.

Location transparency refers to the view of a client making requests. The client has no notion of the location of the target for such requests, only caring that it has an object reference in its local address space. The invocation may route anywhere.

Location transparency has three caveats.

However, three fundamental problems with location transparency exist because that local (same address space) invocation is fundamentally different from remote (cross address space) invocation. These three areas of difference occur as:

1. Latency
2. Memory access
3. Failure mode

Latency differences are not always transparent.

The most obvious of the three differences is latency, although it may be the least significant. The round-trip time (latency) for a request and result in a local address space is virtually guaranteed to be faster than one that travels between different machines over a WAN. This can have some significant impact.

Imagine, if you will, a delicate surgical apparatus with a monitoring system that is with the surgeon in San Diego and a control system is in New York, while the human interface for overseeing the operation is in Houston. Assembling this system from objects that had no concept of the latency involved would be ludicrous. The objects that make sense for this application in a single runtime are vastly different than the objects that are necessary when they operate in multiple runtimes.

Of course, good design would likely avoid such spread between objects if they require tight communication coupling, although it is not clear that good design can avoid all potential problems in a system. Good design minimizes the potential problems to an acceptable level of risk. It is very difficult to undo a bad design without starting over entirely. Reversing a bad design is expensive.

The second most obvious way that location transparency glosses over the difference between local and remote computation is in memory access. Specifically, a pointer in the local address space does not map to a pointer in some other address space.

Memory access is not always transparent.

In some senses, an object reference replaces the pointer. The target language may reinforce the potential for misuse by mapping the reference into a pointer. However, both temporality (persistence beyond the process lifetime) and locality (this address space or some other) distort common notions of equality and identity.

It is certainly possible to legislate pointer use as something *verboten*. Alternatively, an ORB may impose control over all of its memory spaces and provide a distributed shared memory system. This adds additional overhead.

Some vendors have supersets of IDL that include the notion of pointers. There are still some problems. A pointer does not reference across process bounds. For a pointer to arrive in another process and still have meaning, either what it references must travel with it or an adjustment is necessary relative to its target on arrival. Either of these can introduce significant overhead.

The third and perhaps most critical problem is in the failure mode. The failure modes for local processes and distributed processes are fundamentally different. CORBA alerts us to this distinction in that the enum for exceptions classifies them into three categories: success, failure, and maybe. The "maybe" is necessary because distribution introduces indeterminacy if there is a partial failure.

Failure mode is not always transparent.

A single runtime can crash and everything goes away—total failure. For similar behavior from a distributed system, all cooperating runtimes everywhere must crash simultaneously. This does not happen, and the avoidance of such a catastrophic crash is one of the benefits of distributed computing. However, in distributed computing when you know that you are making a remote invocation, you adjust your code accordingly to handle those failure modes. Similarly, you need not expend such efforts if you know that all invocations are local.

A single interface that potentially makes remote and local requests can only optimize for one or the other. If used as a local call, then the failure model needs no special accountancy (because a runtime crash causes everything to crash). If used as a remote invocation, then it is burdened with the

A single interface can optimize for local or remote cases.

additional overhead (and checking) not normally required for same-process invocations.

Although they are not a sur-prise, many people fail to make these distinctions.

People building network applications are usually aware of such problems. Latency of remote operations is a known factor in applications. The problems inherent in cross-address-space memory references are well known. A distributed application programmer knows exactly how to deal with such problems: some of the code always runs local. The failure modes are also well understood.

So the problem is not without solution. These problems are well known and well documented. Knowing that the difference exists is a large part of the solution.

The possibility exists for the application writer to introduce bugs by making assumptions about the local and remote interface calls. Of course, that problem exists today.

CHAPTER 5   *The Dynamic Invocation Interface*

Replace an expensive operation with a cheaper one. Defer an expensive operation, so that it won't be executed as often.
—David Gries

When the submissions for the original CORBA RFP came in, the selection came down to two primary, contentious submissions. One submission was IDL, producing source code to be compiled into the application's clients and implementations. The other took a dynamic approach and did not offer static bindings.

One member made the suggestion that the two responding groups should attempt to merge the specifications.[1] As a result, they decided to go off for 90 days and devise a solution to merge the two proposals. The OMG adopted the resulting proposal, and we now have two approaches to use when we operate on objects. One is static and the other dynamic.

Merging two CORBA proposals provides a richer set of operations: static and dynamic.

It is possible to write a Dynamic Invocation Interface (DII) using IDL, so it did not need to be a part of the ORB. However, making the DII a CORBA standard interface means that code using the dynamic approach is portable across various ORB implementations (at least to some degree). Because the interface is a standard part of the architecture, the IDL compiler is not a necessity for ORB operation, though it is also a standard part of the architecture.

Dynamic requests do not require an IDL compiler.

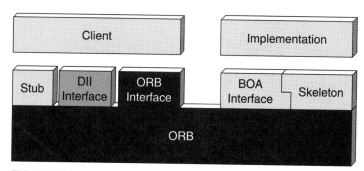

FIGURE 5-1. CORBA components with DII

---

1. This was Jim Green of Microsoft.

The DII makes objects use-
ful that are unknown at
implementation time.

The most interesting feature of a DII is that it may make requests on objects that were unknown at implementation time. This feature is the runtime discovery of objects. It has several nice features because of this property:

- Runtime development is often ideal for rapid prototype development.
- It imposes less development overhead (except, possibly, when compared to incremental compilers) in the traditional code/load/run/debug cycle.
- The dynamic approach may take 80 percent less code than the equivalent compiled code (from research done comparing the two approaches).
- New objects may not require recompiling, which is interesting, in particular, to things that browse.

Various penalties exist for not knowing an object at compilation time. For client programming, having the facility of both static and dynamic models imposes fewer limits on object developers in the long run.

5.1 RUNTIME DISCOVERY

Knowing objects at compile
time can be more efficient.

In the typical static (compiled) implementation, all objects are defined at compile time. One advantage to the foreknowledge of objects is that all of their operations are easier to optimize. A similar performance gain occurs when certain computations occur once (at compile time) as opposed to several or multiple times during runtime.[2] Put another way, compilation allows the compiler to calculate things outside the application runtime so the operation penalties occur beforehand.

A static client must have
compile-time knowledge
of an object to use its
operations.

In a totally static world an object that is unknown at compile time is not very interesting. It may even be unusable if the client has no mechanism by which it may semantically determine the behavior of the object. One misadventure readily occurs when an object reference for a previously unknown type comes into the client's (or server's) possession. It is not totally unknown because all objects derive from the object interface, so its base class is always known. The static environment can only use the operations it knows. Any other operations are not accessible.

Slicing occurs to the leaf
side.

Slicing occurs when inheritance graphs truncate the leaf side. The object representation in a static client truncates to its known type. Forwarding it, forwards only its partial type (the known portion) and the truncated characteristics are lost.

References to unknown
CORBA objects widen to
a known type.

On entry to the client's space, an objref of an unknown type is effectively widened to the node that the client knew before entry. This assumes that the client's runtime is able to construct an instance of an objref to an unknown object (in other words, it may raise an exception if the ORB is aware of the

2. It is not the intent here to overlook the fact that interpreter technology has gained sophistication. Some interpreters may precompile subsets of code, or put source through an optimizer and then run an intermediate code at runtime. The performance distinction is on the decrease.

difficulty). In the worst case, it is widened to the base type: object.[3] Operations not on the base type are then unavailable. An object reference, however, always knows its type, so slicing does not occur. The leaf nodes inaccessible from the client are not lost except to that client.

Clients that anticipate coming across previously unknown types can take corrective measures. Instead of dealing with an instance of the objref, the client can work with a generic object, a Request. Request objects are attainable from an object (which knows its real—most derived—type). The Request object, in essence, is the interface for the DII. (See Example 5-1.)

Static clients may still use the dynamic approach by way of the Request object.

EXAMPLE 5-1. **Create Request object operation**

```
Status create_request(
            in Context          ctx,
            in Identifier       operation,
            in NVList           arg_list,
            inout NamedValue    result,
            out Request         request,
            in Flags            req_flags);
```

5.1.1   Create Request

The Create Request operation on an object returns a status[4] and takes the following six parameters:

1. In Context
2. In Identifier
3. In Argument List
4. InOut Named Value
5. Out Result
6. In Request Flags

Contexts are pseudo-objects (they closely resemble a UNIX or NT shell environment). They contain—that is, their composition consists of—some arbitrary number of names and values (each being a string). Their intent is to define the runtime context.

Context is a pseudo-object collection of names and values as strings.

Context objects are the topic of another techno-religious war. The naysayers state that a context is the weak equivalent of declaring a proper set of parameters on operations. Those that argue for *context* objects say that *they are* dynamic and convenient. Either way, if their use is indiscriminate, much meaningless data may accompany every invocation regardless of its necessity.

Context is a convenience that can be misused.

---

3. One could determine the most derived type by querying it for its interface definition, but it could not instantiate the derived type.
4. The specification states that status is a typedef. It is either an unsigned long or it is a void. Both implementations are conforming. If you are using a Request object, you need to check the implementation of this type in your ORB.

An identifier is a name given as a string.

An Argument List is a list of Named Values.

Details about the context pseudo-objects appear with operational detail in Chapter 6, since it is an ORB operation that creates them.

An identifier is a name. It is a composition of alphabetic, numeric, or underscore characters and may be of arbitrary length. Uppercase and lowercase are not distinct (comparisons treat them as the same value) and digraphs are unique (not equivalent to their equivalently constituent letters or characters).

The Argument List is a list of Named Values.[5] A Named Value is a pair: an identifier (the name) and an Any (the value). A Named Value is a pseudo-object and its C implementation appears in Example 5-2. Each Named Value pair in the list expresses something about the operation (specifically about parameters).

The result is a Named Value for the operation result. The Request is a pseudo-object, which is essentially the DII.

The request flags are of flags type (a bit-mask of type unsigned long). The flags contain parameter passing-mode information (CORBA::ARG_IN, CORBA::ARG_OUT, or CORBA::ARG_INOUT) and may contain other additional information depending on the operation. Create Request accepts a CORBA::OUT_LIST_MEMORY that tells it to associate any ARG_OUT mode memory with the NVList (for management purposes). Setting this flag explicitly requires an NVList. When this flag is not set, the programmer must manage the individual out arguments (the resources do not release when the list releases).

EXAMPLE 5-2. **A Named Value structure**

```
struct  NamedValue
{
Identifier      name;
any             argument;
long            len;
Flags           arg_modes;
};
CORBA_NamedValue     *CORBA_NV_List;      /* C mapping */
```

5.1.2 Invocation Composition

Two operational approaches

The DII (as Request object) has two basic operational modes. One is a minimalist approach and does very little work, requiring that the client do a majority of the work. The other is viewable as being at the completely opposite end of the spectrum in that it has a much more elaborate (fulsome) set of facilities.

Both approaches use an appropriate objref that is of a specific type: that belonging to the object on which the invocation is to occur. From this objref

---

5. A Named Value List (NVList) is a sequence of Named Values. Its operation is discussed in Section 5.1.2.4.

each requests a Request object. The creation of a Request object in this manner effectively retains knowledge of its objref (identity) and knows specific things about the object on which it is going to invoke.[6] The general method constructs a Request object for a specific operation by handing the Request Constructor (operation on the objref) an identifier that specifies the operation. Both approaches then use the Request object to make invocations.

The minimalist approach constructs request messages (invocations) one parameter at a time.

The other approach, somewhat more complex, uses Named Value lists that contain all the necessary information for invocation.

5.1.2.1 The Request Object

The Request object has five operations (Example 5-3), all of which return a Status:

1. Add Argument
2. Invoke
3. Delete
4. Send
5. Get Response

The specification is in C-PIDL, meaning it is the C mapping for the pseudo-object (their implementation does not use IDL).

EXAMPLE 5-3. Request object interface

```
interface Request                        // C-PIDL
{
    Status  add_arg(
                in Identifier    name;
                in TypeCode      arg_type,
                in void          *value,
                in long          len,
                in Flags         arg_flags);

    Status  invoke(n Flags invoke_flags);

    Status  delete();

    Status  send(in Flags invoke_flags);
    Status  get_response(in Flags response_flags);
};
```

---

6. "Effectively" here indicates that this is an implementation detail: it may have direct knowledge or it may have only indirect knowledge via some relation back to the object reference.

Add Argument

The Add Argument operation has five parameters:

1. Name is an identifier. It identifies the operation to invoke.
2. Argument Type is a TypeCode (or half of an Any).
3. Value is a void * (the other half of an Any, in the C mapping).[7]
4. Length is a long and is the length as a function of the number of arguments.[8]
5. Argument Flags may use `CORBA::IN_COPY_VALUE` to indicate that Request should make copies of arguments set as `IN_ARG` (ignoring it for those set as `ARG_OUT` or `ARG_INOUT`). This is besides its having an Argument Mode value set.

Invoke

The Invoke operation instructs Request to execute the operation. The ORB resolves and performs the method. Such an execution is indistinguishable from a stub invocation to the skeleton. Invoke takes a flag parameter.

If successful, the operation places the result in the Named Value Result parameter of the Create Request operation.

Delete

The Delete operation takes no parameters and releases the Request's resources. This includes those whose relationship was inherent from the use of an `IN_COPY_VALUE` flag.

Send

The Send operation instructs Request to execute the operation. It takes a single flag parameter. If `CORBA::INV_NO_RESPONSE` is set, it indicates that the caller does not expect a response and out arguments do not change (are not set). This flag may be set even for operations that are not defined as one way.

Get Response

Get Response takes a flags parameter. The flag may be set to `CORBA::RESP_NO_WAIT`, which indicates that the call should not block if no response is available.

There are additional Request operations on the ORB that operate on a sequence of Request objects. There are also several Named Value List operations. Both sets are in Section 6.1.1.3.

---

7. Splitting the Any into two parts like this is broken because Any has a valid mapping in C.

8. There seems to be no explanation of what a negative length indicates in any of the Named Value, Request, or List operations. I suspect it should have been declared an unsigned long. However, it appears consistently as a long throughout all of the related declarations.

5.1.2.2   The Minimalist Approach

Using the minimalist set of operations, you add each parameter sequentially
from the operation signature. When adding each parameter, it effectively goes
into a list of parameters that become the arguments to the operation request.[9]
On completion (after adding all parameters) an Invoke operation causes the
request to occur. Invocation is possible in either synchronous or deferred synchronous modes.

What we have when we say "deferred synchronous" is the notion of a
nonblocking sender using a synchronous protocol. The receiver resynchronizes on finally accessing the result of the operation. If deferred synchrony is
the preference, the client starts the request by calling Send (instead of Invoke)
and obtains the result later (resynchronizes) by requesting Get Response.
Synchronization defers to when the client requests Get Response.

*Message synchronization
may be deferred until
requesting Get Response.*

This brings us to the heart of another techno-religious war—asynchrony.
A discussion of synchrony, deferred synchrony, and asynchrony came at the
end of Chapter 4.

5.1.2.3   The Complex Approach

The more complex mechanism for invocation composition, which provides
more facilities, operates with objects called Named Values. These operations
use Named Values or NVList operations.

A named value in DII parlance is an object that associates a Name with
data, which is a value parameter. It includes a size (length) of the parameter
and some optional mode flags. A set of operations allows life cycle operations
on lists of Named Values (construction, destruction, and so forth) along with
invocation using these as arguments. It is possible to set up whole sequences
of operation requests via the NVLists. Such requests are either synchronous
or deferred synchronous.

*Named Value Lists are at the
heart of the more complex
approach.*

Their capability is more complex than the intent of this book, so we will
just touch upon their operations. However, it may be useful to point out that
the CORBA specification shows a few rough spots in this particular area.

*Named Values have
blemishes.*

Named Value Lists are pseudo-objects. Their description in the specification is partly IDL and partly not. For instance, a C type (or lack of type) shows
up in some signatures as void *.

The other rough spot is the context. A context parameter appears in many
of the invocations. These appear to place the operation in some context. However, their definitions appear as additional name/value pairs and probably
should be just additional parameters of the Named Value type. Instead they
receive first-class status (a reserved spot) in the invocation signature. The only
argument for contexts is that they are slightly lighter in weight than a Named

*Named Values also have
contexts in signatures.*

---

9. "Effectively" indicates one possible implementation. It does not indicate that it must be implemented in this fashion.

Value. In addition, their values are all strings and they require no length/size indicator (strings terminate with a zero—a C-string style terminal). They also omit the mode flags.

One could argue that mode flags should have been separate Named Value pairs as opposed to be an entity in every Named Value even if they were a requirement for each one.

5.1.2.4   *The Named Value List Interface*

The actual Named Value structure appears only once as an aggregate.

The specification states that this interface's operations use the Named Value structure.[10] However, the specification is in C-PIDL and the Named Value structure seems to occur in only one operation. Other operations show the structure's members as distinct parameters. The operations in the ORB interface that construct Named Value Lists also do not show the structure (Example 5-4).[11]

The Named Value List interface has four operations:

1. Add Item
2. Free
3. Free Memory
4. Get Count

EXAMPLE 5-4. NVList object interface

```
interface NVList                                    // C-PIDL
{
    Status   add_item(
                  in Identifier   item_name,
                  in TypeCode     item_type,
                  in void         *value,
                  in long         value_len,
                  in Flags        item_flags);

    Status   free();
    Status   free_memory();

    Status   get_count(out long count);
};
```

Add Item

Add Item, in the C variant of Pseudo-IDL, shows five parameters:

1. Item Name is an identifier and presumably equates to the name in a Named Value structure.

---

10. This structure appears in Section 5.1.1.
11. These operations are in Chapter 6.

2. Item Type is a TypeCode and presumably corresponds to the Argument Type of the Named Value (or to one half of the members in the C mapping of the Any data type).

3. Value being a void*, equates to the C mapping of the second member of the Any structure.

4. Value Length is a long parameter, corresponding to the Length parameter in a Named Value.

5. Item Flags is a flag-type parameter. Besides the argument passing mode Flags, two additional flags are valid:

The Add Item operation appends a Named Value into the list.

- `CORBA::IN_COPY_VALUE`
- `CORBA::DEPENDENT_LIST`

When `IN_COPY_VALUE` is set, a copy of the argument is made to use instead of using the parameter. The `DEPENDENT_LIST` flag is for use when another Named Value List is the argument to add. This flag indicates that freeing the list should also free the sub-list (the list the operation is adding).

Free
The Free request takes no parameters and releases the list structure and all members' resources. The specification states that this does an implicit request to Free Memory.

Free Memory
Free Memory takes no parameters and releases all resources that list members consume. It does not free the list.

Get Count
Get Count has a single parameter, an out long. The parameter is a Length and indicates the number of items in the Named Value List.

CHAPTER 6   *The ORB*

The term "object" emerged almost independently in various fields in computer science, almost simultaneously in the early 1970s, to refer to notions that were different in their appearance, yet mutually related. All of these notions were invented to manage the complexity of software systems in such a way that objects represented components of a modularly decomposed system or modular units of knowledge representation.
—A. Yonezawa and M. Tokoro

Object request brokers (ORBs) in the generic sense are a class of facilities, of which CORBA is one instance. This is object-oriented middleware, although that name has far less romance.

Unless otherwise indicated, this book assumes the reverse, that an ORB is an instance of a CORBA with the implicit assumption that it is CORBA-compliant. CORBA is the class and ORB is an instance. When we refer to an ORB's domain, we refer to the domain applicable to one instance of a CORBA.

ORB, here, is an instance of a CORBA.

An ORB object, however, is also a pseudo-object within an ORB. It is an IDL interface that is part of the CORBA architecture. It is a pseudo-object that is available everywhere within an ORB (CORBA instance). The ORB, as pseudo-object, offers those operations that require wide availability for clients and implementations alike.

ORB object refers to the ever present ORB interface.

6.1   ORB INTERFACE OPERATIONS

Potentially, ORB interfaces may expand over time if additional operations appear to require pervasive presence (see Example 6-1). Quite a few of the current operations were new in CORBA 2.0.

The operations that are part of the CORBA 2.0 specification are:

- Operations that convert object references to strings and back
- An operation to create a Named Value List
- An operation to create a Named Value List for a specific operation
- An operation to get the default Context
- An operation to initialize the OA (BOA)

- Two operations for resolving initial references
- TypeCode constructors for all major types

EXAMPLE 6-1. ORB object interface

```
module  CORBA
{
    // Security Level 1
    typedef unsigned short  ServiceType;

    const   ServiceType Security = 1;
    // other Service types to be defined

    typedef unsigned long      ServiceOption;

    const   ServiceOption      SecurityLevel1 = 1;
    const   ServiceOption      SecurityLevel2 = 2;
    const   ServiceOption      NonRepudiation = 3;
    const   ServiceOption      SecurityORBServiceReady = 4;
    const   ServiceOption      SecurityServiceReady = 5;
    const   ServiceOption      ReplaceORBServices = 6;
    const   ServiceOption      ReplaceSecurityServices = 7;
    const   ServiceOption      StandardSecureInteroperability = 8;
    const   ServiceOption      DCESecureInteroperability = 9;
    const   ServiceOption      CommonInteroperabilityLevel0 = 10;
    const   ServiceOption      CommonInteroperabilityLevel1 = 11;
    const   ServiceOption      CommonInteroperabilityLevel2 = 12;

    // Service details supported by the implementation
    typedef unsigned long      ServiceDetailType;

    // security mechanism type(s) supported for secure associations
    const   ServiceDetailType   SecurityMechanismType = 1;

    // privilege types supported in standard access policy
    const   ServiceDetailType   SecurityAttribute = 2;

    struct  ServiceDetail
    {
        ServiceDetailType    service_detail_type;
        sequence<octet>      service_detail;
    };

    struct  ServiceInformation
    {
        sequence<ServiceOption> service_options;
        sequence<ServiceDetail> service_detail;
    };

    typedef string             ORBid;
    typedef sequence <string>  arg_list;

    ORB ORB_init(inout arg_list argv, in ORBid orb_identifier);

    interface ORB
    {
        string object_to_string(in Object obj);
        Object string_to_object(in string str);
```

```
Status create_list(in long count, out NVList new_list);
Status create_operation_list(
in OperationDef oper,
out NVList new_list);
Status get_default_context(out Context ctx);

typedef sequence <string>    arg_list;
typedef string               OAid;

BOA BOA_init(inout arg_list argv, in OAid boa_identifier);

typedef string               ObjectId;
typedef sequence <ObjectId> ObjectIdList;

exception InvalidName {};

ObjectIdList list_initial_services();

Object resolve_initial_references(in ObjectId identifier)
          raises (InvalidName);

typedef sequence<Request>    Requests;
Status  send_multiple_requests(inout Requests reqs);
oneway Status send_multiple _requests_oneway(inout Requests reqs);
Status send_multiple_requests_deferred(inout Requests reqs);

boolean poll_next_response();
Status  get_next_response(
inout Flags response_flags,
inout Requests reqs);

TypeCode create_struct_tc(
          in RepositoryId     id,
          in Identifier       name,
          in StructMemberSeq  members);

TypeCode create_union_tc(
          in RepositoryId     id,
          in Identifier       name,
          in TypeCode         discriminator_type,
          in UnionMemberSeq   members);

TypeCode create_enum_tc(
          in RepositoryId     id,
          in Identifier       name,
          in EnumMemberSeq    members);

TypeCode create_alias_tc(
          in RepositoryId     id,
          in Identifier       name,
          in TypeCode         original_type);

TypeCode create_exception_tc(
          in RepositoryId     id,
          in Identifier       name,
          in StructMemberSeq  members);

TypeCode create_interface_tc(
          in RepositoryId     id,
          in Identifier       name);
```

```
TypeCode create_string_tc(
            in unsigned long     bound);

TypeCode create_sequence_tc(
            in unsigned long     bound,
            in TypeCode          element_type);

TypeCode create_recursive_seqeunce_tc(
            in unsigned long     bound,
            in unsigned long     offset);

TypeCode create_array_tc(
            in unsigned long     length,
            in TypeCode          element_type);

boolean get_service_information(   // Security Level 1 addition
            in    ServiceType            service_type,
            out   ServiceInformation     service_information);

Current get_current(); // (PIDL) Security addition for Current support
    };
};
```

Additional data types and one new operation are now part of the specification with the adoption of Security. The data types are those listed under the Security Level 1 comment, down to the type definition of the ORB ID as a string (not including this type definition). The new operation is Get Service Information.

6.1.1   Fundamental Operations

The fundamental operations are discussed here; Security is left for Chapter 12.

6.1.1.1   ORB Initialize

The ORB must be boot-strapped to obtain a first instance.

There also exists a single procedure, which is not implemented on any object, that returns an ORB as a result.[1] This procedure is ORB initialize. It is a procedure because it initializes the ORB, without which no ORB objects are operational. This procedure is the bootstrap mechanism by which ORB initialization occurs at runtime. ORB initialize takes place before any other ORB requests. Besides returning an ORB, the procedure takes two parameters: (1) an in ORB ID and (2) an InOut Argument List.

Each ORB is known by an identifier.

The ORB ID is a string identifier that defines which ORB is to be initialized, since the client may be participating in multiple ORBs. In some cases, a request to ORB initialize may occur with the same parameters. In such cases,

---

1. It is not part of the ORB interface or any other interface.

it should return a reference to the same pseudo-object each time. Multiple calls may occur when the client is multithreaded and requires more than a single reference to the same ORB.

The Argument List is a sequence of strings, essentially designed to replicate the argument vector common for C program command line arguments. It is an `inout` parameter because the anticipation is that only a portion of the command line may be instructions for the ORB and the other parameters are of interest to the client program.

6.1.1.2   *Persistent Object References*

As originally proposed in the OMA, it is useful to have a way to make objrefs take on a form that survives beyond a process lifetime. This means that the objref requires persistence. The idea is that it is useful to send these persistent forms in e-mail messages or to print one on a sheet of paper that could go into a file somewhere.

Sending object references via e-mail was a motivating factor for persistence.

For this to occur easily, the objref requires a form that is visible and to some degree comprehensible. The comprehensibility is primarily to fill a desire for objrefs capable of by-hand transcription—read from one medium and handwritten to another. This persistent and readable form for an objref is a string, where string means only that it is a sequence of printable characters of indefinite length.

The other side of this equation is that one requires a method to take a persistent objref and insert it into a runtime for use. For this to happen, it is necessary to have something that could reconstruct an objref from its persistent form. While the former might easily have been an operation on an object (allowing it to know how to make itself persistent), the reverse is difficult. Keeping both operations together makes them an obvious candidate for an ORB operation.

Persistent object references need reconstitution to make requests on them.

The two operations are: (1) Object to String and (2) String to Object.

The Object to String method takes an objref as an argument and returns a persistent objref, a printable string of characters.

The second of the two operations, String to Object, takes a string argument and returns an object (the base type of all object references). The base returns because we do not know in advance what all the object reference types might be, so we can only refer to them by their common base.

6.1.1.3   *(Named Value) List Operations*

The List operations on the ORB are for use with the DII. The two operations are: (1) Create List and (2) Create Operation List.

These two operations create the Named Value Lists that are available for the more complex calling sequence of the DII. The first of the two is an empty list to which various values are yet to be assigned. The second of the two operations creates a Named Value List that is explicitly bound to an operation on some object.

Create List

The Create List operation takes two parameters and returns a status. The two parameters are: (1) an in Count and (2) an out New List.

The generic Create List operation requires a count parameter so that it creates the correct number of Named Values as part of the list. The out parameter is the new list.

Note that the Request object's Add Item operation may effectively grow the list. In other words, additional Named Value pairs can extend the original list by adding more, one at a time.

Create Operation List

The Create Operation List is explicitly tied to an operation and initializes the list to contain the number of Named Values that the operation requires. This operation also takes two parameters: (1) an in Operation Definition and (2) an out New List. The Operation Definitions are available from the interface repository.

After invocation, memory allocation cleanup is necessary in certain language bindings. Particular attention to memory management rules for your implementation language is necessary. Specific information on this and the associated operations is in the DII's Request object.

6.1.2   Context

Another operation available from the ORB obtains the default context, which is the prevailing context until another is used.

6.1.2.1   *Get Default Context*

The single operation on the ORB is Get Default Context. This operation returns a status and takes a single parameter, an out Context.

6.1.2.2   *Context Interface*

The Context interface (Example 6-2) consists of six operations:

1. Set One Value
2. Set Values
3. Get Values
4. Delete Values
5. Create Child
6. Delete

All of these operations return status (see the details about status in Section 5.1, Runtime Discovery, and the Create Request operation on the object reference earlier in this chapter).

EXAMPLE 6-2. **Context object interface**

```
module  CORBA
{
    interface Context
    {
        Status  set_one_value(in Identifier prop_name, in string value);
        Status  set_values(in NVList values);

        Status  get_values(
                    in Identifier      start_scope,
                    in Flags           op_flags,
                    in Identifier      prop_name,
                    out NVList         values);

        Status  delete_values(in Identifier prop_name);

        Status  create_child(in Identifier ctx_name, out Context child_ctx);

        Status  delete(in Flags del_flags);
    };
};
```

Contexts are property lists and have some commonality with the property service. As mentioned earlier, they also share some characteristics of a shell environment. Almost perversely, the CORBA Environment and Context are virtual role reversals of their name counterparts in UNIX and NT.

Set One Value

Set One Value takes two parameters: (1) Property Name and (2) Value.

This operation sets a single property value in the Context. Each is an identifier (string). The specification states that string is the only value with current support, however, which sounds as if it may change in some future revision.

Set Values

Set Values has a single parameter—Values.

The Values parameter is a Named Value List. This operation also mentions that string is currently the only Value with support and stipulates that the TypeCodes in the list must be set with the TypeCode for string (TC_string). It also states that all flags be set to zero.

The operation can set one or more Context properties in a single request.

Get Values

The Get Values operation is the busiest context operation, with four parameters:

1. An in Start Scope
2. An in Operation Flags
3. An in Property Name
4. An out Values

*Properties may chain
together hierarchically.*

Two characteristics of properties are interesting with this operation. Context properties chain, as the specification says, to other Context's properties. The default context may chain to its user, group, and system context objects. Such chains are hierarchical and occur through the use of the Create Child operation. Searches with Get Values look up the hierarchy starting in the default (or the Start Scope, if one is given). Properties set in a Child override those of its Ancestors (Parent or higher). Valid scope names are implementation-specific.

*Anchored patterns can
search for property names.*

The second interesting characteristic is the ability to do an anchored pattern match by Property Name. The pattern matching has two forms: (1) as <name> and (2) as <name>*. The latter, <name>*, matches <name> and anything to the right of name.

The Start Scope parameter is an identifier that establishes the first scope to search during this request.

Operation Flags are of flags type. A single flag is in the specification: CORBA::CTX_RESTRICT_SCOPE. When this flag is set, the search occurs in a single Context object.

The Property Name parameter is an identifier and a fully qualified name or an anchored pattern. If no Property Name match occurs, the operation returns an error and no Values result.

The Values parameter is a Named Value List and contains the resulting Properties from the search.

The programmer may release Resource allocation during the Get Values operation by requesting the Free operation on the NVList.

Delete Values

The Delete Values operation takes one parameter, Property Name.

Property Name is an identifier that may have a wildcard ("*") character appended. Search occurs within a single Context object. If the operation matches on one or more Names, they are removed from their respective Context objects.

Create Child

Create Child takes two parameters: (1) an in Context Name and (2) an out Child Context.

The Context name is an identifier and names the Context it creates. The new Context is found in the Child Context (of type Context). The new child now chains to this object.

Delete

The Delete operation takes a single parameter, Delete Flags. Delete Flags is a flag type. One flag is currently in the specification: CORBA::CTX_ DELETE_DESCENDANTS. When set, Delete releases the resource for all descendants of this object.

6.1.3   Other ORB Operations

The ORB supports some additional operations. These are TypeCode constructors and some operations that invoke multiple Requests.

The TypeCode operations are mainly of interest to the interface repository, which is discussed in Chapter 9. These operations are widely available, because they are on the ORB pseudo-object and find use elsewhere.

TypeCode operations are widely available from the ORB interface.

6.1.3.1   *TypeCode Constructors*

The TypeCode construction operations are similar to one in the interface repository for creating Type Definitions. The constructors supplement those Type Codes that are constants. The only oddity is that for the creation of a recursive sequence. Sequences are the only IDL types that can currently contain a type that contains the sequence (the offset argument is the offset where the recursion occurs)—see Example 6-3.

Sequences are the only recursive type.

EXAMPLE 6-3. **Recursion in sequence type**

```
struct  bucket
{
    any                 value;
    sequence<bucket>    buckets;
};
```

TypeCode constants are language mapping-specific. The specification also states that they may be implementation-specific. CORBA 1.2 set the initial list of constants available in C. They have seen minimal changes. These constants are as follows:

- TC_null
- TC_void
- TC_short
- TC_long
- TC_ushort
- TC_ulong
- TC_float
- TC_double
- TC_boolean
- TC_char
- TC_octet
- TC_any
- TC_TypeCode
- TC_Principal
- TC_Object
- TC_string
- TC_CORBA_NamedValue

- TC_CORBA_InterfaceDescription
- TC_CORBA_OperationDescription
- TC_CORBA_AttributeDescription
- TC_CORBA_ParameterDescription
- TC_CORBA_ModuleDescription
- TC_CORBA_ConstantDescription
- TC_CORBA_Exception
- TC_CORBA_TypeDescription
- TC_CORBA_InterfaceDef_FullInterfaceDescription

The TypeCodes are also pseudo-objects. They are most useful when they accompany and identify a value; that is, specifically when they are critical to IDL's Any data type.

The TypeCode interface (Example 6-4) has 14 operations:

1. Equal
2. Kind
3. ID
4. Name
5. Member Count
6. Member Name
7. Member Type
8. Member Label
9. Discriminator Type
10. Default Index
11. Length
12. Content Type
13. Parameter Count
14. Parameter

EXAMPLE 6-4. TypeCode object interface

```
module  CORBA
{
    enum     TCKind { tk_null, tk_void,
                      tk_short, tk_long, tk_ushort, tk_ulong,
                      tk_float, tk_double, tk_boolean, tk_char,
                      tk_octet, tk_any, tk_TypeCode, tk_Principal, tk_objref,
                      tk_struct, tk_union, tk_enum, tk_string,
                      tk_sequence, tk_array, tk_alias, tk_except };

    interface TypeCode
    {
        exception   Bounds  {};
        exception   BadKind {};

        // used for all TypeCodes
        boolean     equal(in TypeCode tc);
        TCKind      kind();
```

```
                // used for tk_objref, tk_struct, tk_union, tk_enum, tk_alias and tk_except
                RepositoryId    id()    raises (BadKind);
                Identifier      name()  raises (BadKind);

                // used for tk_struct, tk_union, tk_enum and tk_except
                unsigned long   member_count() raises (BadKind);
                Identifier      member_name(in unsigned long index) raises (BadKind, Bounds);

                // used for tk_struct, tk_union and tk_except
                TypeCode    member_type(in unsigned long index) raises (BadKind, Bounds);

                // used for tk_union
                any         member_label(in unsigned long index) raises (BadKind, Bounds);
                TypeCode    discriminator_type() raises (BadKind);
                long        default_index() raises (BadKind);

                // used for tk_string, tk_sequence and tk_array
                unsigned long   length() raises (BadKind);

                // used for tk_sequence, tk_array and tk_alias
                TypeCode    content_type() raises (BadKind);

                // deprecated methods (from CORBA 1.1)
                long        param_count():
                any         parameter(in long index) raises (Bounds);
        };
};
```

Equal

The Equal operation tests its parameter, a TypeCode. If both TypeCodes respond to all TypeCode operations the same, then the two are equal and the operation returns True. If they do not respond identically in each case, it returns False.

Kind

The Kind operation returns the TCKind enum value corresponding to the TypeCode's type.

ID

The ID operation is valid for object reference, structure, union, alias, and exception TypeCodes. The resulting Repository ID is their global type identity.

Object References and Exceptions always have a Repository ID.

Structure, Union, Enum, and Alias TypeCodes that come from the Repository or from the ORB's Create Operation List method always have Repository IDs. Otherwise, the operation returns an empty string.[2]

---

2. Thus two TypeCodes that are identical except that one has a Repository ID and the other does not (since it is not from the ORB's operation or from the Repository) are not Type-Code::Equal(), by definition.

Name

The Name operation is valid for object reference, structure, union, enumeration, alias, and exception TypeCodes. The operation returns the simple name local to its current scope. The identifier resulting from the operation may not match any Repository Identifier (name) because identifiers are local to a Repository scope. The resulting identifier may also be an empty string.

Member Count

The Member Count operation is valid for structure, union, enumeration, and exception TypeCodes. The specification omits Exception, although it is shown in the IDL comment. Exceptions are similar to structures in that they may have members.

The operation returns the number of members.

Member Name

The Member Name operation takes a single parameter, Index. Index is an unsigned long, and the operation returns the identifier of the member at the index offset. The operation is valid for the same TypeCodes as Member Count.

The identifier result is the member's name in local scope. This has the same caveats about matching Repository names as did the Name operation. This operation may result in an empty string.

Member Type

The Member Type operation is valid only for structure and union TypeCodes. It takes a single unsigned long parameter, Index. The resulting TypeCode identifies the member's type at the offset of the index.

Member Label

The Member Label operation is only valid for union TypeCodes. It takes a single unsigned long parameter, Index. The operation returns the label at the offset of the index. The label is a zero octet for the default member.

Discriminator Type

Discriminator Type is valid for union TypeCodes. It takes no parameters and returns the TypeCode describing the type of the discriminator. Valid types are short, unsigned short, long, unsigned long, char, boolean, or enum. Surprisingly, octet is not in the list of valid types.

Default Index

The Default Index operation is only valid for union TypeCodes. The operation returns the offset of the default label or −1 if no default label exists. While all other Indexes are unsigned long, this one is constrained to report no label, which in turn restricts the placement of the default label.

Length

The Length operation applies only to string, sequence, and array TypeCodes. It returns zero for unbound strings and sequences, and returns the bound for bounded strings and sequences. It returns the number of elements for an array.

Content Type

The Content Type operation applies to sequence, array, and alias. It returns the element type for sequence and array, and returns the original type for alias.

A TypeCode only describes a single dimension of an IDL array. Multi-dimensional arrays require nesting TypeCodes, with the outermost TypeCode describing the left-most (in IDL) index. The innermost array TypeCode describes the right-most (in IDL) index, and its Content Type operation describes the array content. The Content Type describes the next index in all other TypeCodes that describe the multidimensional array.

Deprecated Operations

Parameter Count and Parameter operations are no longer in use. Their original definitions did not describe obtaining Repository IDs for applicable types or the Interface Name for object references.

6.1.4   Multiple Request Operations

Each of these calls operates on a sequence of requests. The intent is that all calls in the sequence occur in parallel, with all requests being made simultaneously. The degree of parallelism or what simultaneity means in this case is system-dependent (Example 6-5).

EXAMPLE 6-5. **Multiple request operation signatures**

```
typedef sequence<Request>    Requests;

Status  send_multiple_requests(inout Requests reqs);

oneway Status send_multiple _requests_oneway(inout Requests reqs);

Status send_multiple_requests_deferred(inout Requests reqs);

boolean poll_next_response();

Status  get_next_response(
          inout Flags response_flags,
          inout Requests reqs);
```

Two flags are specific to these calls, besides the regular mode flags:

- CORBA::INV_NO_RESPONSE
- CORBA::INV_TERM_ON_ERR

The `CORBA::INV_NO_RESPONSE` indicates that the caller does not intend to wait for or receive any response or out parameters. This option applies even if requests are not specifically One Way.

The `CORBA::INV_TERM_ON_ERR` indicates that all requests terminate if one request receives an error.

The results to any of these operations are available through the Request object's Get Response or through the ORB's Get Next Response. Get Next Response returns the next available Request but not necessarily in completion order.

CHAPTER 7 *Object Adapters*

*Identity is that property of an object that
distinguishes each object from all others.*
—Setrag Khoshafian and Razmik Abnous

The object adapter suggests a style of implementation for an object. CORBA specifies a general purpose, do-everything adapter called the Basic Object Adapter (BOA). Basic here indicates general purpose and not minimalist. The CORBA specification mentions a Library Object Adapter. Another specialized adapter may find use in load balancing. Other documents allude to other adapters. Specifically, the work of the ODMG requires another adapter rather than the BOA. The BOA is the only adapter that is currently widely available, however.

7.1 THE ADAPTER'S ROLE

The primary role of an adapter is to centralize certain functionality (style) that is common across a range of implementations. In the BOA it is primarily the style of activation. In a Library Object Adapter, it would be the runtime incorporation; that is, the dynamic loading and linking of a library as the implementation's runtime. In a load-balancing system, several object adapters may conspire to select the appropriate implementation to activate or to aid in implementation migration as loads shift.

*The BOA primarily supports
styles of activation.*

This is not appropriate in the skeleton because such operations frequently require information when the skeleton is not already running. It also has a tighter coupling to the ORB than does a skeleton, due to its involvement with activation of implementations or of objects. It is also good style to put the reused software in a component where it is reusable without creating redundancy.

7.2 BOA

The BOA is perhaps an inappropriate name because it is far from minimal. In fact, it seems almost Baroque. The basic object adapter has an IDL interface. Operations defined in that interface are for object creation and deletion, and to obtain reference data associated with an objref. It has a method to change an implementation and an operation to obtain the principal associated with a request.[1] It also has operations that signal whether an implementation is ready or not and whether a given object is active or not.

The BOA is integral to an object's life cycle.

This means that BOA is involved with various parts of an object's life cycle: creation, destruction, activation, and deactivation. It also provides a hook for persistence storage in that it must track objrefs whether the implementation is active or not and associates some state with an objref that is retrievable on demand.

The BOA has some involvement with security because of its involvement in granting requests to activate an object. It is also involved with administration, allowing implementations to change.

7.2.1   Activation

Process- or thread-related

Servers in CORBA have a notion of inactivity. These servers are programs that activate within a process. However, activation relating to a server may be within a process or thread.

Servers in CORBA are usually clients as well.

Object implementations either reside in the local process or they do not. When they do not, they exist in some other process. These other processes are servers. Server, as in client-server, tends to be only a server. On the other hand, servers in the CORBA sense are virtually always clients, although they also service (or serve) interface requests.

These servers (or implementation run-times) have four distinct styles of activation:

1. Shared
2. Unshared
3. Per method
4. Persistent

7.2.1.1   Shared Server

Objects share one process.

A *shared server* is one that shares a single process for all its subordinate objects. If the server is a shared server, the ORB determines if there is a currently active instance and if so, hands it the message. If no instance exists, the ORB starts a new process with the server before forwarding the message.

7.2.1.2   Unshared Server

Separate process per object

An *unshared server* is one that spawns a new process for each separate object that is active. If the server is an unshared server, the ORB looks to see if an active instance of the server is also active for that specific object. If an instance

---

1. The operation to obtain a principal is deprecated with the adoption of the Common Secure Interoperability proposal.

already exists, the ORB hands it the message. If no instance yet exists for this object, the ORB instantiates a new instance before passing on the message.

7.2.1.3 *Per-Method Server*

A *per-method server* spawns a new process for every invocation of a method regardless of the object on which that method exists. A per-method server first must activate a new instance (start the server in a process) and then hand the message off to the newly started server.

Separate process for each request

7.2.1.4 *Persistent Server*

A *persistent server* does not require explicit activation by the ORB, such as one that is always active in a process from system boot time.

Active from system startup

When a client makes an invocation on an objref, the objref relays that message to the ORB for forwarding to the implementation. When the ORB relays such a message, it looks to see what style of activation the server requires. For a persistent server, the ORB just hands the server the message.

The BOA behaves differently for each server style.

Each style of server has different implications for the developer in terms of security, availability, and concurrency. The idea is that this range of possibilities meets more needs for developers. The server style is a function of the object adapter that the server uses. The adapter is what provides these styles of implementation detail.

Server style affects security, availability, and concurrency.

Along with server activation style there are also implications for object activation within a server. This, too, is a concern of the object adapter, and some discussion occurs in the appropriate method.

The BOA also participates in object activation.

After the initial call, when server and object are active, the call routing theoretically may bypass a BOA process as an optimization (see Figure 7-1).

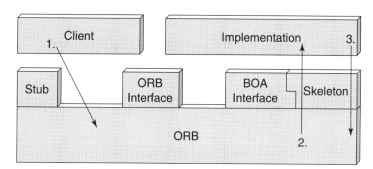

FIGURE 7-1. Theoretical bypass of the BOA

7.2.2 The BOA Interface

The BOA interface (Example 7-1) supports ten operations:

1. Create
2. Dispose
3. Get ID
4. Change Implementation
5. Get Principal
6. Set Exception
7. Implementation Is Ready
8. Deactivate Implementation
9. Object Is Ready
10. Deactivate Object

EXAMPLE 7-1. BOA object interface

```
module  CORBA
{
    interface   InterfaceDef;
    interface   ImplementationDef;
    interface   Object;
    interface   Principal;
    typedef     sequence<octet, 1024>   ReferenceData;

    interface BOA                       // C-PIDL
    {
        Object create(
                    in ReferenceData        id,
                    in InterfaceDef         intf,
                    in ImplementationDef    impl);

        void dispose(in Object obj);

        ReferenceData   get_id(in Object obj);

        void    change_implementation(in Object obj,
                                    in ImplementationDef impl);

        Principal   get_principal(in Object obj, in Environment ev);

        void set_exception(in exception_type major,
                            in string userid,
                            in void *param);

        void impl_is_ready(in ImplementationDef impl);
        void deactivate_impl(in ImplementationDef impl);
        void obj_is_ready(in Object obj, in ImplementationDef impl);
        void deactivate_obj(in Object obj);
    };
};
```

7.2.2.1 Create

The Create operation is the object reference factory. It returns an object and has three parameters:

1. Reference data ID
2. Interface Definition
3. Implementation Definition

The reference data ID is a 1K sequence of octets. The intent is that the implementation uses it to identify a specific object, although it may use it any way it sees fit. The reference data should remain the same throughout that object's lifetime. In other words, the reference data is immutable.

The implementation may use reference data to identify an object.

   The Interface Definition is an interface repository object that specifies the complete detail about the object's interfaces, while the Implementation Definition specifies the complete detail about the object's implementation.

   The Create call produces object references that are distinct even if all three parameters are identical on separate invocations. It is a matter for the implementation, however, to maintain the distinction if it is desirable. An implementation is free to construct any number of object references and treat them all as if they referred to the same object if it so desires.

The BOA's Create call always produces a distinct object reference.

7.2.2.2 Dispose

The Dispose operation instructs the ORB and BOA to forget an object reference, effectively disassociating the parameters that were bound on creation and releasing any resources. It takes a single parameter, Object. All further requests on the object reference will fail after the operation completes.

7.2.2.3 Get ID

The Get ID operation returns reference data and takes a single object parameter. The reference data is the same ID data parameter as occurs in the object's Create call.

   The octet data type (reference data is a sequence of 1,024 such octets) is immutable and does not undergo any change during operation requests. This means that regardless of the endian nature (byte order) or architecture, the ID remains the same and is portable across ORBs. The reference data is always recognizable by its implementation. This is unlike object references, which are opaque and may have many different implementations.

7.2.2.4 Change Implementation

The Change Implementation has no result. It takes two parameters: (1) Object and (2) Implementation Definition.

   The operation associates the new Implementation Definition with the object, disassociating the Implementation Definition from the original Create request.

This operation has very many potential side effects, for instance, synchronization, activation, security, and the implementation's readiness to handle requests for that object.

7.2.2.5   Get Principal

The implementation may use Get Principal[2] to determine the Principal making a request of the implementation. On receipt of a request, the implementation may then interrogate the BOA with this operation to obtain information about the requester. The information that results in the Principal Object result varies, depending on the security in use at that time.

The Get Principal message returns a principal and takes two parameters: (1) Object and (2) Environment.

The Object parameter is the controlling parameter for the request, for which the implementation wants the principal. Giving any other object to this operation will produce entirely speculative results at best. The Environment object is specific to the language mapping.

7.2.2.6   Set Exception

The Set Exception operation allows an implementation to inform the BOA of exceptional conditions potentially occurring outside the normal invocation request. The operation has no result and takes three parameters: (1) Exception Type, (2) Exception Identity, and (3) Parameters.

The Exception Type indicates the kind of exception: none, system, or user. The Exception Identity (in IDL it is a User ID of type string), is the string name, or identity, of the exception. In C-PIDL the Parameters parameter is a void * block of data that contains the parameters for the exception.

7.2.2.7   Implementation Is Ready

The Implementation Is Ready operation has no result and takes one parameter, Implementation Definition.

The four operations (beginning with this one—see Table 7-1) form a protocol that allows the Implementation to inform the BOA of its current state, or an ability to accept requests.

Activation for shared, unshared, and per-method occurs on a first request to an object. In the case of per-method, it occurs on every subsequent request whether the implementation is already active or not. It does not occur for the Persistent server because its activation is by way of some other mechanism. (See Table 7-1.)

In the case of the shared server, the BOA holds calls until the Implementation Is Ready message arrives. The BOA is then free to request object

---

2. Deprecated. See Chapter 13.

TABLE 7-1. Minimum Activation Protocol Agreements

	Shared	*Unshared*	*Per-Method*	*Persistent*
Implementation Is Ready	On starting			On starting
Deactivate Implementation	On terminating			
Object Is Ready		On starting		
Deactivate Object	On deactivating an object	On terminating		

activation or other messages. Objects are active from the time the implementation is ready until a Deactivate Object message informs the BOA otherwise.

In the case of the unshared server, which is a single object per server, the object is active from receipt of Object Is Ready until the BOA receives the contrary Deactivate Object.

The per-method server does not require a minimum set of these messages because servers occur for each method.

Persistent servers make their presence known to the BOA by sending the Implementation Is Ready message. From then on the BOA treats the persistent server as if it were a shared server.

7.2.2.8   Deactivate Implementation

The Deactivate Implementation operation has no result and takes one parameter, Implementation Definition.

The Implementation Definition object is the full description of the object to deactivate as understood by the implementation repository. On deactivation, all further requests should queue until the BOA receives an Implementation Is Ready message after another activation.

7.2.2.9   Object Is Ready

The Object Is Ready operation has no result and takes two parameters: (1) Object and (2) Implementation Definition.

The Object parameter is that of the object now ready to receive requests. The Implementation Definition is the implementation repository object that fully describes the implementation. When the BOA receives this message from the implementation it may forward any queued messages waiting for that object.

7.2.2.10   Deactivate Object

The Deactivate Object operation has no result and takes a single parameter, Object.

The Object is the object no longer active. The BOA must reactivate the object before delivery of any additional messages.

7.3   DYNAMIC SKELETON INTERFACE

The operation of the BOA and its interaction with the skeletons saw an extension in the 2.0 specification. A Dynamic Skeleton Interface (DSI) is now part of the basic architecture. This provides many new capabilities, as shown in Figure 7-2.

A DSI handles multi-language requests.

The Dynamic Skeleton is frequently necessary for implementations of multi-language systems or for dynamic language services. One of the nice features is that the server using this access method might see a substantial reduction in the number of static skeletons it supports.

Servers register a Dynamic Implementation Routine.

The DSI requires the server to register a Dynamic Implementation Routine (DIR). How such registration occurs is an implementation detail. What the server registers is given as an example in both C and C++ mappings. The implementation registers a Dynamic Implementation Routine.

The basic operation follows:

1. A request from a client arrives at the server-side of the ORB (or BOA in the event it is not necessary, for instance, when activation is necessary).
2. The ORB makes an up-call on the DIR, passing in a Server Request object (see Example 7-2).
3. The DIR implementation (in the server) then invokes an Operation Name request on the Server Request parameter and receives the operation name as an identifier.
4. The DIR calls the Parameters operation—even if that operation requires no parameters.
5. If the method is not an attribute operation (Get or Set), the implementation retrieves the Context object if it wants to know the principal of the call.
6. The server executes the operation.

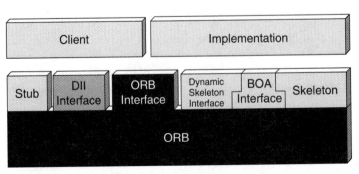

FIGURE 7-2. CORBA components with DSI

7. If any out parameters are part of the invocation, the server sets them in the Named Value List.

8. The DIR may then call either Exception or Result (but not both). If it calls Exception it may not call Result (results are undefined on an exception).[3]

9. If it calls Exception, DIR uses an Exception parameter (see Example 7-3).[4]

10. If it calls Result, the DIR passes an Any with the result.

11. The DIR invocation then returns to the ORB.

Note that the server may invoke the Parameters, Result, and Exception operations once and only once, and then only in the order in the preceding description.

EXAMPLE 7-2. Server Request object interface

```
module   CORBA
{
    interface    ServerRequest
    {
        Identifier        op_name()
        Context           ctx();
        void              params(inout NVList parms);
        Any               result();
    };
};
```

EXAMPLE 7-3. C and C++ mapping examples for Server Request

```
//  C mapping
CORBA_Identifier     CORBA_ServerRequest_op_name(
                         CORBA_ServerRequest req,
                         CORBA_Environment   *env);

CORBA_Context        CORBA_ServerRequest_op_name(
                         CORBA_ServerRequest req,
                         CORBA_Environment   *env);

void     CORBA_ServerRequest_params(
             CORBA_ServerRequest      req,
             CORBA_NVList             parameters,
             CORBA_Environment        *env);

void     CORBA_ServerRequest_result(
             CORBA_ServerRequest      req,
             CORBA_Any                value,
             CORBA_Enviroment         *env);
```

---

3. Both C and C++ mappings show signatures for setting the Result and Exception but they do not appear in the IDL for ServerRequest.

4. C++ must pass an exception as a parameter because it cannot throw one that it did not know at compile time. Other languages may have to resort to the same technique.

```
void      CORBA_ServerRequest_exception(
              CORBA_ServerRequest      req,
              CORBA_exception_type     major,
              CORBA_Any                value,
              CORBA_Environment        *env);

// C++ Mapping
class   ServerRequest
{
    public:
         Indentifier      op_name() throw(SystemException);

         OperationDef_ptr    op_def() throw(SystemException);

         Context_ptr      ctx() throw (SystemException);

         void    params(NVList_ptr parameters)
             throw (SystemException);

         void    result(Any *value) throw (SystemException);

         void    exception(Any *value) throw (SystemException);
};
```

CHAPTER 8

Other Object Adapters and the ODMG

There are two ways of constructing a software design. One way is to make it so simple that there are obviously no deficiencies. And the other way is to make it so complicated that there are no obvious deficiencies.
—Attributed to C.A.R. Hoare

From the beginning, the assumption has been that various styles of adapters are necessary. The object-oriented database vendors may have been the first to draw up requirements for an adapter other than the BOA.

8.1 LIBRARY OBJECT ADAPTER

Although the Library Object Adapter (LOA) has no current definition we can speculate about its potential. Object applications that have only remote objects operate under a handicap. For this type of object, it may be more interesting to place the implementation into a library that operates like a dynamically linked library or shared-object library. The adapter would retrieve objects from their persistent store in files. The adapter would not concern itself with activation. Copying the objects locally once is frequently a good strategy for WAN deployment.

An LOA may concern itself with bringing a shared library local on first use and never afterward.

Currently this functionality is common as part of the general operating system runtime. However, leaving this sort of detail to the operating system keeps it platform-dependent. It may be possible to place a thin layer of service above the runtime linker or loader and allow it to provide a common interface, making library interfaces common across systems. This works particularly well for libraries that support an Application Binary Interface (ABI) that provides interlanguage operation.

An LOA may wrapper existing system tools or may be completely from scratch.

However, for such a service to be generally accepted it must require or impose very little overhead for its operation. Although such a service could make libraries portable across multiple platforms, in practice this kind of universal binary service is extremely difficult to implement. A worst-case scenario to obtain such portability may have the adapter operating as a virtual machine, interpreting all the library's instructions. This would be an enormous burden on the runtime, imposing a great deal of overhead. This may sound far-fetched to some, but it is similar to the Java Applet model.[1]

It is more likely that such an adapter would provide the minimal set of services to support a file-based form of persistence. The overhead may occur during the first call when finding and fetching it from its persistent form consumes extra cycles. Presumably, the succeeding operation would be directly on locally instantiated objects, not requiring any, or very little, ORB intervention.

8.2   OTHER ADAPTERS

Other adapters are mentioned in text occasionally. The adapter most frequently mentioned in such discussions is one that is specific to Persistence. The work of the ODMG suggests such an adapter. Other candidates that are frequently mentioned are for:

- Resource distribution or balancing
- Mobility
- Nonsurvivable objects

The ODMG proposed its own adapter.

Although the Basic Object Adapter can fill these roles, it is not optimal. For instance, the Object Data Management Group (ODMG), a consortium of Object Database Vendors, looked at the BOA and decided that their requirement was more than just that of activation. The ODMG proposed its own Object Adapter (OA), which was different from the BOA but still adhered to the underlying CORBA principles.

8.2.1   Persistent Object Adapter

An ODMG OA may use implicit object references.

An object adapter specific to persistence may operate using implicit reference to objects. On referencing an object, it might copy that object into the local address space, making much of its operation transparent. Additional requirements are necessary for high availability, integrity, and concurrency control. These may be part of the style of such an adapter.

An example of such a system is in the standard proposal from ODMG. The ODMG view of objects is presented in the next section of this book and mentions some of the characteristics of its object adapter.

8.2.2   Load Balancing Object Adapter

Resource balancing or leveling may be useful to other implementation styles.

Resource balancing or leveling requirements also may support a style of implementation that is different from the Basic Object Adapter. This is speculation, however, because no RFI or RFP has been written for such an adapter.

---

1. This is not a comparison with or reference to Java's Remote Method Invocation (RMI), which is a different facility. The Java RMI is similar to a CORBA model that never has to worry about different languages, because the assumption is that Java is the only language.

However, one can imagine a series of objects that have specific resource requirements.[2] On making a request of such an object, the ORB with the help of a specialty OA may track resource consumption. It may then periodically shuffle objects around these resources to maintain an optimal mix between the resources available and their consumers.

Such resource-aware OAs might communicate with each other in such a way that they could forward requests for starting an implementation at a location that currently has more resources available. These OAs also may cooperate with checkpointing, reactivation on failure, or migration of the implementation from one host to another as resources become available or are consumed. There is no requirement that this latter type of OA must conspire with other OAs of its kind. For instance, another alternative is for such OAs to ask available resources to bid for an implementation before activating it.

8.2.3   Mobile Object Adapter

An OA specific to mobility may know more about object location than the BOA. If it supports roaming objects, it may know if objects are currently in contact with the ORB or it may queue requests for those that are not currently available. For migrating objects, it may have special ability so that forwarding pointers are not a requirement to maintain object reference accessibility; in other words, so the references do not grow stale. It also may have special algorithms to garbage-collect these in cooperation with other OAs in the ORB.

A mobile object OA may be aware of objects that are not currently in contact.

8.2.4   Transient Object Adapter

An OA that knows specifically that its objects will never survive their process (are never persistent) may have additional strategies that make it much lighter weight, so that it consumes fewer resources and performs better. It could dispose of any object reference information once the process exits.

8.3   ODMG VIEW

The ODMG vendors provide persistent object storage. Their implementations differ in a variety of ways, but they have agreed on a common set of interfaces. We turn to the ODMG view here because they have a specific object adapter filling their requirements, whereas the BOA does not. The ODMG published two versions of that standard and a third version is on the way.

The ODMG model is similar to CORBA but different. In some senses it is a superset. It also requires its own object adapter. The biggest difference is in the use of this different object adapter. In the BOA model, when an invocation is made on an object reference, you do not know where that message will go or the object's location. With the Object Database Adapter (ODA), when

The ODMG requires a different OA.

---

2. The current strategy is to support this through the Trading Services.

you make a reference on the object, the ODA moves the object into your local address space. The former looks like a network ORB; the latter looks like a local ORB.

8.3.1   The ODMG Difference

Fundamental architecture differences are responsible for the ODMG's creation of a new OA. These architectural differences appear as:

The requirements differ in performance, transactions, and transparency.

- *Performance issues.* Much CORBA infrastructure is exposed, requiring it to be generalized for reusability. Such generalization frequently does not perform as well as a nonreusable implementation of the same service. By hiding much of the infrastructure, persistent storage vendors felt they could achieve better performance.
- *Transactions/Two-Phase Commits.* CORBA presupposes that such services live as an object service above the ORB. The ODMG vendors felt that they do an intrinsically better job when they are incorporated inside their transport.
- *Transparency.* Implementation, Encapsulation, Activation, and Location Transparency are easier when completely hidden from the software writer. The persistent storage vendors are specialists who provide services making objects persistent and returning them from persistence store, and making them active. All of these issues are pretty well hidden. Instead of offering multiple styles of implementations as an activation issue, the ODMG provides implementations with quality of services specifiable. The rest is hidden in the implementation's internals.

Another difference is that the granularity of the objects they anticipate is very fine.

Additional reasons exist for the requirements for a different OA. The ODMG anticipates a finer granularity of objects than those that use the BOA. Its OA does not require every object to register. Instead it has a notion of group activation in which poking one object in the group activates every member. For example, a 1024 by 1024 spreadsheet might register every cell as an object in the BOA. However, it is more efficient to register the spreadsheet itself and cause any single-cell access to activate all cells. Databases have groupings or clusters of objects for efficiency. These groupings may register so that all objects become active on accessing any single member.

Another motivation for an ODA is in the management and control of identity.

8.3.2   Object Definition Language

ODL is a superset of IDL.

Object Definition Language (ODL) is a superset of IDL. ODL interfaces have type and instance properties. A type property provides additional constraints on the type specification. An instance interface has properties, which are either attributes or relationships. ODL Interface Definitions also include operations (Example 8-1).

EXAMPLE 8-1. ODMG ODL interface

```
interface   Employee :
            Person (extent Employees, keys SSN): persistent
{
    attribute               job;
    readonly attribute      SSN;

    relationship    Dept    belongs_to inverse Dept::member_of;

    Salary  salary(in Hours monthly_hours);
};
```

ODL interface types have property specifications (keys, extents, and persistence specifications) and properties as members. An ODL property may be an attribute or a relationship.

ODL adds property specifications.

ODL still looks like IDL. Extent, Keys, and Persistence are properties of the Type. They qualify or further constrain Employee, which is of type Interface.

Extent is a type extent, which includes all instances of that type. All objects that are an instance in the database of the Employee type are the extent of the Employee type. If an interface declaration includes an extent declaration, the database will automatically manage and create an index to members of the extent. In the example, all Employee instances receive indexes.

In the ODMG object model, an object may have a key, name, and identity. Keys typically are useful to index into a table or to establish ordinal values with which ordering (physical or logical) of the objects may occur. Keys may be compound.

ODMG objects may have a Key, Name, and Identity.

Persistence is an indicator. It may be *persistent* or *transient* and indicates whether objects of that class survive their creating process.

Attributes behave exactly like IDL in that it stands for an accessor and mutator pair of operations for a value of the type.

Relationships are a form of reference or link. Relationships have type. For example, department is the name of something having the type Dept. The declaration may also show the inverse of the path. In other words, the example shows how to get from an Employee to a Department and also the inverse declaration that gives the path back from Department to Employee.

Names are a part of all objects. In fact, three properties are available on all ODMG objects:

1. `Boolean has_name()`
2. `names: Set<String>`
3. `type: Type`

There are also two built-in operations:

1. `delete()`
2. `Boolean same_as(oid:Object_id)`

ODL has the notion of atomic (primitives) and structured (constructed) types. ODL extends the IDL type system with types that designate groups. These are structured types. Types with structure are in one of two groups:

1. Collection
2. Structure

Collection types are:

- Set
- Bag
- List
- Array

Types in ODL also have a notion of being mutable or immutable, rather similar to const in C++. Those that are mutable are objects, and those that are immutable are Literals.

All ODL types derive from a denotable object. The complete type hierarchy appears in Figure 8-1.

8.3.3   Object Query Language

OQL makes a query but the programming language acts as DML.

The Object Query Language (OQL) is to persistent object storage what SQL is to relational databases. Database technology frequently has a Data Definition Language (DDL), which is the role ODL fills, a Data Manipulation Language (DML), and a Query Language (QL). The ODMG-93 does not specify a DML because the programming language fills that role. OQL is a dynamic language that allows requests at runtime that were, perhaps, inconceivable at compile time. It is not a complete programming language but it may invoke operations, and operations may invoke it. People familiar with SQL will easily understand how to use OQL. Many of the facilities are either fairly identical or have echoes in the other.

OQL and object flavors of SQL may be headed for a merger.

Unfortunately (though this is currently changing) OQL appears to have some gratuitous differences from the ANSI SQL standard. These are undergoing revision to make them more compatible. The original rationale for some of these differences was to make OQL distinct so that the underlying system was apparent in the language. In other words, you would not mistake OQL for another QL if you were fairly familiar with both languages. This distinction informs users if they are working in the domain of relational algebra for persistent storage. This is something people may wish to impose on objects although it does not map as well as it does for rows and columns in tables.

What is interesting in a relational model is not necessarily interesting to an object database model.

The OODBMS has some specific, characteristic assumptions that accompany it, compared to a relational model. An OODBMS may make certain optimization assumptions that are not generally available to a relational model. In turn, relational models also may make assumptions that are not easy to implement in an OODBMS. The differences between the two underlying technologies are beyond the scope of this book. The most obvious and primary

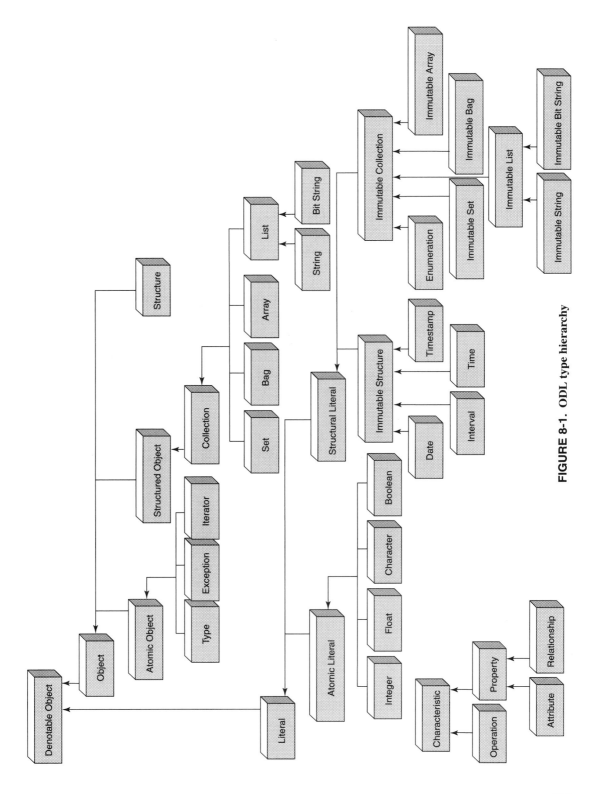

FIGURE 8-1. ODL type hierarchy

131

difference is that OODBMS behaves as a single-level store and an rDBMS does not. Single-level stores make most of the DBMS operations transparent to the programmer. An rDBMS operates as a second-level store.

8.3.4   Client View

Only the ORB should know if a reference points to a BOA object or an ODA object.

An ODMG (with ODA) client most likely links at runtime with a client library that provides a full set of interfaces per the ODMG specification.[3] The client using an ODMG implementation may receive an ODA-specific objref in response to a query on some implementation. It may receive such a reference directly from the ORB, as a request on persistent store, by e-mail or in any of the other ways of transmitting and receiving objrefs. In all cases it is likely to be virtually indistinguishable from a BOA objref. In other words, the client does not need to know it is talking to a totally separate OA. Making an invocation on the ODA object reference delivers the request to the implementation of the object.

8.3.5   Implementations

The implementation side of an ODMG object is more than a skeleton.

Differences between the two models also are more evident on the implementation side. The application writer does not write the ODMG implementation (a persistent store) although they may write some auxiliary operations that the implementation may use. The ODMG ODA is also responsible for ACID properties of its objects and mechanisms such as replication and their own transaction service according to their policies. These implementations are typically of a finer granularity than those of, say, a CORBA, although this is primarily supposition and no such requirement exists.

Let's discuss the auxiliary routines that one may write so that no mistake is read into that statement. An implementation of a spreadsheet object (call it a columnar pad) may in turn use the ODBMS as the implementation for the cells. OQL may navigate through the columnar pad. It may extract or create new entries. The implementation of such things as formulas or macros is more appropriate in auxiliary objects that OQL might apply uniformly across cells. The ODBMS does not have views in the UI sense and so any such formatting or UI work is likely in auxiliary objects as well. The ODBMS vendor may supply the tools to aid in their construction, although that is extraneous to the ODMG-93 standard.

---

3. I use *likely* in this description since this implies dynamic linking.

CHAPTER 9 *Repositories*

> *An object in possession seldom retains the same*
> *charm that it had in pursuit.*
> —Pliny the Younger (Gaius Plinius
> Caecilius Secundus) from *Letters,*
> *book II, letter 15* (c. 61–112 AD)

The CORBA specification mentions two specific repositories: an interface repository and an implementation repository. We will discuss them as conceptually distinct repositories, although there is no requirement that states they must be separate implementations.

A repository is a service that, when presented with a query, returns some object of information. From this description it sounds like a database, and in many respects it is. It may use a lighter-weight mechanism than general databases for its implementation, however, because it supports only a specific application. Databases also generally require more capabilities to satisfy the wider-ranging demands of a multitude of applications.

A repository has query, storage, and retrieval for a specific use.

Flat files could form a repository. A library that dynamically links to a process at runtime also could form the basic infrastructure of a repository. The word *repository* is neutral in that it implies storage and retrieval but not necessarily Atomic, Consistent, Isolated, and Durable (ACID) properties. Some environments may not require such facilities.

9.1 INTERFACE REPOSITORY

The interface repository is a registry of fully qualified interface definitions. The interfaces to the repository as originally defined were for access to information in the repository. Originally there were no interface definitions that stated how to insert information into the repository. The reason was that there may be wide varieties of ways in which information insertion could occur. The 2.0 specification includes the insertion operations. (See Figure 9-1.)

No interface for insertion appears in the original proposal.

The interface repository is a direct complement to the DII. The DII client can browse the interface repository, obtaining the necessary information to construct invocations on an interface.

The interface repository is a direct complement to the DII.

The interface repository may be useful in clarifying the differences between operations by doing a comparison of the accompanying parameters

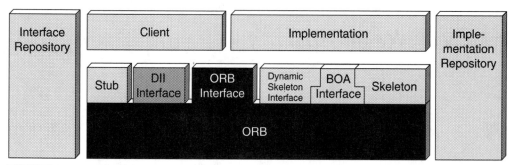

FIGURE 9-1. **CORBA with repositories**

and other operations available on the interface. However, this use is speculative because no rigorous semantics are a part of the repository.[1] It is more
likely that this sort of query is best executing on a service that specializes in
brokering references to specialty interfaces.[2]

9.2   REPOSITORY OBJECT GROUPS

Repository objects add
structure, populate, or both.

A repository represents hierarchical information about interfaces. The objects
in the hierarchy can be classified into three groups. The first structures the
repository and the second populates it. The third is a subgroup of both the
populating group and the structuring group.

The object, itself, is a structuring object. Objects that derive from it, however, populate the repository. This last is the IDL Type Object, which we discuss later in this chapter. The objects that derive from it also will be discussed
later.

The structural group is a set of five objects:

1. Root Interface Repository Objects
2. Container Objects
3. Containment Objects
4. Repository Objects
5. IDL Type Objects

The populating group is a set of eight objects:

1. Module Definition Objects
2. Interface Definition Objects
3. Operation Definition Objects
4. Attribute Definition Objects
5. Exception Definition Objects

---

1. I add the caveat of rigor because some would argue that the names have semantic value. They may
have some value but their meaning can only be interpreted externally and not programmatically.
2. This type of service adds some additional semantics but also has limitations.

6. Typedef Definition Objects
7. Constant Definition Objects
8. Derived IDL Type Objects

The derived IDL Type objects are really the following set of definition objects:

- Structure Definition
- Union Definition
- Enum Definition
- Alias Definition
- Primitive Definition
- String Definition
- Sequence Definition
- Array Definition

The hierarchy is one of containment. Certain objects may contain other objects and some of those objects may contain still other objects. Each level of the containment hierarchy appears in relation to each other in Figure 9-2.

Modules may be useful administratively to segregate or arrange and structure the repository and hierarchies. So Module Definition objects may contain other Module Definition objects.

The repository exists as a containment hierarchy.

Modules may contain other modules.

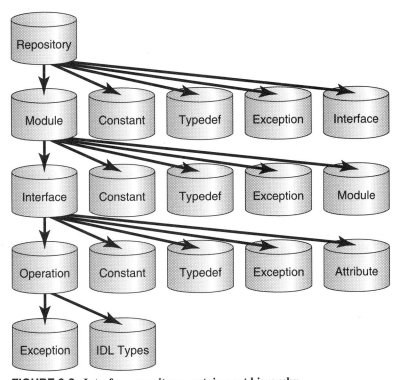

FIGURE 9-2. Interface repository containment hierarchy

9.2.1   Root Repository Object

All objects in the interface repository inherit from the Interface Repository Object (IRObject)—see Example 9-1. This object has one read-only attribute, Definition Kind, and one operation, Destroy. The Definition Kind is a mutator, accessor pair on an enum that describes what it is that is being defined:

- None
- All
- Attribute
- Constant
- Exception
- Interface
- Module
- Operation
- Typedef
- Alias
- Structure
- Union
- Enum
- Primitive
- String
- Sequence
- Array
- Repository

The Destroy operation releases the object and all the resources it consumes.

EXAMPLE 9-1. **Interface repository containment hierarchy**

```
module CORBA
{
    typedef string Identifier;
    typedef string ScopedName;
    typedef string RepositoryId;

    enum DefinitionKind
    {
        dk_none, dk_all,
        dk_Attribute, dk_Constant, dk_Exception,
        dk_Interface, dk_Module, dk_Operation,
        dk_Typedef, dk_Alias, dk_Struct, dk_Union, dk_Enum,
        dk_Primitive, dk_String, dk_Sequence, dk_Array,
        dk_Repository
    };

    interface IRObject
    {
        readonly attribute DefinitionKind def_kind;

        void destroy();
    };
```

9.2.1.1   The IDL Type Interface

The IDL Type is an interface that all objects representing types in IDL support. The IDL Type interface has a single read-only attribute, TypeCode. This provides the mechanism to obtain the TypeCode of all such objects.

9.2.1.2   Special Navigation Interfaces

Two special interfaces establish containment and have more of an administrative reason for being because they do not represent IDL language components. These two interfaces are Contained and Container.

Both inherit from the IR Object. Navigation through the interface repository's Containment hierarchy occurs through operations on these two interfaces.

EXAMPLE 9-2. Contained object interface

```
typedef string VersionSpec;

interface Contained;
interface Repository;
interface Container;

interface Contained : IRObject
{
    attribute RepositoryId     id;
    attribute Identifier       name;
    attribute VersionSpec      version;

    readonly attribute Container     defined_in;
    readonly attribute ScopedName    absolute_name;
    readonly attribute Repository    containing_repository;

    struct Description
    {
        DefinitionKind  kind;
        any             value;
    };

    Description describe();

    void move(
            in Container    new_container,
            in Identifier   new_name,
            in VersionSpec  new_version
    );
};
```

Contained Interface

The Contained Interface has six attributes, three of which are read-only, and two of which are operations (Example 9-2). The attributes are:

1. ID
2. Name
3. Version

4. Defined in Container
5. Absolute Scoped Name
6. Containing Repository

The ID, Name, and Version attributes help to identify the object. The ID identifies it globally. The Name is scoped to its container. The Version differentiates it from other objects of the same name. Modifying any of these three attributes essentially alters the object's identity within the repository.

The Defined in Container is a reference to the object containing this attribute. The Absolute Scoped Name is the name scoped to its containing Repository. The Containing Repository is the root that is found by following all the Defined in Containers up the hierarchy.

The two operations the Contained Interface supports are Describe and Move.

Describe.   Describe has no parameters and returns a Description, which is a structure with two members, Definition Kind and Value.

The Definition Kind describes the kind of the interface's bearer object. The Value is an Any, which contains different structures describing the object depending on its kind. Bearer is discussed in Chapter 14.

Move.   Move has no result and takes three parameters:

1. New Container
2. New Name
3. New Version Specification

The Move operation essentially moves its bearer object to a new container. Objects may be placed in containers either by way of Move (on the Contained Interface) or by Create operations on the Container interface.

Container Interface

The Container interface is far more complicated because it presents operations to work with all the types it may contain in its role as a container. All objects in a container derive from the Contained interface. The Container interface supports eleven operations:

1. Lookup
2. Contents
3. Lookup Name
4. Describe Contents
5. Create Module
6. Create Constant
7. Create Structure
8. Create Union
9. Create Enum
10. Create Alias
11. Create Interface

Lookup. Lookup finds a definition by its Scoped Name, relative to this container. Scoped Names starting with double colons (::) are scoped to the enclosing repository. The operation takes a Scoped Name as parameter and returns a reference to Contained object.

Contents. Contents describes the content of the Container, where the content may be through containment or inheritance. This operation returns a sequence of Contained objects and takes two parameters:

1. Limit Type
2. Exclude Inherited

The Limit Type is a Definition Kind and may be set to All, in which case all objects are part of the result. Otherwise it may be set to an individual kind and only those kinds may be part of the result set.

Exclude Inherited is a boolean indicator of whether or not objects that inherit are part of the resulting set. (See Example 9-3.)

EXAMPLE 9-3. Interface Repository data structures

```
interface ModuleDef;
interface ConstantDef;
interface IDLType;
interface StructDef;
interface UnionDef;
interface EnumDef;
interface AliasDef;
interface InterfaceDef;

typedef sequence<InterfaceDef>   InterfaceDefSeq;
typedef sequence<Contained>      ContainedSeq;

struct StructMember
{
    Identifier   name;
    TypeCode     type;
    IDLType      type_def;
};
typedef sequence<StructMember>   StructMemberSeq;

struct UnionMember
{
    Identifier   name;
    any          label;
    TypeCode     type;
    IDLType      type_def;
};
typedef sequence<UnionMember>    UnionMemberSeq;

typedef sequence<Identifier>     EnumMemberSeq;
```

Lookup Name.   Lookup Name returns a sequence of Contained objects (see Example 9-4). It takes four parameters:

1. Search Name
2. Levels to Search
3. Limit Type
4. Exclude Inherited

The operation finds all objects matching the name of the object. The Name is an identifier.

EXAMPLE 9-4. Container object interface

```
interface Container : IRObject
{
    Contained lookup(in ScopedName search_name);
    ContainedSeq contents(
        in DefinitionKind    limit_type,
        in boolean           exclude_inherited
    );
    ContainedSeq lookup_name(
        in Identifier        search_name,
        in long              levels_to_search,
        in DefinitionKind    limit_type,
        in boolean           exclude_inherited
    );
    struct Description
    {
        Contained            contained_object;
        DefinitionKind       kind;
        any                  value;
    };
    typedef sequence<Description>        DescriptionSeq;
    DescriptionSeq describe_contents(
        in DefinitionKind    limit_type,
        in boolean           exclude_inherited,
        in long              max_returned_objs
    );
    ModuleDef create_module(
        in RepositoryId      id,
        in Identifier        name,
        in VersionSpec       version
    );
    ConstantDef create_constant(
        in RepositoryId      id,
        in Identifier        name,
        in VersionSpec       version,
        in IDLType           type,
        in any               value
    );
    StructDef create_struct(
        in RepositoryId      id,
        in Identifier        name,
        in VersionSpec       version,
        in StructMemberSeq   members
    );
```

```
    UnionDef create_union(
        in RepositoryId         id,
        in Identifier           name,
        in VersionSpec          version,
        in IDLType              discriminator_type,
        in UnionMemberSeq       members
    );
    EnumDef create_enum(
        in RepositoryId         id,
        in Identifier           name,
        in VersionSpec          version,
        in EnumMemberSeq        members
    );
    AliasDef create_alias(
        in RepositoryId         id,
        in Identifier           name,
        in VersionSpec          version,
        in IDLType              original_type
    );
    InterfaceDef create_interface(
        in RepositoryId         id,
        in Identifier           name,
        in VersionSpec          version,
        in InterfaceDefSeq      base_interfaces
    );
};
```

The operation is a request to the object that bears this interface, and Levels to Search limits the search to the object itself or all the objects it contains. Levels to Search is a long. If it is set to −1, then Search looks at this object and all the objects it contains. If Levels to Search is set to 1, then Search only looks at the bearer.

Limit Type and Exclude Inherited operate as they did for the Contents operation.

Describe Contents.   Describe Contents operates as a combination of Describe (in the Contained interface) and Contents. Each object it finds comes with a Description. The operation returns a sequence of Descriptions. A Description is a structure of three members:

1. Contained Object
2. Kind
3. Value

Describe Contents takes three parameters:

1. Limit Type
2. Exclude Inherited
3. Maximum Returned Objects

Limit Type and Exclude Inherited have the same meaning as they held for previous operations.

The Maximum Returned Objects is a long that limits the maximum number of descriptions in the resultant sequence. If it is set to −1 all contained objects are described.

Create Module.   Create Module creates a Module Definition. As do all the Create operations in the Container interface, the Create Module sets the definition's Container to reference the object where creation is invoked, and it sets the Containing Repository to that of the current repository. This operation takes three parameters:

1. Repository ID
2. Name
3. Version Specification

These three parameters are the first three in all Create operations of the Container interface. The Repository ID is a string, the Name is an Identifier, which is a string, and the Version Specification also is a string.

Create Constant.   Create Constant returns a Constant Definition. The operations takes five parameters:

1. Repository ID
2. Name
3. Version Specification
4. IDL Type
5. Value

The IDL Type is the IDL Type object representing the type of the Constant. The Value is an Any containing the value of the Constant.

Create Structure.   Create Structure returns a Structure Definition and takes four parameters:

1. Repository ID
2. Name
3. Version Specification
4. Member Sequence

The Member Sequence is a sequence of structures with three members, one for each member of the structure:

1. Name
2. TypeCode
3. IDL Type Definition

Create Union.   Create Union returns a Union Definition. The operation takes five parameters:

1. Repository ID
2. Name

3. Version Specification
4. Discriminator Type
5. Sequence of Union Members

The Discriminator Type is an IDL type object. A Union Member structure has four members:

1. Name
2. Label
3. Type
4. Type Definition

The Name is an Identifier, Label is an Any, the Type is a TypeCode, and Type Definition is an IDL Type object. One of these structures is in the sequence for each member of the Union.

Create Enum.   Create Enum returns an Enum Definition and takes four parameters:

1. Repository ID
2. Name
3. Version Specification
4. Members

The Members parameter is a sequence of identifiers.

Create Alias.   Create Alias returns an Alias Definition. This operation takes four parameters:

1. Repository ID
2. Name
3. Version Specification
4. Original Type

The Original Type is the IDL Type of the object, which this object aliases.

Create Interface.   Create Interface returns an empty Interface Definition. The operation takes four parameters:

1. Repository ID
2. Name
3. Version Specification
4. Base Interfaces

Base Interfaces is a sequence of Interface Definitions.

The empty Interface Definition bears a Container interface and so the interface may contain such things as Exceptions, Types, and Constants by requesting their creation on the Interface Definition's Container interface. Adding Operations occurs in this same way.

9.2.1.3   The Repository Interface

The Repository Interface is a highly available interface. It is the primary access point for the interface repository (see Example 9-5).

Interface Operations
The interface supports five operations:

1. Lookup ID
2. Get Primitive Definition
3. Create String
4. Create Sequence
5. Create Array

The final three operations return anonymous types. These types do not derive from the Contained interface. Because their construction occurs here, the Contained object does not control their resource allocation.

EXAMPLE 9-5. IDL Type and the Repository object interface

```
interface IDLType : IRObject { readonly attribute TypeCode type; };

interface PrimitiveDef;
interface StringDef;
interface SequenceDef;
interface ArrayDef;

enum PrimitiveKind { pk_null, pk_void,
                     pk_short, pk_long, pk_ushort, pk_ulong,
                     pk_float, pk_double,
                     pk_boolean, pk_char, pk_octet,
                     pk_any, pk_TypeCode,
                     pk_Principal, pk_string, pk_objref
};

interface Repository : Container
{
    Contained lookup_id(in RepositoryId search_id);

    PrimitiveDef get_primitive(in PrimitiveKind kind);

    StringDef create_string (in unsigned long bound);

    SequenceDef create_sequence(
        in unsigned long    bound,
        in IDLType          element_type
    );

    ArrayDef create_array(in unsigned long length, in IDLType element_type);
};
```

Lookup ID.   Lookup ID returns a Contained object. It takes a single parameter as a search ID: the ID of the Repository to search.

Repository ID.   The Repository ID is a string designating the object of the search. All Repository objects have such IDs.

Get Primitive Definition.   Get Primitive Definition takes a single parameter, Primitive Kind, and returns a Primitive Definition.

Create String.   Create String takes a single parameter, Bound, an unsigned long designating the length of the string. The Bound may not be zero. Unbounded strings are available through the Get Primitive operation. This operation returns a String Definition.

Create Sequence.   Create Sequence returns a Sequence Definition and takes two parameters:

1. Bound
2. Element Type

Bound is an unsigned long designating the length of the sequence. Element Type is an IDL Type object.

Create Array.   Create Array returns an Array Definition and takes two parameters:

1. Length
2. Element Type

Length is an unsigned long, and Element type is an IDL Type object.

9.2.1.4   *The Module Definition Interface*

The Module Definition interface has no operations or attributes. It combines the Container and Contained interfaces via inheritance.

The Module Description is the resulting description from the Describe operation on a Module Definition. A Module Description is a structure with four members:

1. Name
2. Repository ID
3. Defined In
4. Version Specification

The Name is an identifier, which is a string, as is the Repository ID of the Module. Defined In is the Repository ID of the container, and Version Specification is a string. (See Example 9-6.)

EXAMPLE 9-6. Module Def, Constant Def, and Type Def object interfaces

```
interface ModuleDef : Container, Contained {    };

struct ModuleDescription
{
    Identifier      name;
    RepositoryId    id;
    RepositoryId    defined_in;
    VersionSpec     version;
};

interface ConstantDef : Contained
{
    readonly attribute  TypeCode    type;
    attribute           IDLType     type_def;
    attribute           any         value;
};

struct ConstantDescription
{
    Identifier      name;
    RepositoryId    id;
    RepositoryId    defined_in;
    VersionSpec     version;
    TypeCode        type;
    any             value;
};

interface TypedefDef : Contained, IDLType {   };
```

9.2.1.5 The Constant Definition Interface

The Constant Definition interface has three attributes, the first being read-only:

1. Type
2. Type Definition
3. Value

The Type is the TypeCode of the constant. Constants are only of simple types.

The Type Definition is the IDL Type definition of the constant. Changing the Type Definition changes the Type. The Value contains the expression value of the constant, which may be different in appearance than its computed value. The TypeCode in the Any must be the Type of the Constant Definition.

The Constant Description is what its Describe interface returns. A Constant Description is a structure with six members:

1. Name
2. Repository ID
3. Defined In
4. Version Specification
5. TypeCode
6. Value

The first four members have the same meanings as the corresponding members in the Module Description. The TypeCode is the Type in the Constant Definition and the Value is the same as the one in the definition.

9.2.1.6 The Typedef Definition Interface

The Typedef Definition interface inherits from IDL Type and Contained. It has no additional operations and no attributes other than those it inherits. It is useful for nonobject types having names. These types are (see Example 9-7):

- Structure
- Union
- Enumeration
- Alias

EXAMPLE 9-7. **Struct Def, Union Def, Enum Def, Alias Def, Primitive Def, String Def, Sequence Def, Array Def, Exception Def object interfaces**

```
struct TypeDescription
{
    Identifier      name;
    RepositoryId    id;
    RepositoryId    defined_in;
    VersionSpec     version;
    TypeCode        type;
};

interface StructDef : TypedefDef { attribute StructMemberSeq members; };

interface UnionDef : TypedefDef
{
    readonly attribute TypeCode     discriminator_type;
    attribute IDLType               discriminator_type_def;
    attribute UnionMemberSeq        members;
};

interface EnumDef : TypedefDef { attribute EnumMemberSeq members; };

interface AliasDef : TypedefDef { attribute IDLType original_type_def; };

interface PrimitiveDef : IDLType { readonly attribute PrimitiveKind kind; };

interface StringDef : IDLType { attribute unsigned long bound; };

interface SequenceDef : IDLType
{
    attribute unsigned long     bound;
    readonly attribute TypeCode element_type;
    attribute IDLType           element_type_def;
};
```

```
interface ArrayDef : IDLType
{
    attribute unsigned long    length;
    readonly attribute TypeCode element_type;
    attribute IDLType          element_type_def;
};

interface ExceptionDef : Contained
{
    readonly attribute TypeCode type;
    attribute StructMemberSeq   members;
};
struct ExceptionDescription
{
    Identifier    name;
    RepositoryId  id;
    RepositoryId  defined_in;
    VersionSpec   version;
    TypeCode      type;
};
```

Primitive types or anonymous types do not inherit from the Typedef Definition. The Typedef describe operation uncharacteristically returns a Type Description, as opposed to a Typedef Description. This structure has five members:

1. Name
2. Repository ID
3. Defined In
4. Version Specification
5. TypeCode

The first four behave as they do in previous descriptions. The TypeCode is the type to which the Typedef applies; that is, the structure, union, enumeration, or alias.

9.2.1.7   *The Structure Definition Interface*

The Structure Definition interface inherits the Typedef Definition interface. It supports a single attribute, Members.

Members is a sequence of Structure Member. Each Structure Member is a structure with three members:

- Name
- TypeCode
- Type Definition

Setting the Members' attribute updates the Type attribute (which it inherits through the Typedef Definition from IDL Type). While setting the Members' attribute, the Type in the Structure Member structure should be initially set to `TC_void` but is otherwise ignored.

Describe returns a Type Description (as in Typedef Definition).

9.2.1.8   The Union Definition Interface

The Union Definition interface, which inherits from the Typedef Definition, supports three attributes, the first as read-only:

1. Discriminator Type is the TypeCode of the union's discriminator.
2. Discriminator Type Definition is the IDL Type bearing that TypeCode.
3. Members is a sequence of Union Member structures.

Each Union Member structure has four members:

1. Name is an identifier. Members that are sequential may have the same name. Members with identical names must have identical Types.
2. Label is an Any and it contains a value that is distinct from any of the other Union Member structures in the sequence. A Label of type octet and value zero is the default label.
3. Type is a TypeCode of the member.
4. Type Definition is its IDL Type.

When setting the Members attribute, the Type in the Union Member structure should initially be set to `TC_void` but is otherwise ignored. Describe returns a Type Description (as in Typedef Definition).

9.2.1.9   The Enumeration Definition Interface

The Enumeration Definition interface inherits from the Typedef Definition and supports a single attribute, Members. Members is an Enumeration Member Sequence, a sequence of identifiers. Each member must possess a distinct name. Describe returns a Type Description (as in Typedef Definition).

9.2.1.10   The Alias Definition Interface

The Alias Definition interface also inherits from the Typedef Definition interface and supports a single attribute, Original Type Definition. The Original Type Definition is an IDL Type that is of the type that this object aliases. Describe returns a Type Description (as in Typedef Definition).

9.2.1.11   The Primitive Definition Interface

The Primitive Definition interface inherits from IDL Type and bears a single attribute, Primitive Kind. Primitive Kind is an enum, with 16 enum members representing the types in Table 9-1 as primitives:

- There are no Primitive Definitions with a Primitive Kind of Null.
- A Primitive Kind of String indicates an unbounded string.
- A Primitive Kind of objref indicates the object type (not one that derives from Object).
- The Repository interface is where one obtains references to Primitive Definitions via its Get Primitive operation.

TABLE 9-1. **Primitive Kind**

Null	Void	Short	Long
Unsigned Short	Unsigned Long	Float	Double
Boolean	Character	Octet	Any
TypeCode	Principal	String	Objref

9.2.1.12   The String Definition Interface

The String Definition interface contains a single attribute, Bound. Bound is an unsigned long and represents the length of a bounded string. Unbounded string definitions are of type Primitive Definition. Bound is never zero but indicates the maximum length (upper bound) of the string.

9.2.1.13   The Sequence Definition Interface

The Sequence Definition interface derives from IDL Type and supports three attributes, the second of which is read-only:

1. Bound
2. Element Type
3. Element Type Definition

Bound is an unsigned long and when it is zero, it signifies an unbounded sequence. Otherwise it is the upper bound (maximum number of elements) of the sequence.

Element Type is a TypeCode and the one read-only attribute. The Element Type Definition is an IDL Type. Sequences are anonymous and do not derive from Typedef Definitions or the Contained interface.

9.2.1.14   The Array Definition Interface

The Array Definition interface derives from IDL Type and supports three attributes, the second of which is a read-only attribute:

1. Length
2. Element Type
3. Element Type Definition

Length is an unsigned long specifying the number of elements in the array. Element Type and Element Type Definition operate as they did for the Sequence Definition interface. In both cases, changing the Element Type Definition changes the Element Type.

9.2.1.15   The Exception Definition Interface

The Exception Definition interface looks much like a structure, which it models. It inherits from Contained and supports two attributes, the first of which is read-only:

1. Type
2. Members

Type is an Exception TypeCode (`tk_except` kind). Members is a sequence of Structure Member structures as in the Structure Definition description.

Calling the Describe operation produces an Exception Description structure, which consists of five members, each of which was described earlier:

1. Name
2. Repository ID
3. Defined In
4. Version Specification
5. Type

9.2.1.16   *The Attribute Definition Interface*

The Attribute Definition interface derives from Contained and has three attributes (see Example 9-8), the first of which is read-only:

1. Type
2. Type Definition
3. Mode

The first two behave the same as in interfaces just described.

EXAMPLE 9-8. **Attribute Def and Operation Def object interfaces**

```
enum AttributeMode {ATTR_NORMAL, ATTR_READONLY};

interface AttributeDef : Contained
{
    readonly attribute TypeCode      type;
    attribute IDLType                type_def;
    attribute AttributeMode          mode;
};

struct AttributeDescription
{
    Identifier      name;
    RepositoryId    id;
    RepositoryId    defined_in;
    VersionSpec     version;
    TypeCode        type;
    AttributeMode   mode;
};

enum OperationMode {OP_NORMAL, OP_ONEWAY};
enum ParameterMode {PARAM_IN, PARAM_OUT, PARAM_INOUT};
```

```
struct ParameterDescription
{
    Identifier      name;
    TypeCode        type;
    IDLType         type_def;
    ParameterMode   mode;
};
typedef sequence<ParameterDescription>  ParDescriptionSeq;

typedef Identifier                      ContextIdentifier;
typedef sequence<ContextIdentifier>     ContextIdSeq;

typedef sequence<ExceptionDef>          ExceptionDefSeq;
typedef sequence<ExceptionDescription>  ExcDescriptionSeq;

interface OperationDef : Contained
{
    readonly attribute TypeCode     result;
    attribute IDLType               result_def;
    attribute ParDescriptionSeq     params;
    attribute OperationMode         mode;
    attribute ContextIdSeq          contexts;
    attribute ExceptionDefSeq       exceptions;
    };

struct OperationDescription
{
    Identifier          name;
    RepositoryId        id;
    RepositoryId        defined_in;
    VersionSpec         version;
    TypeCode            result;
    OperationMode       mode;
    ContextIdSeq        contexts;
    ParDescriptionSeq   parameters;
    ExcDescriptionSeq   exceptions;
};
```

The Mode is an enum having two values:

1. Normal
2. Read-Only

Normal indicates that it is an attribute pair of operation Get and Set. Read-Only indicates only the Get operation is present.

Calling Describe returns an Attribute Description structure, which has six members:

1. Name
2. Repository ID
3. Defined In
4. Version Specification
5. Type
6. Mode

These all behave the same as they do in previous definitions (as one would expect).

9.2.1.17   *The Operation Definition Interface*

The Operation Definition interface derives from Contained and sports six attributes, with the first as read-only:

1. Type
2. Result Definition
3. Parameters
4. Operation Mode
5. Contexts
6. Exceptions

The first two attributes describe the result of the operation being defined.

Parameters is a sequence of structures of type Parameter Description. The Parameter Description structure has four members:

1. Name
2. Type
3. Type Definition
4. Parameter Mode

Parameter Modes are enumerations with three values:

1. Parameter In
2. Parameter Out
3. Parameter In Out

Operation Modes are enumerations with one of two values:

1. Normal
2. One Way

Contexts are sequences of Context Identifiers, which are Identifiers (strings). They describe the list of Contexts for the operation.

Exceptions is a sequence of Exception Definitions and indicates a list of exceptions for the operation.

The Describe operation produces an Operation Description structure, which consists of the following members:

- Name
- Repository ID
- Defined In
- Version
- Result Type
- Operation Mode
- Contexts
- Parameters
- Exceptions

9.2.1.18   *The Interface Definition Interface*

The Interface Definition interface inherits from Container, Contained, and IDL Type, and has one attribute: Base Interfaces. It also supports the following four operations:

1. Is A
2. Describe Interface
3. Create Attribute
4. Create Operation

The Base Interfaces attribute is a sequence of Interface Definitions, which collectively represent all the interfaces from which the current Interface derives (see Example 9-9).

EXAMPLE 9-9. Interface Def object interface

```
typedef sequence<RepositoryId>        RepositoryIdSeq;
typedef sequence<OperationDescription> OpDescriptionSeq;
typedef sequence<AttributeDescription> AttrDescriptionSeq;

interface InterfaceDef : Container, Contained, IDLType
{
    attribute InterfaceDefSeq base_interfaces;

    boolean is_a(in RepositoryId interface_id);

    struct FullInterfaceDescription
    {
        Identifier          name;
        RepositoryId        id;
        RepositoryId        defined_in;
        VersionSpec         version;
        OpDescriptionSeq    operations;
        AttrDescriptionSeq  attributes;
        RepositoryIdSeq     base_interfaces;
        TypeCode            type;
    };

    FullInterfaceDescription describe_interface( );

    AttributeDef create_attribute(
        in RepositoryId    id,
        in Identifier      name,
        in VersionSpec     version,
        in IDLType         type,
        in AttributeMode   mode
    );
```

```
OperationDef create_operation(
    in RepositoryId        id,
    in Identifier          name,
    in VersionSpec         version,
    in IDLType             result,
    in OperationMode       mode,
    in ParDescriptionSeq   params,
    in ExceptionDefSeq     exceptions,
    in ContextIdSeq        contexts
  );
};

struct InterfaceDescription
{
    Identifier        name;
    RepositoryId      id;
    RepositoryId      defined_in;
    VersionSpec       version;
    RepositoryIdSeq   base_interfaces;
  };
};
```

Is A

Is A returns a boolean and takes a single parameter, Repository ID, which identifies an interface.

The operation returns True if the ID is an exact match for this interface or if this interface inherits either directly or indirectly from that of the parameter. Otherwise the operation returns False.

Describe Interface

The Describe Interface operation returns a Full Interface Description structure, which is more comprehensive than the Interface Description resulting from its inherited Describe operation. The resulting structure consists of eight members:

1. Name
2. Repository ID
3. Defined In
4. Version Specification
5. Operations
6. Attributes
7. Base Interfaces
8. Type

The first four behave exactly as previous descriptions state. Operations is a sequence of Operation Description structures. Attributes is a sequence of Attribute Description structures. Base Interface is a sequence of Repository IDs, representing the interfaces that this interface inherits. Type is the Interface's corresponding TypeCode. The inherited Describe operation returns an Interface Description structure, and has the following five members:

1. Name
2. Repository ID
3. Defined In
4. Version Specification
5. Base Interfaces

Create Attribute

The Create Attribute operation returns an Attribute Definition and takes five parameters:

1. Repository ID
2. Name
3. Version Specification
4. Type
5. Attribute Mode

Create Operation

The operation Create Operation returns an Operation Definition and takes eight parameters:

1. Repository ID
2. Name
3. Version Specification
4. Result Type
5. Operation Mode
6. Parameters
7. Exceptions
8. Contexts

9.3 IMPLEMENTATION REPOSITORY

The implementation reposi-
tory is without definition.

The implementation repository presupposes that implementations may collect together in some sort of repository from which they will be invoked. Because the ORB needs to know where implementations exist to make them active, it is not clear that anything more than a path in the local file system (local to the implementation) is necessary. One can envision a library server that passes out Dynamically Loading Libraries to various processes as their implementations become necessary. Some of the speculation results from the fact that an implementation repository is the least well defined.

CHAPTER 10 *Interoperability*

Entia non sunt multiplicanda praeter necessitatem.
—Occam's Razor attributed to William
of Occam (c. 1280–1349)

Interoperability is something computer users want. It also is very important to the goals of the OMA. On the other hand, interoperability is the basis for many arguments that have little or nothing to do with interoperability requirements. The degree to which two things interoperate seems confusing even in ideal circumstances. Fortunately, ORBs can now claim interoperability, and the arguments vanish.

Some arguments for interoperability had little or nothing to do with interoperability.

One of the most confusing points is that people seem to think an ORB should be capable of interoperation with everything in creation. Most of the ORB vendors provide their ORBs for more than just their platforms. In theory, a single vendor could provide its ORB implementation on all platforms that exist. In practice no one is likely to offer it on every platform. Vendors most likely will not offer it for some time to come on specialty systems that are not used in an information-sharing architecture (for example, voice-activated toasters). Vendors of those products may not ever offer ORBs themselves for the same reason. So a universal ORB for interoperability is probably out of the question. Most likely, no ORB will be designed to run on your microwave or toaster oven until there is enough incentive to define a market.[1]

ORBs may interoperate with one another or with special systems. Some forms do not make sense until there is a market.

10.1 ORB DOMAINS

The other big misunderstanding has to do with scope. What is the scope of an ORB? Where are its boundaries? The easy answer is that the scope of an objref (where it is understood) is the domain of its ORB. Presenting an objref from ORB A to a machine in a domain where only ORB B exists raises two immediate questions: What does the object represent? How can I use something I have never heard of before?

It is confusing to talk about doing something meaningful with an unknown objref; an ORB's bound is where its objref has meaning.

---

1. Although ORBs are currently being embedded into medical monitoring devices and the like, it is unlikely than any single ORB vendor will cover the gamut of devices requiring embedded systems.

A client could receive an objref that it has never seen before by way of the persistent form. However, the only way to translate it from string form into usable form would be to present it to a service that understood it. This requires the string form to be presented to its ORB for translation. The reconstitution of an active object reference from a persistent object reference may occur only by presenting it to the ORB in which it belongs. Reconstitution by some other ORB is undefined. Since the client does not belong to ORB A, it has no service through which it can convert or translate the string form into an object in its process.

An alternative means of exchange between ORBs is through the formal service available as one of the CORBAservices (the Externalization Service). This allows object translation into an external form, with a few caveats. This might be of use in exchanging information about objects between different ORBs. The Externalization Service description is in Chapter 14.

There are at least seven domains that require addressing for inter-operability to occur.

The scope of an object reference is within its reference domain. A *domain* is the set of all objects for which a function is defined. *Scope* is the applicable range of operation. At least seven other domains must concur for interoperability to occur, the most common of which are:

1. *Reference Domain*—the scope of an object reference; where it has meaning.
2. *Representation Domain*—the scope of the transporting protocol and message syntax; the place where messages of this form are receivable and interpretable.
3. *Network Addressing Domain*—the scope of addresses for a network; the place where addresses are comprehensible and reachable.
4. *Network Connectivity Domain*—the extent of available paths for messages; the place where the wires exist to interconnect the end points (between object reference and object implementation).
5. *Security Domain*—the extent of the pertinent security policies; the place where protection domains for confidentiality, integrity, accountability, and availability all concur with access.
6. *Type Domain*—the scope of an object's type identity; the place where a specific type is meaningful and known.
7. *Transaction Domain*—the scope of the pertinent transaction service; the locale where the system administrators or other policy makers allow or arrange a single transaction service to interoperate.

ORBs may be distinct in their implementation, such as those of different vendors, but their very definitions may conflict in any of the seven domains just listed. Two ORBs from the same vendor, in use within the same company, may be separate ORBs if they vary by definition in any of these seven domains.

A process is a member of an ORB if it can use an objref. Such a process necessarily has code that participates in that ORB, whether from the same vendor or by another vendor writing code that enables the object reference's scope.

Although an objref is meaningless in one process, say a client in ORB B, the service may be available to this client by way of an ORB B objref. In such a case, some service in ORB B maps the corresponding ORB A object reference into an ORB B reference. The provision of such a service in ORB B may occur through an ORB B object that also belongs to A. In other words, the construction of this object depends on code from both A and B. Within ORB B, this object becomes a surrogate for the corresponding object(s) in A.

A service in one ORB may remap the meaning from a foreign object reference onto one of its object references.

Disregard for the moment the problems of bootstrapping the object in both ORBs, particularly the name collisions that may occur during compilation from having two implementations for standard ORB components. Let us look at a trivial implementation of such a surrogate object.

A local surrogate for a foreign object acts as a gateway, translating between the two ORBs. For two ORBs to communicate, a message travels from a client stub in ORB A to a service object. This service object acts as a surrogate in ORB A for the implementation in ORB B. This surrogate translates the request into ORB B lingo. The surrogate also has an ORB B client stub that relays the request through invocation to the implementation in ORB B. The surrogate lives in and is a part of both ORBs and has an implementation skeleton from ORB A and a client stub for ORB B. On completion, the call path is the reverse for the return result (see Figure 10-1).

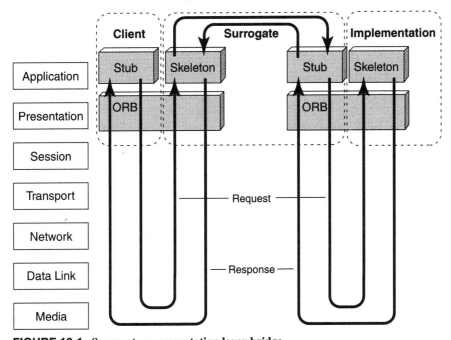

FIGURE 10-1. Surrogate as presentation layer bridge

The adoption of common protocols reduces the work necessary by a gateway or surrogate.

The adoption of common protocols reduces the work necessary by a gateway or surrogate.

Surrogates may translate all foreign objects or there might be many specializing surrogates.

Specialty protocols for specific environments may be added as ESIOPs.

Describes marshaling and unmarshaling

The detail can be useful background.

This gateway approach requires translation and encoding when the request crosses an ORB boundary going in either direction. The surrogate also may need to translate or at least find the appropriate stub to call the request into the correct target if it handles all requests between ORB A and ORB B. Depending on the request, this could be trivial or it could be expensive. Part of the problem depends on how close the underlying implementations happen to be. Because CORBA masks the underlying implementation, they can be quite far apart.

This gateway approach is not really the only one available, or is it? Actually, no. OMG never stated that two vendors could not conspire to use the same protocol if they desired. This form of consensus is the major reason that OMG has accomplished as much as it has to date. As a result, multiple vendors could agree among themselves on what underlying protocols to use.

Now what? You could build a single surrogate that did translation for all objects. This is very hard. You could build a surrogate for each type of object. This is a lot of work. However, CORBA now includes interoperability that came from a proposal for a universal network object (UNO for short).[2] This proposal, shown in Figure 10-2, specifies a general inter-ORB protocol (a GIOP) that is the message format and syntax for interoperation. The proposal includes an internet inter-ORB protocol (the IIOP) that states how GIOP messages map to TCP/IP. All ORBs must support the GIOP/IIOP protocols to conform.

The proposal also specifies that various other profiles (types of protocols) may be added. These add-on profiles are for Environment-Specific Interoperability Protocols (ESIOPs). Some ORBs may wish to support specialty ESIOPs to leverage skills, resources, or other cost factors that already may exist in these environments.

This adoption provides a path between ORBs through which invocations may occur. The specification is a very lightweight transport service. It specifies how data is marshaled and unmarshaled by common data representation (CDR) and the primitives necessary for packaging a request in one ORB and unpackaging it in a different ORB.

Much of the specification is for people who are building ORBs, not for people who are building an object's implementation. Still, a little conceptual background is always useful, particularly when comparing implementations, because the specification allows a number of different implementations to interoperate.

---

2. The term *universal network object* is no longer in use, since it came from an early form of the specification prior to adoption. It is mentioned here for historical continuity. I still get requests about what became of UNO.

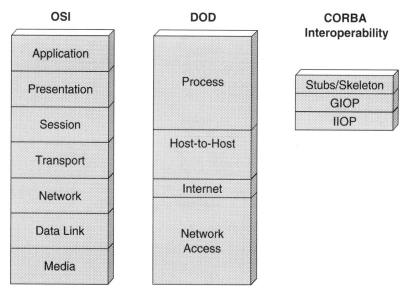

FIGURE 10-2. CORBA interoperability's relation to OSI
            and DOD protocols

10.2 INTEROPERABILITY VOCABULARY AND CONCEPTS

Domain-to-domain operation occurs through a mapping component that the specification calls a bridge. This seems an unfortunate term because a bridge in networking parlance is a link-level mechanism that translates between two link-level protocols. Bridges do not inspect the network header and so may pass packets from different protocols with equal ease. As is so often the case, the best terms are already in use, so we end up overloading these with terms that have multiple meanings.

An IIOP bridge is not a network bridge.

Another networking term, *gateway,* may be more applicable, although it tends to signify a single machine that frequently performs hardware and software translation between two networks. Most gateways do care about the protocols above the Link-Layer, but not always.

Neither term is accurate. Bridge is used in the specification, although Presentation Layer Bridge, perhaps, is even more appropriate.

As Figure 10-3 shows, a network bridge is at the data link layer. A router exists primarily at the network layer. Gateways may span the continuum. CORBA, from a protocol standpoint, exists above the session layer. A bridge in CORBA, an inter-ORB bridge, therefore, exists in the presentation or application layers, or both.

An inter-ORB bridge exists at the application and presentation layers.

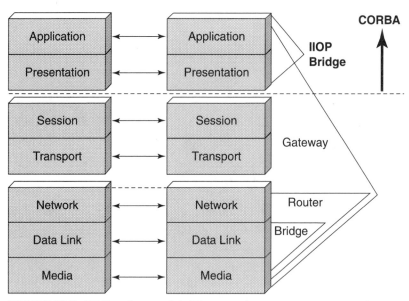

FIGURE 10-3. IIOP and network bridges

An ORB-built bridge is in-line; a service bridge is request-level.

If the bridging occurs in the ORB core, the bridge is an in-line bridge. If the bridge is a service on top of CORBA, it is a request-level bridge. Figure 10-1 shows a request-level bridge because the translation occurs in an implementation after the receiving skeleton and before invoking the stub (forwarding).

Intermediate and direct translation

Two more distinctions are useful. If the translation that an inter-ORB bridge undertakes is to an intermediate form, that bridge is a mediated bridge. However, if the bridge translates directly into the target ORB's form, it is an immediate bridge.

When a bridge enforces some policy domain, it is a policy-mediated bridge.

The extent of a domain is largely administrative. For example, domain boundaries for security are set up through an administrative effort dictated by operational policy. Such domain boundaries constrain operations in accordance with that policy that meet the organizational objectives or goals. In such cases, complete transparency of ORB boundaries for interoperability is not desirable. Some administrative constraints are desirable and require policy enforcement. Such bridges are policy-mediated bridges, because an intermediate policy is more desirable than a transparent mapping directly from the source into target ORB policy.

Inter-ORB bridges require four things:

1. A way to represent null references (they may be arguments to operations but do not support invocation)
2. A way to signify type so that strongly typed systems may preserve their integrity
3. A way to determine the protocol(s) in use
4. A means of determining what ORB services are available

An inter-ORB bridge that is also a secure bridge has two additional requirements:

1. A trust model that establishes a secure context across the bridge
2. A trust mechanism by which correspondents gain access to each other's private session keys

Such trust mechanisms are necessary to decrypt incoming protocol elements with the incoming side's mechanism and reencrypt them into outgoing protocol elements with the outgoing side's mechanism.[3]

The means by which the protocol (GIOP/IIOP) provides this is through the definition of an Interoperable Object Reference (IOR). The internals of the IOR are for the ORB builder; the IOR is opaque to the ORB application programmer. The tagged profile is a description of the characteristics of the referenced object. There is at least one per protocol if the object supports more than one. The profile information is complete enough to determine all the characteristics and conduct an invocation in that protocol. (See Example 10-1.)

Much of the information that bridges require is in the IOR.

EXAMPLE 10-1. Module IOP

```
module IOP
{
    typedef unsigned long            ProfileId;
    const ProfileId TAG_INTERNET_IOP =        0;
    const ProfileId TAG_MULTIPLE_COMPONENTS =   1;

    struct TaggedProfile
    {
        ProfileId           tag;
        sequence<octet>     profile_data;
    };

    struct IOR
    {
        string                      type_id;
        sequence<TaggedProfile>     profiles;
    };

    typedef unsigned long       ComponentId;
    struct                      TaggedComponent
    {
        ComponentId     tag;
        sequence<octet> component_data;
    };
```

---

3. In general this is considered very difficult if not impossible to achieve with assurance; that is, in a provable, secure way. On a case-by-case basis for a well-defined subset of features, construction of such a bridge may be possible, but it is not done commonly.

```
            typedef sequence<TaggedComponent>  MultipleComponentProfile;

            typedef unsigned long       ServiceID;

            struct ServiceContext
            {
                ServiceID               context_id;
                sequence<octet>         context_data;
            };
            typedef sequence<ServiceContext>    ServiceContextList;

            const ServiceID TransactionService = 0;
    };
```

The Profile ID indicates the protocol.

The Profile ID signifies the protocol. The assignment of unique Profile IDs falls to OMG administration. Two assignments are specifically for the GIOP; namely, IIOP and Multiple Components. The protocol determines the content of the Profile.

An empty profile indicates a Null reference.

An empty set of profiles indicates a Null reference. Multiple Components indicate that the Profile fully encapsulates a Multiple Component Profile (MCP). Depending on the protocol's definition, each component in an MCP may indicate a service in the ORB and its characteristics. The ORB Component IDs are protocol-specific. The Type IDs are type information according to the interface repository. Thus, the IOR encapsulates the four types of information necessary to an Inter-ORB Bridge.

The specification includes the details of encoding for a persistent IOR in string form. While this does not necessarily make their content comprehensible to a foreign ORB, at least such ORBs are able to parse the string and identify that it is an IOR.

Some of this terminology needs cleaning up.

While we are discussing the terminology, two differences require pointing out. First, in the CORBA vernacular, a proxy is a component that represents a cross-domain ORB object. This is what appears as a surrogate in Figure 10-1. Proxies do not fill the role of object references; rather, their role is that of reference. These terms are more accurate. I chose to diverge earlier because the word *reference* is overloaded with semantics from programming languages, and people new to IDL are generally steeped in the pre-existing meanings. Also, some vendors refer to their object references (stubs) as proxies.

Correct bridge operation requires a service context.

Along with the IOR, ORBs have the notion of service contexts. These contexts are "auto-magically" part of the invocation (implicit) and necessary for correct bridge operation. The CORBA defines one such context for Object Transaction Services (in CORBAservices). The Security mechanism defines an additional implicit context.

10.3   GENERAL INTER-ORB PROTOCOL

The GIOP is responsible for message layout and type.

The GIOP specifies seven message layouts and message types, shown in Table 10-1. The common data representation (CDR) details the alignment and

TABLE 10-1. GIOP's Seven Message Types

TypeName	Originator	Enum Value
Request	Client	0
Reply	Implementation	1
Cancel Request	Client	2
Locate Request	Client	3
Locate Reply	Implementation	4
Close Connection	Implementation	5
Message Error	Both	6

byte order of primitive data types, the composition of constructed types, and the format and layout of the various pseudo-objects (see Figure 10-4). It defines everything with octets and sequences of octets. A byte in a GIOP message indicates the byte order of the message. It also defines how to encapsulate an opaque octet sequence in CDR.

All message headers are given in the spec in IDL. Message bodies are not, except for their length, which is in the header. The Message Header's magic four-character array contains the letters GIOP (see Example 10-2). Message Size indicates the length in octets of the message following the header. Size zero messages is on reserve for future use. Message formats reference an Object Key. This is an opaque data type, the translation of which is only comprehensible to the server (Implementation).

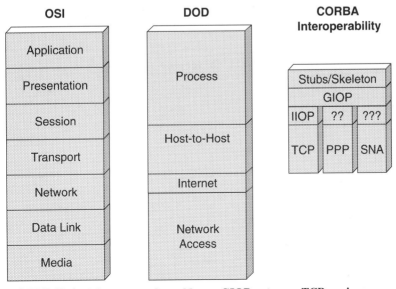

FIGURE 10-4. Other protocols could map GIOP onto non-TCP sessions

EXAMPLE 10-2. Module GIOP

```
module GIOP
{
    enum MsgType
    {
        Request, Reply,
        CancelRequest, LocateRequest,
        LocateReply, CloseConnection,
        MessageError
    };

    struct MessageHeader
    {
        char            magic[4];
        Version         GIOP_version;
        boolean         byte_order;
        octet           message_type;
        unsigned long   message_size;
    };

    struct RequestHeader
    {
        IOP::ServiceContextList service_context;
        unsigned long           request_id;
        boolean                 response_expected;
        sequence<octet>         object_key;
        string                  operation;
        Principal               requesting_principal;
    };

    enum ReplyStatusType
    {
        NO_EXCEPTION, USER_EXCEPTION,
        SYSTEM_EXCEPTION, LOCATION_FORWARD
    };

    struct ReplyHeader
    {
        IOP::ServiceContextList service_context;
        unsigned long           request_id;
        ReplyStatusType         reply_status;
    };

    struct CancelRequestHeader { unsigned long request_id; };

    struct LocateRequestHeader
    {
        unsigned long   request_id;
        sequence<octet> object_key;
    };

    enum LocateStatusType
        { UNKNOWN_OBJECT, OBJECT_HERE, OBJECT_FORWARD };

    struct LocateReplyHeader
    {
        unsigned long    request_id;
        LocateStatusType locate_status;
    };
};
```

The GIOP insists on certain transport assumptions. For instance, the transport is connection-oriented, reliable, may appear as a byte stream, and obtains connections following the connection model of TCP/IP; that is, the transport's connection service maps well to that of TCP.

10.4   INTERNET INTER-ORB PROTOCOL

The IIOP maps the GIOP into a TCP/IP session. The IIOP specifies a profile. This profile is the instruction to GIOP to use the IIOP protocol for its connection (see Example 10-3).

IIOP maps GIOP into a TCP/IP session.

Everything in the IIOP profile is self-explanatory. The two members, host and port, are equivalent to those in a TCP connection. The Object Key extends the addressing to the object level. The intercepting server, or whatever it is that is listening at that host on that port, understands the construction of the Object Key's sequence of octets. For instance, the sequence may be that of the Reference Data that is a parameter to the BOA's Create operation.

EXAMPLE 10-3. Module IIOP

```
module IIOP
{
    struct Version
    {
        char    major;
        char    minor;
    };

    struct ProfileBody
    {
        Version          iiop_version;
        string           host;
        unsigned short   port;
        sequence<octet>  object_key;
    };
};
```

10.5   ENVIRONMENT-SPECIFIC INTER-ORB PROTOCOL

The first Environment-Specific Inter-ORB Protocol (ESIOP) is one specific to DCE. It is currently the only definition of an ESIOP. It is similar in form to the GIOP but maps more directly to DCE. (See Figure 10-5.)

The first ESIOP is DCE-CIOP.

The DCE-CIOP (Common Interoperability Protocol) is a DCE derivative or subset. It maps more effectively to inter-ORB operation than does DCE directly. Work is currently underway to see if a more direct approach is available for interoperation between CORBA and a DCE environment. All the current efforts are focusing on creating an RFP for such interoperation, so it is far too early to tell exactly what the end product will be.

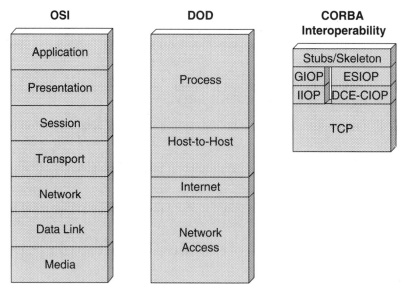

FIGURE 10-5. ESIOP's relation to IIOP, DOD, and OSI protocols

The DCE ESIOP uses NDR and not CDR encoding, and does not inter-operate with vanilla DCE. It also enables significant reuses of DCE infrastructure for ORB construction (see Example 10-4). Other ESIOPs will occur as their requirements arise.

EXAMPLE 10-4. Module DCE CIOP

```
module DCE_CIOP
{
    struct InvokeRequestHeader
    {
        boolean                  byte_order;
        IOP::ServiceContextList  service_context;
        sequence<octet>          object_key;
        string                   endpoint_id;
        string                   operation;
        CORBA::Principal         principal;
        sequence<string>         client_context;
    };

    enum InvokeResponseStatus
    {
        INVOKE_NO_EXCEPTION,
        INVOKE_USER_EXCEPTION,
        INVOKE_SYSTEM_EXCEPTION,
        INVOKE_LOCATION_FORWARD,
        INVOKE_TRY_AGAIN
    };
```

```
struct InvokeResponseHeader
{
    boolean                   byte_order;
    IOP::ServiceContextList   service_context;
    InvokeResponseStatus      status;

    // if status = INVOKE_NO_EXCEPTION,
    // result then inouts and outs follow

    // if status = INVOKE_USER_EXCEPTION or
    // INVOKE_SYSTEM_EXCEPTION, an exception follows

    // if status = INVOKE_LOCATION_FORWARD, an
    // IOP::MultipleComponentsProfile follows
};

struct LocateRequestHeader
{
    boolean                   byte_order;
    sequence<octet>           object_key;
    string                    endpoint_id;
    string                    operation;

    // no body follows
};
};
```

CHAPTER 11   *OLE, COM, and DCOM*

Get the facts first. You can distort them later.
—Mark Twain

This particular topic is large enough for an entire book; it is critical enough to condense here to its essentials. Each of the three is an acronym—OLE is Object Linking and Embedding, COM stands for Common Object Model, and DCOM is Distributed Common Object Model.

In short, OLE links, placing references to one or more objects inside some compound object, or it embeds, placing one object inside another. COM, initially, involves more access specification and details the binary layout of such objects so that they are accessible directly through multiple languages. COM is an application binary interface (ABI) but it also describes how such objects appear and, to some degree, how they behave. The ABI is a well-defined binary form similar to a virtual function table. DCOM is a distributed version of both the OLE and COM specifications and defines the protocol to which DCOM objects respond.

OLE is links and embedding, COM is a binary interface, DCOM is a distributed object model.

Although this description is somewhat short, it is enough to contrast the primary differences and illustrate interoperation (see Figure 11-1). Early on, OMG members decided that because of the widespread appearance of OLE and COM on the desktop, there was an immediate requirement to provide a mapping between CORBA and COM or OLE objects. At the time, DCOM did not exist, although some talk of Distributed OLE occasionally appeared in the press.

Because legacy desktops use these technologies, it is important to provide a bridge.

In January of 1996 a standard for interoperation, called COM-CORBA Inter-working, became official. This standard was originally larger in scope but was divided into two parts: Part A (presented here) and Part B, which is not yet a standard although it should be by the time this book is in print.

Another part of the CORBA-to-desktop bridge has the name of Compound Presentation and Compound Interchange Facility. This facility is more the equivalent of the distributed linking and embedding of objects that occurs within nondistributed OLE. The facility derives from the original and, perhaps, more widely known IBM name, OpenDoc. It provides a specification to the interfaces for compound objects and supports the construction of objects having functions similar to OLE/COM objects. The CORBA version does not require a bridge because these compound objects adhere to the CORBA model.

The CORBAfacilities model is based on OpenDoc.

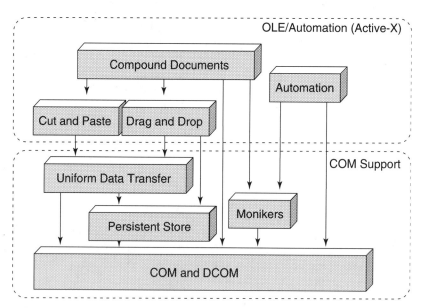

FIGURE 11-1. OLE, COM, and DCOM facilities

11.1   DIFFERENCES

Historically, the two solved different problems.

Several of the differences between the two models stem from their original design. OLE and COM's original designs were to do specific things within a single (nondistributed, homogenous by default) multitasking environment. Their behavior evolved over time to its current level of support. CORBA, from the beginning, has been both distributed and heterogeneous.

There are several differences, some subtle and some not subtle at all.

COM interfaces, which only have methods, can be composed with Microsoft Interface Definition Language (MIDL) or directly in the target language because the binary layout is well known. OLE Automation objects, which have methods and properties, can be defined in ODL. Automation is implemented by way of COM but because it appears somewhat different from COM, it is covered distinctly. One primary difference is that calls to automation objects have runtime-type checking. This makes automation somewhat equivalent to the use of DII. Additionally, automation properties may be only a subset of the COM types, since there is no support for user-constructed types.

There is some equivalency between the various interface definition languages.

Both MIDL and ODL are now passé to some degree because the IDL for DCOM supersedes them. However, this CORBA-to-COM mapping facility maps to the older subset (before DCOM) because it provides interworking to the large amounts of legacy code.

A big difference is CORBA supports multiple inheritance.

The two object models, COM and CORBA, are similar in some respects and different in others. One difference is that CORBA supports multiple inheritance (MI) and COM supports only single inheritance. On the other hand, a CORBA interface is the object's class definition, but a COM class may be a composition of a set of COM interfaces (an aggregate). The two object models also have some similarities. The CORBA object reference is the rough equivalent of the COM interface pointers. COM interfaces are the functional equivalent of CORBA interfaces.

CORBA interfaces register with and are accessible from the interface repository. COM objects are available through the system registry. Automation objects optionally may register in a binary Type Library.

Registration of interfaces occurs in both.

11.2   INTERFACE MAPPING

Mapping from one model to the other occurs by way of a bridge. The bridge code is an intermediate server of the client's object type that translates and delegates an invocation into the target object's type.

Mapping between the models occurs by way of a bridge.

The adoption takes four interface-mapping models into consideration:

1. COM interface to CORBA object
2. Automation interface to CORBA object
3. CORBA interface to COM object
4. CORBA interface to Automation object

Since COM/Automation (not DCOM) is inherently a single-user environment and CORBA implies (but does not require) a distributed environment, we first look at the mappings from COM and Automation Client to CORBA objects.

11.2.1   Presenting a CORBA Object as a COM Interface

While some mappings work better than others, the COM interface to a CORBA object is relatively straightforward, as shown in Figure 11-2.

The COM primitive types map almost directly to CORBA primitives. The constructed COM types (enumerators, arrays, strings, structures, and unions) map to CORBA constructed types with minor fiddling. The COM

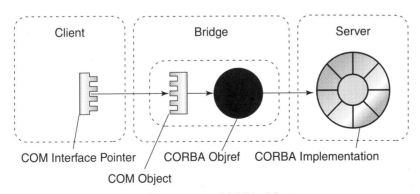

FIGURE 11-2. COM interface access to CORBA object

Interface pointer also maps fairly well to a CORBA object reference. COM's Get and Set operations map to CORBA attributes.

11.2.1.1 *Mapping CORBA Inheritance to COM*

Because CORBA supports multiple inheritance and COM does not, special rules are necessary for the ORB implementer when providing a COM-to-CORBA interface mapping.

Single inheritance maps directly to a single COM v-table, which contains the complete CORBA inheritance graph. Multiple inheritance is more difficult. A mix-in may occur as a COM aggregate. Obtaining the COM interface occurs through invocation of a Query interface, with each interface's UUID. However a mix-in is indistinguishable from extension in IDL, so a compromise occurs with the following rules:

Ordering rules are needed.
- A CORBA IDL interface that has no parent maps to an MIDL interface whose parent is the Unknown interface (`IUnknown`).
- A CORBA IDL interface with a single parent maps to an MIDL interface that derives from the CORBA parent's mapping.
- A CORBA IDL interface with multiple parents maps to an MIDL interface deriving from the Unknown interface.
- CORBA interface operation mappings precede attribute mappings.
- Operation mappings within an interface are in lexicographic order by bytes in machine-collating sequence by operation name.
- Attribute mapping order follows operation ordering with the Get immediately preceding the Set operation (if there is one; that is, it is not a read-only attribute), sorting by attribute name.

11.2.2 Automation Interface to CORBA Object

Automation mappings to and from CORBA, shown in Figure 11-3, impose more limitations than the COM mappings do. Some primitive types, such as the OLE Currency type or CORBA's unsigned integer types, require special case mappings that may introduce a loss of precision or range.

Constructed types do not have an equivalent in Automation, so they must occur as special cases, such as a COM object with its own interface. Automation Type Libraries dynamically map to CORBA interface repositories. Automation interface pointers map to CORBA object references, while Get and Put properties in Automation map to CORBA attributes.

11.2.2.1 *Mapping CORBA Inheritance to Automation*

CORBA MI suffers a similar fate with an Automation interface.
Automation suffers similar problems with MI as did COM. The following rules apply to mapping to Automation.

- A CORBA IDL interface that has no parent maps to an ODL interface whose parent is the Dispatch interface (`IDispatch`).

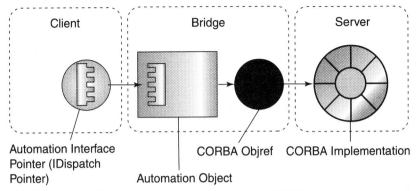

FIGURE 11-3. OLE Automation interface access to CORBA object

- A CORBA IDL interface with a single parent maps to an ODL interface that derives from the CORBA parent's mapping.
- A CORBA IDL interface with multiple parents maps to an ODL interface that derives through single inheritance from the first parent. The first parent is distinguished by sorting the parent's Interface Repository IDs lexicographically by bytes in machine collating order.
- CORBA interface operation mappings precede attribute mappings for any single interface.
- Operation mappings within an interface are in lexicographic order by bytes in machine collating sequence by operation name.
- Attribute mapping order follows operation ordering, with the `propget` immediately preceding the `propput` operation (if there is a `propput`; that is, it is not a read-only attribute), sorting by attribute name.
- A CORBA IDL interface with multiple parents (multiple inheritance) maps the operations and attributes it introduces first, according to the preceding rules. Immediately following this are the ordered operations of parent interfaces, excluding the first parent's, which uses the inheritance mapping.

11.2.3   CORBA Interface to COM Object

The operation of mapping from a CORBA client to a COM service, shown in Figure 11-4, is a reverse of the earlier COM-client-to-CORBA service. The differences are primarily in types not analogous to CORBA types—certain pointer types, some unions, and a `SAFEARRAY`. Each of these requires some special handling.

CORBA interface to COM object is the reverse of COM-to-CORBA.

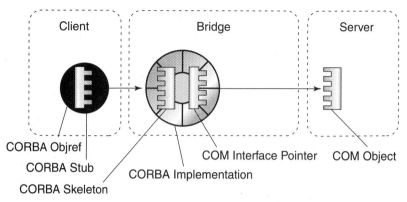

FIGURE 11-4. CORBA interface access to a COM object

COM objects that do not expose an interface specification require one or must be customized.

Some additional complications exist because COM object construction may occur directly in the target language (C or C++, for example) and, therefore, do not expose an interface specification. These constructs are available because COM supports custom marshaling. However, if such a construct can be expressed in formal terms, using MIDL, ODL, or a Type Library, mapping its interface may occur to the hand-translation of the formalism. Otherwise, the only thing left is to devise some custom interworking mechanism.

Finally, MIDL, ODL, and the Type Libraries are not consistent with each other and some are not available on certain platforms.[1]

11.2.4   CORBA Interface to Automation Object

Automation and the Type Libraries are type-constrained.

Mapping may occur through a predefined interface.

The mapping for a CORBA client interface to an Automation server, shown in Figure 11-5, is perhaps the easiest to solve in the respect that the type system for Automation and the Type Libraries is the most constrained.

Automation types typically map directly to CORBA types. When Automation has a type that does not match, its mapping may occur through a predefined CORBA interface, such as when, for example, the Automation CURRENCY type maps as a CORBA interface Currency.

Automation interfaces and IDispatch pointers (references) map directly to CORBA interfaces and object references. Automation request signatures (operations) map directly to CORBA interface request signatures. Automation properties map to CORBA interface attributes.

---

1. The specification says that MIDL is not available on WIN16 platforms.

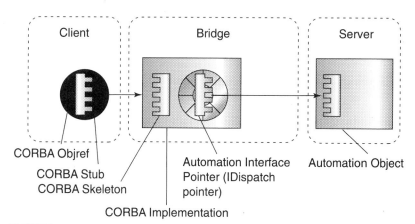

FIGURE 11-5. CORBA interface to an OLE Automation object

11.3   INTERFACE IDENTITY MAPPING

CORBA Interface Repository IDs require a mapping to COM Interface IDs. COM Interface IDs are DCE UUIDs. The mapping uses an MD5 hashing algorithm because of its wide popularity and because of its uniform distribution. The MD5 algorithm operates on 128 bits but here it effectively uses 118 bits.

COM Interface IDs are DCE UUIDs.

Byte 8 (where byte 0 is least significant and 8 is most significant) has modifications according to the divisions shown in Table 11-1. These divisions currently divide the DCE UUID name space. In NCS 1.5, the other bits in byte 8 are family indicators. To avoid collision with other autogeneration techniques, family 29 indicates an Interface ID (IID) for COM and CORBA interworking.

The upper two bits of byte 9 avoid collisions when autogenerating IIDs for multiple types: dual, COM, and Automation. These upper two bits find use as shown in Table 11-2. However, these bits should never be used as interface determiners. In other words, programmers should not inspect the bits to determine the interface type.

The one exception to this mechanism is necessary to permit developers to implement existing COM interfaces. In this case, the Repository ID is a DCE UUID and corresponds directly to the COM IID (not a dual or Automation interface).

TABLE 11-1. Byte 8 Encodings in a DCE UUID

0xxxxxxx	the NCS 1.4 name space
10xxxxxx	a DCE 1.0 UUID name space
110xxxxx	in use by Microsoft
1111xxxx	unspecified

TABLE 11-2. **The High-Order Two Bits in Byte 9**

00	unspecified
01	generated COM IID
10	generated Automation IID
11	generated dual interface Automation IID

11.3.1   Identity in Each Object Model

The meaning of identity is different between the two models.

There are issues about identity between the two models. The primary difference between the two appears to be that CORBA object identity applies to a unique instance that exhibits consistency of state. A COM object's identity applies to an instance of an implementation with, initially, a default "empty" (or arbitrary) state.

The next distinction is the scope of the identity. CORBA is specifically for the distribution of objects, and COM is not (see Table 11-3). The scope of COM interfaces identity exists within a single process.

TABLE 11-3. **Scope of the CORBA and COM Identities**

CORBA Identity	*COM Identity*
Objects have object references that encapsulate identity in an opaque fashion.	A COM instance is one whose interface(s) results from a request on `IClassFactory::CreateInstance`, which takes no parameters to describe the initial state.
Object identities are unique at least within the domain of one ORB's instance.	
Object references reliably denote a specific object, having operations, behavior, and state.	COM's identity is only inherent through its collection of one or more interfaces, which has limits in the determination of equivalence.
Identities are immutable over the lifetime of the object.	A COM object's identity has limitations to the scope and extent of the active process. Persistent identity, while not part of the model, may be built in as part of an implementation.
Object references may be persistent in an external string form. That form may find use later in reinternalizing the reference by presenting it back to the ORB in the reference domain.	
An object reference invocation is independent of the object's location or activity; that is, the object does not need to be active.	COM has no built-in notion of class equivalence between two interface pointers.
Object references do not possess a notion of relation or share a notion of reference counting.	A COM object's identity and state are separate from and independent of a COM class instance. For instance, the interesting state for a document object may be a document file persisting in the file system, and it may be in use simultaneously by different class instances.
Object references may be equivalent. Queries are available to make that determination, although they are only equivalent when the request is unambiguously true.	

CHAPTER 12 *Security*

Not all objects are equal.
—Wallace Stevens

Security is part of the underlying OMA. It is pervasive. However, by degree it depends on the transport, operating systems, and physical media on which it exists. A chain of security is only as secure as its weakest link.

Security is pervasive throughout CORBA.

The ORB, by itself, offers only trivial security without the aid of an underlying secure infrastructure. It is able to check that parameters meet requirements and that the correct target receives a request. This is very minimal security.

When its installation is on top of more secure features in the network and hardware it may leverage those depending on the implementation. The design of security is flexible to the point of being able to support a wide variety of security mechanisms.

The OMG security specification poses a security reference model. This is a meta-model describing a framework on which the construction of many different security models may occur. This specification also describes an architecture that shows how the various facilities and components may choose to interact.

The basic security areas are:

Areas of concern for security.

- *Confidentiality*—disclosure only to recipients with the appropriate authorization
- *Integrity*—consistency of data, with correct delivery and modification only with the appropriate authorization
- *Accountability*—maintenance of accountable actions that involve security
- *Availability*—access to legitimate users
- *Legitimate Use*—use of resources only by authorized personnel

The terminology is different, depending on who is describing these area. Each area requires coverage. The services that generally safeguard systems fall into the following five generic categories:

1. *Authentication Service*—provides an assurance of an identity of an entity (a person or system) that may or may not be local. Its identity is vouched for, or authenticated, by the service.
2. *Authorization Service*—assigns privilege to an identity. This generally applies to an identity and the granting of their right(s).
3. *Confidentiality Service*—makes sure that only the authorized entity receives information or has it disclosed.
4. *Integrity Service*—prevents data from modification, deletion, or substitution without authorization.
5. *Nonrepudiation Service*—prevents a receiver or sender from falsely denying the receipt or transmission of data. It provides proof of transactions.

Correctly behaving interfaces do not provide assurance.

Last but not least, security is greatly concerned with assurance, which is the amount or level of trust that can be measurably (provably) placed in a system. Assurance is the degree to which the services just listed provide their safeguards. On the other hand, assurance is not an automatic provision of correctly behaving interfaces. True conformance for a secure ORB requires correct implementation.

12.1 GENERAL SECURITY

The basic model, shown in Figure 12-1, presents two immediate areas as primary concerns: client and target object.

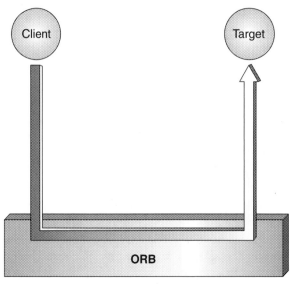

FIGURE 12-1. Client and target in a security association

The client and target are in a security association. Decisions governing the association may occur in both places, which means there are four places for making decisions about things such as access control:

The basic model has four security decision points.

1. Client
2. Client invocation
3. Target invocation
4. Target object

Both client and target may make their own access decisions either on startup or first invocation. The ORB also may make decisions on client invocation (a request on an object reference) and target invocation (an ORB handing the request to an object). The security model views the client request as a client invocation on the ORB and the ORB's invocation on the target. These invocation points are security control (decision) points.

The model addresses replies as well as requests, although we present it as request invocation.

Each of these decision points may participate according to a security policy. Access decision functions enforcing such policies may examine attributes and context information and simply respond affirmatively or negatively at these points.

Two sets of attributes, shown in Figure 12-2, are primary considerations for such decision points:

Decision-making examines two attribute sets.

1. Initiator privilege attributes
2. Target control attributes

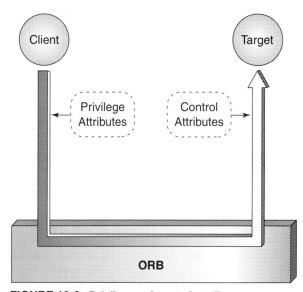

FIGURE 12-2. Privilege and control attributes

Initiator privileges are the attributes of a Principal.

Initiator privilege attributes are the attributes of a Principal. A Principal is a user or entity that the system can ascertain with some degree of confidence. For this confidence to occur, a Principal requires registration and authentication.

A Principal is a registered entity with a valid identity.

In other words, the person or entity is known to the system in advance (registration), and some method is available to validate the claim of identity (authentication). Such entities are known to the security services by their security name.

Principals may have more than one identity.

A Principal has at least one and possibly several identities, such as access, audit, accounting, group, or repudiation identities. Different identities may be useful for various functions or policies of the system. A Principal that causes an action is an *initiator*.

Principals have privilege attributes that may include a variety of features:

- Identity, which may be for access, auditing, accounting, and so on
- A role, which may relate to the task at hand or job function
- A group, which may relate to organizational structure
- Clearance, which may be a security classification or rating
- Capabilities, which may limit accessible targets

Targets have control attributes that may include features such as:

- Labels, which is a means of classifying objects by rules
- Access control lists, which establish who has access by identity or by privileges

Immediate targets may make other requests, becoming intermediate clients.

The situation becomes more complex when a single object does not satisfy an initiator's request. Request chains occur when an immediate target makes requests on other objects. This is delegation, or how privileges may delegate along with a request through intermediate objects, which in turn become clients. Such intermediate clients may or may not wish to pass along information originating with the initiator.

All of this information, the services available, and the policies governing various operations are available to both clients and objects so they can determine and establish policies.

Policies apply to domains.

Policies effect policy domains. A policy domain is the set of objects to which a policy applies. Policy domains may appear hierarchical, overlap, federate, and layer. Each domain has a domain manager. The domain manager is of interest to clients and targets that wish to participate in the domain.

There is no requirement for the construction of security services solely within the ORB. Many services that offer additional control are available as ORB objects similar to the offerings in the CORBAservices.

The ORB may delegate security to external services.

ORBs also may provide interfaces for services but delegate the operations to external entities. The ORB may provide interfaces but not implementations of security services, allowing other systems to control the security aspects of the system. A Security Replaceability Ready ORB is one that chooses this form of delegation. Because of its design, it understands how to make correct requests on the external security service on behalf of its participants.

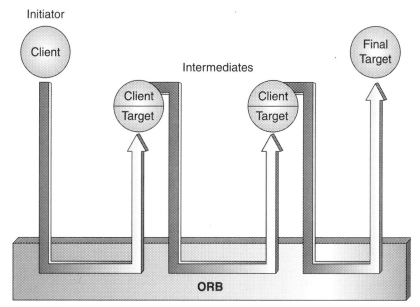

FIGURE 12-3. Intermediates in a request chain delegation

One of the key objects in security came from the Object Transaction Service (OTS). The OTS transparently transfers a transaction context along with transaction invocations, as discussed in Chapter 22. This object is the current object. The current object's role expands, encompassing security, and it becomes the vehicle by which information such as the client's privileges and credentials accompany requests. The impact on the Current object appearing in the Object Transaction Service is trivial.

The current object is a context transmitting credentials and privileges.

In the current design, the ORBs have certain defaults to establish security. The ORB may automatically place information in the current object to pass along to the target. These defaults, however, may be overridden. The client may choose to only allow certain credentials to hand off on invocation. The client also may choose to set certain attributes on a specific object reference. Both of these mechanisms in combination allow the client to control security attributes of the Principal.

Clients may modify the default information in the current object.

The application also may choose to make application decisions directly from the information it receives from the ORB instead of just allowing the ORB to handle decisions. These provide additional control points to the security model.

Figure 12-4 illustrates some of the following decision and control operations:

1. The client asks the ORB about various security environment issues, such as policy domains, policies, and default conditions.

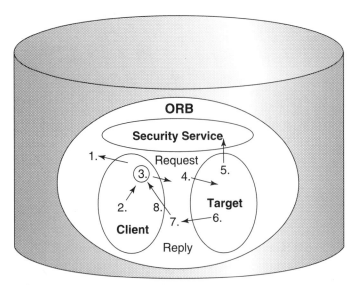

FIGURE 12-4. Decision and control operations

2. The client may decide to alter some of the attributes on the object reference.
3. Invoking the object reference passes control to the ORB, where it may fill in default values that the client did not fill in or alter. The ORB may reject the request according to security policies (and their consequent decisions) currently in force.
4. The ORB decides about invoking the object, and either transfers in the request or rejects it based on security invocation requirements.
5. The object activates and may query the security services or the ORB about services available, overriding defaults, and so forth. Between 5 and 6, where the application satisfies the request, it may make decisions about security issues.
6. The object passes the result back to the ORB, which checks the response according to the security and policies in force and decides to accept the request.
7. Using initiator-side policies, the ORB decides whether to return the result to the client. By doing so it completes the request.

Intermediate objects may alter information.

Similarly, intermediate objects may choose to alter what is passed on during delegation, when they make invocation on other intermediates or on the final target.

If the client or application is unaware of security, default values apply to the security association of the call. The ORB still checks initiator privileges on receiving the request and target controls before handing it off to the object.

12.2   SECURITY INTERFACES

The security specification proposes three levels of security, which it refer- *Security has three functional*
ences as security functionality Level Zero, Level One, and Level Two. Security *levels.*
Level Zero offers none of the main functionality level support but has replaceability interfaces that allow the later addition of security. The specification
references this as a security-ready ORB, which does not meet minimum
requirements for CORBA security compliance (Level One) but does provide
the appropriate migration path for adding this security later.[1]

12.2.1   Level One Security

Security Level One is an entry-level or basic security. Applications running on *Level One is basic security.*
a secure ORB do not have to actively participate. Participation is optional.
Level One offers:

- Secure invocation between client and target
- Message protection
- Access control
- Unrestricted delegation

Level One security is primarily available through defaults or through existing
interfaces (having new operations since security's adoption). The service
interface is small.

12.2.2   Level Two Security

Security Level Two is for security-aware applications that want more control
over their options. This level extends the interfaces to support these options.
Level Two includes the offerings of Level One with a greater degree of application involvement in their enforcement.

The only optional functionality is a provision for a nonrepudiation ser- *Nonrepudiation is the only*
vice. Nonrepudiation is a provision that prevents a Principal (client or target) *optional functionality.*
from falsely denying the occurrence of an activity, such as the sending or
receiving of a request. It provides proof of transactions.

The interfaces in the security specification are not an entire nonrepudia- *Nonrepudiation support*
tion service. They do offer evidence generation and collection services. They
do not offer storage and verification of evidence.

Security extends the CORBA module's interfaces to support security pol- *Policy and replaceability*
icy and replaceability, which are Security Level Two features. Policy manage- *support are in Level Two*
ment is a general service that security uses to manage security policy domains. *functionality.*
Other services, such as administration, are likely to use it in the future.

---

1. We skip the details about replaceability's "appropriate migration path" because it is detail primarily of interest to ORB implementers and not application builders. The exception is that it is
vaguely interesting to application builders when their application construction occurs on a Level
Zero ORB and they are interested in utilizing the secure functionality once added.

Although policy domains are mandatory for Level Two functionality, replaceability is optional. Example 12-1 details the extensions to CORBA.

EXAMPLE 12-1. Policy, Domain Manager, and Construction Policy object interfaces

```
module  CORBA
{
    // Security Level 2 additions
    enum    PolicyType
    {
        ClientInvocationAccess,
        TargetInvocationAccess,
        ApplicationAccess,
        ClientInvocationAudit,
        TargetInvocationAudit,
        ApplicationAudit,
        Delegation,
        ClientSecureInvocation,
        TargetSecureInvocation,
        NonRepudiation,
        Construction
    };

    // Interfaces to support basic management infrastructure
    interface    Policy
    {
        // Features common to all Policies
    };

    interface    DomainManager
    {
        // Features common to all Domain Managers

        sequence<DomainManager> get_domain_managers();

        // get policies for objects in this domain
        Policy  get_domain_policy(in PolicyType policy_type);
    };

    interface    ConstructionPolicy : Policy
    {
        void    make_domain_manager(in InterfaceDef object_type);
    };
};
```

12.2.2.1 *Policies*

Policies show up in interfaces as a list of primary policy types about which an ORB knows. An ORB may extend these policies, derive specializations, or choose to offer additional policies. The current list of policies includes the following:

- Client invocation access
- Target invocation access
- Application access
- Client invocation audit
- Target invocation audit
- Application audit
- Delegation
- Client secure invocation
- Target secure invocation
- Nonrepudiation
- Construction

Applications bind policies to objects when creation of an object reference occurs by calling Create on the BOA. The details of how this occurs are left to the implementation. The object at creation enters an association of what may be several domains: the Security Policy, Security Technology, and Security Environment. The application may even be unaware of some or all of these domains.

Policies are bound to applications on creation of an object reference.

The Security Policy domain is the set of policies that apply to that object, while the Security Technology domain is the set of technology and services that are available to enforce and control the security aspects. This allows a layer of generic APIs that may hide technology that has no domain manager or may have no objects. Specifically, the services include creating and handling secure associations, including keys, and message protection services for integrity and confidentiality.

Security Technology domain

The Security Environment domain is the large picture from an ORB viewpoint. It includes the security covering all members of the ORB and all things that may be outside the ORB but have influence, such as a gateway to another ORB and different security environments. For example, in an environment in which the underlying transport already uses encryption on messages, the ORB need not do any encryption directly.

Security Environment domain

The object reference interface is a primary means to determine what domain managers and policies apply to an object. It is of most use to clients and applications. Another mechanism, the Current object, is also a means to determine information about how policies apply to an object in a specific execution context. For instance, the Current object enables different policies to apply to the same object, depending on which thread in the client makes an invocation. The ORB uses this interface.

Policy information is accessible through the object reference and the Current object.

Client and Target Invocation Access

Invocation access includes policies for client invocation access and target invocation access. An access decision for client invocation is yes or no. The client has the right to make an invocation on this object reference. The access decision for the target is yes or no (as are all such decisions); the question being, does this invocation have the right to invoke this target. The policies about how those decisions occur come from the policy object that the policy domain manager owns.

Application Access

Application access is similar to invocation access in that it may control access. Under such a policy, an application can make access decisions about granting access to certain functions. The functions may be of any granularity, such as single requests or large functional-component services. These specific policies may differ even further from the others in that their management may be through the application instead of a domain manager.

Client and Target Invocation Audit

Client and target invocation audit policies control and administer things such as the nature of events to audit and their criteria for selecting events.

Application Audit

Application audit policies may be part of the applications domain rather than the general Security Policy domain. The application may establish the criteria for events and their selection.

Delegation

Delegation policies administer the nature or type of delegation that may occur. They also may govern what credentials go to intermediates or propagate across the chain. They may control the selection of intermediates to be of a type that participates according to the applicable delegation policy.

Client and Target Secure Invocation

Client and target secure invocation policies govern issues such as mutual authentication and quality of protection.

Authentication validates an identity. It may be the client's identity to a target and may validate the target's identity to the client. When it does both, it is *mutual authentication*. Quality of protection (QOP) determines issues such as privacy, integrity, and confidentiality.

Nonrepudiation

Nonrepudiation policies control the rules for the generation and verification of evidence.

Construction

Construction policy controls the creation of domains, which may contain or apply to one or more objects. Depending on the specifics of the construction policy, a domain creation may occur to handle the details of the object.

12.2.2.2   Interceptors

Interceptor objects interpose on the invocation path, intercepting requests or messages. Interfaces for interceptors are a requirement for ORBs to implement replaceability, overriding the default services with another set of security services.[2] These interfaces (see Example 12-2) are useful to the implementer of an ORB and third-party security service providers. Specifically, third-party security vendors may make available a wide variety of pluggable security options, which their customers can choose among to get the combination of security that they require.

Interceptors are hooks for replaceable security services.

EXAMPLE 12-2. **Interceptor object interfaces**

```
module   CORBA
{
    // new interfaces for Replaceability Conformance

    interface    Interceptor
    {
        // Generic interceptor operations (management, etc.)
    };

    interface    RequestInterceptor : Interceptor        // PIDL
    {
        void     client_invoke(inout Request request);
        void     target_invoke(inout Request request);
    };

    interface    MessageInterceptor : Interceptor        // PIDL
    {
        void     send_message(
                    in Object    target,
                    in Message   msg
                 );

        void     receive_message(
                    in Object    target,
                    in Message   msg
                 );
    };
};
```

A request interceptor operates on an operation request. It is useful for making invocation decisions, checking invocation rights, or performing other operations that apply to the entire request as a unit.

A message interceptor operates on a lower level and may treat the message as a structureless buffer. This level of interface is necessary for performing operations such as encryption for privacy. Request and message interceptors are presented in Figure 12-5.

---

2. An ORB of Level Zero Functionality may be only *security read,* in which case the interceptors are available and all or most security will come from the externally provided services.

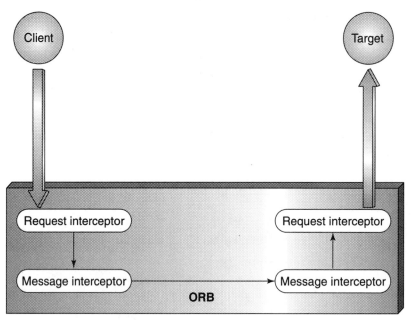

FIGURE 12-5. Request and message interceptors

12.2.2.3   *Current Object*

The Current object is the context of the current thread of control.

The Current object, whose first chronological appearance was in the Object Transaction Services, is now in the general ORB definitions. Both the OTS Current object and that of security derive from this general instance. In both cases, the Current object is the context of the current thread of control. (See Example 12-3.)

   More detail about the security form appears with its interface in the following sections. Information about the OTS Current object is discussed in Chapter 22.

EXAMPLE 12-3. Current object interface

```
module  CORBA
{
    // New interface to support Current Pseudo-Object

    interface   Current                          // PIDL
        {
        };
};
```

12.3 SECURITY MODULE INTERFACES

The core interfaces supporting security are in a separate module.

12.3.1 Security Names, Families, and Mechanisms

Every Principal that participates in a security domain has at least one security name. Such a name acts as the identity of a Principal within a security domain. When the domain authenticates the Principal, the Principal hands in its security name and some set of authentication attributes, depending on the mechanism in use.

Security names are a Principal's identity with a domain.

Families are groups of related rights or characteristics. OMG reserves the first eight (0-7) family identifiers and currently defines two: one of identity attributes and the other of privilege attributes (see Example 12-4). The family with identifier 0 is for the standard privilege attributes. Attributes, such as those for Privilege, are comprehensible (usable and interpretable) by family.

Families are groups with related privileges.

Rights families and audit families are user-extensible. They are extensible families. User- and vendor-extensible families, however, can narrow the applicability of the attributes for portability.

The families of rights and audit are user-extensible.

Security mechanisms are for identifying the security association between objects. Currently, there is no standard definition for these mechanisms apart from the definition of security as it applies to IIOP for out-of-the-box security interoperability. These definitions are in Chapter 13.

Security mechanisms establish security associations between objects.

EXAMPLE 12-4. Security data types

```
module  Security
{
    typedef     string       SecurityName;
    typedef     sequence<octet> Opaque;

    // extensible families for standard data types
    struct  ExtensibleFamily
    {
        unsigned short      family_definer;
        unsigned short      family;
    };

    //  security association mechanism
    typedef     string  MechanismType;
    struct      SecurityMechandName
    {
        MechanismType       mech_type;
        SecurityName        security_name;
    };

    typedef sequence<MechanismType> MechanismTypeList;
    typedef sequence<SecurityMechandName> SecurityMechandNameList;

    // security attributes
    typedef     unsigned long   SecurityAttributeType;
```

```
// identity attributes: family = 0
const    SecurityAttributeType         AuditId = 1;
const    SecurityAttributeType         AccountingId = 2;
const    SecurityAttributeType         NonRepudiationId = 3;

// priviledge attributes; family = 1;
const    SecurityAttributeType         Public = 1;
const    SecurityAttributeType         AccessId = 2;
const    SecurityAttributeType         PrimaryGroupId = 3;
const    SecurityAttributeType         GroupId = 4;
const    SecurityAttributeId           Role = 5;
const    SecurityAttributeType         AttributeSet = 6;
const    SecurityAttributeType         Clearence = 7;
const    SecurityAttributeType         Capability = 8;

struct  AttributeType
{
    ExtensibleFamily              attribute_family;
    SecurityAttributeType         attribute_type;
};

typedef sequence<AttributeType> AttributeTypeList;

struct  Attribute     // the value of this attribute can be
{       // interpreted only with knowledge about this type
    AttributeType         attribute_type;
    Opaque                defining_authority;
    Opaque                value;
};

typedef     sequence<Attribute> AttributeList;

// Authentication return status
enum     AuthenticationStatus
{
    SecAuthSuccess, SecAuthFailure,
    SecAuthContinue, SecAuthExpired
};

// Association return status
enum     AssociationStatus  {     SecAssocSuccess,
                                  SecAssocFailure,
                                  SecAssocContinue };
```

12.3.2   Security Data Types

Many of the data types that are necessary for building security services are
also those types that the application developer uses to determine what services
are available or to make selections of optional service.

One example is information about security associations, which are asym-
metric. Different security mechanisms may find use for the request and reply
paths, as Example 12-5 shows. Authentication may be of one association member or mutual.

Many of the data types relate to Access, Audit, and Delegation. These
areas have the most complete definitions in the current specifications.

EXAMPLE 12-5. Security data types

```
// Authentication method
typedef     unsigned long    AuthenticationMethod;

// Credential types which can be set as the Current default
enum    CredentialType
{
    SecInvocationCredentials,
    SecOwnCredentials,
    SecNRCredentials
};

// Declaration related to Rights
struct  Right
{
    ExtensibleFamily        rights_family;
    string                  right;
};
typedef     sequence<Right> RightsList;

enum    RightsCombinator    { SecAllRights, SecAnyRight };

// Delegation related
enum    DelegationState { SecInitiator, SecDelegate };

// pick up from TimeBase
typedef     TimeBase::UtcT          UtcT;
typedef     TimeBase::IntervalT     IntervalT;
typedef     TimeBase::TimeT         TimeT;

// security features available on credentials
enum    SecurityFeature
{
    SecNoDelegation,
    SecSimpleDelegation,
    SecCompositeDelegation,
    SecNoProtection,
    SecIntegrity,
    SecConfidentiality,
    SecIntegrityAndConfidentiality,
    SecDetectReplay,
    SecDetectMisordering,
    SecEstablishTrustInTarget
};

// Security feature-value
struct  SecurityFeatureValue
{
    SecurityFeature     feature;
    boolean             value;
};

typedef sequence<SecurityFeatureValue> SecurityFeatureValueList;
```

```
// Quality of protection (QOP) which can be specified
// for an object reference and used to protect messages
enum    QOP
{
    SecQOPNoProtection,
    SecQOPIntegrity,
    SecQOPConfidentiality,
    SecQOPIntegrityAndConfidentiality
};

// Association options which can be administered on secure
// invocation policy and used to initialize security context
typedef      unsigned short      AssociationOptions;

const   AssociationOptions  NoProtection = 1;
const   AssociationOptions  Integrity = 2;
const   AssociationOptions  Confidentiality = 4;
const   AssociationOptions  DetectReplay = 8;
const   AssociationOptions  DetectMisordering = 16;
const   AssociationOptions  EstablishTrustInTarget = 32;
const   AssociationOptions  EstablishTrustInClient = 64;

// Flag to indicate whether association options being
// administered are the "required" or "supported" set
enum    RequiresSupport { SecRequires, SecSupports };

// Direction of communication for which
// secure invocation policy applies
enum    CommunicationDirection
{
    SecDirectionBoth,
    SecDirectionRequest,
    SecDirectionReply
};

// AssociationOptions-Direction pair
struct   OptionsDirectionPair
{
    AssociationOptions       options;
    CommunicationDirection   direction;
};

typdef  sequence<OptionsDirectionPair>    OptionsDirectionPairList;

// Delegation Mode which can be administered
enum    DelegationMode
{
    SecDelModeNoDelegation,     // i.e., use own credentials
    SecDelModeSimpleDelegation, // delegate received credentials
    SecDelModeCompositeDelegation       //delegate both
};

// Association options supported by a given mech type
struct   MechandOptions
{
    MechanismType            mechanism_type;
    AssociationOptions       options_supported;
};

typedef  sequence<MechandOptions>           MechandOptionsList;
```

```
// Audit
struct AuditEventType
{
    ExtensibleFamily        event_family;
    unsigned short          event_type;
};

typedef sequence<AuditEventType>    AuditEventTypeList;

typedef unsigned long       SelectorType;

const    SelectorType    Intface = 1;
const    SelectorType    Obj = 2;
const    SelectorType    Operation = 3;
const    SelectorType    Initiator = 4;
const    SelectorType    SuccessFailure = 5;
const    SelectorType    Time = 6;

// Values defined for audit_needed and audit_write are:
//        Interface: object reference
//        Object: object reference
//        Operation: op_name
//        Initiator: Credentials
//        SuccessFailure: boolean
//        Time: utc time on audit_write; time picked up from
//              environment in audit_needed if required
struct  SelectorValue
{
    SelectorType        selector;
    any                 value;
};

typedef sequence<SelectorValue> SelectorValueList;
};
```

12.3.3   Basic Operation

For the application developer, the basic set of operations flows essentially in this order:

1. Determine security features
2. Establish Principal's credentials
3. Select security attributes
4. Make secure invocation
5. Targets and intermediate targets control issues
6. Audit application
7. Evidence generation and verification
8. Locate applicable policies

12.3.3.1   Determine Security Features

The application needs to determine what features are available so it can make a determination about what set or subset of features it will use.

12.3.3.2   *Establish Principal's Credentials*

Principal authentication may occur through an external service or through the
ORB security service (see Example 12-6). Under external authentication,
Current is set with the appropriate credentials.

EXAMPLE 12-6. **Security Level Two Module—Principal Authenticator, Credentials, and Required**
**   Rights object interfaces**

```
module SecurityLevel2
{
    // forward declaration of interfaces
    interface    PrincipalAuthenticator;
    interface    Credentials;
    interface    Object;
    interface    Current;

    interface    PrincipalAuthenticator
    {
        Security::AuthenticationStatus   authenticate(
            in Security::AuthenticationMethod   method,
            in string                           security_name,
            in Security::Opaque                 auth_data,
            in Security::AttributeList          privileges,
            out Credentials                     creds,
            out Security::Opaque                continuation_data,
            out Security::Opaque                auth_specific_data
        );

        Security::AuthenticationStatus   continue_authentication(
            in Security:Opaque                  response_data.
            inout Credentials                   creds,
            out Security::Opaque                continuation_data,
            out Security::Opaque                auth_specific_data
        );
    };

    interface    Credentials
    {
        Credentials copy();

        void set_security_features(
            in Security::CommunicationDirection direction,
            in SecurityFeatureValueList         security_features
        );

        SecurityFeatureValueList get_security_features (
            in Security::CommunicationDirection direction
        );

        boolean set_privileges (
                in boolean                      force_commit,
                in SecurityAttributeList        requested_privileges,
                out SecurityAttributeList       actual_privileges
        );
```

```
    SecurityAttributeList get_attributes(
            in SecurityAttributeTypeList    attributes
    );

    boolean    is_valid( out UtcT expiry_time );

    boolean    refresh( );
};
typedef    sequence<Credentials>    CredentialsList;

interface    RequiredRights
{
    void    get_required_rights(
        in CORBA::object               obj,
        in CORBA::Identifier           operation_name,
        in CORBA::InterfaceName        interface_name,
        in Security::RightsList        rights,
        in Security::RightsCombinator  rights_combinator
};
```

Internal to the ORB, the security name, authentication data, and privileges go to a Principal Authenticator, which creates credentials. If no authentication data accompanies the request, the credentials will contain those necessary for invoking public services.

If the authentication process is not a single-step process, such as that used in log on when a name and password are entered first, the Principal Authenticator returns an indication to continue for the next phase. Then the requester invokes the continuation.

Credentials contain security attributes. These attributes occur in two forms, unauthenticated and authenticated.

Credentials for which no authentication occurs are public. The authenticated credentials include identity and privilege attributes. Note that privilege attributes are client-side, whereas control attributes are target-side.

An object has three kinds of credentials.

1. *Own credentials*—integral to the object.
2. *Invocation credentials*—most often set transparently, they apply when the object invokes another.
3. *Received credentials*—attributes that an object shares with another. They may arrive as part of the delegation to an intermediate object.

12.3.3.3   *Select Security Attributes*

These select the attributes and security features for further application. They compile the set of things such as privileges for use during operation.

12.3.3.4   *Make Secure Invocation*

Based on the features, attributes, and credentials the application selects, it then makes a secure invocation and applies them.

12.3.3.5   *Targets and Intermediate Targets Control Issues*

Intermediates, during delegation, and targets then apply credentials and so on to the way the call chain proceeds. Both access and delegation control occur here.

12.3.3.6   *Audit Application*

If the application chooses to audit the application activities, these may occur in this space.

12.3.3.7   *Evidence Generation and Verification*

If nonrepudiation requires supporting evidence, the application may participate in generation and verification of such evidence.

12.3.3.8   *Locate Applicable Policies*

On receiving a request for an object, the current policies in force at that time are necessary. Finding those that apply and interpreting and enforcing them come next.

12.3.4   Credentials Object

The Credentials interface specifies six operations:

1. Set Security Features
2. Get Security Features
3. Set Privileges
4. Get Attributes
5. Is Valid
6. Refresh

12.3.4.1   *Set Security Features*

The Set Security Features operation sets the current feature value for a given communication direction. Security is not symmetric—different features may appear on the invocation and response.

The operation takes two parameters, Communication Direction and a sequence of Security Feature Values.

The Security Feature Value is a structure containing a Feature-Value pair. If the Feature is active (or on) the Value (a Boolean) is true. If the Feature is inactive (or off) the Value is false.

Security Features are enumerators with 10 values:

1. No Delegation
2. Simple Delegation
3. Composite Delegation

4. No Protection
5. Integrity
6. Confidentiality
7. Integrity and Confidentiality
8. Detect Replay
9. Detect Misordering
10. Establish Trust in Target

12.3.4.2   Get Security Features

The Get Security Features operation takes a single parameter, Communication Direction, and returns a sequence of Security Feature Values that apply to that given direction.

12.3.4.3   Set Privileges

The Set Privileges operation returns a Boolean and takes three parameters:

1. In Force Commit
2. In Requested Privileges
3. Out Actual Privileges

The Force Commit parameter is a Boolean that indicates whether attributes apply immediately or can be deferred until required. The Requested Privileges are those desired. They may be a Role or for a set of Capabilities. A null parameter indicates that the default set should take precedence. The Actual Privileges are the set of privileges that are actually granted (that the request may obtain).

12.3.4.4   Get Attributes

The Get Attributes operation takes a single parameter, Attributes, and returns a sequence of Attributes as result.

The parameter is the set of privilege attributes and identities that fill the current requirement. The result is the same set of attributes as applicable to the current credentials.

12.3.4.5   Is Valid

Is Valid is useful for testing the state of time-expiring credentials.

12.3.4.6   Refresh

The Refresh operation is for updating credentials that lapse. After expiration they may be capable of renewal; if so, this occurs by using the refresh operation.

12.3.5   Security Object

Security associations are bindings between client and target established by an ORB.

The security association between client and target is a binding. The ORB determines what constitutes the binding through security services and may consider both static and dynamic properties and the policies in effect. The binding is between the object reference to the target and the various elements in the client's context. Exposure of the binding information on the client-side is by way of the Security object and on the target-side via the Current object. Multiple bindings may exist between client and target.

The Security object is a direct extension of the object base class (see Example 12-7). It has eight operations and no attributes. The operations are:

1. Override Default Credentials
2. Override Default QOP
3. Get Security Features
4. Get Active Credentials
5. Get Policy
6. Get Security Mechanism
7. Override Default Mechanism
8. Get Security Names

EXAMPLE 12-7. Security Level Two—Object and Current object interfaces

```
// interface Object derives from Object providing
// additional operations on the objref for this
// security level
interface   Object : CORBA::Object                 // PIDL
{
    void override_default_credentials( in Credentials creds );

    void override_default_QOP( in Security::QOP qop );

    Security::SecurityFeatureValueList
    get_security_features(
            in Security::CommunicationDirection    direction;
    );

    Credentials get_active_credentials( );

    Security::MechanismTypeList get_security_mechanisms();

    void override_default_mechanism(
            in Security::MechanismType   mechanism_type
    );

    Security::SecurityMechandNameList get_security_names();
};

// interface Current derives from SecurityLevel1::Current
// providing additional operations on Current for this
// security level. This is implemented by the ORB.
interface   Current : SecurityLevel1:Current        //PIDL
```

```
{
    void    set_credentials(
                    in Security::CredentialType cred_types,
                    in Credentials              creds
    );

    Credentials get_credentials(
                    in Security::CredentialType cred_type
    );

    readonly attribute CredentialList received_credentials;
    readonly attribute Security:SecurityFeatureValueList
                        received_security_features;

    CORBA::Policy    get_policy(
                    in CORBA::PolicyType policy_type
    );

    readonly attribute RequiredRights required_rights_object;
    readonly attribute PrincipalAuthenticator
                                    principal_authenticator;
};
```

12.3.5.1 *Override Default Credentials*

Override Default Credentials has no result and takes a single parameter, Credentials, that contains the new set of credentials to use for subsequent operations.

A client may decide to narrow or reduce the set of credentials to pass during invocation. Such a reduction takes place by way of the object reference.

The same may apply for intermediate targets when they forward requests. They may wish to manipulate the set of credentials in use as their defaults.

Overriding defaults typically nullifies the current binding or security association, so it may be necessary to establish a new security association afterwards.

12.3.5.2 *Override Default QOP*

Override Default QOP has no result and takes a single parameter, Quality of Protection (QOP), which establishes the Quality of Protection in use. QOP is an enum with the following values:

- No Protection
- Integrity
- Confidentiality
- Integrity and Confidentiality

12.3.5.3 *Get Security Features*

Get Security Features takes a single parameter, Communication Direction, and returns a sequence of Security Feature Values that informs the client of the security requirement details necessary for the object.

If Communication Direction is set for both directions (Request and Reply), it receives the cumulative features. Otherwise it gets those for the specific direction.

12.3.5.4   *Get Active Credentials*

Get Active Credentials takes no parameters and returns Credentials, which is a sequence that may be a subset of the current credentials applicable to the current invocation.

12.3.5.5   *Get Policy*

Get Policy takes a single parameter, Policy Type, and returns the Policy object that currently applies for this object.

12.3.5.6   *Get Security Mechanism*

Get Security Mechanism is a rare and seldom useful feature because ORBs and object can handle all this transparently. However, in some cases the application may desire to do some negotiation for the security mechanism to use. In such cases, the Get and Override Security Mechanism calls aid that negotiation.

This operation takes no parameter and returns the set of security mechanisms as a sequence of Mechanism Types. The Mechanism Type is currently a string.

12.3.5.7   *Override Default Mechanism*

Override Default Mechanism has no result and takes a single parameter, Mechanism Type. Presumably if an application wants to negotiate several changes it must request this operation multiple times. Depending on the implementation, however, requesting subsequent operations may affect the type in the request.

12.3.5.8   *Get Security Names*

Get Security Names takes on parameters and returns the sequence Security Mechanisms and Names. This is a sequence of structures that has two members, Mechanism Type and Security Name.

12.3.6   Security Current Object

The Current object for Security Level Two inherits from Current in Security Level One. The Current object for Security Level One supports a single operation, Get Attributes (see Example 12-8).

EXAMPLE 12-8. Security Level One—Current object interface

```
module SecurityLevel1
{
    interface   Current: CORBA::Current              // PIDL
    {
        Security::AttributeList get_attributes (
                in Security::AttributeListType attributes
        );
    };
};
```

12.3.6.1   Get Attributes

The Get Attributes has a single parameter, Attributes, which is a sequence of the desired attributes. It returns a sequence of attributes. The attribute result gives the current set of applicable security attributes. At the client the result is generally the attributes of the Principal. At the target they are the received attributes.

If the Principal was not previously authenticated, the result is a single attribute of the type Public.

The Security Level Two Current object supports an additional three operations:

1. Set Credentials
2. Get Credentials
3. Get Policy

and has three read-only attributes:

1. Received Credentials
2. Received Security Features
3. Required Rights

Set Credentials

Set Credentials allows an application to override the credentials that associate with Current automatically during initialization, authentication, and invocation.

The operation returns no result and takes two parameters:

1. Credential Type
2. Credentials

Credential Type is one of three enumerators:

1. Invocation Credential
2. Own Credential
3. Nonrepudiation Credential

Invocation Credentials may change to reduce those for a client or to set the credentials during delegation by an intermediate object.

The type may be Own Credentials if the application authenticates itself again or is participating in composite delegation and its current credentials require modification for further invocations.

Nonrepudiation Credentials may be identical to those for invocation, but they may require setting depending on the policy and implementation in effect.

Get Credentials

Get Credentials takes a single parameter, Credential Type, and returns a sequence of Credentials. This is useful for reducing the credentials that are then current.

Get Policy

Get Policy takes a single parameter, Policy Type, and returns a Policy of the type of the parameter.

Received Credentials

Received Credentials on the target object gets the invocation's inbound credentials. These may be the:

- Client's (for simple delegation)
- Client's and/or intermediates (where and when merging credentials is useful)
- Lists of credentials for objects in the call chain

At the client, the call produces the current credentials.

Received Security Features

The Received Security Features attribute returns a sequence of Security Feature Values. This is the Security Feature Value as previously described.

Required Rights

The Required Rights are available for inspection by Access Decision objects that need to determine the rights of a particular interface. The operations on this object can interrogate the Rights to make such decisions.

12.3.7   Security Auditing

Security Audits find support in two interfaces (see Example 12-9):

1. Audit Decision
2. Audit Channel

EXAMPLE 12-9. **Audit Channel and Audit Decision object interfaces**

```
interface   AuditChannel
{
    void    audit_write(
        in Security::AuditEventType    event_type,
        in CredentialsList             creds,
        in Security::UtcT              time,
        in Security::SelectorSequence  descriptors,
        in Security::Opaque            event_specific_data
    );
};

interface   AuditDecision
{
    boolean audit_needed
            in Security::AuditEventType    event_type,
            in Security::SelectorValueList value_list
    );

    readonly attribute AuditChannelaudit_channel;
};
};
```

12.3.7.1   Audit Decision Interface

The Audit Decision has a single read-only attribute, Audit Channel. It also has a single operation, Audit Needed.

Audit Needed

Audit Needed returns a Boolean decision about whether to write an audit record for a particular event. The operation takes two parameters:

1. Audit Event Type
2. Value List

An Audit Event Type is a structure of two members:

1. Extensible Family
2. Event Type

The Extensible Family describes the event family. The Event Type is an unsigned short designating the particular event.

The Value List parameter is a sequence of Selector Values. A Selector Value is a structure with two members:

1. Selector Type
2. Value

In the specification, six Selector Types have definitions.[3] The Value accompanying each of these is an Any. The six Types and their respective Values are:

1. *Interface*—object reference
2. *Object*—object reference
3. *Operation*—operation name
4. *Initiator*—credentials
5. *Success Failure*—Boolean (true or false)
6. *Time*—UTC time

If presenting an event to the Audit Needed operation results in a True decision, then the application is to write a record via the Event Channel given as attribute.

12.3.7.2   *Audit Channel Interface*

The Audit Channel interface supports a single operation, Audit Write.

Audit Write
Audit Write has no result. The operation takes five parameters:

1. Audit Event Type
2. Credentials List
3. Time
4. Selector Values
5. Event Specific Data

The Audit Event Type is the parameter to the Audit Decision object's Audit Needed operation. The Credentials List is a sequence of Credentials. They should be the credentials for the principals participating in or causing the event. If credentials do not accompany the request, then the Audit Channel will use the Own credentials from Current. Time is the time of the event given as a UTC structure. Chapter 14 on CORBAservices has more details. The sequence of Selector Values acts as descriptors for the audit trail. Event Specific Data is of type Opaque (a sequence of octets). This is Event Type specific data and resolution of the Extensible Family for this Event Type should include knowledge about coding and decoding of this opaque data.

---

3. These are described in Chapter 14.

CHAPTER 13 *Common Secure Interoperability*

*A distributed system is one in which the failure of
a computer you didn't even know existed can
render your own computer unusable.*
—Leslie Lamport [1992]

This topic is part of the security mechanism, which was discussed in Chapter 12. However, it applies specifically to interoperability of security by way of GIOP/ IIOP and its adoption came after that of the general security mechanism. For these reasons, its treatment here is separate.

13.1 CSI LEVELS

Three CSI levels, or types of policy, for security are part of the specification and are presented in Table 13-1.

TABLE 13-1. CSI Level 0, 1, and 2 Delegation

CSI Level 0	Identity policy with no delegation
CSI Level 1	Identity policy with unrestricted delegation
CSI Level 2	Identity and Privilege policy with controlled delegation

13.2 SECURITY PROTOCOLS

The CSI describes three security protocols for interoperability, as shown in Table 13-2. One combination of the two (CSI level and security protocol) is mandatory for conforming implementations, with the others being additional profiles of conformance.

The SPKM protocol only supports CSI Level 0. The GSS Kerberos protocol supports CSI Level 0 or CSI Level 1, whereas the CSI-ECMA protocol supports CSI Levels 0, 1, and 2. Table 13-3 shows the various levels of support.

TABLE 13-2. **CSI Security Protocols**

SPKM Protocol	Simple Public-Key GSS-API Mechanism[a]
GSS Kerberos Protocol	Kerberos V5[b]
CSI-ECMA Protocol	A SESAME profile-based[c] subset of the ECMA GSS-API Mechanism[d]

[a] IETF RFC 2025 of October 1996 (replacing Internet draft draft-ietf-cat-spkmgss-06.txt of January 1996). The GSS-API V2 (Generic Security Services) is defined in IETF RFC 2078 of January 1997 (replacing IETF RFC 1508 of September 1993).

[b] IETF RFC 1510 of September 1993 and RFC 1964 of June 1996 containing Kerberos V5 use with and updates for the GSS-API.

[c] IETF Internet draft draft-ietf-cat-sesamemech-02.txt of November 1996.

[d] ECMA 235 (ECMA GSS-API Mechanism Standard) specifies the full ECMA GSS-API, and ECMA 219 (Authentication and Privilege Attribute Security Application) includes details on key distribution.

TABLE 13-3. **Security Protocol Level Support**

	SPKM Protocol	*GSS Kerberos Protocol*	*CSI_ECMA Protocol*
CSI Level 0	supported	supported	supported
CSI Level 1	unsupported	supported (mandatory)	supported
CSI Level 2	unsupported	unsupported	supported

13.3   CRYPTOGRAPHIC PROFILE

A cryptographic profile is necessary to make everything adhere. However, current US export controls stymie easy selection of a best-fit cryptographic algorithm. The mandatory conformance for CSI Level 1 with the GSS Kerberos protocol with MD5 means that data integrity support is available but not confidentiality.[1] Other cryptographic profiles definitely will find support because this form does not suit all requirements.

13.4   KEY DISTRIBUTION

Support of cryptography is an issue of key distribution. Clients, targets, and trusted authorities require a key to lock and unlock information. Because of the widespread interest in both e-mail and the World-Wide Web, public key systems are gaining popularity. The protocols currently in use do not have the delegation and privilege extensions necessary for CORBA's complete security capabilities, however. Such extensions may not come along for some time.

---

1. MD5 stands for Message Digest 5. This profile specifies the use of the Kerberos mechanism with a DES encrypted MD5 message digest for data integrity.

Other models of key distribution exist. Besides a public key there is a secret key model. A hybrid model also exchanges keys between principals in a single domain using secret keys and between trusted authorities (across domains) with public keys. When a secret key use is in support of CSI, it is Kerberos V5. When a public key is used, it is either an SPKM or ECMA derivative.

13.5   SECURE INTER-ORB PROTOCOL

The Secure Inter-ORB Protocol (SECIOP) is a specific reference that applies the CSI to the GIOP/IIOP protocols. As Figure 13-1 shows, the SECIOP layer sits beneath the GIOP and can establish a secure association between client and target by transmitting security tokens that are transparent to the application.

The placement of SECIOP allows it to transmit GIOP messages and message fragments securely. The SECIOP protocol defines all the tags necessary to relay the detail about CSI Level and Cryptographic profiles, key establishment and protection algorithms, as well as security names and security domain information.

CORBA
Interoperability

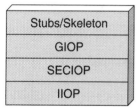

FIGURE 13-1.   SECIOP as it applies to GIOP/IIOP

CHAPTER 14 *CORBAservices*

Try to solve a problem in terms of simpler ones.
—David Gries [1981]

The Common Object Services Specification (COSS) Volume I, which has a publication date of March 1, 1994 [OMG-1994], details the general design principles that define a Common Object Service (now called CORBAservices). This document describes the interfaces and operations of three general-purpose CORBAservices: naming, events, and life cycles.

CORBAservices: Common Object Services Specification [OMG-1995], which came out March 31, 1995, includes specifications for concurrency control, externalization, relationships, transactions, and persistent object storage.

Additional services are time and security (from RFP3); licensing, properties, and query (from RFP4); and change management and trading (from RFP5). All but change management were in adoption at the time of this writing.

The general design principles have eight categories: service design, interface style consistency, key issues, accommodation of future services, service dependencies, relation to CORBA, relation to the OMA, and conformance to standards. We will discuss each briefly.

The first object services were published in spring of 1994.

14.1 CORBASERVICES ARCHITECTURE

CORBAservices stipulates the requirements of its architecture:

- Object-oriented and declared in IDL
- Explicitly identified extensions
- Explicit operation sequencing dependencies
- No implementation descriptions
- Completeness
- Preciseness

It also has the following list of goals:

- Independent and modular
- Minimal duplication
- Fully public interfaces for interaction

- Consistent
- Extensible
- Stable
- Configurable
- Precision
- Secure
- Performant
- Scaleable
- Portable

Quality of service is not currently specifiable in IDL.

The quality of service provided by an interface is a definite requirement that is not currently specifiable in IDL for an interface specification. However, the details are under discussion and may be available by the time this book reaches print.

Relationships between objects come in two flavors: significant and non-significant.

14.1.1   Audience and Bearer

The CORBAservices architecture, in a draft form, uses two terms to describe CORBAservices objects and their relationship to the rest of the CORBA object world. These terms are Audience and Bearer.

Audiences have three specific categories of interfaces:

1. Functional
2. Management
3. Constructive

Bearers, on the other hand, may be one of two categories of objects:

1. Specific
2. Generic

The 1995 document does not mention any of these terms. They are useful, however, which is why we use them here. Perhaps they were omitted because they complicate and specialize the vocabulary too much or because they were not defined before the document was published.

The Audience and Bearer terminology are a bit confusing at first glance. Audience in most senses is a client of a CORBAservice, and a Bearer is the server of such a service.

Audience and Bearer apply to auxiliary or additional interfaces.

The terms apply to services and their use because these are secondary, or auxiliary services. The primary services are those for which an object exists; in other words, the services necessary for whatever application is being composed. The provision of such secondary services is mostly a convenience and not functionally necessary to accomplishing the business.

The difference is apparent in the example of a bank (an Account object) and a bank customer. The Account object has three methods—deposit, withdraw, and balance—that are the only operations necessary to whatever application we are currently constructing. The customer knows about an account, and the bank knows nothing of the customer.

Suppose, however, that the Account object is a Bearer; that is, it offers a secondary service of event notification for NSF checks. If the customer happens to be an Audience for such a service, then the bank (Account) has a method by which it can notify the customer about such events. Of course an NSF notification is really a primary service, or it should be because it is part of the business operating factors for banks.

Let's move it into a more practical example of a secondary service. Consider the customer appearing as an icon in the GUI. This particular icon has a net worth figure in its representation. Assume the Account is a Bearer for event notification on a change in balance and the customer object is an audience for such a service. In other words, every time something modifies the balance, the icon may update because it receives notice if the account's balance changes. This occurs through this secondary service because the client receives notification when such a change occurs, assuming it registers for such notifications.

An example of a secondary service

An even better example might be if the customer happens to be a Bearer of a change of address event notification and the Account happens to be an Audience of such an event service. The customer may generate an event stating that the address has changed and the bank can immediately inquire about the change to update its records. In this case the client of the account service provides the service, and the client-server model tends to blur a bit. Audience and Bearer are analogous to client and server, respectively, but are specific to the use of CORBAservices, which are system services (internal) and not primary business services.

Interfaces in CORBAservices also have divisions by the kind of audience and kind of bearer. Audiences exhibit interests in functional, management, or construction interfaces. Bearers are interesting in specific or generic ways.

A functional interface, here, is an interface that provides the object service. Management interfaces are interesting to an Audience managing a specific CORBAservice. Construction interfaces are the interfaces that an Audience uses to construct or compose services it wants to use, something like a connection protocol.

On the bearer side, objects are specific or generic. A generic object provides a primary service and bears a CORBAservice as a secondary service. The almost canonical example is that all objects may bear the life cycle interfaces because these probably are pervasive. Such bearers, therefore, are generic objects and are not explicitly relations of the CORBAservice (the secondary service).

A specific object is one that exists independently to provide CORBA-services. For instance, a name object may exist explicitly as a name repository. An event object may exist explicitly as an event manager. Here these so-called secondary services really are not secondary. They are the primary reason for an object's existence.

14.2   CORBASERVICES GENERAL DESIGN PRINCIPLES

The principles guiding the design of CORBAservices fall into two categories, Service and Interface style. The next two sections describe these principles.

14.2.1   Service Design Principles

There are nine service design principles:

1. *Build on CORBA Concepts*—the COS must support and be based on the general principles extended by the CORBA. They include the following:
   - Separate interface from implementation
   - Multiple interface inheritance
   - Objects referenced by interface type
   - Clients interact with interfaces and not implementations
   - Subtyping of interfaces may extend, evolve, or specialize services

2. *Basic and Flexible*—the services in the COS should be:
   - *Minimal*—doing one thing well
   - *Simple*—being only as complicated as necessary

3. *Generic*—providing general and wide use without making assumptions, such as:
   - *Client type*—few, if any assumptions must be exposed in the service about the client of such a service
   - *Request data types*—few, if any assumptions must be exposed in the signatures of operations

4. *Allow Local and Remote Implementation*—the service must not make assumptions about clients being local or remote. It should allow easy implementation in remote process as well as in locally shared libraries.

5. *Quality of Service Is an Implementation Characteristic*—the COS must not assume or exhibit knowledge about the quality of a service, which is an implementation detail, at least for the moment. Stated differently, the interface to a COS should not preclude any implementations providing different quality of services.

6. *Objects Often Conspire*—frequently in various COS, different objects may conspire to provide a service. This may occur in producer-consumer or client-server relations. The COS should not preclude other forms of conspiracy intentionally and should anticipate a variety of forms.

7. *Callback Interface Use*—a variety of services require callback interfaces and such support should be available to a client.

8. *No Global Identifier Space Assumed*—all identifiers in COS occur within some context. This avoids disallowing certain types of implementations. Identifiers generated by a service for a client are unique within some scope. The assumption that an ID is not globally unique does not preclude the scope from being defined as global.

9. *Finding and Using a Service Is Orthogonal*—determining the location of a service occurs at a higher architectural level than the use of that service. This does not preclude implementations. Different applications may find and use such services in some policy-specific manner.

14.2.2   Interface Style Consistency

Interface Style Consistency has three principles:

1. *Use of Exceptions and Results*—exceptions only indicate exceptional conditions, whereas operation results occur through the return parameters.
2. *Explicit versus Implicit Operations*—distinct services are available through distinct operations requests. This makes service requests explicit, whereas passing a flag (as mode) parameter is more characteristic of implicit operations conducted by a multimode operation.
3. *Use of Interface Inheritance*—COS use of inheritance is strictly to partition a set of operations into a subset of all available operations. The example in the COS is that an interface given a client may not be one that includes the administrative operations available for the service.

14.3   KEY ISSUES

There are four key design issues:

1. *Naming Service*—the naming service as described shares some commonality with other distributed computing services, however, this service is minimal in keeping with the general design principle of being basic and flexible. For instance, Naming Contexts are similar to property lists and the name service itself is similar to a trading service, however, the services here are simple and orthogonal.
2. *Universal Object Identity*—the COS services do not require the concept of a universal object identity.
3. *Life Cycle Dependency on Future Services*—the current COS service specifies a client model of the life cycle. It does not currently support graphs of object relationships although it anticipates the need to do so in the future.
4. *Reliability, Performance, Scalability, and Portability*—consideration for each of these issues occurs separately and distinctly as necessary for each COS service.

14.4   ACCOMMODATION OF FUTURE SERVICES

The possibility exists that the standard services adoptions to date may need to evolve when change management (versioning) and internationalization gain acceptance. These issues are factors in the design without making commitments to any one particular style of service.

14.5   SERVICE DEPENDENCIES

Services must limit dependencies.

The current services minimize dependencies on external software availability. For example, the naming service can be implemented with other distributed name services such as those of Distributed Computing Environment (DCE) or Open Network Computing (ONC). Internally, the life cycle depends on naming. Events do not have dependencies.

14.6   RELATION TO CORBA AND OMA

No COS object introduces extensions to CORBA.

Life cycles expects CORBA implementations will support object relocation.

Name Objects are pseudo-objects, which are objects in the language mapping but have no objref, meaning they are not IDL objects. They are, however, defined in Pseudo IDL (PIDL) so that their interfaces are consistent within the CORBA framework.

The COS adheres to the OMA and Reference models.

14.7   CONFORMANCE TO EXISTING STANDARDS

Although the standards in existence at the time did not support object-oriented interfaces and did not readily map to object interfaces, the existing standards were a great influence on the writing of the COS. The naming service specification appears to be compatible with X.500, DCE CDS, and ONC NIS and NIS+.

The specifications were broadly conforming to ISO/IEC/CCITT ODP standards:

- CCITT Draft Recommendations X.900, ISO/IEC 10746 Basic Reference Model for Open Distributed Computing
- ISO/IEC JTC1 SC21 WG7 N743 Working Document on Topic 9.1—ODP Trader

CHAPTER 15 *Naming Services*

Naming things properly—so that they reflect their semantics—is often treated lightly by most developers, yet it is important in capturing the essence of the abstractions we are describing.
—Grady Booch [1994]

. . . the natural object is always the adequate *symbol.*
—Ezra Pound, from "A Retrospect," in *Literary Essays of Ezra Pound* (1918)

Names are ubiquitous in human endeavor. Everyone can be identified by name, and objects deserve the same treatment. A CORBA name service identifies objects by name when presented with an object reference. It also may do the reverse, which is possibly more interesting. When presenting with a name for an object, the service gives back an object reference.

A name service may provide scoping information when an unqualified name is given, in which case any of several objects may satisfy the request. A more qualified name may be given, which narrows the object down to a service-specific object. A fully qualified name may be given, which narrows the field down to a specific object. Various gradients of specificity may be available.

Name qualification tightens a name's scope.

The names may be well-known public names, if some standards body should decide to name well-known public objects. Names may be well known as provided by the vendors of the objects. Or, names may be private to an organization or even an individual.

Names may be well known or private.

The names provided by the service may be object names or operation names. Naming for objects is likely to become as ubiquitous as the use of the interface and implementation repositories. While names are not a requirement to operate, they are a mechanism through which people can decipher and manage complexity. Trying to carry around a hundred interface definitions in your head is more difficult than remembering that many names.

Names may apply to objects or operations.

Good names immediately inform and set expectations. Bad names can be hell to unravel and may lead to many wild-goose chases before comprehension dawns.

15.1   THE NAMES OF NAMES

Name binding is relative to a naming context.

Naming services requires a few definitions before proceeding. The attachment or association of a name to an object is *name binding*. Name bindings are always relative to a scope, which is a *naming context*. Names are unique to their naming context. More than one name may bind to an object, either sharing context or in different contexts. Object names are optional, and objects may exist that are not bound to names.

Name resolution determines an object bound to a name in a context.

Name resolution is the determination of the object bound to a name within a context. When a name *binds,* it associates to an object within a specific or default context. A *default context* is likely an act of administrative detail and finds use when no explicit context is specifically given. Object names are never absolute names.

Name contexts are objects and bind to names.

Name contexts are objects and, therefore, may bind to names. The binding of contexts to other contexts creates a naming graph. A naming graph is a directed graph with contexts as nodes and labeled edges. Complex names that reference objects may be composed by traversing such a graph, which describes a *compound name*. A compound name is a path through a naming graph.

15.1.1   Names

The naming services consist primarily of two structures, (1) a name component and (2) a binding, and two interfaces, (1) a naming context and (2) a binding iterator.

15.1.1.1   Name

A name in the naming service is a composition, or a sequence of name components. Each name component consists of two string attributes, (1) ID and (2) Kind. The ID is the name associated with the object. The Kind is for categorizing the object and may be any meaningful string, such as executable, object file, command file, shell script, ASCII text, printer, e-mail, spreadsheet, and so forth. Either or both attributes may be understandable to people. Names may follow convention or they may be arbitrary.

This name object, however, is not an ORB object. It is a very lightweight, frequently passed by value as a parameter (see Example 15-1). It is a pseudo-object, so its description is in PIDL. The interface to names and the name service operates as if it were an IDL interface mapped into the current language binding.

However, it is not possible to pass a reference to a pseudo-object as one would expect to do with an IDL object. The COS specifies operations to convert a name reference into an objref and back for those times when passing a name by reference is desirable. Such operations may be a part of a library.

EXAMPLE 15-1. Name and binding structures

```
module CosNaming
{
    typedef string  Istring;
    struct NameComponent
    {
        Istring      Id;
        Istring      Kind;
    };

    typedef sequence<NameComponent> Name;

    enum    BindingType {noobject, ncontext};

    struct  Binding
    {
        Name          binding_name;
        BindingType binding_type;
    };

    typedef sequence<Binding>    BindingList;

    interface        BindingIterator;
```

15.1.1.2   *Binding*

The binding structure has two members, Binding Name and Binding Type. Bindings also may have names. The two types of bindings are Object and Context. The binding type is an enum.

15.1.1.3   *Naming Context Interface*

The Naming Context interface consists of 10 operations (see Example 15-2):

1. Bind
2. Rebind
3. Bind Context
4. Rebind Context
5. Resolve
6. Unbind
7. New Context
8. Bind New Context
9. Destroy
10. List

Both Bind and Rebind have no result and take two parameters: (1) Name and (2) Object.

EXAMPLE 15-2. **Naming Context object interface**

```
interface    NamingContext
{
    enum NotFoundReason
    {
        missing_node,
        not_context,
        not_object
    };

    exception    NotFound
    {
        NotFoundReason        why;
        Name                  rest_of_name;
    };

    exception CannotProceed
    {
        NamingContext    ctx;    // The spec has "cxt", which
                                 // I think is an error
        Name                  rest_of_name;
    };

    exception  InvalidName      {};
    exception  AlreadyBound     {};
    exception  NotEmpty         {};

    void    bind(in Name n, in Object o)
        raises (NotFound, CannotProceed,
                InvalidName, AlreadyBound);
    void    rebind(in Name n, in Object o)
        raises (NotFound, CannotProceed, InvalidName);

    void    bind_context(in Name n, in NamingContext nc)
        raises (NotFound, CannotProceed,
                InvalidName, AlreadyBound);
    void    rebind_context(in Name n, in NamingContext nc)
        raises (NotFound, CannotProceed, InvalidName);

    Object  resolve(in Name n)
        raises (NotFound, CannotProceed, InvalidName);

    void    unbind(in Name n)
        raises (NotFound, CannotProceed, InvalidName);

    NamingContext    new_context();
    NamingContext    bind_new_context(in Name n)
        raises (NotFound, CannotProceed,
                InvalidName, AlreadyBound);

    void    destroy() raises (NotEmpty);

    void    list(
                in  unsigned long     how_many,
                out BindingList       bl,
                out BindingIterator   bi);
};
```

Bind

Bind associates a name and object within a naming context. Bound naming contexts do not participate in compound name resolution.

Rebind

Rebind binds a name and object even when the name is already in use within a naming context. Again, naming contexts bound with rebind do not participate in compound name resolution.

Both Bind Context and Rebind Context have no return value and take two parameters: (1) Name and (2) Naming Context.

Bind Context

Bind Context binds a name to a context object. Context objects that bind in this way may participate in compound name resolution.

Rebind Context

Rebind Context works like rebind except the object is a naming context and the Context object may participate in compound name resolution.

Resolve

Resolve locates an exact match within the naming context, returning its object reference, which the application must narrow appropriately. The Resolve operation takes a single parameter, Name.

Unbind

Unbind removes a name from a naming context. The operation has no return result and takes a single parameter, Name.

New Context

New Context returns an unbound naming context and takes no parameter.

Bind New Context

Bind New Context returns a bound naming context and takes a single parameter, Name.

Destroy

Destroy deletes a naming context. This operation has no result and takes no parameters.

List

List allows iteration through a sequence of bindings in a naming context. It has no return result and takes three parameters: (1) in How Many, (2) out Binding List, and (3) out Binding Iterator.

How Many is an unsigned long indicating the maximum number of bindings to return in the Binding List. The Binding List is a sequence of Binding structures. The Binding Iterator is the reference to the object used to iterate through the binding list.

15.1.1.4   Binding Iterator

The Binding Iterator interface (see Example 15-3) consists of three operations:
(1) Next One, (2) Next N, and (3) Destroy.

Next One

Next One has a boolean result, which is false when no more bindings are
available. This operation takes a single parameter, out Binding.

Next N

Next N has a boolean result and takes two parameters: (1) in How Many and
(2) out Binding List. How Many is an unsigned long indicating the maximum
number of bindings to return in the Binding List.

Destroy

The destroy operation detroys the Binding Iterator.

EXAMPLE 15-3. Binding Iterator object interface

```
interface BindingIterator
{
    boolean     next_one(out Binding b);
    boolean     next_n(
                      in unsigned long how_many,
                      $out BindingList bl);

    void destroy();
    };
};
```

CHAPTER 16 *Relationships*

An object by itself is intensely uninteresting.
— Grady Booch [1994]

No object is an island. True, it is fairly self-sufficient (encapsulated) but it also is true that the developer may not be able to predict every future use. What this means is that objects always interact with other objects. They may inherit from an object, or another object may inherit from them. They may use other objects, or other objects may use them. Objects are always in relationships with other objects.

Objects are always in relations with other objects and not always predictably.

When these relationships are invariant (never changing), the object can be constructed in such a way that it knows everything there is to know about them. Such built-in knowledge, however, is not a transient or dynamic quality—the object knows these things from the time it was first defined. It is an integral part of the object.

Two things can change:

1. A developer may find a new use for an object and reuse it.
2. An object may have temporary relations about which it does not require previous knowledge.

An example might be the relationship between a car and a person. The person may own the car, be a passenger in a car, or drive the car. The person may be hit by the car. The person may notice a car. Each is a somewhat different relationship between person and car. They generally are not true simultaneously. Driving a car and being hit by the car at the same time is exceedingly difficult. Owning a car and being hit by a car is not so difficult to imagine. Even owning a car may be a transitory relationship, however, because one might sell the car. Driving a car is not often something a person stops doing.

The semantics of two relationships may differ.

Table 16-1 includes descriptions of relationships. In each, at least two entities are involved. Entities in a relationship are related by the roles they have in that relationship. Ownership implies an owner role and a property role.[1]

---

1. Actually it implies owner and owned, which in this case is specialized as property. The counterexample might be, Do you own your own life? Is that property?

TABLE 16-1. **Relationships Have at Least Two Entities in Relation**

Relation	Entity	Other Entity
Ownership	Owner	Property
Transport	Passenger	Vehicle
Transport	Driver	Vehicle
Vehicle accident	Victim	Vehicle
Observation	Observer	Observed

Hard-wiring relationships decreases their flexibility and limits their reuse.

All these relationships can be built into an object, but that makes the object more complicated and, therefore, harder to change or maintain. Another reason not to build the relationships into an object is that the entities are not always the same. For instance, a company could own a car, or the company may own only trucks. This means that a lot of the same code (expressing owners) would need to occur in Person and Company, and both cars and trucks require similar support for expressing owned-by. Ideally, you write code such as this once in an object that knows how to deal with such information and then reuse it wherever the information is of interest.

Relationships are graphs.

Relationships are expressible as graphs. The relationship itself is the arc. The objects involved in the relationship are nodes. The way in which the nodes participate are roles.

The preceding paragraph describes the entire CORBAservices Relationship Service. The Relationship Service describes objects for relationships, roles, and nodes, as well as operations that provide a means to traverse the graphs described by such relations.[2]

Degree and cardinality are essential to relationships.

Relationships also have two characteristics called degree and cardinality. *Degree* is the number of roles required to form a relationship. *Cardinality* refers to the number of relationships with which a role may be involved. This is often used as maximum cardinality, the maximum number of relations that may involve that role.

An example of degree is the three-way relationship in our legal system: judge, plaintiff, and defendant. For such a relationship to exist, each of these three must participate. Ownership, on the other hand, has a degree of two (binary): owner and property.

An example of cardinality is a vehicle, which has one driver (one-to-one) at any time but may have zero or more passengers (zero-to-many or zero-to-four, depending on precision).

Relationships also may have attributes. For instance, a claim number or trial name may be attached to the adjudication relationship.

2. Note that relationships, roles, and nodes are the primary objects, since the service also describes a Factory Object for each of these three, as well an object called Identifiable Object. Additional objects are also defined and will be noted as they appear.

Entities also may participate in more than a single relationship. For example, the owner of a vehicle may be the driver at times and the passenger at other times without relinquishing ownership.

The Relationship Service has essentially three different parts, which the specification calls levels of service. The first, the Base Service, includes the essentials necessary to establish and manage relationships. The second, the Graph Service, is useful for managing collections of relationships as graphs. The third level of service, Specific Relationships, provides the ability to express what usually is not expressed in an interface: containment and reference.[3] More discussion of this will occur at the end of this section.

Relationships are simple, graphs, or specific.

One other component is included in the Relationship Service. It fell here because this was the first service that found this component was necessary. The specification calls it Object Identity, although it is really a means of ascertaining if two references to objects actually reference the same object. The Relationship Service includes it for use by things such as graph traversal, where one may want to know that different entities in the graph actually reference back to the same object. An example of this may be when someone creates a backup of the objects in a graph and does not want to use up physical storage space with duplicate copies of an object.

Relationships also require some notion of identity.

16.1   OBJECT IDENTITY SERVICE

All nodes created in the Relationship Service inherit the Identifiable Object interface. The interface (see Example 16-1) is relatively simple, although its explication can be quite complex and is frequently misunderstood.

16.1.1   Identifiable Object Interface

The Identifiable Object interface has a single read-only attribute and a single operation. The attribute is an Object Identifier, which happens to be an unsigned long named Constant Random ID. The operation's name is Is Identical and it takes an identifiable object as a parameter and returns a Boolean.

EXAMPLE 16-1. Identifiable Object interface

```
ModuleCosObjectIdentity
{
    typedef     unsignedlongObjectIdentifier;

    interface   IdentifiableObject
```

---

3. For an implementation to be conforming, only Service Level One is required. Conforming can also be levels One and Two, or levels One, Two, and Three. Level One is the service, and Two and Three are additional features called profiles.

```
    {
        readonly attribute ObjectIdentifier constant_random_id;
        boolean  is_identical(in IdentifiableObject other_object);
    };
};
```

Comparing two pointers does not work in a distributed system.

Sameness, which is what this interface is about, is often an implementation-specific test. A common shortcut for testing sameness is to test whether two references point to the same address. This works well in a single runtime but is problematic in different runtimes, especially when location is transparent.

This is also subject to religious wars and debate. For example, several people complain that such identity ought to be part of every object reference instead of being an add-on service. Unfortunately there are a number of problems with this approach. The problems certainly are solvable but they have unpleasant side effects and ramifications. For instance, one could assign a universally unique identifier to all objects. Administering such unique identities is very problematic, however.

The question also arises about the cost of querying such an operation. While it may have trivial overhead while in the same runtime, it can be quite expensive to go over the network. Such an identity could be carried around in the reference, but it adds overhead to a lightweight object (the object reference) that in many cases may not require such a service, not to mention the added complexity when one considers that object references may be made persistent.

One could cache such information in the reference on first use but this brings up another issue. If the service is made intrinsically available, it may be used automatically without much planning. In other words, it may encourage people to use the operation as they would use pointer equality testing.

As with all such questions there are pluses and minuses on both sides of the argument.

16.1.1.1   *Constant Random ID*

With that in mind, the attribute is useful for quickly determining whether two objects are identical. The attribute is constant throughout the life of the object, meaning it never changes. It is also expected to be of random distribution because it will commonly find use as a hash key (or other) where random distribution produces the best result.

Two objects with different constant random IDs are guaranteed to be different.

It is not guaranteed to be unique. Another, different object may return the same number. However, if two objects return different Object Identifiers, they are guaranteed to be different. This not does not solve the entire equation but is very effective and requires very little overhead.

16.1.1.2   *Is Identical*

The operation solves the rest of the equation at the potential expense of performance. It returns True if the object reference parameter is the same implementation instance as the instance whose operation is invoked.

16.1.1.3 Base Relationship Service

The base service consists of interfaces for:

- Roles
- Role Factories
- Relationships
- Relationship Factories
- Relationship Iterators

Three steps are required to create a trivial relationship:

1. Create or gather all objects that are to participate in the relationship.
2. For each type of Role necessary to the relationship, pass in the Related Object (the one participating in the Role) to the Role Factory's Create operation.
3. Once all Roles are created, pass them all into the appropriate Relationship Factory.

Out pops the Relationship (see Example 16-2).

EXAMPLE 16-2. Relationship and Relationship Factory object interfaces

```
#include    <ObjectIdentity.idl>

module  CosRelationships
{
    interface    RoleFactory;
    interface    RelationshipFactory;
    interface    Relationship;
    interface    Role;
    interface    RelationshipIterator;

    typedef      Object             RelatedObject;
    typedef      sequence<Role>     Roles;
    typedef      string             RoleName;
    typedef      sequence<RoleName> RoleNames;

    struct NamedRole { RoleName name; Role aRole; };
    typedef sequence<NamedRole>     NamedRoles;

    struct RelationshipHandle
    {
        Relationship    the_relationship;
        CosObjectIdentity::ObjectIdentifier constant_random_id;
    };
    typedef      sequence<RelationshipHandle>    RelationshipHandles;

    interface RelationshipFactory
    {
        struct NamedRoleType
        {
            RoleName     name;
            ::CORBA::InterfaceDef    named_role_type;
        };
```

```
    typedef      sequence<NamedRoleType>       NamedRoleTypes;

    readonly    attribute    ::CORBA::InterfaceDef    relationship_type;
    readonly    attribute    unsigned short           degree;
    readonly    attribute    NamedRoleTypes           named_role_types;

    exception   RoleTypeError             { NamedRoles culprits; };
    exception   MaxCardinalityExceeded  { NamedRoles culprits; };
    exception   DegreeError     { unsigned short    required_degree; };
    exception   DuplicateRoleName         { NamedRoles culprits; };
    exception   UnknownRoleName          { NamedRoles cluprits; };

    Relationship    create(in NamedRoles named_roles)
        raises (
            RoleTypeError,
            MaxCardinalityExceeded,
            DegreeError,
            DuplicateRoleName,
            UnknownRoleName);
};

interface    Relationship : CosObjectIdentity::IdentifiableObject
{
    exception   CannotUnlink { Roles offending_roles };

    readonly    attribute    NamedRoles   named_roles;

    void        destroy() raises (CannotUnlink);
};
```

16.1.2   Role Factory Interface

The Role Factory supports only a single operation (see Example 16-3). However, it has four read-only attributes:

1. *Role Type*—an interface definition.[4] It is the type of Role that a factory creates. Note that this Role Type is derived from the Role interface and is the specific subtype of Role that the factory creates.
2. *Maximum Cardinality*—the maximum number of relationships in which a role may participate.
3. *Minimum Cardinality*—the minimum number of relationships in which a Role must participate.[5]
4. *Related Object Types*—this attribute consists of a sequence of Related Types. The factory can construct Roles for use with any of the object types found in the related types. In other words, the created Role must support at least one of the Related Objects interfaces in order to be a valid Role.

---

4. These (as `InterfaceDef`) are more fully described in Chapter 9. Suffice it to say they describe an Interface Type.

5. Unlike maximum cardinality, the minimum cardinality cannot be enforced because during construction they start below their minimum. However, Roles support an operation on their minimum and can report if this is the case.

The Create Role operation on this factory takes a Related Object as a parameter and returns a Role.

EXAMPLE 16-3. Role, Role Factory, and Relationship iterator object interfaces

```
interface   Role
{
    exception   UnknownRoleName {};
    exception   UnknownRelationship {};
    exception   RelationshipTypeError {};
    exception   CannotDestroyRelationship { RelationshipHandles offenders; };
    exception   ParticipatingInRelationship
                {
                    RelationshipHandles the_relationships;
                };

    readonly    attribute   RelatedObject    related_object;

    RelatedObject    get_other_related_object(
                    in RelationshipHandle rel,
                    in RoleName target_name)
        raises (UnknownRoleName, UnknownRelationship);

    Role    get_other_role(in RelationshipHandle rel, in RoleName target_name)
        raises (UnknownRoleName, UnknownRelationship);

    void    get_relationships(
                    in unsigned long        how_many,
                    out RelationshipHandles    rels,
                    out RelationshipIterator   iterator);

    void    destroy_relationships() raises (CannotDestroyRelationship);
    void    destroy() raises (ParticipatingInRelationship);

    boolean check_minimum_cardinality();

    void    link(in RelationshipHandle rel, in NamedRoles named_roles)
        raises (
            RelationshipFactory::MaxCardinalityExceeded,
            RelationshipTypeError);
    void    unlink(in RelationshipHandle rel) raises (UnknownRelationship);
};

interface   RoleFactory
{
    exception   NilRelatedObject    {};
    exception   RelatedObjectTypeError {};

    readonly    attribute   ::CORBA::InterfaceDef    role_type;
    readonly    attribute   unsigned long max_cardinality;
    readonly    attribute   unsigned long min_cardinality;
    readonly    attribute   sequence<::CORBA::InterfaceDef> related_object_types;

    Role    create_role(in RelatedObject related_object)
        raises (NilRelatedObject, RelatedObjectTypeError);
};
```

```
interface RelationshipIterator
{
    boolean    next_one(out RelationshipHandle rel);
    boolean    next_n(in unsigned long how_many, out RelationshipHandles rels);

    void    destroy();
};
};
```

16.1.3   Role Interface

The Role interface has a single read-only attribute for its Related Object (the object that assumes this role). The Related Object is one that conforms to the Role Type of its creating factory.

The interface also has eight operations:

1. Get Other Related Object
2. Get Other Related Role
3. Get Relationships
4. Destroy Relationships
5. Destroy
6. Check Minimum Cardinality
7. Link
8. Unlink

16.1.3.1   *Get Other Related Object (Get Other Related Role)*

These operations take a relationship handle as one parameter. A relationship handle is an IDL structure having a role name (string) and an interface definition for the named role. It also takes a role name for the target Role. Essentially, both operations traverse the relationship and retrieve the role of the given target name. Get Other Related Role returns the Role, and Get Other Related Object returns the Related Object of that target Role.

16.1.3.2   *Get Relationships*

This operation takes three parameters:

1. How Many
2. Relationships
3. Iterator

How Many is an in unsigned long signifying the number of relationships to return. Relationships is an out sequence of relationship handles. Iterator is an out relationship iterator for retrieving relationship handles.

The Get Relationships operation is useful for retrieving all relationships. If there are more relationships than the number requested via How Many, the iterator can access the remainder. If there are no additional relationships, the iterator is null.

16.1.3.3   Destroy Relationships

This operation effectively destroys all relationships associated with a Role.

16.1.3.4   Destroy

This operation destroys the Role unless a relationship is still in effect. If a relationship is still extant, an exception is thrown.

16.1.3.5   Check Minimum Cardinality

This operation tests to see if the Role satisfies the minimum cardinality. If so, it returns True; otherwise it returns False.

16.1.3.6   Link and Unlink

Neither of these operations should be public. These two operations, according to the specification, are strictly for use by the Relationship Service itself. Link is for use by the Role factory in its creation of Roles. Unlink is for use by the Role's Destroy implementation.

The Link operation takes a relationship handle and a sequence of Named Roles that represent the related objects in that relationship. The Unlink operation takes a relationship handle for the relation that it is disconnecting from the Role.

16.1.4   Relationship Factory Interface

The Relationship factory consists of three read-only attributes and one operation. The attributes are:

- *Relationship Type*—an interface definition for the relation that defines the type the factory may construct and may be a subtype of Relationship
- *Degree*—an unsigned short for expressing the number of degrees
- *Named Role Types*—a sequence of the requisite Named Role Type, which is a structure with a name and an interface definition. Both names and types are requirements.

The single operation is Create, which takes a sequence of Named Roles as a parameter and results in a Relationship. A Named Role is defined as a structure containing a name (string) and a role.

During invocation, Create's implementation effectively uses the Link operation to inform each Role of its involvement in the Relationship. A Role may refuse to participate if it violates the Role's self-enforced cardinality constraint. The number of Roles passed into Create must equal the Degree or an exception is raised.

Role Names associate Role objects with one of the formal roles expected by the relationship. The Role Names passed to Create must be the same as those in the factory's Named Role Types attribute or an exception is raised.

The types of each Role passed to Create must conform to the factory's Named Role Types attribute or an exception is raised. The names of the Roles passed to Create must be unique within the scope of the Relationship type.

16.1.5 Relationship Interface

A Relationship interface is even simpler than its factory. It has a single read-only attribute and a single operation. The attribute is a sequence of Named Roles that correspond to those used in the factory's Create operation.

Relationship's operation is Destroy. On invocation, its implementation presumes to call the Unlink operation on its associated Roles.

16.1.6 Relationship Iterators

The Relationship Iterator is an interface that has three operations:

1. *Next One*—has an out parameter of a relationship handle type. If no more relationships exist, the operation returns False; otherwise it returns True.
2. *Next N*—has an unsigned long for the number to fetch and an out parameter that is a sequence of relationship handles. The number requested is the maximum number to return. If no more relationships are found, the operation returns False, otherwise True.
3. *Destroy*—destroys the iterator.

16.2 GRAPH RELATIONSHIP SERVICE

This level of service adds the following list of seven objects to the service.

1. Nodes
2. Node Factories
3. Role—a specialization of Role from the Base Service
4. Edge Iterators
5. Traversals
6. Traversal Criteria
7. Traversal Factories

A graph is at least two nodes with a connecting edge.

In general, nodes and edges define a graph. A graph is composed of a set of nodes and a set of edges. A node is a hub from which one or more edges radiate. An edge always connects two nodes. Tracing a path from node to edge to node, and so on, is a traversal. A traversal that arrives back at a previous node without traversing the same edge is a cycle.

A traversal object can follow edges to nodes according to its traversal criteria.

In the graph service (see Example 16-4), a node collects an object and its set of roles. The relationships between roles are edges. Given a node, a traversal object can be constructed that can traverse the graph starting from that Node. The manner or order in which traversal takes place is given by defining Traversal Criteria (see Example 16-5). The Traversal object acts like an iterator, returning directed edges.

EXAMPLE 16-4. Graphs—Traversal Factory object interface

```
#include     <Relationships.idl>
#include     <ObjectIdentity.idl>

module CosGraphs
{
    interface    TraversalFactory;
    interface    Traversal;
    interface    TraversalCriteria;
    interface    Node;
    interface    NodeFactory;
    interface    Role;
    interface    EdgeIterator;

    struct  NodeHandle
    {
        Node    the_node;
        ::CosObjectIdentity::ObjectIdentifier    constant_random_id;
    };
    typedef     sequence<NodeHandle>     NodeHandles;

    struct  NamedRole
    {
        Role    the_role;
        ::CosRelationships::RoleName     the_name;
    };
    typedef     sequence<NamedRole>     NamedRoles;

    struct  EndPoint
    {
        NodeHandle    the_node;
        NamedRole     the_role;
    };
    typedef     sequence<EndPoint>  EndPoints;

    struct  Edge
    {
        EndPoint      from;
        ::CosRelationships::RelationshipHandle  the_realtionship;
        EndPoints     relatives;
    };
    typedef     sequence<Edge>  Edges;

    enum    PropagationValue   { deep, shallow, none, inhibit };
    enum    Mode               { depthFirst, breadthFirst, bestFirst };

    interface   TraversalFactory
    {
        Traversal    create_traversal_on(
                        in NodeHandle          root_node;
                        in TraversalCriteria   the_criteria;
                        in Mode                how);
    };
```

EXAMPLE 16-5. Traversal, Traversal Criteria, and Node object interfaces

```
interface Traversal
{
    typedef     unsigned long   TraversalScopeId;

    struct   ScopedEndPoint
    {
        EndPoint            point;
        TraversalScopeId    id;
    };
    typedef     sequence<ScopedEndPoint>    ScopedEndPoints;

    struct  ScopedRealtionship
    {
        ::CosRelationships::RelationshipHandle  scoped_relationship;
        TraversalScopeId    id;
    };

    struct  ScopedEdge
    {
        ScopedEndPoint          from;
        ScopedRelationship      the_relationship;
        ScopedEndPoints         relatives;
    };
    typedef     sequence<ScopedEdge>    ScopedEdges;

    boolean     next_one(out ScopedEdge the_edge);
    boolean     next_n(in short how_many, out ScopedEdges the_edges);

    void        destroy();
};

interface   TraversalCriteria
{
    struct  WeightedEdge
    {
        Edge                    the_edge;
        unsigned long           weight;
        sequence<NodeHandle>    next_nodes;
    };
    typedef     sequence<WeightedEdge>  WeightedEdges;

    void    visit_node(in NodeHandle a_node, in Mode search_mode);

    boolean     next_one(out WeightedEdge the_edge);
    boolean     next_n(in short how_many, out WeightedEdges the_edges);

    void        destroy();
};

    interface   Node : ::CosObjectIdentity::IdentifiableObject
    {
    typedef     sequence<Role> Roles;

    exception   NoSuchRole {};
    exception   DuplicateRoleType   {};
```

```
    readonly   attribute   ::CosRelationships::RelatedObject   related_object;
    readonly   attribute   Roles   roles_of_node;

    Roles   roles_of_type(in ::CORBA::InterfaceDef role_type);

    void    add_role(in Role a_role) raises (DuplicateRoleType);

    void    remove_role(in ::CORBA::InterfaceDef of_type) raises (NoSuchRole);
};
```

EXAMPLE 16-6. Node Factory, Role, and Edge Iterator object interfaces

```
    interface NodeFactory
    {
        Node    create_node(in Object related_object);
    };

    interface   Role : ::CosRelationships::Role
    {
        void    get_edges(
                    in long             how_many,
                    out Edges           the_edges,
                    out EdgeIterator    the_rest);
    };

    interface   EdgeIterator
    {
        boolean     next_one(out Edge the_edge);
        boolean     next_n(in unsigned long how_many, out Edges the_edges);

        void        destroy();
    };
};
```

16.2.1   Node Factory Interface

The Node Factory interface (see Example 16-6) has a single operation, Create
Node. This operation takes a related object as parameter and returns a node
that will have a related object attribute initialized to this parameter.

16.2.2   Node Interface

A Node object has two read-only attributes and three operations. The
attributes are:

1. Related Object
2. Roles of Node

Related Object is mentioned as a node factory parameter. The Related Object is
the same as defined for Relationship's Base Service. It is the object that is participating in the relationship under one or more roles, although the nature of the
relationship service is such that objects are not aware they are participating.

Roles of Node is a sequence of all roles that the node collects (participates). Here Role is the Graph specialized Role, which derives from the basic Relationship service Role covered in the next section.

The operations are:

1. Roles of Type
2. Add Role
3. Remove Role

The Roles of Type operation returns a sequence of Roles matching the parameter, which is a Type description in the form of an interface definition. This operation returns Roles matching either the type or its subtypes.

The Add Role operation takes a Role parameter. It adds the parameter to the node's collection unless the Role, its supertype, or subtype are already in the collection. If the Role already exists, the operation raises an exception.

The Remove Role operation takes an interface definition as a parameter to describe the type of Role to remove from the node's collection.

16.2.3   Role Interface

The Role object in the Graph service derives from the Role in the Base service. It has a single operation, Get Edges, which takes three parameters:

1. An in parameter stating How Many
2. An out sequence of edges
3. An out edge iterator

How Many is the maximum size of the sequence of edges. If there are more edges than requested by How Many, an Iterator is returned from which additional edges can be accessed. If no additional edges are available, the iterator is null.

16.2.3.1   Edges

The Graph service defines an edge as a structure with three members. An edge consists of the following:

1. An endpoint with the name From. The singular endpoint is the Role and its related object.
2. An Edge, which is a relationship handle as defined in the Basic service under Role.
3. A sequence of endpoints, which are the relative endpoints.

16.2.3.2   Endpoints

Endpoints are defined by the Graph service to be a structure with two members, a Node Handle and a Named Role.

Node Handle

A Node Handle is defined by the Graph service as a structure of two members:

1. A reference to a Node object
2. A random constant ID

The random constant ID is defined by the Object Identity service.

Named Role

A Named Role is defined by the Graph service as a structure of two members:

1. A reference to the Role object
2. A Role Name

Role Names are defined in the Basic service.

16.2.4   Edge Iterator Interface

An edge iterator interface supports three operations:

1. Next One
2. Next N
3. Destroy

An edge iterator object results from an invocation of the Graph service Role's Get Edges operation.

16.2.4.1   Next One

The Next One operation has an out parameter of type edge. If there are no more edges, the operation returns False; otherwise it returns True.

16.2.4.2   Next N

The Next N operation takes two parameters:

1. An in of How Many
2. An out sequence of edges found

It returns at most the number requested by How Many. If there are no more edges, it results in a False; otherwise True.

16.2.4.3   Destroy

The Destroy operation destroys the iterator.

16.2.5   Traversal Factory Interface

The traversal factory interface consists of one operation, Create Traversal On. This single operation takes three in parameters:

1. A node handle, which is the root node from which the traversal starts
2. A traversal criteria object, which instructs the traversal on which nodes it must visit and which edges it must emit
3. A mode, which describes the order by which the traversal shall proceed—depth first, breadth first, or by Best First, where Best is a determination of weighted edges

16.2.6   Traversal Interface

Traversal objects iterate through graphs of relationships. A Traversal object defines a scope for the graph it traverses. The assignment of such a scope occurs through the Traversal object's assigning of identifiers to the nodes and edges it returns. These identifiers are unique within the scope of the Traversal object.

16.2.6.1   Traversal Scope

Traversal objects iterate through scoped edges, which are determined at traversal creation time according to the criteria and mode. Scoped edges are directed edges.

Scoped Edge

A scoped edge is a structure consisting of three scoped members:

1. A scoped end point, which establishes direction because it represents the From or starting point
2. A scoped relationship
3. A sequence of scoped end points relative to the first member

Each has scope by possessing an Identifier.

16.2.6.2   Scoped End Point

A scoped end point is a structure of two members:

1. An end point
2. A traversal scope ID

Traversal scope IDs are unsigned longs. An end point is as it is defined for the Graph service's Role.

16.2.6.3   Scoped Relationship

A scoped relationship is a structure of two members:

1. A relationship handle
2. A traversal scope ID

The relationship handle is defined in the Basic service under Role.

16.2.6.4   The Traversal Interface

The traversal interface has three operations:

1. Next One
2. Next N
3. Destroy

These behave much like the previous occurrences of like-named operations.

Next One
Next One has a scoped edge as an out parameter and a Boolean result.

Next N
Next N has an in parameter designating How Many to retrieve and an out parameter that is a sequence of scoped edges. A Boolean result occurs saying whether or not the request was successful.

Destroy
Destroy has no parameters and no returns.

16.2.7   Traversal Criteria Interface

The traversal criteria is effectively a call-back, queried by the Traversal object in order to determine edges to emit. They are associated during traversal construction by its factory.

The interface supports four operations:

1. Next One
2. Next N
3. Destroy
4. Visit Node

The first three also behave much like their previously occurring counterparts.

16.2.7.1   Next One and Next N

The out parameters for the Next operations are weighted edges. A weighted edge is a structure with three members:

1. An edge
2. A weight
3. A sequence of node handles

The weight is an unsigned long and is ignored except for best first traversals. The sequence of node handles is a list of the next nodes.

16.2.7.2   Destroy

Destroy releases any resources associated with the traversal criteria object.

16.2.7.3 *Visit Node*

The Visit Node operation takes two parameters, a node and a mode. The Node is the node from which the traversal criteria will iterate. Mode establishes the mode of iteration (the search mode) to use.

The Traversal object uses Visit Node to traverse the graph. On calling Visit Node, it continues by requesting one of the Next operations (Next One or Next N) to get the edges from the current node.

The Best First mode sorts the weighted edges in ascending order. If traversal calls Visit Node while weighted edges remain for the previous node, they are discarded. Only a single node's edges are served at a time.

16.3 CONTAINMENT AND REFERENCE

Containment and reference are two of the most common object relationships.

The specification states that because containment and reference are so common, the specification includes them. Each is in its own module. Each is composed of three interfaces: one relationship and two roles. The relationships inherit from the Base service's Relationship. The roles inherit from the Graph service Roles. None of these interfaces introduces any operations.

The specifications go on to detail the attributes of the factories that create such objects.

Containment supports two Roles: Contains and Contained (see Example 16-7). Reference supports two roles, References and Referenced (see Example 16-8).

EXAMPLE 16-7. **Containment Relationship, Contains Role, and Contained In Role object interfaces**

```
#include    <Graphs.idl>

module  CosContainment
{
    interface   Relationship : ::CosRelationships::Relationship {};

    interface   ContainsRole : ::CosGraphs::Role    {};

    interface   ContainedInRole : ::CosGraphs::Role {};
};
```

EXAMPLE 16-8. **Reference Relationship, References Role, and Referenced By Role object interfaces**

```
#include    <Graphs.idl>

module  CosReference
{
    interface   Relationship : ::CosRelationships::Relationship {};

    interface   ReferencesRole: ::CosGraphs::Role    {};

    interface   ReferencedByRole: ::CosGraphs::Role {};
};
```

CHAPTER 17 *Event Services*

The tendency of an event to occur varies
inversely with one's preparation for it.
—David Searles

Typically, an event is a communication between two or more entities about the occurrence of a state transition. It is not the transition itself, although the transition may trigger it. It may convey no message at all, simply informing the receiving entity about the transition. For this to occur, the two entities must previously agree to make such an occurrence mean something. This agreement comes through registration, in which one entity registers with the other.

Events typically indicate a state transition.

17.1 PUSH AND PULL

Moving a little further along in sophistication, two styles of access, push and pull, are available, as shown in Figure 17-1.

This is made possible by an object that interposes itself between the supplier and consumer, which is the event channel. The event channel acts like a mailbox between the supplier and consumer.

An event channel object interposes itself between consumer and supplier.

In the Push style of event, the supplier pushes a message into the event channel regardless of whether a consumer is waiting for the message or even available to receive the message. The event channel will push the message to all consumers that have signed up for push events.

Push is a supply-side initiated event notice.

In the Pull style of event, a consumer attempts to receive an event message from the channel. The consumer pulls the event from the event channel, which in turn pulls it from the server, if a server is available for pull-style events.

Pull is a request for event notice.

The Pull consumer may find a message or it may not and it has a choice of blocking or nonblocking reads. If it chooses to wait (blocking) until an event posting occurs, it may do so. If the consumer wants to check back without waiting for a message to be posted (nonblocking), it continues on with whatever it wants to do and may look at some later point for an event.

A Pull may or may not find a notice and block if a notice is not present.

The data in the event channel may be generic for a generic channel, meaning the consumer will have to determine the event's type on receipt. Or it may be typed and use a typed channel where the consumer knows the type of the message before receiving it.

Event data may be generic or specific.

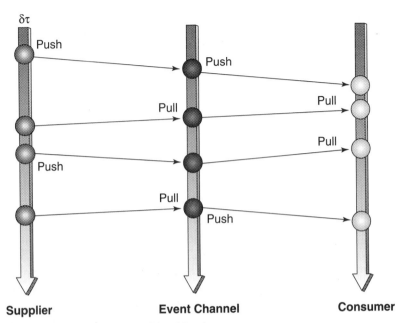

FIGURE 17-1. **Push-and-Pull combinations**

Suppliers and consumers do not have to be both Push or both Pull for any given event channel.

Suppliers and consumers are free to mix and match the Push and Pull styles of event use. There may be multiple suppliers as well as consumers. This is a feature of decoupling the event channel as a separate object interposing itself between the producer and consumer of events. An event supplier may push to the channel, and consumers may pull that event from the channel.

An event channel with at least one Push Consumer or at least one Pull request, has an event due. If at least one Pull Supplier previously registers (before the request in either of the above cases), the channel attempts to satisfy the event by pulling from a Pull Supplier.

17.2   EVENT SERVICES

The definition of event services consists of four modules:

1. Event communication
2. Event channel administration
3. Typed event communication
4. Typed event channel administration

The latter two mirror the first two except they are for typed events. A brief summary of the differences between the two occurs later in this chapter.

17.2.1   Basic Operation

The Basic operation runs as follows:

- A request occurs on an Event Channel factory for an Event Channel.[1]
- An Event Channel is the result of the factory request.
- An Event Channel interface has three operations:
  1. For Consumers
  2. For Suppliers
  3. Destroy
- A Consumer Administration object is the result of For Consumers, and a Supplier Administration object is the result of For Suppliers.
- Proxy Suppliers of both Push and Pull types are available from the Consumer Administration object.
- Proxy Consumers of both Push and Pull types are available from the Supplier Administration object.
- A Consumer looking for a Push Supplier may register via a connect operation on the Proxy Push Supplier.
- A Consumer looking for a Pull Supplier may register via a connect operation on a Proxy Pull Supplier.
- A Supplier looking for a Push Consumer may register via a connect operation on a Proxy Push Consumer.
- A Supplier looking for a Pull Consumer may register via a connect operation on a Proxy Pull Consumer.

17.2.2   Event Channel Administration

Event Channel Administration consists of seven interfaces:

1. Event Channel
2. Consumer Administration
3. Supplier Administration
4. Proxy Push Consumer
5. Proxy Pull Consumer
6. Proxy Push Supplier
7. Proxy Pull Supplier

17.2.2.1   Event Channel

The Event Channel operation has three operations:

1. For Consumers
2. For Suppliers
3. Destroy

---

1. The specification does not include any detail about Event Channel Factories or Factory finders. Both are left as implementation detail.

The For Consumers operation takes no parameters and returns a Consumer Administration object. The For Suppliers operation takes no parameters and returns a Supplier Administration object. The Destroy operation releases the Event Channel and all the resources it consumes.

17.2.2.2 *Consumer Administration*

The Consumer Administration interface has two operations:

1. Obtain Push Supplier
2. Obtain Pull Supplier

Neither operation takes parameters. The first returns a Proxy Push Supplier, which is for connecting Push Consumers to the Event Channel. The second returns a Proxy Pull Supplier, which is for connecting Pull Consumers to the Event Channel.

17.2.2.3 *Supplier Administration*

The Supplier Administration interface has two operations:

1. Obtain Push Consumer
2. Obtain Pull Consumer

Neither operation takes parameters.

   The first returns a Proxy Push Consumer, used for connecting Push Suppliers to the Event Channel.

   The second returns a Proxy Pull Consumer, which is for connecting Pull Suppliers to the Event Channel.

17.2.2.4 *Proxy Push Consumer*

The Proxy Push Consumer interface has a single operation that returns one result, Connect Push Supplier. This operation takes a Push Supplier as a parameter and connects that object to the Event Channel.

   Passing a nil Push Supplier to the connect prevents anyone from disconnecting the Supplier with a call to disconnect supplier on the Supplier.

17.2.2.5 *Proxy Pull Consumer*

The Proxy Pull Consumer interface has a single operation that returns one result, Connect Pull Supplier. This operation takes a Pull Supplier as a parameter and connects that object to the Event Channel.

17.2.2.6 *Proxy Push Supplier*

The Proxy Push Supplier interface has a single operation that returns one result, Connect Push Consumer. This operation takes a Push Consumer as a parameter and connects that object to the Event Channel.

17.2.2.7   *Proxy Pull Supplier*

The Proxy Pull Supplier interface has a single operation that returns one result, Connect Pull Consumer. This operation takes a Pull Consumer as a parameter and connects that object to the Event Channel.

Passing a nil Pull Consumer to the connect prevents anyone from disconnecting the Consumer with a call to disconnect consumer on the Consumer (see Example 17-1).

EXAMPLE 17-1. Event Channel Administration object interfaces

```
#include    "CosEventComm.idl"

module  CosEventChannelAdmin
{
    exception    AlreadyConnected {};
    exception    TypeError        {};

    interface    ProxyPushConsumer : CosEventComm:PushConsumer
    {
        void    connect_push_supplier(in CosEventComm::PushSupplier push_supplier)
            raises (AlreadyConnected);
    };

    interface    ProxyPullSupplier : CosEventComm::PullSupplier
    {
        void    connect_pull_consumer(in CosEventComm::PullConsumer pull_consumer)
            raises (AlreadyConnected);
    };

    interface    ProxyPullConsumer : CosEventComm::PullConsumer
    {
        void    connect_pull_supplier(in CosEventComm::PullSupplier pull_supplier)
            raises (AlreadyConnected, TypeError);
    };

    interface    ProxyPushSupplier : CosEventComm::PushSupplier
    {
        void    connect_push_consumer(in CosEventComm push_consumer)
            raises (AlreadyConnected, TypeError);
    };

    interface    ConsumerAdmin
    {
        ProxyPushSupplier    obtain_push_supplier();
        ProxyPullSupplier    obtain_pull_supplier();
    };

    interface    SupplierAdmin
    {
        ProxyPushConsumer    obtain_push_consumer();
        ProxyPullConsumer    obtain_pull_consumer();
    };
```

```
interface   EventChannel
{
    ConsumerAdmin   for_consumers();
    SupplierAdmin   for_supplier();

    void    destroy();
};
};
```

17.2.3   Event Communication

Event Communication consists of four interfaces (see Example 17-2):

1. Push Consumer
2. Push Supplier
3. Pull Supplier
4. Pull Consumer

EXAMPLE 17-2. Push Consumer, Push Supplier, Pull Supplier, and Pull Consumer object interfaces

```
module  CosEventComm
{
    exception   Disconnected {};

    interface   PushConsumer
    {
        void    push(in any data) raises (Disconnected);
        void    disconnect_push_consumer();
    };

    interface   PushSupplier
    {
        void    disconnect_push_supplier();
    };

    interface   PullSupplier
    {
        any     pull() raises (Disconnected);
        any     try_pull(out boolean has_event)
            raises (Disconnected);
        void    disconnect_pull_supplier();
    };

    interface   PullConsumer
    {
        void    disconnect_pull_consumer();
    };
};
```

17.2.3.1   Push Consumer

The Push Consumer interface supports two operations:

1. Push
2. Disconnect Push Consumer

Neither operation returns results.

Push takes a single data parameter, Any. A Push Supplier communicates with consumers via the Push interface. The input parameter is the event data.

Calling Disconnect Push Consumer terminates the connection, and releases resources and the Push Consumer's object reference.

17.2.3.2   Push Supplier

The Push Supplier interface supports a single operation, Disconnect Push Supplier, which takes no parameter and returns no result. The operation terminates the connection, releasing resources and the Push Supplier object.

17.2.3.3   Pull Supplier

The Pull Supplier interface supports three operations:

1. Pull
2. Try Pull
3. Disconnect Pull Supplier

The Pull operation takes no parameters and returns an Any. Pull is a blocking receive.

The Try Pull operation takes one parameter, an out Boolean that signifies if an event is available. Try Pull also returns an Any. If event data was available, the Any contains that data. If no event data was available, the Any contains a long with an arbitrary value.

The Disconnect Pull Supplier operation terminates the connection, releasing resources and the Pull Supplier object reference.

17.2.3.4   Pull Consumer

The Pull Consumer interface supports a single operation, Disconnect Pull Consumer, which takes no parameter and returns no result. The operation terminates the connection, releasing resources and the Pull Consumer's reference.

17.2.4   Typed Event Communication

In Typed Event communications an object reference to an interface is available. The suppliers and consumers already agree what the interface is; in other words, they conspire beforehand to operate with such an interface.

In Typed Push mode (see Example 17-3), the Interface comes from the consumer, so consumers and suppliers exchange a Typed Push Consumer and a Push Supplier. The supplier, when pushing, invokes Get Typed Consumer

Consumer and supplier conspire to exchange the typed interface for the event.

on the Typed Push Consumer, which returns an object reference to the interface. This interface's operations must have no return results, and all parameters must be In parameters. The supplier then may invoke operations on the interface once it obtains a Typed Event Channel.

EXAMPLE 17-3. Typed Event Channel Administration object interfaces

```
#include    "CosEventComm.idl"
#include    "CosTypedEventComm"

module  CosTypedEventChannelAdmin
{
    exception   InterfaceNotSupported   {};
    exception   NoSuchImplementation    {};

    typedef  string    Key;

    interface   TypedProxyPushConsumer :
            CosEventChannelAdmin::ProxyPushConsumer,
            CosTypedEventComm::TypedPushConsumer
    {
    };

    interface   TypedProxyPullSupplier :
            CosEventChannelAdmin::ProxyPullSupplier,
            CosTypedEventComm::TypedPullSupplier
    {
    };

    interface   TypedSupplierAdmin : CosEventChannelAdmin::SupplierAdmin
    {
        TypedProxyPushConsumer  obtain_typed_push_consumer(
                in Key support_interface)
            raises (InterfaceNotSupported);

        ProxyPullConsumer   obtain_typed_pull_consumer(in Key uses_interface)
            raises (NoSuchImplementation);
    };

    interface   TypedConsumerAdmin : CosEventChannelAdmin::ConsumerAdmin
    {
        TypedProxyPullSupplier  obtain_typed_pull_supplier(
                in Key supported_interface)
            raises (InterfaceNotSupported);

        ProxyPushSupplier   obtain_typed_push_supplier(in Key uses_interface)
            raises (NoSuchImplementation);
    };

    interface   TypedEventChannel
    {
        TypedConsumerAdmin      for_consumers();
        TypedSupplierAdmin      for_suppliers();

        void    destroy();
    };
};
```

In Typed Pull mode, the interface comes from the supplier, so consumers and suppliers exchange a Typed Pull Supplier and a Push Consumer. The consumer obtains the interface by calling Get Typed Supplier on the Typed Pull Supplier. Once it obtains this interface it may invoke its operations.

The interface that suppliers and consumers conspire to use in the Typed Pull mode has some additional requirements:

For every interface that supplier and consumers agree to use in the Type Push mode, there is another interface named Pull<Interface Name>. The <Interface Name> is a Key parameter, in which Key is the string name of the interface. For each operation on such an interface, two additional operations appear in the Pull<Interface Name> (Pull<Key>) version:

- Pull<operation name>
- Try<operation name>

For the Pull and Try variants of the operation, all the operation's In parameters appear in this variant as Out parameters.

When invoking Pull<operation>, the operation blocks until event data (coming from the Out parameters) is available.

When invoking Try<operation>, it has a Boolean result that indicates event availability. If there is event data, the result is true and the Out parameters contain event data. If there is no event data, the result is false and the Out parameters' content is up to the imagination.

17.2.5 Typed Event Channels

Everything operates much as you might expect, given the way the untyped service operates and the fact that this version conspires to exchange references to interfaces.

Five primary administration interfaces are useful in setting up typed event channels. The five interfaces are:

1. Typed Event Channel
2. Typed Consumer Administration
3. Typed Supplier Administration
4. Typed Proxy Pull Supplier
5. Typed Proxy Push Consumer

17.2.5.1 Typed Event Channel

The Typed Event Channel interface starts the setup or construction of typed channels.[2] Like the Event Channel, the Typed Event Channel supports three operations:

---

2. Again both factories of Typed Event Channels and finders are left to the imagination.

1. For Consumers
2. For Suppliers
3. Destroy

The For Consumers operation returns a reference to a Typed Consumer Administration interface. The For Suppliers operation returns an object reference to a Typed Supplier Administration interface. Destroy releases all resources of the Typed Event Channel.

17.2.5.2   Typed Consumer Administration

The Administration interfaces obtain appropriate proxies much as they did for the untyped, or generic, Event Channel. The Typed Consumer Administration interface has two operations:

1. Obtain Typed Pull Supplier
2. Obtain Typed Push Supplier

The Obtain Typed Pull Supplier operation returns a Typed Proxy Pull Supplier. The Obtain Typed Push Supplier operation returns only a Proxy Push Supplier.

Both operations take a single parameter, Key, which is a string identifying the name of the interface that suppliers and consumers conspire to use for these typed events. Note that for the Typed Proxy Pull Supplier, the Key is Pull<Key>.

The Typed Proxy Pull Supplier supports this interface (is a bearer of the interface Pull<Key>). The Pull Supplier supports the interface (is a bearer of this interface) for Pull Consumers. Pull Consumers may use the generic operations or the Pull<operation> as previously defined.

The Typed Push Supplier, on the other hand, uses the interface as given by <Key>, as opposed to the Pull<Key>. The Typed Push Supplier uses operations from this interface instead of the Push operations.

The Proxy Push Supplier only guarantees to invoke operations on this interface alone. It ignores all others, becoming a typed event filter.

17.2.5.3   Typed Supplier Administration

The Typed Supplier Administration interface supports two very similar operations:

1. Obtain Typed Push Consumer
2. Obtain Typed Pull Consumer

The Obtain Typed Push Consumer operation returns a Typed Proxy Push Consumer. The Obtain Typed Pull Consumer operation returns only a Proxy Pull Consumer.

Both operations take a single parameter, Key, a string identifying the name of the interface that suppliers and consumers conspire to use for these typed events. Note that for the Proxy Pull Consumer, the interface name in Key is Pull<Key>.

The Typed Proxy Push Consumer supports this interface (is a bearer of the interface Pull<Key>) for suppliers to invoke. The Pull Supplier supports the interface (is a bearer of this interface) for Pull Consumers.

The Proxy Pull Consumer, on the other hand, uses the interface as given by Pull<Key>, as opposed to the <Key> alone. The Proxy Pull Consumer uses operations from this interface instead of the generic Pull operations. The Proxy Pull Consumer only guarantees to invoke operations on this Pull<interface> alone. The Proxy Pull Consumer ignores all others, becoming a typed event filter.

17.2.5.4   *Typed Proxy Pull Supplier*

The Typed Proxy Pull Supplier interface has no operations. However, it supports the generic Pull and Try Pull operations as well as the Typed Pull operations (it inherits from both Proxy Pull Supplier and Type Pull Supplier). It also supports the connection and disconnection of Pull consumers, exactly as the generic event channel does.

17.2.5.5   *Typed Proxy Push Consumer*

The Typed Proxy Push Consumer interface has no operations. However, it supports the generic connection, disconnection, and Push operations as well as the Typed Push operations (it inherits from both Proxy Push Consumer and Type Push Consumer).

17.2.5.6   *Typed Push Consumer Interface*

The Typed Push Consumer interface supports a single operation, Get Typed Consumer.

The object reference result from the Get Typed Consumer operation supports the interface given as Key to the Typed Push Consumer interface's operation Obtain Typed Push Consumer (see Example 17-4).

The interface also may support the generic operations but they are not vital if only typed operations will be in use. In such cases, the operations may throw No Implementation.

17.2.5.7   *Typed Pull Supplier Interface*

The Typed Pull Supplier interface supports a single operation, Get Typed Supplier.

The Object reference result from the Get Typed Supplier operation supports the interface given as Key to the Typed Pull Supplier interface's operation Obtain Typed Pull Supplier (see Example 17-4).

The interface is of the form Pull<Key> with the extra operations for each generic operation (of the form Pull<operation name> and Try Pull<operation name>. As with the Typed Push Consumer, generic operations can throw a No Implementation exception on invocation of a generic operation.

EXAMPLE 17-4. **Typed Push Consumer and Typed Pull Supplier object interfaces**

```
#include    "CosEventComm.idl"

module CosTypedEventComm
{
    interface    TypedPushConsumer : CosEventComm::PushConsumer
    {
        Object  get_typed_consumer();
    };

    interface    TypedPullSupplier : CosEventComm::PullSupplier
    {
        Object  get_typed_supplier();
    };
};
```

CHAPTER 18

Life Cycle Service

> *Less is more.*
> —Mies van der Rohe

An object's life cycle runs from its creation until it is deleted or destroyed. In between, it may be cloned, replicated, or duplicated, or it may move. Life Cycle Services assist the client in conducting these types of operations if the object is willing; that is, if it is a Bearer or Audience of such services.

Life cycles include construction, destruction, copy, and move.

This raises a number of interesting questions in a CORBA environment. For instance,

- What does it mean to create a new object in an environment where you have only references to objects?
- What does *move* mean in a location-transparent environment?

The solution is economical.

Creation in a CORBA environment occurs through factories. One asks an appropriate factory to construct an object of a type fitting the current requirements. The Life Cycle Service also specifies an interface called a Factory Finder to help in the location of appropriate factories. Factories participate not only in the creation but also in the copying and moving of CORBA objects.

Creation occurs at a factory, and factory finders help locate appropriate factories.

In addition to the Factory Finder interface, the Life Cycle Service specifies the Life Cycle interface (supporting the operations Copy, Move, and Remove) and a Generic Factory interface.

The Life Cycle Object supports Copy, Move, and Remove.

The Generic Factory interface may be either a general creation service with which application implementations register or part of an implementation itself.

The basic Life Cycle Service declares the following three interfaces (see Example 18-1):

1. Factory Finder
2. Life Cycle Object
3. Generic Factory

EXAMPLE 18-1.   Life Cycle module

```
#include    "Naming.idl"

module  CosLifeCycle
{
    typedef     Naming::Naming     Key;
    typedef     Object             Factory;
    typedef     sequence<Factory>  Factories;
    typedef     struct NVP {
                    Naming::Istring name;
                    any             value;
                } NameValuePair;
    typedef     sequence<NameValuePair> Criteria;

    exception   NoFactory          { Key search_key };
    exception   NotCopyable        { string reason; };
    exception   NotMovable         { string reason; };
    exception   NotRemovable       { string reason; };
    exception   InvalidCriteria    { Criteria invalid_criteria; };
    exception   CannotMeetCriteria { Criteria unmet_criteria; };

    interface   FactoryFinder
    {
        Factories   find_factories(in Key factory_key)
            raises (NoFactory);
    };

    interface   LifeCycleObject
    {
        LifeCycleObject copy(
                        in FactoryFinder there,
                        in Criteria criteria)
            raises (NoFactory, NotCopyable, InvalidCriteria, CannotMeetCriteria);

        void    move(in FactoryFinder there, in Criteria the_criteria)
            raises (NoFactory, NotMovable, InvalidCriteria, CannotMeetCriteria);

        void    remove() raises (NotRemovable);
    };

    interface   GenericFactory
    {
        boolean     supports(in Key k);

        Object      create_object(in Key k, in Criteria the_criteria)
            raises (NoFactory, InvalidCriteria, CannotMeetCriteria);
    };
};
```

18.1 CREATION SERVICES

In any case, the general (anticipated) sequence of operation from a client's view is that the client will ask the factory finder to procure a list of factories. The Key is a name from the naming service (composed of 1 to *n* name components) and thus contains an ID and a Kind.

Clients query finders by name (ID and Kind).

The result of the Find is a sequence of factories, each supporting the Generic Factory's interface. The client may select one factory from the result and request that it create an object according to its criteria. Creation, therefore, takes place at a location that is within the scope of the factory (the location or set of locations where the factory may cause the creation of an object).

Finders return sequences of factories.

The location of such factories, wherever they may be, is the notion of *there* in operations such as Copy and Move. In other words, things can move or copy to locations within the scope of a factory.

Locations couple tightly to factory scope.

18.1.1 Factory Finder Interface

The Factory Finder interface supports a single operation, Find Factories. This operation returns a sequence of factories and takes a single parameter, Key, a CORBAservices Object Naming Service Name.

18.1.2 Generic Factory Interface

The Generic Factory offers a primitive Factory interface from which the construction of more interesting factories is straightforward.

The Create operation again takes a Key and an additional Criteria parameter that is similar to Key. Its content is implementation-specific; however, it is a Named Value Pair (a composition of a Name Component's name string and an Any value).

Creation's Criteria parameter has an implementation-specific content.

Because naming is the first OMG-defined location service, it is frequently applicable, such as in the Key. However, locations may resolve through traders (brokers) or through an interface or implementation repositories, since such things also may have names. This is the most flexible approach because the object naming service's design of Name objects is suitably lightweight so it need not impose much burden. Such Names are pseudo-objects specifically to make them as lightweight as is possible.

The Generic Factory interface supports two operations:

1. Supports
2. Create Object

18.1.2.1 Supports

The Supports operation returns a Boolean and takes a single parameter, Key, which is a Naming Service Name here, as elsewhere. If the factory supports the creation of objects of that Key type, the operation returns True; otherwise it returns False.

18.1.2.2   Create Object

The Create Object operation returns an object and takes two parameters:

1. Key
2. Criteria

The Key is an Object Naming Service Name. Criteria is a sequence of Name-Value Pairs. Name is a string, and Values are an Any. The Criteria's specification is an implementation detail.

One interesting note is that Name-Value Pairs may find an extension in the future that allows certain pairs opaque treatment, letting them pass through to other objects for evaluation.

The resulting object may be safely narrowed to the specific type necessary using the Type-Safe narrow operation.

18.2   COPY, MOVE, AND REMOVE SERVICES

Copy and Move work from here to there.

Copy, Move, and Remove are operations available from a Life Cycle object. Copy and Move semantically perform their operations from *here* to *there*. The *here* is implicit to both operations; the assumption is that the bearer's location is always the *here* part of the semantic. *There* is within the scope of a factory finder, which the operation receives as a parameter. In addition, both Copy and Move operations take a Criteria parameter (as did Create, defined previously).

Remove takes no parameters and returns no result. This facilitates the widest variety of semantics for Remove.

18.2.1   Life Cycle Object

The Life Cycle Object interface supports three operations:

1. Copy
2. Move
3. Remove

18.2.1.1   Copy

The Copy operation returns a Life Cycle Object and takes two parameters:

1. There
2. Criteria

Passing a Nil as There allows the object to determine the factory scope.

The There parameter is a Factory Finder location, meaning it is at a location of a factory as found by the finder using the criteria to locate such a factory.[1] Passing a Nil object as There allows the object to find its factory.

---

1. The specification states that the criteria is likely important to the factory, leaving it open for something other than the factory to also evaluate the criteria in a particular implementation. This applies to Move as well.

A copy of the bearer of the operation is made at the discovery location.

18.2.1.2   Move

The Move operation has no return result and takes two parameters:

1. There
2. Criteria

The There, to which the bearer object moves, is again the discovery location as found by the Factory Finder. Passing a Nil object as There allows the object to find its factory. The Criteria is the criteria the finder uses in locating such a factory.

The result of the operation is that the bearer relocates to the found factory's scope.

18.2.1.3   Remove

The Remove operation returns no result and takes no parameters. The net result is the releasing of resources for the Life Cycle Object. If the object does not wish to give up the ghost it should raise the Not Removable exception.

18.3   COMPOUND LIFE CYCLE

An addendum to the original specification is necessary for the support of object graphs as occurs with the CORBAservices Relationship Service. The Compound Life Cycle adds six new interfaces, reflecting its newer requirements:

Compound Life Cycle supports the life cycle of graphs.

1. Operations Factory
2. Operations
3. Node
4. Role
5. Relationship
6. Propagation Criteria Factory

In addition, there are three interfaces for Reference relationships and three for Containment relationships.

Graph relations include reference or containment.

18.3.1   Compound Life Cycle Interfaces

Since the general semantics of each of these operations are the same, the following sections cover the items that are unique to various interfaces. Containment and Reference are separate in the next section. Most of the other information necessary to this portion of the Life Cycle Service is in the Relationship Service or the Name Service.

A general summary is necessary to explain the important distinctions of the Compound Life Cycle to the general service.

Objects in a graph are nodes that may be roles.

Graph operations operate from starting node and traverse the graph.

Traversal information

Node and Role operations may occur to meet the operation's semantics.

The first distinction is that the general Life Cycle services reflect the client's view. Individual objects that are the bearers of these interfaces are the most likely to implement the operations.

Objects that are currently in relationships (as defined by the COS Relationship Services) are not individuals. Instead they are members of graphs. In these, the relationships are the edges of the graph while the objects are the nodes. Additionally, nodes may participate in the relationship as one or more roles.

When a client makes a Life Cycle request to an object that is participating in a graph, that object may choose to delegate the request to a bearer of the Compound Life Cycle interface services. It makes this request on an Operations interface. As part of the request, it passes in its Compound Life Cycle node as a parameter. This node becomes the starting node for graph traversal.

The Operations interface walks the graph, conducting the necessary requests to each relevant participant. (This may occur during a second pass through the graph, after all constituents were identified first.) It navigates the graph by obtaining a Graph Traversal object from the Relationship Service's Traversal Factory. Part of the request to create a Traversal object is a Traversal Criteria, also part of the Graph services.

During traversal, the nodes may be the first target of the operation underway (Copy, Move, or Remove). Role operations may occur at the same time as that of the nodes (Copy or Move, since Remove is in the Relationship Service). After nodes, it may act on the Relationships (Role operations may occur here as well, since roles define each relationship).

EXAMPLE 18-2. Compound Life Cycle—Operations Factory object interface

```
#include    <LifeCycle.idl>
#include    <Relationships.idl>
#include    <Graphs.idl>

module  CosCompoundLifeCycle
{
    interface    OperationsFactory;
    interface    Operations;
    interface    Node;
    interface    Role;
    interface    Relationship;
    interface    PropagationCriteriaFactory;

    enum    Operation { copy, move, remove };

    struct  RelationshipHandle
    {
        Relationship                          the_relationship;
        ::CosObjectIdentity::ObjectIdentifier constant_random_id;
    };

    interface  OperationsFactory
    {
        Operations  create_compound_operations();
    };
```

18.3.1.1   Operations Factory

The Operations Factory interface supports a single operation, Create Compound Operations, which takes no parameter and returns an Object reference to an Operations interface (see Example 18-2).

Note that it is likely that this factory is a discoverer of factory finders, and the immediate target for Copy and Move operations. The same methods of operation essentially hold for Compound and general Life Cycle objects.

18.3.1.2   Operations Interface

The Operations interface has four operations:

1. Copy
2. Move
3. Remove
4. Destroy

The first three operations operate on graphs of objects. Destroy releases the resources that the Operations object holds.

Copy, Move, and Remove all take a Compound Life Cycle node reference as their first parameter. This becomes the starting node for the traversal that Operations undertakes. Both Copy and Move take Life Cycle factory finders (the destination of the operation) and Criteria as their second and third parameters, respectively. The Criteria is from the general Life Cycle services.

18.3.1.3   Node Interface

The Node interface supports three operations (see Example 18-3):

1. Copy Node
2. Move Node
3. Remove Node

Copy Node takes four parameters:

1. An in Factory Finder
2. An in Criteria
3. An out New Node
4. An out sequence of Roles

Factory Finder is the immediate target of the Copy Node. Criteria is from the general services. The New Node is the copy. Nodes begin life alone, meaning they are not part of a relationship, and may participate in a variety of roles once they are in relationships. The sequence of roles is from the original Node (the source of the copy).

EXAMPLE 18-3. Compound Life Cycle—Operations and Node object interfaces

```
interface    Operations
{
    Node     copy(
                 in Node starting_node,
                 in ::CosLifeCycle::FactoryFinder there,
                 in ::CosLifeCycle::Criteria      the_criteria)
         raises (
             ::CosLifeCycle::NoFactory,
             ::CosLifeCycle::NotCopyable,
             ::CosLifeCycle::InvalidCriteria,
             ::CosLifeCycle::CannotMeetCriteria);

    void     move(
                 in Node starting_node,
                 in ::CosLifeCycle::FactoryFinder there,
                 in ::CosLifeCycle::Criteria      the_criteria)
         raises (
             ::CosLifeCycle::NoFactory,
             ::CosLifeCycle::NotCopyable,
             ::CosLifeCycle::InvalidCriteria,
             ::CosLifeCycle::CannotMeetCriteria);

    void     remove(in Node starting_node) raises (::CosLifeCycle::NotRemovable);

    void     destroy();
};

interface    Node: ::CosGraphs::Node
{
    exception    NotLifeCycleObject   {};

    void     copy_node(
                 in ::CosLifeCycle::FactoryFinder there,
                 in ::CosLifeCycle::Criteria the_criteria,
                 out Node new_node,
                 out Roles roles_of_new_node)
         raises (
             ::CosLifeCycle::NoFactory,
             ::CosLifeCycle::NotCopyable,
             ::CosLifeCycle::InvalidCriteria,
             ::CosLifeCycle::CannotMeetCriteria);

    void     move_node(
                 in ::CosLifeCycle::FactoryFinder there,
                 in ::CosLifeCycle::Criteria the_criteria)
         raises (
             ::CosLifeCycle::NoFactory,
             ::CosLifeCycle::NotCopyable,
             ::CosLifeCycle::InvalidCriteria,
             ::CosLifeCycle::CannotMeetCriteria);

    void     remove_node() raises (::CosLifeCycle::NotRemovable);

    ::CosLifeCycle::LifeCycleObject get_life_cycle_object()
         raises (NotLifeCycleObject);
};
```

Move Node takes two parameters:

1. Factory Finder
2. Criteria

Afterwards, the node and all its resources are in the scope of the Factory Finder given as the destination. No Node needs returning since the reference still points to the Node and no new one came into existence.

Remove Node takes no parameters and has no return. It releases resources the Node object is consuming.

18.3.1.4   Role Interface

The Role interface consists of three operations:

1. Copy Role
2. Move Role
3. Get Life Cycle Propagation Value

Copy and Move behave similarly. Each takes two parameters:

1. Factory Finder
2. Criteria

Copy returns a result, which is a reference to the new Role. Factory Finder and Criteria behave as they do in previous requests.

The Life Cycle Propagation operation returns a propagation value. The operation takes four parameters:

1. An in Operation
2. An in Relationship Handle
3. An in Role Name
4. An out Same For All

An Operation is an enum with three values:

1. Copy
2. Move
3. Remove

The operation returns a Propagation Value to the Role (the Role Name) for the life cycle Operation (enum) and the Relationship (a Relationship Handle). If the Role guarantees that all relationships it participates in have the same value, then the Boolean Same For All is set True; otherwise it is False.

The Relationship Handle is a structure containing a reference to the relationship and a Constant Random ID. An explanation of Constant Random IDs is in Chapter 16.

18.3.1.5   *Relationship Interface*

The Relationship interface has three operations:

1. Copy Relationship
2. Move Relationship
3. Get Life Cycle Propagation Value

These operations do for Relationships what the Role Interface operations do for Role.

The Copy Relationship operations return a reference to the new copy of the relationship. Both Copy and Move take the parameters Factory Finder and Criteria, which operate as they did for previous operations. Copy has an additional parameter as well, New Roles.

The copy of the relationship is the same as the original except that the Named Roles in the copy match those in the sequence New Roles.

The third operation returns the Propagation Value and takes four parameters:

1. Operation
2. From Role Name
3. To Role Name
4. Same For All

The result is the propagation value From Role Name to Role Name for the life cycle Operation (enum). Same For All is a Boolean. If the From Role Name guarantees that all propagation values are the same for all relationships in which it participates, Same For All is set True; otherwise it is False.

18.3.1.6   *Propagation Criteria Factory Interface*

The Propagation Criteria Factory interface (see Example 18-4) creates a Traversal Criteria for the Relationships service (its definition is there). The Graph Relationship service provides a Graph Traversal service that supports the registration of Traversal Criteria objects. The Graph Traversal service uses the Traversal Criteria object to obtain information necessary for conducting its traversal. The Graph Traversal service uses the object this factory creates for that purpose.

EXAMPLE 18-4. Role, Relationship, and Propagation Criteria Factory object interfaces

```
interface    Role : ::CosGraphs::Role
{
    Role    copy_role(
                in ::CosLifeCycle::FactoryFinder    there,
                in ::CosLifeCycle::Criteria         the_criteria)
        raises (
            ::CosLifeCycle::NoFactory,
            ::CosLifeCycle::NotCopyable,
            ::CosLifeCycle::InvalidCriteria,
            ::CosLifeCycle::CannotMeetCriteria);
```

```
        void    move_role(
                    in ::CosLifeCycle::FactoryFinder    there,
                    in ::CosLifeCycle::Criteria         the_criteria)
            raises (
                ::CosLifeCycle::NoFactory,
                ::CosLifeCycle::NotMovable,
                ::CosLifeCycle::InvalidCriteria,
                ::CosLifeCycle::CannotMeetCriteria);

        ::CosGraphs::PropagationValue life_cycle_propagation(
                    in Operation                    op,
                    in RelationshipHandle           rel,
                    in ::CosRelationships::RoleName to_role_name,
                    out boolean                     same_for_all);
    };

    interface   Relationship: :: CosRelationships::Relationship
    {
        Relationship    copy_relationship(
                    in ::CosLifeCycle::FactoryFinder    there,
                    in ::CosLifeCycle::Criteria         the_criteria,
                    in ::CosGraphs::NamedRoles          new_roles)
            raises (
                ::CosLifeCycle::NoFactory,
                ::CosLifeCycle::NotCopyable,
                ::CosLifeCycle::InvalidCriteria,
                ::CosLifeCycle::CannotMeetCriteria);

        void    move_relationship(
                    in ::CosLifeCycle::FactoryFinder    there,
                    in ::CosLifeCycle::Criteria         the_criteria)
            raises (
                ::CosLifeCycle::NoFactory,
                ::CosLifeCycle::NotMovable,
                ::CosLifeCycle::InvalidCriteria,
                ::CosLifeCycle::CannotMeetCriteria);

        ::CosGraphs::PropagationValue life_cycle_propagation(
                    in Operation op,
                    in ::CosRelationships::RoleName from_role_name,
                    in ::CosRelationships::RoleName to_role_name,
                    out boolean same_for_all);
    };

    interface   PropagationCriteriaFactory
    {
        ::CosGraphs::TraversalCriteria   create(in Operation op);
    };
};
```

This interface supports a single operation, Create. It returns a Graph
Relationship's Traversal Criteria and it takes a single parameter, Operation,
which is an enum indicating which operation the traversal is to occur on.

18.3.2   Containment Interfaces

Containment and Reference interfaces have no operations.

The Containment and References interfaces define no new operations. They mix in Life Cycle and Containment interfaces or Life Cycle and Reference interfaces. The Containment and References interfaces (see Example 18-5) from which these inherit are in the Relationship services.

EXAMPLE 18-5. Compound Life Cycle—Containment interfaces

```
#include     "Containment.idl"
#include     "CompoundLifeCycle.idl"

module  CosLifeCycleContainment
{
    interface    Relationship :
        ::CosCompoundLifeCycle::Relationship,
        ::CosContainment::Relationship
    {};

    interface    ContainsRole :
        ::CosCompoundLifeCycle::Role,
        ::CosContainment::ContainsRole
    {};

    interface    ContainedInRole :
        ::CosCompoundLifeCycle::Role,
        ::CosContainment::ContainedInRole
    {};
};
```

One of their primary purposes is to establish semantics for the value returned from the Get Life Cycle Propagation Value operations shown in the following tables. There are three Containment interfaces:

1. Relationship
2. Contains Role
3. Contained in Role

The Contains Role operation Life Cycle propagation returns the values for operations shown in Table 18-1. The Contained in Role operation Life Cycle propagation returns the values for operations shown in Table 18-2.

TABLE 18-1. Propagation from Contains to Contained

Operation	Propagation from Contains Role to Contained in Role
copy	deep
move	deep
remove	deep

TABLE 18-2. **Propagation from Contained to Contains**

Operation	Propagation from Contained Role to Contains Role
copy	shallow
move	shallow
remove	shallow

18.3.3   Reference Interfaces

There are three Reference interfaces (see Example 18-6):

1. Relationship
2. References Role
3. Referenced by Role

The References Role operation Life Cycle propagation returns the values for operations shown in Table 18-3. The Referenced by Role operation Life Cycle propagation returns the values for operations shown in Table 18-4.

EXAMPLE 18-6. **Compound Life Cycle—Relationship, References Role, Referenced by Role object interfaces**

```
#include    "Reference.idl"
#include    "CompoundLifeCycle.idl"

module  CosLifeCycleReference
{
    interface   Relationship :
        ::CosCompoundLifeCycle::Relationship,
        ::CosReference::Relationship
    {};

    interface   ReferencesRole :
        ::CosCompoundLifeCycle::Role,
        ::CosReference::ReferencesRole
    {};

    interface   ReferencedByRole :
        ::CosCompoundLifeCycle::Role,
        ::CosReference::ReferencedByRole
    {};
};
```

TABLE 18-3. Propagation from References to Referenced By

Operation	Propagation from References Role to Referenced By Role
copy	shallow
move	shallow
remove	shallow

TABLE 18-4. Propagation from Referenced By to References

Operation	Propagation from Referenced By Role to References Role
copy	none
move	shallow
remove	shallow

CHAPTER 19 *Object Query Service*

> *Never dismiss as obvious any fundamental principle,*
> *for it is only through conscious application of such*
> *principles that success will be achieved.*
> —David Gries

The Object Query Service (OQS) provides predicate-based query capability for ORB objects. The queries may be directed to a single object or collections of objects. The response may return a single object or collections of objects. Because the OQS specification predates the CORBAservices Collection Service, it specifies a minimalist service for Collections.

The query service is designed to leverage existing declarative languages including predicates. Its design also allows one to query arbitrary values and operations, invoking various ORB services. The design includes the nesting and federating of services of various resource managers, so it can assume data-warehousing-style query capabilities.

Although the OQS design is intentionally Query Language (QL) independent, there is no exact match between the primary standards. However, the OQS specification for querying draws heavily from ANSI SQL-92 Query and ODMG's OQL-93. In addition, the ongoing ANSI X3H2 (the committee working on adding object capabilities to SQL3) and ODMG are collaborating in order to merge the variations and remove differences. The ODMG OQL-93 is very similar to the SQL-92. That coupled with X3H2's agreement to work with ODMG to make SQL a superset of OQL at least appears to be moving forward correctly.

OQS draws on ANSI SQL and ODMG OQL.

Meanwhile, the OQS specification states that providers of OQS should base their system on at least one of the standards—SQL-92 Query or OQL-93—to be compatible.[1]

The OQS specifies two services, the Query Collection service and the Query service.

---

1. However, this is left to the implementer to decide; the exact details are in the Object Management Group's specification.

19.1   GENERAL OPERATION AND NESTING

Queries are made to an evaluator and provide the combined result to the client.

The typical scenario is a client making requests. These requests are made to a Query Evaluator that processes the request. In processing the request, it may interact with an object, which could be some other query system (not OQS), or another Query Evaluator. In processing a request, the Query Evaluator evaluates the query predicate and may perform operations on objects through that object's published interface. When a Query Evaluator combines all of its results, it returns that result back to its caller.

Query Evaluators may be arranged hierarchically.

A client may query a Query Evaluator, which in turn queries a Collection. Such a Collection is known as a Queryable Collection and inherits from both Collection and Query Evaluator. The Queryable Collection is an object that is a Query Evaluator. The Queryable Collection must evaluate its query and in processing may perform still other operations, and so on, ad infinitum. This nesting may be arbitrarily deep.

The Query Evaluator may act as a front-end to some other non-OQS query service. It may translate the request into terms or operations that the foreign service comprehends. In doing this, the Evaluator is free to leverage as much of the other implementation as it deems necessary. This is particularly useful when the foreign service is optimized for a special type of query or service.

The OQS includes interfaces that create and manipulate collections of objects. A queryable collection is the scope to which a Query applies and may be the result. Collections themselves include interfaces to manipulate members (elements). They may be homogenous or arbitrarily heterogeneous, and are not limited to type extents. Collections may map onto foreign collections (non-OQS collections).

In addition, collections can create iterators that help manipulate members. The iterators provide standard interfaces for navigation through collections regardless of their size, composition, management, distribution, or heterogeneity. Such common interfaces make databases such as data marts or data warehouses into reality.

A side effect, however, results from the specialization that the combination of nesting and collection-as-scope provide. A collection could be asked to add some arbitrary object that it knew nothing about. So collections may choose to not do so when the arbitrary object is outside of its scope. If collections had to add any arbitrary object as a member, they could not specialize and would require general-purpose Query Evaluators, losing the benefits of the current nesting design.

19.1.1   Type Extents and Extensibility

Each language has its own type extent. IDL, SQL-92, and OQL-93 all have some differences in the types they support. So do the languages for which IDL mappings are defined, such as C, C++, Smalltalk, and Ada-95. SQL-92

Query defines language bindings for Ada, C, COBOL, Fortran, Mumps, Pascal, and PL/I. OQL-93 bindings exist for C++ and Smalltalk.

The Query Collection Service module contains IDL definitions for mapping the data types of SQL-92 and OQL-93. Without going into all of the detail, the module defines a Value union of all of these data types and declares a Value Type enum that is used as the union's discriminator. So in many instances, an Any may continue an `Any::value` of the Value union. The following list describes the types[2] this union supports[3]:

Query Collection Service has IDL for mapping data types to SQL-92 and OQL-93.

- Boolean
- Char
- Octet
- Short
- UShort
- Long
- ULong
- Float
- Double
- String
- Object
- Any
- Small Int
- Integer
- Real
- Double Precision
- Character
- Decimal
- Numeric

In addition to these data types, the module also defines IDL for Field Value and Record to assist in the mapping of Query Collections onto relational systems.

Specializing the Query Collection into a variety of collections is possible. For example, the specification mentions ANSI C++ Standard Template Library (STL), ODMG's set, list, bag, and varray, as well as variations of relational collections.

19.2   QUERY COLLECTION SERVICE

The Query Collection Service defines Queryable Collections. It is composed of three interfaces (see Examples 19-1 and 19-2):

1. Collection Factory
2. Collection
3. Iterator

---

2. Assume that these types will be extended with the new set of IDL types, for example, longlong.

3. See the code in the CosQueryCollection module to see their IDL mappings.

EXAMPLE 19-1.   OQS—Collection Factory object interface

```
module  CosQueryCollection
{
    exception   ElementInvalid  {};
    exception   IteratorInvalid {};
    exception   PositionInvalid {};

    enum    ValueType { TypeBoolean, TypeChar, TypeOctet,
                TypeShort, TypeUShort, TypeLong, TypeULong,
                TypeFloat, TypeDouble, TypeString, TypeObject,
                TypeAny, TypeSmallInt, TypeInteger, TypeReal,
                TypeDoublePrecision, TypeCharacter, TypeDecimal,
                TypeNumeric };
    struct  Decimal
    {
        long      precision;
        long      scale;
        sequence<octet> value;
    };
    union Value switch (ValueType)
    {
        case TypeBoolean:         boolean b;
        case TypeChar:            char c;
        case TypeOctet:           octet o;
        case TypeShort:           short s;
        case TypeUShort:          unsigned short us
        case TypeLong:            long l;
        case TypeULong:           unsigned long ul;
        case TypeFloat:           float f;
        case TypeDouble:          double d;
        case TypeString:          string str;
        case TypeObject           Object obj;
        case TypeAny:             any a;
        case TypeSmallInt:        short si;
        case TypeInteger:         long I
        case TypeReal:            float r;
        case TypeDoublePrecision: double dp;
        case TypeCharacter:       string ch;
        case TypeDecimal:         Decimal dec;
        case TypeNumeric:         Decimal n;
    };

    typedef     boolean     Null;
    union   FieldValue switch (Null)
    {
        case false: Value    v;
    };
    typedef     sequence<FieldValue>     Record;

    typedef     string Istring;
    struct      NVPair {Istring name; any value; };
    typedef     sequence<NVPair>     ParameterList;

    interface   Collection;
    interface   Iterator;

    interface   CollectionFactory
    {
        Collection  create(in ParameterList params);
    };
```

EXAMPLE 19-2.   QOS—Collection and Iterator object interfaces

```
interface   Collection
{
    readonly    attribute   long    cardinality;

    void    add_element(in any element) raises (ElementInvalid);
    void    add_all_elements(in Collection elements) raises (ElementInvalid);

    void    insert_element_at(in any element, in Iterator where)
        raises (IteratorInvalid, ElementInvalid);

    void    replace_element_at(in any element, in Iterator where)
        raises (IteratorInvalid, PositionInvalid, ElementInvalid);

    void    remove_element_at(in Iterator where)
        raises (IteratorInvalid, PositionInvalid, ElementInvalid);
    void    remove_all_elements();

    any    retrieve_element_at(in Iterator where)
        raises (IteratorInvalid, PositionInvalid);

    Iterator    create_iterator();
};

interface   Iterator
{
    any    next() raises (IteratorInvalid, PositionInvalid);

    void    reset();

    boolean more();
};
};
```

19.2.1   Collection Factory Interface

The Collection Factory has a single operator, Create.

19.2.1.1   Create

Create returns a Collection and takes one parameter, Parameter List, which is
a sequence of Name-Value Pairs. The Name-Value Pair is a structure with two
members:

1. Name—a string
2. Value—an Any

One of the Name-Value Pairs must have a pair with the members set as:

```
"initial_size" for Name; and
a Value of type long
```

This Value indicates to the Factory the "estimate" or best-guess about the number of elements in the Collection.

A Collection starts out empty but grows dynamically (if required) in size and elements. Other parameters in the Parameter List may include hints for such things as indexing, ordering, and so forth.

19.2.2   Collection Interface

The Collection interface has one read-only attribute, Cardinality, and eight operations:

1. Add Element
2. Add All Elements
3. Insert Element At
4. Replace Element At
5. Remove Element At
6. Remove All Elements
7. Retrieve Element At
8. Create Iterator

The Cardinality attribute describes the maximum cardinality of the Collection, in other words, the maximum number of Elements in the collection set.

Except for Create Iterator, all the operations manipulate Elements in the Collection. An Element (singular) is always an Any. Elements (plural) are always Collections.

19.2.2.1   *Add Element*

The Add Element request has no result and takes one parameter, an Element. It adds it to the Collection in an undefined order.

In almost all cases, after adding, inserting, or removing elements, the behavior of all extant iterator instances is undefined.

As was mentioned previously (as a side effect of nesting and scope), the Collection may choose to raise an Element Invalid exception if it chooses not to add the element (decides it is out of scope).

19.2.2.2   *Add All Elements*

Add All Elements has no result and takes a Collection as a parameter. It adds all of the Elements in the Collection parameter to its Collection in iterator order from the source Collection. The destination Collection's iterators are undefined. An Element Invalid exception may be raised the same as for Add Element.

19.2.2.3   *Insert Element At*

The insert Element At request has no result and takes two parameters:

1. Element
2. Iterator

The Element is an Any and will be inserted to the Collection at the location to which the Iterator currently points. All extant Iterators (except the one used in the operation) become undefined. An Element Invalid exception may be raised the same as for Add Element.

19.2.2.4 *Replace Element At*

The Replace Element At operation exhibits behavior similar to Insertion. Replace Element At has no result and takes two parameters:

1. Element
2. Iterator

The Element is an Any and will replace the one in the Collection at the location to which the Iterator currently points. An Element Invalid exception may be raised the same as for Add Element.

19.2.2.5 *Remove Element At*

The Remove Element At operation has no result and takes one parameter, Iterator. This operation removes the Element from the Collection to which Iterator currently points. The behavior of all extant Iterator instances for this Collection is undefined.

19.2.2.6 *Remove All Elements*

The Remove All Elements operation has no result and no parameters. This operation removes all Elements from the Collection. The behavior of all extant Iterators for this Collection is undefined.

19.2.2.7 *Retrieve Element At*

The Retrieve Element At request returns an Element (an Any) and takes an Iterator as a parameter. The operation returns the Element to which the Iterator points.

19.2.2.8 *Create Iterator*

The Create Iterator operation takes no parameters and returns an Iterator. The resulting Iterator points to the first of the Collection.

19.2.3 Iterator Interface

The Iterator interface has three operations:

1. Next
2. Reset
3. More

None of these operations takes parameters.

19.2.3.1 Next

The Next operation advances the Iterator by one Element and returns the new Element (as an Any). If the Iterator does not point to an Element it raises a Position Invalid exception.

19.2.3.2 Reset

Reset sets the Iterator to point to the first of the Collection. It has no result.

19.2.3.3 More

More returns a Boolean, true if there are more Elements and false if not.

19.3 QUERY SERVICE

The OQS specification defines:

- Query Language Types
- Query Evaluators
- Queryable Collections
- Query Managers
- Query Objects

19.3.1 Query Language Types

A set of seven interfaces describes the base set of Query Language Types that interact in this service.

The Query Language Type includes the seven interfaces, as shown in Figure 19-1. This type graph is for the OQS provider to create its own Interface type for its Query Language. The language is expected to inherit from one of the leaves: SQL-92 Query, OQL-93, or OQL-93 Basic.

For instance, if a provider supports a proprietary Object Query, which supports SQL-92 and OQL-93 Basic, their language interface declaration would appear as (see Example 19-3):

```
interface  ObjectQuery : SQL_92Query, OQL_93Basic {  };
```

19.3.2 Query Evaluator Interface

The Query Evaluator interface has two read-only attributes and a single operation. The attributes are:

- QL Type
- Default QL

The operation is Evaluate.

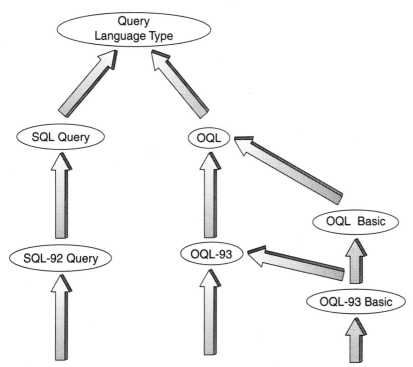

FIGURE 19-1. Query Language Types

EXAMPLE 19-3. QOS—Query Module

```
module  CosQuery
{
    exception    QueryInvalid              { string why; };
    exception    QueryProcessingError      { string why; };
    exception    QueryTypeInvlaid          {};

    enum    QueryStatus { complete, incomplete };

    typedef    CosQueryCollection::ParameterList    ParameterList;
    typedef    CORBA::InterfaceDef QLType;

    interface    QueryLanguageType                  {};
    interface    SQLQuery : QueryLanguageType        {};
    interface    SQL_92Query : SQLQuery              {};
    interface    OQL : QueryLanguageType             {};
    interface    OQLBasic : OQL                      {};
    interface    OQL_93 : OQL                        {};
    interface    OQL_93Basic : OQL_93, OQLBasic      {};

    interface    QueryEvaluator
    {
        readonly    attribute    sequence<QLType> ql_types;
        readonly    attribute    QLType default_ql_types;
```

```
    any     evaluate(
                        in string query,
                        in QLType ql_type,
                        in ParameterList params)
                    raises (QueryTypeInvalid, QueryInvalid, QueryProcessingError);
};

interface   QueryableCollection : QueryEvaluator, CosQueryCollection::Collection
{
};

interface   QueryManager: QueryEvaluator
{
    Query   create(in string query, in QLType ql_type, in ParameterList params)
        raises (QueryTypeInvalid, QueryInvalid);
};

interface   Query
{
    readonly    attribute   QueryManager    query_manager;

    void    prepare(in ParameterList params) raises (QueryProcessingError);

    void    execute(in ParameterList params) raises (QueryProcessingError);

    QueryStatus get_status();

    any     get_result();
};
};
```

The first attribute is a sequence of QL Types that the Query Evaluator interface supports. A QL Type is an Interface Definition[4] for a Query Language Type interface. The second attribute is the default QL Type.

19.3.2.1 *Evaluate*

The Evaluate operation returns an Any and takes three parameters:

1. Query string
2. QL Type
3. Parameter List

The Query is a string, as opposed to an instance of the Query object. QL Type is the QL to use for this evaluation. Parameter List, as defined for the Query Collection Service, is a sequence of Name-Value Pairs.

The operation evaluates the query and performs all processing necessary. If the QL Type is null, the operation assumes the default QL Type for query processing.

The resulting Any may have a Collection or a subtype, an Object, or any data type.

---

4. That is of type `InterfaceDef`.

19.3.3   Queryable Collection Interface

The Queryable Collection interface derives from both Query Evaluator and Query Collection. It does not introduce any new operations.

19.3.4   Query Manager Interface

The Query Manager specializes the Query Evaluator interface. It has a single operation adding the ability to create Query objects to its behavior. Its single operation is Create.

19.3.4.1   Create

The Create operation returns a Query object and takes three parameters:

1. Query string
2. QL Type
3. Parameter List

These parameters are the same as those defined for the Evaluate operation on the Query Evaluator.

19.3.5   Query Object Interface

The Query interface consists of one read-only attribute and four operations. The single attribute identifies the Query's Query Manager. The attribute is a Query Manager. The four operations on the Query object are:

1. Prepare
2. Execute
3. Get Status
4. Get Result

19.3.5.1   Prepare

Prepare has no result and takes a single parameter, Parameter List. This operation provides a window in which things such as preprocessing or query optimization may take place. Such preparation may occur as a collaboration between the Query and its Query Manager.

19.3.5.2   Execute

Execute also has no result and takes a single parameter, Parameter List.

The specification makes no claims about the relationship of the Parameter List for this operation and that which is a parameter to Prepare. It does, however, state that if the Execute request occurs on a Query before preparation occurs, it will prepare and then execute the Query.

Query execution also may be a collaboration by Query and the Query Manager.

19.3.5.3   *Get Status*

Get Status takes no parameters and returns a Query Status. Query Status is an enum with two values:

1. Complete
2. Incomplete

19.3.5.4   *Get Result*

Get Result takes no parameters and returns an Any, which is the result of the query.

CHAPTER 20 *Properties Service*

Know the properties of the objects that
are to be manipulated by a program.
—David Gries

The Object Properties Service (OPS) provides a way to associate objects with typed, Name-Value Pairs. Such information acts much like an object's attributes, in that they have Get and Set operations. Properties also have operations to dynamically add and delete properties. Attributes do not. They do not change an object's type; in fact, an object is not aware of its properties.[1]

Properties are like attributes, but may be transient.

Properties are a sequence of type Property. A Property is a structure that consists of a Name—given as a string—and a Value—given as an Any. The interfaces in OPS deal with Properties; that is, always as sequences of type Property. The interfaces make their objects distinct by referring to them as Property Sets, which is reflected in both interface names as well as operation names.

Properties are lists of typed Named-Value Pairs.

A specialization of a Property Set is available through a Property Set definition.[2] This object is a name-value-mode triple. Modes are a characteristic of a Property (stating its mutation characteristics).

Property Set Definitions are Properties with modes.

The association of object to its properties is cited as an implementation detail. An obvious mechanism to make such an association would be by using the Object Relationship Service.

20.1 THE OPS INTERFACE

The OPS supports six interfaces (see Example 20-1):

1. Property Set Factory
2. Property Set Definition Factory
3. Property Set
4. Property Set Definition
5. Property Iterator
6. Property Names Iterator

---

1. An object's type is declared by its interface. Interfaces are composed of operations and attributes. The property is an association outside of the interface and, therefore, does not change the object's type.
2. I use Definition even though the actual name is PropertySetDef.

EXAMPLE 20-1.   Property Service data types

```
module  CosPropertyService
{
    typedef string  PropertyName;

    struct  Property
    {
        PropertyName    property_name;
        any             property_value;
    };

    struct  PropertyDef
    {
        PropertyName        property_name;
        any                 property_value;
        PropertyModeType    property_mode;
    };

    struct  PropertyMode
    {
        PropertyName        property_name;
        PropertyModeType    property_mode;
    };

    typedef sequence<PropertyName>  PropertyNames;
    typedef sequence<Property>      Properties;
    typedef sequence<PropertyDef>   PropertyDefs;
    typedef sequence<PropertyMode>  PropertyModes;
    typedef sequence<TypeCode>      PropertyTypes;

    interface   PropertyNameIterator;
    interface   PropertiesIterator;
    interface   PropertySetFactory;
    interface   PropertySet;

    exception   ConstraintNotSupported  {};
    exception   InvalidPropertyName      {};
    exception   ConflictingProperty      {};
    exception   PropertyNotFound         {};
    exception   UnsupportedTypeCode       {};
    exception   UnsupportedProperty      {};
    exception   UnsupportedMode          {};
    exception   FixedProperty            {};
    exception   ReadOnlyProperty         {};

    enum ExceptionReason
    {
        invalid_property_name, conflicting_property,
        property_not_found, unsupported_type_code,
        unsupported_property, unsupported_mode,
        fixed_property, read_only_property
    };

    struct  PropertyException
    {
        ExceptionReason     reason;
        PropertyName        failing_property_name;
    };
    typedef sequence<PropertyException> PropertyExceptions;
```

```
exception MultipleExceptions
{
    PropertyExceptions exceptions;
};
```

20.1.1   Property Set Factory Interface

The Property Set Factory has three operations, all of which return Property Sets:

1. Create Property Set
2. Create Constrained Property Set
3. Create Initial Property Set

20.1.1.1   *Create Property Set*

Create Property Set takes no parameters. The specification says that the state of such a Property Set is an implementation detail; that is, if it is initialized to some value or null, or if it is constrained.

20.1.1.2   *Create Constrained Property Set*

Create Constrained Property Set is an operation that takes two parameters:

1. Property Types
2. Properties

These parameters are used to constrain the Property Set such that the result may only contain Properties that have the characteristics of the parameters.

Property Types is a sequence of Type Codes and constrains the types of values in the Properties of the result Property Set. Properties is the sequence of Property structures and constrains the Properties that are allowable. The modes associated with this set are an implementation detail.

20.1.1.3   *Create Initial Property Set*

Create Initial Property Set takes one parameter, Initial Properties. This parameter is a sequence of Property structures and initializes the resulting Property Set to contain those Properties.

20.1.2   Property Set Definition Factory Interface

The Property Set Definition Factory interface (see Example 20-2) is much like the Property Set Factory interface, in that it has three operations, all of which return Property Set Definitions:

1. Create Property Set Definition
2. Create Constrained Property Set Definition
3. Create Initial Property Set Definition

EXAMPLE 20-2. Property Factories and Property Set interface

```
interface    PropertySetFactory
{
    PropertySet      create_propertyset( );

    PropertySet      create_constrained_propertyset(
                    in PropertyTypes   allowed_property_types,
                    in Properties      allowed_properties)
        raises (ConstraintNotSuppported);

    PropertySet      create_initial_propertyset(
                    in Properties      initial_properties)
        raises (MultipleExceptions);

};

interface    PropertySetDefFactory
{
    PropertySetDef  create_propertysetdef( );

    PropertySetDef  create_constrained_propertysetdef(
                    in PropertyTypes   allowed_property_types,
                    in Properties      allowed_properties)
        raises (ConstriantNotSupported);

    PropertySetDef  create_initial_propertysetdef(
                    in Properties      initial_properties)
        raises (MultipleExceptions);
};

interface    PropertySet
{
    void    define_property(
            in PropertyName   property_name,
            in any            property_value)
        raises (InvalidPropertyName, ConflictingProperty, UnsupportedTypeCode
            UnsupportedProperty, ReadOnlyProperty);

    void    define_properties(
            in Properties    nproperties)
        raises (MultipleExceptions);

    void    get_all_property_names(
            in unsigned long           how_many,
            out PropertyNames          property_names,
            out PropertyNamesIterator  rest);

    void    get_property_value(
            in PropertyName   property_name
        raises (PropertyNotFound, InvalidPropertyName);

    boolean get_properties(
            in PropertyNames      property_names,
            out Properties        nproperties);

    void    get_all_properties(
            in unsigned long           how_many,
            out Properties             nproperties,
            out PropertiesIterator     rest);
```

```
      void    delete_properties(
                  in PropertyName     property_name)
         raises (PropertyNotFound, InvalidPropertyName, FixedProperty);

   boolean delete_all_properties( );

   boolean is_property_defined(
               in PropertyName     property_name)
         raises (InvalidPropertyName);
   };

   interface   PropertySetDef : PropertySet
   {
      void    get_allowed_property_types(out PropertyTypes property_types);

      void    get_allowed_properties(out propertyDefs property_defs);

      void    define_property_with_mode(
                  in PropertyName property_name,
                  in any property_value,
                  in PropertyModeType property_mode)
           raises (
                       InvalidPropertyName,
                       ConflictingProperty,
                       UnsupportedTypeCode,
                       UnsupportedProperty,
                       UnsupportedMode,
                       ReadOnlyProperty);

      void    define_properties_with_modes(in PropertyDefs property_defs)
           raises (MultipleExceptions);

      PropertyModeType    get_property_mode(in PropertyName property_name)
           raises (PropertyNotFound, InvalidPropertyName);

      boolean     get_property_modes(
                     in PropertyNames property_names,
                     out PropertyModes property_modes);

      void    set_property_mode(
                  in PropertyName property_name,
                  in PropertyModeType property_mode)
           raises (InvalidProperty, PropertyNotFound, UnsupportedMode);

      void    set_property_modes(in PropertyModes property_modes)
           raises (MultipleExceptions);
   };

   interface   PropertyNamesIterator
   {
      void      reset();
      boolean   next_one(out PropertyName property_name);
      boolean   next_n( in unsigned long how_many, out PropertyNames property_names );
      void      destroy();
   };
```

```
interface   PropertiesIterator
{
    void        reset();
    boolean     next_one(out Property aproperty);
    boolean     next_n(in unsigned long how_many, out Properties nproperties);
    void        destroy();
};
};
```

A Property Set Definition is a structure of three members:

1. Property Name—same as for Property, a string
2. Value—same as for Property, an Any
3. Property Mode Type

The Property Mode Type is an enum with five defined values:

1. *Normal*—no restrictions apply; a client may change values or delete the Property.
2. *Read-Only*—a client may only get the Property's state but is allowed to delete the Property.
3. *Fixed Normal*—a client may change values but may not delete the Property.
4. *Fixed Read-Only*—a client may only get the Property's state. It may not be deleted.
5. *Undefined*—a special case that signifies a Property is not found during a multiple get mode operation. Attempting to set this mode for a Property raises an Unsupported Mode exception.

20.1.2.1   *Create Property Set Definition*

Create Property Set Definition takes no parameters. The initial state of the resulting Property Set Definition is an implementation detail.

20.1.2.2   *Create Constrained Property Set Definition*

Create Constrained Property Set Definition takes a Property Types parameter (a sequence of Type Codes) and a Property Definitions parameter (the plural indicates a sequence of Property Definition structures). The resulting Property Set Definition has both constraints and modes set.

20.1.2.3   *Create Initial Property Set Definition*

Create Initial Property Set Definition takes a single parameter, a sequence of property definition structures. The result has Properties, constraints, and modes initialized.

20.1.3   Property Set Interface

The Property Set interface has 11 operations:

1. Define Property
2. Define Properties
3. Get Number of Properties
4. Get All Property Names
5. Get Property Value
6. Get Properties
7. Get All Properties
8. Delete Property
9. Delete Properties
10. Delete All Properties
11. Is Property Defined

20.1.3.1   Define Property

Define Property adds or mutates a Property to the Property Set. This operation returns no result and takes two parameters:

1. Name—the string name of the Property
2. Value—an Any that contains the Value of the Property

If the Property already exists, this operation checks the Type Code of the Value parameter to make sure it is correct. If it is correct, then the existing Property's Value is overwritten.

   To change a Property Value's Type Code, Delete Property must delete the Property. Then use the Define Property request with the same Name and the new Value (new Any).

20.1.3.2   Define Properties

The Define Properties operation takes a sequence of Properties as its parameter. It has no result. This operation adds new Properties or modifies those that already exist. It makes similar checks to Define Property.

   This is considered a batch operation. In OPS, such operations raise the Multiple Exceptions exception if any individual Define fails.

   A side note on so-called batch commands may be appropriate here. The batch commands generally operate on a set, a batch or bunch of things such as names, properties, property definitions, or modes). The specification points out that such operations are not atomic. Actually, I'd say the failure is not atomic. Essentially a batch operation applies itself to every member in the set even if one or more of the operations normally would raise an exception.

   Instead of failing and stopping, the operation accumulates exceptions and then raises an exception named Multiple Exceptions after application to each set member. The specification does not indicate that a batch command encountering only a single failure will raise the more specific exception, so I assume it is still a Multiple Exception. Either way, in order to determine exactly what failure occurred, you need to examine each possible set member individually.

20.1.3.3   Get Number of Properties

The Get Number of Properties operation returns an unsigned long indicating the number of properties in this property set.

20.1.3.4   Get All Property Names

The Get All Property Names operation has no result and takes three parameters:

1. How Many
2. Property Names
3. Property Name iterator

How Many is an in unsigned long indicating the size of the sequence of Property Names. Property Names is an out sequence of (up to How Many) Property Names. Property Name iterator is an out iterator that can access any remaining names if there are more than what is given in How Many. The iterator is null if there are no additional Property Names.

20.1.3.5   Get Property Value

The Get Property Value operation takes a Name parameter and returns an Any.

20.1.3.6   Get Properties

The Get Properties operation takes two parameters:

1. Property Names
2. Properties

Property Names is an in sequence of Names of the Properties to return.

Properties is an out sequence of property structures that the Name lookup found. The operation returns a Boolean. True indicates that a Property was found for each Name. False indicates that one or more Names did not match a Property or were not valid Names. Such a failure still returns a corresponding property, but the Values Type Code is set to `tk_void`.

To determine whether a resulting Property with a `tk_void` value is valid or an indication of error, a Get Property by name is necessary for each such Property. If the Property is invalid, this operation will raise an exception.

20.1.3.7   Get All Properties

Get All Properties takes three parameters:

1. How Many
2. Properties
3. Properties iterator

How Many is an in unsigned long that indicates the size of the sequence of Properties.

Properties is an out sequence of (up to How Many) Property structures.

Properties iterator is an out iterator that can access any remaining Property structures if there are more than what is given in How Many. The iterator is null if there are no additional Property structures.

20.1.3.8   Delete Property and Delete Properties

These two operations are virtually identical. The first, Delete Property, takes a single Property Name, and the second a sequence of Property Names. The basic difference is that the second is a batch command and, therefore, can raise the Multiple Exception on an error.

20.1.3.9   Delete All Properties

The Delete All Properties operation is slightly different from the preceding two because it returns a Boolean. The Boolean for this operation is similar to the one for Get Properties.

Here a False indicates that some of the Properties had a Fixed Mode and so they cannot be deleted. If the exact cause of the failure is necessary, then you can count what is left (Get Number of Properties) for the out sequence of Names, Get All Property Names, and then Delete Property for each Name.

20.1.3.10   Is Property Defined

This operation takes a Name parameter and returns a Boolean if the Name matches a current member of the Property Set.

20.1.4   Property Set Definition Interface

The Property Set Definition interface inherits from the Property Set interface. It adds operations to get constraints, get and set modes, and define properties with modes.

As a side effect, if you have a Property Set that returns False to a Delete All Properties request and if it happens that the Property Set is really a Property Set Definition Object, you can narrow it, change the modes if they failed because some were set as Fixed, and then delete the Properties.

The Property Set Definition interface also has the notion of batch commands that raise a Mixed Exception.

The Property Set Definition interface supports eight operations:

1. Get Allowed Property Types
2. Get Allowed Properties
3. Define Property With Mode
4. Define Properties With Modes
5. Get Property Mode
6. Get Property Modes
7. Set Property Mode
8. Set Property Modes

20.1.4.1   *Get Allowed Property Types*

This operation takes a single parameter, an out sequence of Property Types. It returns no result.

The sequence is a list of all Property Types (Type Codes) that constrain this Property Set. If the out parameter is empty, there are no Property Type constraints set. However, if Properties are constrained, the Types are indirectly constrained to be the same as the allowed Properties. This operation does not report those.

20.1.4.2   *Get Allowed Properties*

Get Allowed Properties takes a single parameter, an out sequence of Property Definitions. It returns no result.

The sequence is a list of all supported Property Definitions. If it is empty, then no constraints exist unless the set's Property Types are under constraint.

20.1.4.3   *Define Property With Mode*

The Define Property With Mode adds to or modifies the Property Definitions in the Set. The operation has no result but it takes three parameters:

1. Property Name
2. Property Value
3. Property Mode

On invocation, the operation checks to determine if the Property already exists. If it does and if its Mode is such that it can be overwritten, then it overwrites it. If such a Property does not already exist, it is added to the Set.

20.1.4.4   *Define Properties With Modes*

This is a batch operation that takes a sequence of Property Definition structures as input. It effectively modifies on a match or adds on no match for each Property Definition in the sequence.

One or more failures raises the exception, Multiple Exceptions. If more information is a requirement then each will require separate definition via the previously mentioned operation.

20.1.4.5   Get and Set for Mode and Modes

All four of these operations are fairly obvious. Get Mode takes a Property Name and returns a Property Mode Type. Get Modes has two parameters:

1. An in sequence of Names
2. An out sequence of Property Modes

Being a batch command, the potential exists that Multiple Exceptions will be raised as an exception and more information may be obtained by accessing each individual Property Definition to get their Modes.

   Set Mode takes two parameters:

1. Property Name
2. Property Mode

Set Modes takes a sequence of Property Modes and raises the exception for such batch operations, Multiple Exceptions.

20.1.5   Property and Property Names Iterator Interfaces

The iterators have the same operation names and the same result types. Each Iterator interface has four operations:

1. Reset
2. Next One
3. Next N
4. Destroy

20.1.5.1   Reset

Reset, in both iterators, positions the iterator relative to the first Property or Property Name in the Property Set.

20.1.5.2   Next One

The Next One operation takes an out parameter of the type being iterated. In other words, Property Iterator takes a Property, and Property Name takes a Property Name (string). In both cases this operation returns a Boolean. If the result is true, the out parameter has the next valid entry in the Set. If the result is false, there are no more entries in the Set and the out Parameter is undefined.

20.1.5.3   Next N

The Next N operation takes two parameters in both interfaces. The first is How Many (the number of entries from the Set to be placed into the out parameter). The second parameter is an out parameter, which is a sequence of the Set's type. In other words, a sequence of type Property or a sequence of type Property Name. This operation on both interfaces returns a Boolean. If Set members were returned and How Many was not set to zero, they return True. They return False if there are no more members in their respective Sets.

20.1.5.4   Destroy

Destroy, in both, destroys the iterator, releasing its resources back to the system.

CHAPTER 21   *Time*

> *Time is the coin of your life. It is the only coin*
> *you have, and only you can determine how it*
> *will be spent. Be careful lest you let other*
> *people spend it for you.*
> —Carl Sandburg

The Object Time Service is actually a set of two services, the Basic Time Service (BTS) and the Timer Event Service (TES). The BTS is a core service that the TES depends on.

The specification embodies the Universal Time Coordinated (UTC) representation from X/Open DCE Time Service. The UTC finds broad support and is broadcast from the National Bureau of Standards radio station (WWV).

Both Time and Timer services derive from the X/Open DCE Time Service.

UTC is Greenwich Time Zone and has the characteristics shown in Table 21-1. Another component of the time, as defined for UTC, is the specification of its inaccuracy in 100-nanosecond units.

21.1   BASIC TIME SERVICE

The Basic Time Service has three interfaces:

1. UTO
2. TIO
3. Time Service

A Universal Time Object (UTO) is a unit of time. A Time Interval Object (TIO) is a duration, or length of time. The Time Service is primarily the operations for obtaining or creating Time and Interval Objects.

The time service supports both units and intervals.

TABLE 21-1. Universal Time Coordinated Characteristics

Time Unit	100 nanoseconds (10^{-7} seconds)
Base Time	15 October 1582 00:00:00[a]
Approximate Range	30,000 AD

[a] The reason this date was selected is that in October of 1582 the calendar changed from Gregorian to Julian. In order to transform from one to the other, October of 1582 has several missing days—specifically 5 through 14. So the 15th is the first day after this gap. Since that day (October 15, 1582) all days have been consecutively numbered.

21.1.1   UTO Interface

The UTO has four read-only attributes and four operations. The attributes are:

1. Time
2. Inaccuracy
3. Time Displacement Factor
4. UTC

The first three attributes are the constituent members of the fourth, which is a structure (see Example 21-1).

EXAMPLE 21-1. Time module

```
module  Time
{
    struct  ulonglong
    {
        unsigned long    low;
        unsigned long    high;
    };
    typedef      ulonglong     TimeT;
    typedef      TimeT         InaccuracyT;
    typedef      short         TdfT

    struct  UtcT
    {
        TimeT            time;       // 8 octets
        unsigned long    inacclo;    // 4 octets
        unsigned short   inacchi     // 2 octets
        TdfT             tdf;        // 2 octets
    };

    struct  IntervalT
    {
        TimeT        lower_bound;
        TimeT        upper_bound
    };

};
```

Time dates from October 15, 1582 and is 64 bits.

Time is a 64-bit representation of Time since the base date: 15 October 1582 00:00:00. The proposal was written prior to extending the types in IDL with 64-bit data types and so notes that the current configuration will change. When the specification is updated it will become an unsigned long long. It is currently a structure with two long members, one high and one low.

Inaccuracy is 48 bits.

Inaccuracy is a 48-bit value expressing inaccuracy per the X/Open specification for their implementation of UTC. Here again, IDL extensions to types cause this to be an unsigned long (low) and unsigned short (high) and were expected to change.

The Time Displacement Factor (coded as a TDF in IDL) is a representation of Time Zone as a displacement factor in the number of seconds from the Greenwich Meridian. It is a 16-bit short and likely will not change. TDFs are positive to the East of the meridian and negative to the West.

Time Zone is a Displacement in seconds from Greenwich Meridian.

The UTC attribute returns the binary representation of the Universal Time Coordinated, which is currently a structure with the three attributes cited and four members: time structure, high and low inaccuracy, and TDF.[1] The specification states that this structure should be considered opaque and that it is primarily exposed to allow marshaling of the structure. The four operations (see Example 21-2) on a UTO are:

1. Absolute Time
2. Compare Time
3. Time to Interval
4. Interval

EXAMPLE 21-2. UTO, TIO, and Time Service object interfaces

```
#include    <Time.idl>

module   CosTime
{
    enum    TimeComparison    {EqualTo, LessThan, GreaterThan, Indeterminate};
    enum    ComparisonType    {Interval, Mid};
    enum    OverlapType       {Container, Contained, Overlap, NoOverlap};

    exception   TimeUnavailable {};

    interface   TIO;

    interface   UTO
    {
        readonly    attribute    Time::TimeT        time;
        readonly    attribute    Time::InaccuracyT  inaccuracy;
        readonly    attribute    Time::TdfT         tdf;
        readonly    attribute    Time::UtcT         utc_time;

        UTO    absolute_time() raises (CORBA::DATA_CONVERSION);

        TimeComparison  compare_time(
                in  ComparisonType  comparison_type,
                in  UTO             uto)
            raises (CORBA::BAD_PARAM);
```

---

1. Note that the data types for the UTC and for Time Intervals are in the Time module because they will find use even when the interfaces are not a requirement.

```
    TIO     time_to_interval(
                in ComparisonType    interval_type,
                in UTO               uto)
        raises (CORBA::BAD_PARAM);

    TIO     interval() raises (CORBA::DATA_CONVERSION);
};

interface   TIO
{
    readonly    attribute   Time::IntervalT time_interval;

    Overlap     overlap(in TIO interval, out TIO overlap) raises (CORBA::BAD_PARAM);

    UTO         time();
};

interface   TimeService
{
    UTO universal_time() raises (TimeUnavailable);
    UTO secure_universal_time() raises (TimeUnavailable);

    UTO new_universal_time(
            in Time::TimeT          time,
            in Time::InnaccuracyT   inaccuracy,
            in Time::TdfT           tdf)
        raises (CORBA::BAD_PARAM);

    UTO uto_from_utc(in Time::UtcT utc);        // no exception in spec???

    TIO new_interval( in Time::TimeT lower, in Time::TimeT upper)
        raises (CORBA::BAD_PARAM);
};
};
```

21.1.1.1   *Absolute Time*

The Absolute Time request has no parameters and returns a UTO that contains the absolute time. This operation takes the relative time in the invocation object and adds it to the current time producing the absolute time with which it initializes the resulting UTO.

21.1.1.2   *Compare Time*

Compare Time takes two parameters and returns a Time Comparison. The two parameters are:

1. Comparison Type
2. UTO

Comparison Type is an enum with two values:

1. Interval
2. Mid

An Interval comparison is a fuzzy compare. It compares the times, taking their inaccuracy into account. In other words, it considers time to be the fuzzy value of the error envelope and may be indeterminate.

Mid comparisons ignore the inaccuracy and compare the midpoints for each time value. A Mid compare is never indeterminate.

The second parameter of the Compare Time operation is the UTO against which the invocation object will compare against itself. The result, a Time Comparison, is an enum with four values:

1. Equal To
2. Less Than
3. Greater Than
4. Indeterminate

Indeterminate occurs in considering error envelopes for Interval compares. When two error envelopes overlap, they result in an indeterminate comparison. The envelope extent is symmetric with Time at the midpoint—time minus inaccuracy to time plus inaccuracy. For such an Interval compare to return equal, the two objects are equal and both have zero inaccuracy values.

The time within the invocation object is always the first value in the equality equation. Thus, this time is less than that time, where this is the current object and that is the parameter of the operation.

21.1.1.3   *Time to Interval*

Time to Interval takes two parameters and returns a TIO. The two parameters are:

1. Comparison Type
2. UTO

The Comparison Type is an enum with two values as described under the previous operation.

The UTO parameter describes one endpoint of the interval, while the time in the invocation object describes the other endpoint.

The TIO result is the interval between the object and the UTO parameter. If the Comparison Type is Mid, the TIO is the interval between midpoints. If the Comparison Type is Interval, the TIO is the interval that spans the complete error envelopes for both UTOs.

21.1.1.4   *Interval*

The Interval operation takes no parameters and the return result is a TIO, which is the interval for the width of the object's error envelope. The TIO has a lower bound of UTO minus the inaccuracy and an upper bound of UTO plus the inaccuracy.

21.1.2   TIO Interface

The TIO interface has one read-only attribute, Time Interval, and three operations:

1. Span
2. Overlap
3. Time

Time Interval is a data structure that has two members, both of which are equivalent to the Time member of the UTC structure. The first is the lower bound of the Interval and the second is the upper bound. Each is a 64-bit data type (these are structures in the initial specification and will be changing soon).

21.1.2.1   *Span*

The Span operation takes two parameters and returns an Overlap Type. The two parameters are:

1. An in Interval TIO
2. An out Span TIO

The Overlap Type expresses the relation between two intervals. The first interval in the equation expressed is always the invocation object and the second is the parameter. An Overlap Type is an enum with four values:

1. Container
2. Contained
3. Overlap
4. No Overlap

A Container value states the relationship such that the first interval encompasses the second completely. A Contained value states their relationship is reversed: the second interval encompasses the first. An Overlap value states that the two intervals share some commonality; that is, overlap to some extent. A No Overlap value states that they are completely distinct and share no common time.

The in TIO Interval is the second object in the equation, as mentioned. The out TIO is the Interval that spans across both TIOs.

21.1.2.2   *Overlap*

The Overlap request takes the same two parameters (one in and one out TIO) and also returns an Overlap Type.

Everything behaves just as it did for the Span operation with one exception. If the Interval Type is No Overlap, the out TIO represents the Interval between the object and the parameter TIO.

21.1.2.3   *Time*

The Time operation is the reverse equivalent to the `UTO::Interval` operation. Time takes no parameters and has a UTO result.

The UTO result is the Interval expressed as a UTO whose Inaccuracy is
equivalent to the length of the Interval. In other words, the Time of the UTO is
set to the Time at the midpoint of the Interval. The UTO's Inaccuracy is set to
one-half of the span of the Interval, so that `UTO.Time` minus the Inaccuracy
equals TIO's lower bound and `UTO.Time` plus Inaccuracy equals the TIO's
upper bound.

21.1.3   Time Service Interface

The Time Service interface provides services to obtain time, construct a UTO,
and construct a TIO, although it has five operations:

1. Universal Time
2. Secure Universal Time
3. New Universal Time
4. UTO from UTC
5. New Interval

The Time Service interface has no attributes.

21.1.3.1   *Universal Time*

The Universal Time request takes no parameters and returns a UTO. The UTO
represents the current time and an estimate of its potential inaccuracy. The
time is not guaranteed to be secure. If the Time Service is able to return a
Time, one is available from this interface.

21.1.3.2   *Secure Universal Time*

The Secure Universal Time takes no parameters and returns a UTO. If a value
is returned, then the UTO has a guarantee that it was securely acquired. If no
such guarantee can be made, the operation raises a Time Unavailable exception. An appendix in the specification provides a guideline as to how time
acquisition by this service should occur in order to guarantee its security.

21.1.3.3   *New Universal Time*

The New Universal Time takes three parameters and returns a UTO representing the new time. The three parameters are:

1. Time
2. Inaccuracy
3. Time Displacement Factor

These are the three components of a UTC (this operation behaves much as the next one). This is a UTO constructor for creating arbitrary times, such as are required for the Timer Event Service. Having these separate allows one to treat the UTC structure as opaque because the individual components are available from a UTO as read-only attributes in addition to this factory operation.

21.1.3.4   *UTO from UTC*

The UTO from UTC operation takes a single parameter and returns a UTO. The single parameter is a UTC.

This operation is provided so that a UTC received over-the-wire, say from a Time service broadcasting UTCs, can be used to construct UTOs. Similarly, one can obtain a UTC from the read-only attribute on the UTO in the event a UTC needs to be sent over-the-wire or elsewhere that a UTO may not be desirable.

21.1.3.5   *New Interval*

The New Interval operation is a factory operation for TIOs. It takes two parameters and returns a TIO. The two parameters are:

1. Lower Bound
2. Upper Bound

These parameters are both Time values (the Time component from a UTC).

21.2   TIMER EVENT SERVICE

The Timer Event Service manages Timer Event Handlers (see Example 21-3). The service has two interfaces:

1. Timer Event Handler
2. Timer Event Service

EXAMPLE 21-3. **Timer Event Handler and Timer Event Service object interfaces**

```
#include    <Time.idl>
#include    <CosTime.idl>
#include    <CosEventComm.idl>

module  CosTimerEvent
{
    enum    TimeType        { Absolute, Relative, Periodic };
    enum    EventStatus     { TimeSet, TimeCleared, Triggered, FailedTrigger };

    struct  TimeEventT
    {
        Time:UtcT   utc;
        any         event_data;
    };
```

```
interface   TimerEventHandler
{
    readonly    attribute   EventStatus status;

    boolean     time_set(out CosTime::UTO uto);

    void        SetTimer(          // probably should be set_timer
                    in  TimeType        time_type,
                    in  CosTime::UTO    trigger_time)
        raises (CORBA::BAD_PARAM);

    boolean     cancel_timer();

    void        set_data(in any data);
};

interface   TimerEventService
{
    TimerEventHandler   register(
            in CosEventComm::PushConsumer   event_interface,
            in any                          data)
        raises (CORBA::NO_RESOURCE);

    void    unregister(in TimerEventHandler timer_event_handler)
        raises (CORBA::INV_OBJREF);

    CosTime::UTO    event_time(in TimerEvent timer_event);
};
};
```

21.2.1   Timer Event Handler Interface

The Timer Event Handler Interface has one read-only attribute, Event Status, and four operations:

1. Time Set
2. Set Timer
3. Cancel Timer
4. Set Data

Event Status is an enum with four values:

1. Time Set
2. Time Cleared
3. Triggered
4. Failed Trigger

The value Time Set indicates that an event is set for some future time. The Time Cleared value indicates that no time is set and if it was, it was cleared prior to triggering. Triggered indicates that an event already occurred and the data was sent via the event channel. Failed trigger indicates a trigger occurred but the data failed to go over the event channel.

When a periodic event is scheduled, Triggered never occurs. When a periodic event triggers, it resets immediately to Time Set.

21.2.1.1   *Time Set*

Time Set returns a Boolean and has one parameter, an out UTO. If the time is set for an event yet to come, the operation returns True; otherwise it returns False. The UTO always contains the current Timer's value.

21.2.1.2   *Set Timer*

Set Timer takes two parameters and has no result. The parameters are:

1. Time Type
2. Trigger Time

Time Type is an enum having three values:

1. Absolute
2. Relative
3. Periodic

Absolute indicates that the time is the time at which the event is to occur. Relative indicates that the time given is relative to the current time. Periodic is a relative time that indicates the amount of time between each successive triggering of the event. A periodic event continues to occur until reset.

The Trigger Time parameter is a UTO that indicates the time the timer should use.

When set, any previous timer current timer setting is canceled.

If the Time component of the UTO is zero and its type is Relative, the Timer will use the last relative time it had set.

21.2.1.3   *Cancel Timer*

The Cancel Timer operation has no parameters and returns a Boolean. It returns True if an event was set and if it was able to cancel it; otherwise it returns False.

21.2.1.4   *Set Data*

The Set Data operation has no result and only one parameter, Any, which contains the data that is to be handed off to the Event Channel every time the event triggers.

21.2.2   Timer Event Service Interface

The Timer Event Service is a registry of Timer Events. It registers and unregisters such events. This interface has three operations:

1. Register
2. Unregister
3. Event Time

21.2.2.1   Register

The Register operation has two parameters and returns a Timer Event Handler. The two parameters are:

1. Event Object
2. Any

The Event Object is a CORBAservices event channel of Push Consumer type. The Any contains the data that will be passed to the Event channel when the event triggers. Data delivery occurs with a Push onto the channel.

   The Set Time operation on the resulting Timer Event Handler requires invocation for an event to actually occur. At initialization, the Timer Event Handler is set to current absolute time, with its state set to Time Cleared.

21.2.2.2   Unregister

The Unregister operation takes one parameter and has no result. The parameter is Timer Event Handler. On requesting Unregister, the service may release all resources associated with the Timer Event Handler. Any further attempts to use the handler will raise an exception.

21.2.2.3   Event Time

The Event Time operation takes one parameter and returns a UTO. The parameter is a Timer Event, which is a structure with two members:

1. UTC
2. Any

This structure is what an event requester receives when an event occurs from a Timer Event. The UTC contains the actual time the event triggered. The inaccuracy members contain the difference between the time the Timer was set for and the actual time of the event.

   The Any contains the data that the requester associated to the event by requesting its delivery.

   The resulting UTO contains the time corresponding to the Timer Event parameter.

21.3   CAVEATS ABOUT TIME

Some additional notes in the specification are worth keeping in mind because they can have far-ranging impact. The first caveat we have already mentioned and will not discuss in further detail—the criteria for implementing secure time.

   The second caveat is that the formulation of time (based on the UTC) presupposes that the Time is immediately available. In other words, for the element of inaccuracy to have any bearing on reality, that time and its inaccu-

racy must be immediately available. The specification warns that interposing
a proxy between the Time Service and the client introduces unaccounted
latency, which essentially skews the inaccuracy and makes it inaccurate.

The specification makes two suggestions in this regard. One, disallow
proxies between clients and the Time Service. Two, make a special proxy that
is smart enough so that it can compensate for the additional latency.

The third caveat is really the same as the second but interesting enough on
its own to warrant a special mention. This is that for the Time Service to operate
(specifically without proxies) correctly and most reliably, the Time Service
should be in the local runtime with the objects using the Time Services.

An additional note is that it is expected that since UTOs are first class
objects, not pseudo-objects, they cannot be sent over-the-wire. If their references are passed, invocation on the reference introduces some latency that
should be considered. As mentioned earlier, part of the reason for the UTC is
that it may be passed over-the-wire.

CHAPTER 22

Transaction Services

> *A transaction is an atomic set of activities that are*
> *performed either fully or not at all.*
> —Ivar Jacobson

The basic service is virtually transparent to the client through inheritance. When an implementation uses it in this manner, the service and ORB handle all of the details. Such a transactional client need do very little. In this mode, the client needs only to state when a transaction starts and when it ends. In the nonbasic mode, it can get relatively complex quite quickly. The complexity comes from the additional objects that are included to provide a large combination of options that the client may use if it wants control over the transactions.

The client needs only to state when transactions begin and end.

A transaction is said to have ACID properties. ACID is the acronym for atomic, consistent, isolated, and durable.

- *Atomic*—the transaction occurs as a single unit. If it fails, all of its effects are undone (rolled back).
- *Consistent*—a transaction always ends with the same result and in a consistent manner, preserving its invariants.
- *Isolated*—a transaction's intermediate states are not visible to other transactions (so other transactions cannot use states that may roll back). It appears serial even if execution is concurrent.
- *Durable*—the effects of a completed transaction are persistent.

The OTS provides support for flat transactions and nested transactions. The OTS is compatible if it supports at least flat transactions.

OTS supports nested transactions.

Flat transactions have a Begin, followed by one or more steps and then an end (terminator).

Nested transactions allow subtransactions to occur within a transaction. The initial transaction is the relative *parent* of a subtransaction, or *child*. Transactions may have multiple subtransactions which are known as *siblings*. Together, all of the subtransactions and their parent are known as a *family*. Subtransactions may nest to any arbitrary level. When multiple levels exist, those coming before are ancestors of a current subtransaction. Those nesting within the current subtransaction are descendants.

22.1   TRIVIAL SCENARIO

A transactional client (transaction originator) has a Current object. The Current object is a pseudo-object that is constructed locally.[1] Calling Begin on the Current object starts the transaction.

The client makes one or more operation requests, with at least one occurring on a recoverable object.

To terminate the transaction the client may choose to commit or rollback, and so invokes the operation of that name on the Current object. This is all that needs to occur from the client's perspective in what is known as the implicit mode of operation.

Actually, even from the server-side there is not a whole lot more that occurs. When the client requests Begin on the Current object the Transaction Service conspires with the ORB to construct a Transaction Context that identifies the current thread with this transaction.

When the client makes a transactional request, the transaction context is automatically propagated by the service to the recoverable, or transactional objects. That leaves only a few steps out of what happens. At some point, one or more recoverable servers has registered one or more transaction resources with the OTS.

When the client requests Commit, the OTS basically asks all registered resources if they are ready to commit. If they all respond in the affirmative, the OTS tells them to go ahead. If one or more respond negatively, the OTS asks them to roll back and raises a rolled back exception to the client's Commit request.

If the client requests a roll back (instead of a Commit) then the OTS informs all of the resources to roll back any changes.

22.2   OBJECTS IN OTS

A number of objects and entities play together to form this service. The primary ones are:

- Context Object
- Transactional Object
- Recoverable Object
- Current Object
- Control Object
- Transaction Factory
- Terminator Object
- Coordinator

---

1. It is not required to be a pseudo-object but the design allows it.

22.2.1   Context Objects

The ORB conspires with the transaction service to associate and propagate a Context object for each thread that issues a transaction (in a transactional client). The transactional client and ORB know to conspire because the client makes requests on OTS Services. Figure 22-1 shows the components in a transaction service.

Context objects are null and do not need to be propagated unless a transaction is requested. Once a transaction starts, the ORB propagates the context to operations that are transactional; that is, those that inherit from a Transactional object.

If the transaction originator (the thread that requested Begin) starts a subtransaction, the transaction context is updated to reflect that the thread of execution is in a subtransaction. On termination of a subtransaction, the transaction context changes to reflect the way it was prior to the subtransaction Begin. On making an invocation, the transaction context is effectively copied (initialized by the OA) into the called object. If the called object is in another thread, the transaction context does not retain any notion of previous state. In other words, a transaction context that the ORB copies into a new process has a null state prior to invocation and caller state directly after invocation, even if it was called by a subtransaction. All of these operations occur implicitly. In other words, the OTS and ORB make sure this occurs.

Only during a transaction invocation are contexts other than null during implicit propagation.

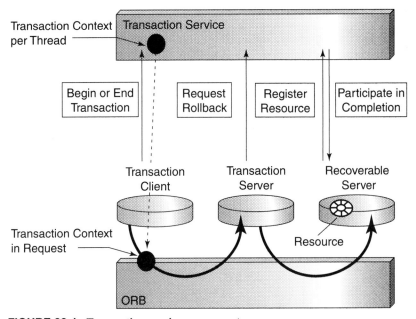

FIGURE 22-1. **Transaction service components**

Explicit propagation occurs by passing a control object.

Explicit propagation of Context occurs via the control object. The Control object may be explicitly passed as a parameter to others that need explicit transaction contexts. Section 22.2.5 on control objects treats this in more detail.

22.2.2 Transactional Objects

Transactional objects are affected from within a transaction.

Transactional objects (TOs) are objects that are affected when invocation occurs within a transaction. Some Persistent data is associated with TOs. The association may be indirect or direct. A direct association may be one in which the objects contains the data. Requests on TOs are transactional requests.

OTS does not disallow non-transactional requests.

However, although the OTS is concerned with transaction requests (and transactional objects) it does not disallow nontransactional requests. This is true even within a transaction. Nontransactional requests are made on non-transactional objects.

A single interface may mix transactional support.

Objects also may choose to mix their transactional support, observing transactional behavior on some requests and nontransactional behavior on others. A single IDL interface may support transactional and nontransactional operations.

Transactional objects are necessary to the implementation of transactional servers and recoverable servers.

The Transactional Object interface has no operations or attributes. All of its behavior is implicit.

22.2.3 Recoverable Objects

Recoverable objects derive from TOs.

A recoverable object is a transactional object. There is no recoverable interface. Recoverable objects differ in that they have a direct association to a persistent state that a transaction can affect. Such objects experience effects at the outcome of a transaction—they commit or roll back.

Recoverable objects register their resource.

Recoverable objects also differ because they register a resource with the OTS. The resource has an interface. If the resource supports nested transactions, the resource is registered as being aware of subtransactions.

The OTS and recoverable objects follow a particular protocol to coordinate the outcome of transactions. Part of the participation requires the recoverable object to maintain state in stable storage during certain key operations. In the event of a failure, the recoverable object participates in a recovery protocol that is determined by the contents (or lack thereof) of its stable store.

22.2.3.1 Transactional Servers

Transactional servers consist of TOs.

A transactional server is a collection of one or more objects having behavior that a transaction affects (transactional objects). However, transactional servers have no recoverable state. It can cause a transaction to roll back but it does not participate in transaction completion.

22.2.3.2   Recoverable Servers

A recoverable server is a collection of one or more objects having recoverable state; that is, inheriting from transactional objects. Recoverable servers participate in the OTS protocols: they register resources and drive the commit protocols of the resources, thus directly participate in transaction completion.

Recoverable servers consist of recoverable objects.

22.2.4   Current Object

The Current object (see Example 22-1) may be a pseudo-object; in other words, expressed but not implemented in IDL. A transactional client that requests transactions and has little or no interest in controlling the transaction may use only the Current object. It also provides operations that allow more explicit control. However, its primary operations are those to begin and terminate—commit or roll back—transactions.

The Current object mainly commits or rolls back a transaction.

The additional operations offer a client more explicit control over the transaction. The client may obtain the transaction's name, its current status, or set the time-out value for the transaction. It may also obtain a control object and suspend or resume the transaction, thus altering the transactions context.

22.2.4.1   Interface Operations

The Current interface has 10 operations:

1. Begin
2. Commit
3. Roll Back
4. Roll Back Only
5. Get Status
6. Get Transaction Name
7. Set Time-out
8. Get Control
9. Suspend
10. Resume

Begin

The Begin operation starts a new transaction and sets the transaction context to reflect this new status. If the thread was already running a transaction, this new transaction becomes its child (a subtransaction). If it is a subtransaction, an exception is raised if its parent's transaction is running against a resource that does not support nesting.

Commit

The Commit operation terminates the current transaction.[2] If this is a flat transaction or the originating parent (ancestor), the transaction context is set to null. If this is a child (subtransaction) the context is set back to what it was at the invocation of Begin for this child. All terminating operations treat the restoration of the transaction context in this same manner.

EXAMPLE 22-1. OTS—Current object interface

```
module  CosTransactions
{
    enum     Status
    {
        StatusActive,
        StatusMarkedRollback,
        StatusPrepared,
        StatusCommitted,
        StatusRolledback,
        StatusUnknown,
        StatusNoTransaction
    };

    enum     Vote     { VoteCommit, VoteRollback, VoteReadOnly };

    exception    TransactionRequired         {};
    exception    TransactionRolledBack       {};
    exception    InvalidTransaction          {};

    exception    HeuristicRollback           {};
    exception    HeuristicCommit             {};
    exception    HeuristicMixes              {};
    exception    HeuristicHazard             {};

    exception    WrongTransaction            {};

    exception    SubtransactionUnavailable       {};
    exception    NotSubtransaction           {};
    exception    Inactive                    {};
    exception    NotPrepared                 {};
    exception    NoTransaction               {};
    exception    InvalidControl              {};
    exception    Unavailable                 {};

    interface    Control;
    interface    Terminator;
    interface    Coordinator;
    interface    Resource;
    interface    RecoveryCoordinator;
    interface    SubtransactionAwareResource;
    interface    TransactionFactory;
    interface    TransactionalObject;
    interface    Current;
```

---

2. In reality, calling commit at the client originator does not terminate until all participants are in agreement to commit (or roll back, which raises an exception).

```
// The Current Interface defines a pseudo-object (PIDL)
interface    Current : CORBA::ORB::Current
{
    void    begin() raises (SubtransactionUnavailable);
    void    commit(in boolean report_heuristics)
        raises ( NoTransaction, HeuristicMixed, HeuristicHazard);
    void    rollback() raises (NoTransaction);

    Status  get_status();
    string  get_transaction_name();

    void    set_timeout(in unsigned long seconds);

    Control     get_control();
    Control     suspend();
    void        resume(in Control which) raises (InvalidControl);
};
```

The Commit operation takes a Boolean parameter that instructs it whether or not to raise heuristic exceptions (these are covered later).

Roll Back
The Roll Back operation requests that the transaction roll back.[3] The specification notes that the roll back operation may be available only from the transaction originator in some implementations.[4]

Roll Back Only
Roll Back Only effectively modifies the transaction so that a Roll Back is its only possible outcome. How this is done is implementation detail but since the coordinator object has a similar operation (and the specification says they behave identically), one might imagine that it informs the coordinator, who will see that the outcome can only roll back.

Get Status
The Get Status returns an enum for one of possibly seven states:[5]

1. Active
2. Marked for Roll Back
3. Prepared
4. Committed
5. Rolled Back
6. Unknown
7. No Transaction

---

3. This is poorly distinguished from the Roll Back Only. It appears that this requests the transaction and all subtransactions to roll back. Roll Back Only appears to instruct the target of the transaction (recoverable server) to only allow a roll back as the final outcome.

4. The caveat being that, for portability, this may be the only place a developer should use it.

5. There is no reason given why Get Status, Get Transaction Name, and Get Control are not read-only attributes.

Get Transaction Name

The Get Transaction Name returns a string form describing the transaction. There is no indication how this name is set or constructed. An additional note states that the operation is intended for debugging.

Set Time-out

The Set Time-out operation takes one parameter (an unsigned long) that is used to indicate a time-out value in seconds. The time-out value is for the top-level transaction from the time of the request to Begin. The specification makes a point of stating that a parameter of zero is equivalent to there being no application time-out.

Get Control

The Get Control operation returns a Control object for the current transaction.

Suspend

The Suspend operation returns a control object, which is passed as a parameter to the Resume operation. It disassociates the current thread from the current transaction. The scope of the Control object returned is dependent on the implementation but is at least valid in the same thread. Suspension of the transaction does not affect the transaction; that is, it does not cause the transaction to roll back.

Resume

The Resume operation takes a Control object as a parameter. If the Control object is null, it disassociates the current thread from the current transaction. If the Control object parameter is within scope (it comes from an execution environment consistent with the current environment) it associates the thread with the transaction and the transaction context in force at the time the Control object was obtained.

22.2.5 Control Object

Clients control transactions with Control objects.

Control objects are for explicit client control of a transaction. In fact, if the client chooses to propagate its own transaction context instead of allowing the OTS and ORB to do this, the client uses the Control object as the representation of its transaction context.

Control objects are obtained from a Transaction Factory in the case of a new transaction, or from the result of a Get Control or Suspend operation on the Current object. A Control object is passed as a parameter to the Current object's Resume operation, since it establishes current transaction context.

Control objects have two operations, which take no parameters:

1. Get Terminator
2. Get Coordinator

The operations return a Terminator or Coordinator object respectively.

22.2.6   Transaction Factory

A Transaction Factory interface (see Example 22-2) is useful for constructing
Control objects. Transaction Factories have no attributes and a single operation,
Create. This operation takes a time-out value (an unsigned long) as a parameter
and returns a Control object.

EXAMPLE 22-2. OTS object interfaces

```
interface  TransactionFactory
{
    Control     create(in unsigned long time_out);
};

interface   Control
{
    Terminator     get_terminator() raises (Unavailable);
    Coordinator    get_coordinator() raises (Unavailable);
};

interface   Terminator
{
    void    commit(in boolean report_heuristics)
        raises (HeuristicMixed, HeuristicHazard);
    void    rollback();
};

interface   Coordinator
{
    Status  get_status();
    Status  get_parent_status();
    Status  get_top_level_status();

    boolean     is_same_transaction(in Coordinator tc);
    boolean     is_related_transaction(in Coordinator tc);
    boolean     is_ancestor_transaction(in Coordinator tc);
    boolean     is_descendant_transactionIn Coordinator tc);
    boolean     is_top_level_transaction();

    unsigned long   hash_transaction();
    unsigned long   hash_top_level_tran();  //spec shows tran not transaction

    RecoveryCoordinator register_resource(in Resource r) raises (Inactive);

    void    register_subtran_aware(in SubtransactionAwareResource r)
        raises (Inactive, NotSubtransaction);

    void    rollback_only() raises (Inactive);

    string  get_transaction_name();

    Control     create_subtransaction() raises (SubtransactionUnavailable, Inactive);
};
```

```
interface   RecoveryCoordinator
{
    Status  replay_completion(in Resource r) raises (NotPrepared);
};

interface   Resource
{
    Vote    prepare();
    void    rollback() raises (HeuristicCommit, HeuristicMixed, HeuristicHazard);

    void    commit()
        raises (NotPrepared, HeuristicRollback, HeuristicMixed, HeuristicHazard);

    void    forget();
};

interface   SubtransactionAwareResource : Resource
{
    void    commit_subtransaction(in Coordinator parent);
    void    rollback_subtransaction();
};

interface   TransactionalObject { };//spec shows interface is empty
};
```

22.2.7   Terminator Object

This Terminator object provides the behavior to terminate a transaction. The Terminator interface has no attributes and two operations:

1. Commit
2. Roll back

The commit operation takes a Boolean parameter, issued to instruct Commit whether to raise heuristic exceptions if they occur. The client issues a Commit if it believes the transaction was successful. Roll back requests the transaction to be aborted.

22.2.8   Coordinator

The Coordinator interface provides central control for the OTS.

The Coordinator interface has 15 operations that provide the central control for the OTS. Typical access to this interface is from a recoverable object but all transaction participants may use it. Objects that bear a Coordinator interface associate with a single transaction. An implementation may choose to limit the scope of a coordinator to a single thread.

22.2.8.1   *Interface Operations*

The operations on the Coordinator interface are:

- Get Status
- Get Parent Status
- Get Top-level Status

- Is Same Transaction
- Is Related Transaction
- Is Ancestor Transaction
- Is Descendent Transaction
- Is Top-level Transaction
- Hash Transaction
- Has Top-level Transaction
- Register Resource
- Register Subtransaction Aware
- Roll Back Only
- Get Transaction Name
- Create Subtransaction

Get Status
The Get Status operation behaves identically to the operation of the same name that appears in the Current interface. It returns one of the same seven states.

Get Parent Status
The Get Parent Status operation behaves as does Get Status. If the request comes from the top-level transaction it is identical. If the request comes from a subtransaction, it returns the parent's status.

Get Top-level Status
The Get Top-level Status operation behaves the same way as the two preceding operations. It always returns the status of the first ancestor.

Is Same Transaction
The Is Same Transaction operation takes a coordinator as parameter. If both the object on which this operation is invoked and the coordinator parameter apply to the same transaction or subtransaction, it returns True.

Is Related Transaction
The Is Related Transaction returns True if its object and the coordinator passed in as a parameter are members of the same transaction family.

Is Ancestor Transaction
The Is Ancestor Transaction operation returns True if the target of the invocation is an Ancestor of (the same as) the coordinator parameter.

Is Descendent Transaction
The Is Descendent Transaction operation returns True if the target of the invocation is a descendent of (or equal to) the coordinator parameter.

Is Top-level Transaction
The Is Top-level Transaction operation returns True if the target of the invocation has no parent transaction. This operation takes no parameter.

Hash Transaction

The Hash Transaction operation returns a hash code (preferably of uniform distribution) for the current transaction, which is the one associated with the target of the invocation.

Such hash codes are used to quickly tell if two transactions are not the same; that is, if they have different hash codes. If two codes are the same, the Is Same Transaction operation can be called, to check the identities of the transaction, potentially going over the wire to do so. A similar mechanism is found in the CORBAservices Relationships part of the specification (called the CORBAservices Object Identity service).

Hash Top-level Transaction

The Hash Top-level Transaction operation is the same as calling Hash Transaction if done from the top-level transaction.

Register Resource

The Register Resource operation takes a Resource object as a parameter. A recoverable server calls this operation to register a resource that will participate in the transaction associated with the coordinator on which this request is made.

If the current coordinator is one from a subtransaction and the resource supports the Subtransaction Aware Resource, the register invocation operates exactly like the Register Subtransaction Aware operation and registers the resource directly to the subtransaction. If this is a subtransaction, the resource will not receive Prepare or Commit requests until the top-level transaction (ancestor) terminates.

The Register Resource operation returns a recovery coordinator that may be used by the resource to recover. The Resource should store the recovery coordinator in stable storage. In the event of a failure the Resource will want to retrieve this object.

Register Subtransaction Aware

The Register Subtransaction Aware operation takes a Subtransaction Aware Resource object as parameter. The invocation must occur during a subtransaction or an exception is raised. This operation cannot register a resource as a participant to the transaction.

Roll Back Only

The Roll Back Only operation modifies the object such that a Roll Back is the only possible outcome for termination. This operation operates exactly like the operation of the same name in the Current object.

Get Transaction Name

The Get Transaction Name operation operates just like the operation of the same name in the Current object. It returns a printable string that describes the current transaction. The operation is support for debugging.

Create Subtransaction

The Create Subtransaction operation creates a new subtransaction.[6] The operation returns the subtransaction-specific Control object.

22.2.9   Recovery Coordinator Object Interface

The Recovery Coordinator Object supports a single operation, Replay Completion, which takes a Resource object as a parameter and returns a Status (one of the seven states mentioned in the Current object description of Get Status).

Once the Resource has seen the Prepare operation, this request may be made. It indicates to the coordinator that something has gone awry (potentially after a failure occurs), alerting it that the Resource has not done a Commit or Roll Back. The coordinator then may reissue the Prepare request in preparation for a Commit or Roll Back.

22.2.10   Resource Interface

The Resource interface supports five operations, none of which takes parameters:

1. Prepare
2. Roll Back
3. Commit
4. Commit One Phase
5. Forget

22.2.10.1   Prepare

Prepare is the only operation with a result—a Vote. The Vote is an enum with a value of Commit, Roll Back, or Read-only.

The Resource responds with a commit when all of the data that it needs to commit is written to stable storage. This also includes an indication to itself of its intent to commit. After this response, the transaction service will request either a Commit or Roll Back operation on this Resource at some later time.

The Resource responds with a Read-only if the transaction did not affect any data. The transaction service need not perform any additional actions on the Resource after a read-only vote and the Resource can forget all knowledge about the current transaction.

The Resource responds with a Roll Back for a variety of reasons, such as being unaware of any transaction (perhaps after a failure) or not having enough storage to commit the state. Given this response the transaction must roll back. The transaction service need not perform any additional actions on the Resource after a Read-only vote and the Resource can forget all knowledge about the current transaction.

------

6. The OTS is not required to support subtransactions, so an exception may be raised.

22.2.10.2   *Roll Back*

The Roll Back operation instructs the Resource to roll back all changes for the transaction. If it does not know about the transaction, then it should do nothing.

22.2.10.3   *Commit*

The Commit operation instructs the Resource to commit all of the changes made for the transaction. If the Resource has no knowledge of the transaction, then it should do nothing.

22.2.10.4   *Commit One Phase*

A Commit One Phase on the Resource instructs it to commit all of the changes made for the transaction. In the event it cannot commit, it raises a Transaction Rolled Back exception.

Generally, the transaction service uses a two-phase commit—Prepare to Commit, which returns either a vote of Commit or Read-only, followed by a Commit request. Prepare and Commit are the two phases. However, in a transaction where only a single Resource is involved, one can retain ACID properties with a one phase commit.

Applications that choose to use the commit one phase do not call Prepare.

22.2.10.5   *Forget*

The Forget request is made only after a heuristic exception is raised in response to a Commit or Roll Back request. It instructs the Resource that it may forget all about the transaction.

22.2.10.6   *Heuristic Exceptions*

At least twice, heuristic exceptions were alluded to but not explained. Sometimes (depending on the application) it seems wise to invest a transaction participant with the ability to use a heuristic in order to determine to commit or roll back without determining the consensus vote first.

Such a heuristic decision is rare and occurs only during exceptional circumstances, and then maybe only if we are very confident we are making a correct choice; that is, when we know that no integrity will be lost one way or the other. For instance, a heuristic may be used as a temporary recovery for a communication failure after having been asked to Prepare. The heuristic may decide that it is safer to roll back the data.

In the event it is later determined that the heuristic made a wrong choice, one of four exceptions may be raised:

1. *Heuristic Roll Back*—the exception raised when the Resource receives a request to commit a transaction that it already chose to Roll Back.
2. *Heuristic Commit*—when a Resource receives a Roll Back request for a transaction after it already did a Commit.

3. *Heuristic Mixed*—an exception stating that some relevant changes were committed while others were rolled back.
4. *Heuristic Hazard*—an exception that states a heuristic decision may have been made but we do not know everything. It is also an indication that the transaction is not known to be in a mixed state (otherwise the mixed exception would have been raised). In other words, for those updates we may know about, they were all either committed or rolled back.

22.2.11   Subtransaction Aware Resource Interface

The Subtransaction Aware Resource is a specialization of the Resource. Resources bearing this object can participate in subtransactions and receive notification of subtransaction completion if they register as such with the coordinator. Registration occurs when a Resource passes in a reference to this interface to the Coordinator via the Register Subtransaction Aware operation.

Recoverable objects that support subtransactions generally register a Resource with the top-level coordinator by passing a reference in the Register request. Recoverable objects that desire finer control may choose to register for the top-level transaction and then register for a particular subtransaction. This latter allows the object to view the completion result of the subtransaction and then make changes to the transaction based on that subtransaction's completion. Rather than just wanting to know when a subtransaction completes, it actually wants to do something specific on its completion, say, after it commits.

The Subtransaction Aware Resource has two operations:

1. Commit Subtransaction
2. Roll Back Subtransaction

Neither of these operations is requested unless the Resource registered as subtransaction aware.

22.2.11.1   *Commit Subtransaction*

The Commit Subtransaction is requested when the subtransaction commits. The Coordinator of the subtransaction's parent is the parameter to the operation. Subtransactions are relative transactions and only commit relative to their ancestors. If any ancestor rolls back, then this commit may be undone.

22.2.11.2   *Roll Back Subtransaction*

Roll Back Subtransaction notifies the resource that the subtransaction terminates with a Roll Back.

CHAPTER 23 *Concurrency Control*

Everything should be made as simple
as possible, but not simpler.
—Albert Einstein

The Concurrency Control Service (CCS) mediates multiple client interactions on a resource. Resources may or may not be objects. In essence, concurrency control coordinates access to the resource across operations that may conflict. This occurs by serializing the access of operations that are in conflict if they were to occur at the same time.

Concurrency control serializes concurrent access to resources.

23.1 LOCKS AND LOCK SETS

The CCS coordinates a client's resource access through the acquisition of locks on those resources. The set of locks associated with a resource is a *lock set*. If the resource is an object, it internally creates the lock set. If the resource is not an object, then the lock set is external to the resource, in an object that holds the lock set for the resource. The clients determine which lock set to associate with a resource.

If the resource is not an object, the lock is external to the resource.

23.1.1 Lock Modes

To some degree, lock modes are a performance consideration. Having only one category of access essentially serializes multiple requests, allowing only one access to a resource at any time and (possibly) the least concurrency. While this is effective, it is not as efficient if there is a potential for multiple nonconflicting accesses to occur simultaneously. For example, multiple readers could access an object or other resources and not be in conflict. However, there is conflict if a client writes to the record at the same time other clients are reading the record. As a result, clients could read a partially updated record.

Five lock modes are available through CCS.

The modes offered by CCS are:

1. Read
2. Write
3. Upgrade
4. Intention Write
5. Intention Read

23.1.1.1 Read

Read Locks do not conflict with themselves, allowing multiple concurrent readers. They do, however, conflict with Writers.

23.1.1.2 Write

Write Locks conflict with everything, meaning that concurrent readers or writers are disallowed.

23.1.1.3 Upgrade

Upgrade Locks are read locks that conflict with themselves as well as with write locks. These are interesting to clients that need to read a resource just before writing it. Such operations are frequently necessary if the client wants to change only a portion of the resource or to determine that the resource has not changed.

   If only read and write locks are available, two clients that want to read and then write a resource could deadlock. This occurs when they both acquire read locks but then neither is able to acquire the write lock. By first acquiring an upgrade lock, no other client can obtain an upgrade. Obtaining the write lock then may occur without deadlock.

23.1.1.4 Intention Write and Read

An intention lock is another mechanism to provide efficient locking, specifically with variable granularity. For example, a database may choose to provide locking at different levels of resource granularity for different performance requirements. It may choose to provide locking at the following levels:

1. *Database-level*—implementing very few locks but serializing all access to the database
2. *Table- (or file) level*—requires more locks (implementation overhead) but allows concurrent access to other tables
3. *Record-level*—possibly is another order of magnitude in overhead for the lock mechanism but potentially supports many more simultaneous accesses
4. *Field-level*—very high lock management overhead but the greatest potential for concurrent access

Such hierarchical resources invite potential conflicts if two resources acquire locks at different levels of the hierarchy for potentially conflicting access. For instance, one client may obtain a read lock on a field to read its data at the same moment another client obtains a lock on the record, containing that field, to delete the record.

   An intention lock is used on the larger-grained portions of the resource to state that an intent exists to lock a subset (smaller grained) of that resource.

For example, in a database with variable levels of control granularity, such as database, file, and record locks, a client intending to update a record acquires an Intention Write on the database, an Intention Write on the file, and a Write Lock on the record.

An intention read lock has the least conflicts of all locks, whereas write locks have the most conflicts. They conflict with all other modes. Lock conflicts are outlined in Table 23-1. Lock requests that are in conflict queue in first-in-first-out (FIFO) order.

TABLE 23-1. Lock Conflicts

Requested	Intention Read	Read	Upgrade	Intention Write	Write
Acquired:					
Intention Read					Conflict
Read				Conflict	Conflict
Upgrade			Conflict	Conflict	Conflict
Intention Write		Conflict	Conflict		Conflict
Write	Conflict	Conflict	Conflict	Conflict	Conflict

23.2 LOCKS AND TRANSACTIONS

The CCS design works explicitly with the CORBAservice Object Transaction Service (OTS) and supports explicit means for their support. CCS supports both OTS clients and non-OTS clients and, hence, coordinates access to resources regardless of whether the client is a transaction client.

The CCS design works for the transaction service and nontransaction clients.

The transaction client (specifically an OTS client) requires some additional capabilities from the CCS. One such requirement is for conflict resolution to occur in a slightly different fashion. A second provides multiple possession semantics. A third is to provide support for implementing two-phase transactional locking.

23.2.1 Conflict Resolution in Nested Transactions

Nested transactions, or transactions that have one or more subtransactions, require slightly different conflict resolution to make them effective and logically simple. In support of nested transactions, the CCS may grant requests that are otherwise conflicting when not made within a nested transaction. For example, a child transaction may acquire a lock for a resource that is already locked by its parent. The child may release that lock without causing the parent to lose its lock on the resource.

CCS grants some requests for nested transactions that would otherwise be in conflict.

Normally, one transaction cannot observe the effects of a transaction that might not commit (abort). However, nested transactions include the relations between parent and child such that a parent cannot abort without causing all of its children to abort, and a child cannot abort without causing its parent to abort. Transactions that cannot abort without causing a related transaction to abort are committed relative to the other transaction.

Therefore, transactions that are committed relative to each other do not survive the observation of a transaction that might abort because if one aborts they all must. This allows them to acquire otherwise conflicting locks.

23.2.2 Multiple Possession Semantics

Clients may hold multiple locks on the same resource.

Multiple possession semantics makes it easier for a client to hold multiple locks on the same resource. This applies to locks of different and the same modes. In the case of multiple locks of the same modes, the lock effectively maintains a count to track how many of this particular lock a client holds. This capability specifically enables the special style of conflict resolution in use for OTS nested transactions.

23.2.3 Two-Phase Transactional Locking

CCS supports transaction-duration locking, a special case of strict two-phase locking, with its operations. Developers also may implement less strict locking for transactions in special cases. They should observe great care in doing so, however, because it is particularly easy to run afoul.

Two-phase locking grows and shrinks.

The point of transaction locking is to avoid viewing any intermediate results of a transaction. Two-phase locking acquires and never drops locks during the growing phase (first phase), and releases locks but does not acquire new ones in the shrinking phase (second phase). With CCS, locks are dropped after the transaction is complete and no new locks can be acquired during this operation.

The form that is weaker and more vulnerable to contaminating the required isolation allows the transaction to drop individual locks after those locks are no longer required to ensure serialization. One needs to take great care to make sure that this is appropriate for the application.

23.2.3.1 Client Categories

CCS supports three kinds of client.

The final item of note is that OTS clients operate in one of two modes: implicit or explicit. Three client categories find support—nontransactional clients, implicit transactional clients, and explicit transactional clients:

1. *Nontransactional clients*—acquire locks on behalf of the current thread
2. *Implicit transactional clients*—acquire locks on behalf of the current transaction
3. *Explicit transactional clients*—acquire locks by referencing the current transaction to the transaction's coordinator object

Generally, the implicit transactional clients and the nontransactional clients use the same sets of interfaces, while the explicit transactional requirements use a slightly different set for Lock Sets.

23.2.3.2   Lock Set Factory Interface

The Lock Set Factory interface (see Example 23-1) offers four creation-type operations:

1. Create
2. Create Related
3. Create Transactional
4. Create Transactional Related

Create takes no parameters and returns a lock set. Create Related takes a lock set as a parameter to identify which Lock Set the new one will relate. Create Transactional takes no parameters and results in a transactional lock set for explicit transactional clients. Create Transactional Related takes a transactional lock set as a parameter to identify the relation and returns a transactional lock set.

23.2.3.3   Lock Set and Transactional Lock Set interfaces

Both Lock Set and Transactional Lock Set interfaces offer identical operations, except that the transactional variety requires explicit reference to the OTS transaction coordinator. The operations on these interfaces are:

- Lock
- Try Lock
- Unlock
- Change Mode
- Get Coordinator

Lock

The Lock call takes a mode parameter to identify the kind of access required. If the lock is already held in a conflicting mode by another client, the call blocks the thread of control until the conflicts resolve.

If a transactional client blocks and the transaction aborts, an OTS transaction exception occurs, informing the client that the transaction is rolling back.

Try Lock

This operates like Lock except it is nonblocking. This operation has a Boolean result, which is false when the lock cannot be so acquired. It takes a mode parameter to identify the access requirement (as does Lock).

EXAMPLE 23-1. Concurrency Control Module

```
#include    "CosTransactions.idl"

module CosConcurrencyControl
{
    enum    lock_mode   { read, write, upgrade, intention_read, intention_write };

    exception   LockNotHeld {};

    interface   LockCoordinator
    {
        void    drop_locks();
    };

    interface   LockSet
    {
        void        lock(in lock_mode mode);
        boolean     try_lock(in lock_mode mode);

        void    unlock(in lock_mode mode) raises (LockNotHeld);

        void    change_mode(in lock_mode held_mode, in lock_mode new_mode)
            raises (LockNotHeld);

        LockCoordinator get_coordinator(in CosTransactions::Coordinator which);
    };

    interface   TransactionalLockSet
    {
        void        lock(in CosTransactions::Coordinator current, in lock_mode mode);
        boolean     try_lock(in CosTransactions::Coordinator current, in lock_mode mode);

        void    unlock(in CosTransactions::Coordinator current, in lock_mode mode)
            raises (LockNotHeld);

        void    change_mode(
                in CosTransactions::Coordinator current,
                in lock_mode    held_mode,
                in lock_mode    new_mode)
            raises (LockNotHeld);

        LockCoordinator get_coordinator(in CosTransactions::Coordinator which);
    };

    interface   LockSetFactory
    {
        Lockset                 create();
        LockSet                 create_related(in Lockset which);

        TransactionalLockSet    create_transactional();
        TransactionalLockSet    create_transactional_related(
                                    in TransactionalLockSet which);
    };
};
```

Unlock

Unlock also takes a mode parameter and drops a single lock, or effectively decrements the lock count if it holds multiple locks of that same mode.[1]

Change Mode

The Change Mode operation takes two mode parameters: the current mode and the new mode. In changing mode, it acts like the Lock operation in that it blocks on conflict and returns on successful acquisition of the new mode.

If multiple locks of the current mode are held by the client, only one will change to the new mode. If the client is transactional and the transaction aborts, the roll back exception occurs.

Get Coordinator

The Get Coordinator operations for both Lock Set and Transactional Lock Set interfaces are identical in that they both require a reference to the OTS Transaction Coordinator. The operation returns a Lock Set Coordinator.

23.2.3.4   *Lock Coordinator Interface*

The Lock Coordinator offers only a single operation, Drop Locks, which takes no parameters and returns no result. The intent is that transactional clients, both implicit and explicit, will call this operation after committing or aborting.

This call must be made by an aborting nested transaction but needs only to be called once for a transaction family when that family commits.

---

1. Whether the locks are actually counted is an implementation detail but the behavior is effectively that of a counted lock.

CHAPTER 24

Persistence Service

> *Persistence saves the state and class of an object*
> *across time or space.*
> —Grady Booch

The Persistent Object Service (POS) is a generalized set of service interfaces that provide a variety of different types of persistent services to objects. It is composed of six entities:

1. Persistent Identifier (PID)
2. Persistent Object (PO)
3. Persistent Object Manager (POM)
4. Persistent Data Service (PDS)
5. Protocols
6. Data Store

In the basic scenario of operation, an object that wants to participate in the service has a PID, which is an identifier relative to the data storage type that it uses for persistence. A PID may specialize to designate a finer granularity of type within the data storage if such is a requirement. Different objects may have different data storage types, allowing different means of storage. For example, one storage type may be an OODBMS, another may specify an rDBMS, still another may specify some file system interface.

Persistent objects have an ID (PID) relative to its persistent storage type.

This translates to the ability to allow both single-level and two-level stores as the occasion requires. Single-level storage appears transparent to the client because disk and memory are indistinguishable. The client accesses an object and has no idea if it was already in memory or brought from disk at the time of access. Two-level storage makes a distinction between the object transient state (in memory) and its persistent state (on disk). Two-level stores are necessary to support the majority of storage systems currently in use, such as relational database systems, or flat files.

Single-level and two-level storage

Depending on the implementation, persistent objects may implement a direct connection and interoperation with the data storage or they may delegate such operations through the POM. This also allows more variety in how much detail and control a client needs to see. (See Figure 24-1.)

Persistent objects

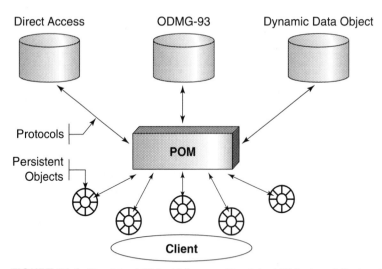

FIGURE 24-1. **Persistent Object Manager, Persistent Object, and Protocols**

Clients may have control over persistence.

An implementation may provide the client with a highly detailed view (a very fine granularity of control) of the PDS or none at all. In other words, the client may view the object as the bearer of PO interfaces. The client may not have any view of such interfaces. This is not an all or nothing proposal because a variety of exposures and granularities may be apparent to the client. Objects that bear a PO interface anticipate a client audience. A PO interface is expressly for client control of persistent storage.

Protocol implementation

Depending on what PDS is in use with the persistent object, the object must implement the protocol necessary to interact with the specific PDS. If the POM plays a role, the object must understand and implement the protocol of the POM and the POM, in turn, must understand and implement the protocols for the appropriate PDS.

24.1 PID INTERFACE

The PID has a Data Store Type attribute.

The PID has one operation and one attribute. The attribute is a string that signifies the data store. The operation returns the string form of the PID.[1] The format of the PID string is implementation-specific and, therefore, has no format definition.

PID specialization

The vision is that the PID may be specialized when the data store contains more than just a single object. For instance, the object may be specialized to declare a specific database within a data store. It may also specialize to specify which segment or cluster, and which OID.

---

1. This is actually somewhat puzzling. It is not clear why the PID string form was not declared a read-only attribute on the interface, at least because it does not raise any exceptions of its own.

EXAMPLE 24-1. PID object interface

```
module  CosPersistencePID
{
    interface   PID
    {
        attribute   string  datastore_type;

        string      get_PIDstring();
    };
};
```

Like most CORBA objects, a PID is obtainable from a factory. The PID factory does not have any explicit definition (apparently agreement could not be reached at the time). However, an example of a PID factory is given. It is clear from Example 24-1 that a variety of operations might be useful in various circumstances. The various Create operations show creation by Key, the PID string, or a combination of the two. In the latter case, the assumption is that the Key is useful for creation and the Key is ignored in the PID string. The Key in the PID string is useful when objects move between data stores that require different PID interfaces.

An example PID factory is part of the specification.

24.2   PO INTERFACE

The PO is useful for an object to pass control of persistence to the client (see Example 24-2). The PO has five operations, which directly reflect the operations available to an object from the POM interface. These operations are:

An implementation may hand a PO object to the client to control.

1. Connect
2. Disconnect
3. Store
4. Restore
5. Remove

Each of the five operations takes a PID as its parameter. The PID acts as a reference to a location within the data store. Each operation, therefore, takes place between the object bearing the PO and the location within the data store to which the PID refers.

As with the PID, a PO Factory is a presumption without adopting a specification. The example factory cites a Create operation taking a PID string and POM identifier string.

A PO Factory example exists but not standard interfaces.

24.2.1   Interface Operations

The PO operations appear again in the POM and PDS interfaces. The latter two, however, take an additional object reference as a parameter. The PO gives the client direct control of persistence.

EXAMPLE 24-2. PO and SD object interfaces

```
#include    <CosPersistencePDS.idl>

module  CosPersistencePO
{
    interface   PO
    {
        attribute   CosPersistencePID::PID  p;

        CosPersistencePDS::PDS  connect(in CosPersistentPID::PID p);

        void    disconnect(in CosPersistentPID::PID p);

        void    store(in CosPersistentPID::PID p);

        void    restore(in CosPersistentPID::PID p);

        void    delete(in CosPersistentPID::PID p);
    };

    interface   SD
    {
        void    pre_store();
        void    post_restore();
    };
};
```

24.2.1.1   *Connect*

Connection establishes a relation between the object and data store. On connection, the persistent data may receive updates as operations occur on the object.

The connection operation, the only one to return a result, returns an object reference to the PDS. Depending on the data store, this may or may not be useful. It is useful when the protocol requires the client to invoke additional operations on the PDS directly.

24.2.1.2   *Disconnect*

Disconnect disassociates the object and data store. The object and data store must completely synchronize on disconnect. Further use of such an object is undefined, leaving it for the implementation to determine. Of course being undefined carries the warning that such use is not portable even if an implementation were to allow further use of an object after invoking the disconnect operation.

24.2.1.3   *Store*

The Store operation causes the persistent store to synchronize with the object. In other words, the persistent state of the object moves by copy from the object into persistent store.

24.2.1.4   Restore

The Restore operation causes the object to synchronize with the persistent store. The state held in the persistent store moves by copy from persistent store into the object.

24.2.1.5   Remove

The Remove operation deletes the object's persistent data from the data store.

24.2.2   Synchronized Data Interface

Objects that are under control of their client regarding their persistence also, occasionally, may have some additional synchronization requirements. These issues are usually not obvious to the client, so the object bearing a PO interface may choose to bear a Synchronized Data (SD) interface. The audience (client) of a Synchronized Data interface is the POM.

An additional interface is available with early and late synchronization operations.

The SD interface has two operations, neither of which takes parameters or returns results:

1. Prestore
2. Postrestore

Both are useful when synchronizing the object's transient data with the data to make persistent.

An example is a sequence of operations in which a client calls PO store on the object, which in turn delegates the call directly to the POM. The POM, seeing the request to store, first calls prestore on the object, which writes its cache (transient data) into the appropriate (persistent) space. On completion of the prestore call, the POM completes the store by copying the persistent part of the object off to the PDS.

Similarly, on a client invocation of the restore call, the object again directly delegates to the POM. The POM first calls the PDS to fetch the appropriate data. After writing it into the object, the POM next calls postrestore on the object's SD interface, telling the object that it is okay to write the persistent state into the cache as a refresh.

24.3   POM INTERFACE

The POM operations (see Example 24-3) exactly match the image of the PO except that each operation requires an object reference as a parameter (in addition to the PIDs). The object calls the POM when delegating a client request through from a PO. However, the object may choose not to allow the client a PO interface, and the implementation may invoke the POM itself directly and not just at the behest of a client. In both such cases, the presumption is that the object reference is that of the implementation.

The POM has the same operations as a PO.

EXAMPLE 24-3. POM object interface

```
#include    "CosPersistencePDS.idl"

module CosPersistencePOM
{
    interface   Object;

    interface   POM
    {
        CosPersistencePDS::PDS   connect(
                in Object o,
                in CosPersistencePID::PID p);

        void    disconnect(
                in Object o,
                in CosPersistencePID::PID p);

        void    store(
                in Object o,
                in CosPersistencePID::PID p);

        void    restore(
                in Object o,
                in CosPersistencePID::PID p);

        void    delete(
                in Object o,
                in CosPersistencePID::PID p);
    };
};
```

However, a persistent object can conspire within the confines of the POS and pass the client an object reference to the POM with which it has registered. The client can then directly call the POM without delegating through the PO. In such cases, the client would pass in the object reference for the object it wished the POM to use as the controlling parameter of the operation.[2]

The POM hides the PDS behind its abstraction.

The whole point of the POM is to provide a layer of abstraction between the object and the PDS so that the PDS may change without reimplementing the object. This being the case, the POM must know all the PDSs with which it must interact, as well as the protocols and data stores associated with each. The specification claims that more learning is necessary about how these associations occur before they are specifiable. Currently there is no specification for how a POM determines which PDSs are available. There is no specification describing how it determines which sets of protocols go with which sets of data stores, or which are in use by individual objects. An example is administratively setting this up in a registry for the POM to consult.

---

2. Note that in this scenario the SD interface is also interesting, probably more so than in the one given by the specification because the object is given no chance to fend for itself in this scenario. It is somewhat questionable to allow the client to access the POM directly, however.

24.4   PDS INTERFACE

The PDS serves as a higher-level interface for a data store. The data store also probably has interfaces, which occasionally may receive direct calls (according to the protocol), as opposed to an indirect invocation through the PDS. However, the primary role of the PDS is to act as intermediary between the object and the data store.

The PDS is an abstraction over the data store that mediates between object and store.

An object that uses a specific protocol can interoperate with a PDS that supports that protocol. The PDS is responsible for moving data to and from the object and to and from the data store. The protocol of the PDS may be such that it makes an explicit request on the object to stream out its data. The protocol also may use hidden (nonpublic) interfaces that implicitly move data, such as a call to map the object's persistent data into persistent virtual memory.

The PDS interface declaration is virtually identical to the POM (see Example 24-4). There are five operations, each taking an object reference and a PID as parameters and only the connect operations returning a reference to the PDS as a result. In the case of the PDS, however, the meaning of each operation is not specifically nailed down. This is because the operations at this level may require supplemental (additional) calls to accomplish an operation. Such supplemental calls are part of the protocol. These operations retain their general meaning.

EXAMPLE 24-4. PDS object interface

```
#include    "CosPersistencePID.idl"

module CosPersistencePDS
{
    interface   Object;

    interface   PDS
    {
        PDS connect(
                in Object o,
                in CosPersistencePID::PID p);

        void    disconnect(
                in Object o,
                in CosPersistencePID::PID p);

        void    store(
                in Object o,
                in CosPersistencePID::PID p);

        void    restore(
                in Object o,
                in CosPersistencePID::PID p);

        void    delete(
                in Object o,
                in CosPersistencePID::PID p);
    };
};
```

24.5   PROTOCOLS

Three additional protocols are current.

Three protocols (or two and a half, depending on how you choose to view it) are part of the specification. The protocols are:

1. Direct Access (DA)
2. ODMG-93 (inherits from the DA protocol)
3. Dynamic Data Object (DDO)

These are interesting but only a summary will be provided here. For complete detail you should consult the specifications. Other protocols may occur as a need arises. The first three represent the most desirable at the time of the POS specification, since each had adherents.

24.5.1   DA Protocol

The design of the DA protocol provides direct access to persistent data through typed attributes. These attributes are data objects, which a subset of IDL called the Data Definition Language (DDL) defines.

DDL appears like IDL minus operations.

The DDL specification appears as an interface with no operations but supports attribute declaration. DDL-defined objects are interfaces and, therefore, CORBA objects, having data object references. Such interfaces may include data object references as attributes, enabling complex data graph descriptions through DDL. Interfaces defined in the specification (see Example 24-5) are:

- PID DA
- DA Object
- DA Object Factory
- DA Object Factory Finder
- PDS DA
- Dynamic Attribute Access (DAA)
- PDS Clustered DA

EXAMPLE 24-5. PDS DA object interfaces

```
#include    "CosPersistencePDS.idl"

module  CosPersistencePDS_DA
{
    typedef string      DAObjectID;

    interface   PID_DA : CosPersistence::PID
    {
        attribute   DAObjectID  oid;
    };
```

```
interface   DAObject
{
    boolean     dado_same(in DAObjectID d);
    DAObjectID  dado_oid();
    PID_DA      dado_pid();

    void        dado_remove();
    void        dado_free();
};

interface   DAObjectFactory
{
    DAObject    create();
};

interface   DAObjectFactoryFinder
{
    DAObjectFactory find_factory(in string key);
};

interface   PDS_DA : CosPersistencePDS::PDS
{
    DAObject    get_data();
    void        set_data(in DAObject new_data);

    DAObject    lookup(in DAObjectID id);

    PID_DA      get_pid();
    PID_DA      get_object_pid(in DAObject dao);

    DAObjectFactoryFinder   data_factories();
};

typedef sequence <string>   AttributeNames;

interface   DynamicAttributeAccess
{
    AttributeNames  attribute_names();
    any             attribute_get(in string name);
    void            attribute_set(in string name, in any value);
};

typedef     string ClusterID;
typedef     sequence<ClusterID> ClusterIDs;

interface   PDS_ClusterDA : PDS_DA
{
    ClusterID   cluster_id();

    string      cluster_kind();

    ClusterIDs  clusters_of();

    PDS_ClusterDA   create_cluster(in string kind);
    PDS_ClusterDAopen_cluster(in ClusterID cluster);
    PDS_ClusterDAcopy_cluster(in PDS_DA source);
};
};
```

The implication is that all IDL objects requiring persistence have a parallel DA Data Object (DADO) created with DDL.

A DAA manipulates attributes by name, while the Cluster DA allows associative creation and access of objects.

The last two interfaces mentioned above may be slightly less than obvious. The DAA interface is a DDL equivalent to the DII. While the DII is useful for the manipulation of DADOs, the DAA is more explicitly tuned to operations on the DADOs by referencing attributes by name. The last interface mentioned is the PDS Cluster DA interface.

This interface allows the creation and access of associative groupings of objects. The groups associate through a Kind string parameter on creation. One may open, copy, or create a cluster. They may be queried for their kind and have an operation that queries for all clusters in a data store. Each cluster has a cluster ID, which may be individually queried or returned in a sequence when asking for all clusters in the data store.

24.5.2   ODMG-93 Protocol

The ODMG-93 protocol is very close to the DA protocol. ODL is used instead of DDL, and the ODMG-93 has its own program language mapping. They are so close that a DA protocol is easy to implement directly on top of an ODMG-93 PDS, providing support for DA objects as well as ODMG-93 objects. The latter offers a much finer control over persistent operations.

24.5.3   DDO Protocol

The DDO protocol is data store neutral. It is a single interface (see Example 24-6) with two attributes, a data type and a PID. The rest of the operations are in two sections. The first find use in determining the data item, the second manipulate some number of properties associated with each data item.

EXAMPLE 24-6. DDO object interface

```
#include    "CosPersistencePID.idl"

module  CosPersistenceDDO
{
    interface   DDO
    {
        attribute   string  object_type;
        attribute   CosPersistencePID::PID  p;

        short   add_data();
        short   add_data_property(in short data_id);

        short   get_data_count();
        short   get_data_property_count(in short data_id);

        void    get_data_property(
                    in short    data_id,
                    in short    property_id,
                    out string  property_name,
                    out any     property_value);
```

```
        void    set_data_property(
                    in short    property_id,
                    in string   property_name,
                    in any      property_value);

        void    get_data(
                    in short    data_id,
                    out string  data_name,
                    out any     data_value);

        void    set_data(
                    in short    data_id,
                    in string   data_name,
                    in any      data_value);
    };
};
```

24.6   DATA STORE

The data store (DS) is the piece of the architecture that is most tightly bound
to the underlying persistence mechanism if it exists. The DS example in POS
is one possible data store. It is a record-oriented data store.

It may be the case that this part of the architecture may not exist in an
implementation. This might be the case for an implementation that is strictly
for an OODBMS data store. An example might be one in which the DA or
ODMG-93 protocols are a part of the OODBMS itself and no additional layer
is necessary.

*Data Store is obviated by an
OODBMS using built-in DA
or ODMG-93 protocols.*

The data store specification is the DS Call Level interface (CLI) and is
compatible (as far as is possible) with the X/Open CLI, IDAPI, and ODBC.
Dynamic Data Objects (DDOs) front for the CLI, and if it uses the DDO protocol, the PDS can delegate directly to the CLI interface (see Example 24-7).

*The data store CLI derives
from IDAPI and ODBC.*

EXAMPLE 24-7. DS CLI object interfaces

```
#include    "CosPersistenceDDO.idl"

module  CosPersistenceDS_CLI
{
    interface   UserEnvironment
    {
        void    set_option(in long option, in any value);
        void    get_option(in long option, out any value);
        void    release();
    };

    interface   Connection
    {
        void    set_option(in long option, in any value);
        void    get_option(in long option, out any value);
    };
```

```
interface   ConnectionFactory
{
    Connection  create_object(in UserEnvironment user_envir);
};

interface   Cursor
{
    void    set_position(in long position, in any value);

    CosPersistenceDDO::DDO       fetch_object();
};

interface   CursorFactory
{
    Cursor  create_object(in Connection connection);
};

interface   PID_CLI : CosPersistencePID::PID
{
    attribute   string  datastore_id;
    attribute   string  id;
};

interface   Datastore_CLI
{
    void    connect(
                in Connection connection,
                in string datastore_id,
                in string user_name,
                in string authentication);

    void    disconnect(in Connection connection);

    void    get_connection(
                in string datastore_id,
                in string user_name);

    void    add_object(
                in Connection connection,
                in CosPersistenceDDO::DDO data_object);

    void    delete_object(
                in Connection connection,
                in CosPersistenceDDO::DDO data_object);

    void    update_object(
                in Connection connection,
                in CosPersistenceDDO::DDO data_object);

    void    retrieve_object(
                in Connection connection,
                in CosPersistenceDDO::DDO data_object);

    void    select_object(
                in Connection connection,
                in string key);

    void    transact(
                in UserEnvironment user_envir,
                in short completion_type);
```

```
    void    assign_PID(in PID_CLI p);

    void    assign_PID_relative(
                in PID_CLI source_pid,
                in PID_CLI target_pid);

    boolean     is_identical_PID(
                    in PID_CLI  pid1,
                    in PID_CLI  pid2);

    string  get_object_type(in PID_CLI p);

    void    register_mapping_schema(in string schema_file);

    Cursor  execute(
                in Connection connection,
                in string command);
    };
};
```

The DS CLI specification defines seven interfaces:

1. User Environment
2. Connection
3. Connection Factory
4. Cursor
5. Cursor Factory
6. PID CLI
7. Data Store CLI

Both the User Environment and Connection interfaces are used to get and set options. Each takes an option parameter and a value. The User Environment also has a release operation to release the resources associated with the environment.

Both the Connection and Cursor factories have a single operation: Create. The Connection Factory takes a User Environment as a parameter and returns a Connection. The Cursor Factory takes Connection as a parameter and returns a Cursor.

The Cursor interface has two operations. The first sets the position of the cursor and takes a position and a value as parameters. The second is a fetch object operation, which returns the next DDO object following the current position of the cursor.

The PID CLI interface has no operations and two attributes. The interface inherits directly from the PID. Its two attributes are data store ID, which identifies the specific data store, and ID, which identifies an element within the data store.

The data store CLI interface is large and has 15 operations:

1. Connect
2. Disconnect
3. Get connection

4. Add object
5. Delete object
6. Update object
7. Retrieve object
8. Select object
9. Transact
10. Assign PID
11. Assign PID relative
12. Is Identical PID
13. Get object type
14. Register mapping schema
15. Execute

The first eight operations are fairly straightforward and are best left to the specification for their exact semantic. Of these seven, those that operate on an object do so on a DDO type of object.

Transact is for committing or rollback on add, update, or delete.

Assign PID relative assigns values from a source PID to a Target PID for the data store ID and element ID. It is an implementation detail whether or not the exact values are copied or if the target is changed according to an internal (to the data store) algorithm.

The Is Identical PID tests two PIDs to determine if all of their attributes are identical (same PDS, same data store, same IDs). Get Object Type returns the string type of the PID. Register Mapping Schema registers schema information. It is generally a composition of individual mappings between pairs of object type and data store type.[3]

The execute operation executes a command on the data store, given as a string. The result is a cursor. If objects (DDOs) are to be returned as a result of the command, they are available at the cursor.

---

3. I say "generally" because this is an example of what may be in such a schema file, and the actual content and composition is implementation-specific.

CHAPTER 25

Licensing Service

> *Before attempting to solve a problem, make*
> *absolutely sure you know what the problem is.*
> —David Gries

The Object Licensing Service (LS) consists of two interfaces:

1. License Service Manager
2. Producer-Specific License Service

One of the driving factors that underlies its entire design is flexibility. A multitude of licensing schemes and strategies are in use today. Each reflects one of an exceedingly large number of business philosophies about what constitutes appropriate compensation for the use of intellectual property. LS is designed so that a company or software producer can implement virtually any current strategy via these two interfaces.

The licensing service may support any number of licensing schemes, allowing implementation control over each.

The audience for the licensing service is an object or collection of objects that wish to control the use of their services with licensing. The specification calls these objects the Producer Client because they are clients of the LS and license the intellectual property of their Producer. A simpler name might have been *application.* This probably was not used because what we think of as a single application may be composed of multiple objects, each of which may wish to be licensed separately.

As an implementation service it is not very visible to the client.

Regardless of name, these objects require the ability to get in touch with some object (a license service) that understands the specific licensing policies that apply. This is done through the License Service Manager. A License Service Manager object finds a Producer-specific License Service object (one that understands the specific policies that apply to the product) and returns a reference to that object.

The License Service Manager coordinates the licensing process.

The Producer-specific License Service object and its client then conspire to manage whatever licensing scheme is appropriate over the appropriate duration.

All operations on both interfaces provide a challenge/response so that they can, if they wish, ascertain the authenticity of the requester or responder. One specific request by the license service client passes a Principal to the license service. Both of these aspects are subject to revisions because this mechanism was adopted prior to the adoption of the security service. The

All operations provide challenge/response to validate requests.

specification admits that it expects these specifics to change. We do not know exactly how, however.

The specification states that virtually all parameters may be left null if the specific licensing policy to be implemented does not require them. In covering the detail about the operations for each interface, these options will appear in the explanations.

Administrative interfaces are not specified.

There are bound to be many administrative aspects of the LS both for setup (at installation time) and for ongoing administration or management. This service, however, does not include any interfaces that deal with these issues. Therefore, they are currently implementation-dependent and likely shall vary. They are independent, however, and should not affect the currently specified functional interfaces (see Example 25-1).

EXAMPLE 25-1. Licensing data types

```
#include     <CosEventComm.idl>
#include     <Property.idl>
#include     <PropertyStore.idl>
module  CosLicensingManager
{
    exception    InvalidProducer          {};
    exception    InvalidParameter         {};
    exception    ComponentNotRegistered   {};

    typedef     Object  ProducerSpecificNotification;

    enum     ActionRequired  { continue, terminate };
    enum     Answer          { yes, no };

    struct  Action
    {
        ActionRequired        action;
        Answer                notification_required;
        Answer                wait_for_user_confirmation_after_notification;
        unsigned long         notification_duration;
        ProducerSpecificNotification    producer_notification;
        string                notification_text;
    };

    struct  ChallengeData
    {
        unsigned long         challenge_index;
        unsigned long         random_number;
        string                digest;
    };

    struct Challenge
    {
        enum    challenge_protocol    { default, producer_defined };

        unsigned long   challenge_data_size;

        any             challenge_data;
    };

    typedef     any     LicenseHandle;
```

25.1 LICENSE SERVICE MANAGER INTERFACE

The License Service Manager interface has a single operation. Its sole job is to obtain an appropriately specific reference to the LS to use. The single operation is Obtain Producer-Specific License Service (see Example 25-2). This finder operation (shorter than retyping the name everywhere and more comprehensible than OPSLS, the method's acronym) returns a Producer-specific License Service and takes two parameters:

1. An In Producer Name
2. An InOut Challenge

The Producer Name is a string. The intent of this parameter is that the Manager may use it, depending on the licensing policy requirements, to further determine the appropriate license service.[1] It may contain instance-specific information that reveals the nature of the current licensing requirement or general information, such as the name of the company that is the Producer, the owner of the intellectual property rights that are being licensed.

EXAMPLE 25-2. **Producer-Specific License Service and License Service Manager object interfaces**

```
interface    ProducerSpecificLicenseService
{
    readonly    attribute    string  producer_contact_info;
    readonly    attribute    string  producer_specific_license_info;

    LicenseHandle    start_use (
                        in Principle      principle,
                        in string         component_name,
                        in string         component_version,
                        in Property::PropertyList    license_use_context,
                        in CosEventComm::PushConsumer    call_back,
                        inout Challenge    challenge)
            raises (InvalidParameter);

    void    check_use (
                        in LicenseHandle          handle,
                        in Property::PropertyList    license_use_context,
                        out unsigned long    recommended_check_interval,
                        out Action    action_to_be_taken,
                        inout Challenge    challenge)
            raises (InvalidParameter);

    void    end_use(
                        in LicenseHandle    handle,
                        in Proprty::PropertyList    license_use_context,
                        inout Challenge    challenge)
            raises (InvalidParameter);
};
```

---

1. Some determination already may have taken place, depending on how the requesting object found the reference to the Manager.

```
interface   LicenseServiceManager
{
    ProducerSpecificLicenseService  obtain_producer_specific_license_service(
                                    in string          producer_name,
                                    inout Challenge    challenge)
        raises (InvalidProducer, InvalidParameter);
};
};
```

The InOut Challenge parameter is an IDL structure with three members:

1. Challenge Protocol
2. Challenge Data Size
3. Challenge Data

Challenge Protocol is an enum with two values:

1. Default
2. Producer-defined

The Default value indicates that the Challenge protocol is to be the standard one that the service implements. The specification offers up one based on *shared secrets* using MD5.[2]

The Producer-defined value indicates that the service should use some other specific protocol, which the LS and Producer have conspired in implementing.

The Challenge Data Size parameter, an unsigned long, is a hint that may be useful specifically in the event that a Producer-defined challenge protocol is in operation.

The Challenge Data member is an Any. In the event the default challenge protocol is in use, this Any will contain a Challenge Data structure. In a producer-specific protocol, it may contain virtually anything. The Challenge Data structure for the default challenge protocol consists of three members:

1. Challenge Index
2. Random Number
3. Digest

The Challenge Index and Random Number are both unsigned longs. The Digest is a string.

25.1.1   Default Challenge Protocol

The default challenge protocol suggests one way of using this data structure member. An appendix in the specification details this particular use. The placement in an appendix apparently was due to the expectation that Security

---

2. RFC 1321 by R. Rivest, which produces a 128-bit signature of any arbitrary message.

Services would eventually do away with or alter the nature of such detail. However, it stills bears relaying and is not explicitly superseded to date.

The Challenge Index is meant to index shared secret sets. The specification states that to be compliant, the implementation must support a minimum of four shared secret sets, indexes 0 through 3. Each shared secret set refers to one *forward secret* value and one *reverse secret* value. Both secret values are known only by the producer.

The producer generates a challenge by forwarding a challenge data structure with forward secret value, a random number and the message digest (MD5) of all parameters.

The license service authenticates the legitimacy of the message and returns the appropriate reverse secret value and the same random number along with a message digest of all of its parameters, which the producer can authenticate.

25.2   PRODUCER-SPECIFIC LICENSE
SERVICE INTERFACE

The Producer-Specific License Service interface has two read-only attributes and three operations. The two attributes are:

1. Producer Contact Information
2. Producer-Specific License Service Information

The intent of these attributes is in the specification but no detail is given about their implementation. Both are strings and presumably the former can be read by humans.

The Producer Contact Information attribute is said to contain information that the client may wish to display to the human user. For instance, it may state information about the license service, version, and release of the licensing mechanism, which the user may want to relay to administrators or to a help desk in the event of some problem with license access.

The Producer-Specific License Service Information is said to contain information that may cause the LS client to alter its behavior on interacting with objects bearing such information. For example, it may contain version information that indicates only certain licensing challenge algorithms are available for use.

The three operations available from this interface are:

1. Start Use
2. Check Use
3. End Use

Before going into the specifics of each operation, here is a short summary of their interaction.

When a client (Producer) starts up and wishes to use some licensing strategy, it contacts a Manager to get a specific license server. The Manager returns an object to the client that represents the specific LS it desires. This client (the LS audience) is then responsible for issuing the requests. On starting to use the licensed software, it issues a Start Use. During its operation the client may periodically issue Check Use. On terminating the license session (relinquishing the license or exiting the licensable software) the client issues an End Use. The manner and periods in which the client uses these, accompanied by the parameters each request uses, determine the licensing strategy that the software employs.

25.2.1 Start Use

Start Use informs the Producer-Specific License Server that some aspect of the product is in use. It takes six parameters and has a license handle as a result. The parameters are:

1. In Principle[3]
2. In Component Name
3. In Component Version
4. In License Use Context
5. In Call Back Event
6. InOut Challenge

The Principle identifies the requester of the license. The Component Name is a string that identifies the product seeking a license. The Component Version is a string identifying the version of the product requesting the license.

The License Use Context is a CORBAservices Property List. This parameter appears in all three requests of the Producer-Specific License Service. This property list is used to convey information about the user's runtime context.[4] The specification cites a whole list of examples for the property list. Here are some of the potential properties that an LS may use: Host Name or Node Name, User ID, Network Protocol, Date, Time, Process ID, Public Key, Hardware Model or Description, or Operating System.

The Call Back Event is a CORBAservices Push Consumer Event Channel. The client forwards this event channel so the LS can call back to the client with an event notification, if that is a part of the license strategy. The InOut Challenge parameter was described earlier.

The resulting license handle is an Any. The license handle is a parameter for both Check Use and End Use and associates these operations with the same licensing session begun by requesting Start Use.

---

3. As noted earlier, the approval of Security for the ORB will likely change this parameter.

4. This parameter may also change in light of the Security adoption. The Context that Security describes now conveys information similar to what this parameter anticipates. Since the LS changes are not out as of this date, we document their original intent.

25.2.2   Check Use

The Check Use operation has no result and takes five parameters:

1. In License Handle
2. In License Use Context
3. Out Recommended Check Interval
4. Out Action to Be Taken
5. InOut Challenge

The license handle comes from the Start Use operation. It continues the current license session through this association.

The License Use Context is a CORBAservices property list and has the same description as that of the Start Use request. It may be the same or a different property list.

The Recommended Check Interval is an unsigned long.[5] Generally, this parameter is a suggestion to the producer client about how often it should request Check Use. Its specific meaning, however, may be modified by the Action to Be Taken parameter.

Action to Be Taken is advice from the Producer-Specific License Server to the producer client. Action is a structure composed of six members:

1. Action Required
2. Notification Required
3. Wait for Confirmation After Notification
4. Notification Duration
5. Producer-Specific Notification
6. Notification Text

The Action Required member is an enum with two values:

1. Continue
2. Terminate

This advice, in essence, expresses the state of the license. Continue indicates the license is still valid and processing may continue. Terminate indicates that processing should stop according to the current licensing policy.

Both Notification Required and Wait for Confirmation After Notification are enumerators called Answer. Answer has two values, Yes and No. Notification Required set Yes is an indication that the producer client should notify the user of the license.

Wait for Confirmation After Notification is only interesting if the previous member was set to Yes. If it was set Yes and this member is set Yes, then the producer client is expected to await some acknowledgment by the user after receiving the notification.

---

5. This should change to a CORBAservices Time Interval Object in the future but the Time Services came after the License Service.

Notification Duration is interesting when the Notification Required is Yes and Wait for Confirmation is No. In this case, the Duration (an unsigned long) is set to the amount of time to wait after notification before processing continues. The specification does not state the granularity of this duration.

Producer-specific Notification is an object reference. Obviously, the Producer-Specific License Server and the producer client need to collaborate on the type of the object, what it does, and what requests it excepts. Examples given by the specification include: policy information or instructions, or time and date of license expiration.

The final member of the Action Required structure, Notification Text, is a string. This member may contain the text for notification if such an action is indicated.

The Challenge parameter in Check Use operates the same as its previous description.

25.2.3 End Use

The End Use operation has no result and takes three parameters. The operation is used by the producer client to notify the Producer-Specific License Server that a license session is terminating. The three parameters are obvious:

1. In License Handle
2. In License Use Context
3. InOut Challenge

All of these function in the capacities previously mentioned in Sections 25.2.1 and 25.2.2 and need no additional elaboration.

CHAPTER 26 *Externalization Service*

*The absolute natures or kinds are known severally
by the absolute idea of knowledge.*
—Plato, from *Dialogues, Parmenides,*
134 (c. 428–348 BC)

The externalization service provides a means to stream out an object's state (externalize) and later, to stream it back in (internalize). The in and out may occur on different objects, effectively performing a copy from one object to another. Where the stream goes (and exists) between externalize and internalize operations is an implementation detail except in one case, when explicit file operations externalize to a file and then internalize from the file.

Externalization and internalization stream object state out of and back into objects.

26.1 EXTERNALIZATION INTERFACES

Nine externalization interfaces have been defined:

1. Stream
2. Stream Factory
3. File Stream Factory
4. Streamable
5. Streamable Factory
6. Stream I/O
7. Node
8. Relationship
9. Role

The first three are for the client's use. The second three are used by the service (the Stream object or the Stream I/O object). The last three are used also by the general stream service when Relationship service graphs connect a series of streamable objects and they are all to be streamed, such as a container of objects.

26.1.1 Stream

The client must have a reference to a Stream (an object bearing the Stream interface) or it must create one via a factory. Much of the externalization interface plays well with the Life Cycle Services and so Factory Finders are used.

26.1.2   Stream Factories Interfaces

Two types of factories exist:

1. Stream Factory
2. File Stream Factory

Both have a single operation, Create, which returns a Stream (see Example 26-1). In the case of the File Stream Factory, the Create operation takes a file name parameter.

26.1.3   Stream Interface

The Stream interface has five operations:

1. Externalize
2. Internalize
3. Begin Context
4. End Context
5. Flush

EXAMPLE 26-1. **Stream, Stream Factory, and File Stream Factory object interfaces**

```
#include    "LifeCycle.idl"
#include    "Stream.idl"

module CosExternalization
{
    exception   InvalidFileNameError      {};
    exception   ContextAlreadyRegistered  {};

    interface   Stream : CosLifeCycle::LifeCycleObject
    {
        void    externalize(in CosStream::StreamableObject theObject);

        CosStream::Streamable internalize(in CosLifeCycle::FactoryFinder there)
            raises (CosLifeCycle::NoFactory);

        void    begin_context() raises (ContextAlreadyRegistered);
        void    end_context();

        void    flush();
    };

    interface   StreamFactory
    {
        Stream  create();
    };

    interface   FileStreamFactory
    {
        Stream  create(in string theFileName) raises (InvalidFileNameError);
    };
};
```

Externalize takes the reference to a streamable object and Internalize takes a reference to a Life Cycle Factory Finder.

Begin and End Context operations are for externalizing multiple objects to a stream. The client invokes the Begin Context before the first and End Context after the last object.

The Flush operation essentially performs a Commit after Externalize so that the client can go about its business.

26.1.4   Simple Service Interfaces

An object that participates in the service (is willing to externalize its data or internalize some external data) is streamable. Streamable objects are bearers of the streamable interface (see Example 26-2).

EXAMPLE 26-2. **Streamable and Streamable Factory object interfaces**

```
#include    "LifeCycle.idl"
#include    "ObjectIdentity.idl"
#include    "CompoundExternalization.idl"

module  CosStream
{
    exception   ObjectCreationError     {};
    exception   StreamDataFormatError   {};

    interface   StreamIO;

    interface   Streamable : CosObjectIdentity::IdentifiableObject
    {
        readonly attribute CosLifeCycle::Key   external_form_id;

        void    externalize_to_stream(in StreamIO targetStreamIO);

        void        internalize_from_stream(
                        in StreamIO sourceStreamIO,
                        in FactoryFinder there)
            raises (
                CosLifeCycle::NoFactory,
                ObjectCreationError,
                StreamDataFormatError);
    };

    interface   StreamableFactory
    {
        Streamable  create_uninitialized();
    };
```

26.1.5   Streamable Interface

The Streamable interface has one read-only attribute, External Form ID, which is a Life Cycle Key. This contains enough information for a Factory Finder to find a factory that can make an equivalent streamable object for internalization to an uninitialized object.

The Streamable interface also has two operations:

1. Externalize to Stream
2. Internalize from Stream

When a client makes a request on a Stream to externalize an object, the Stream invokes the object's Externalize to Stream operation and passes it a target parameter. The target is a Stream I/O interface (see Example 26-3). The object then participates. The description is in Section 26.1.6.

When a client requests a Stream to internalize an object, it passes a factory finder to the Stream. It uses the factory finder to locate an appropriate factory, which constructs uninitialized, essentially stateless, streamable objects. The streamable factory has a single operation, Create Uninitialized, which returns a reference to a streamable object.

The Stream then asks that streamable object to Internalize from Stream, passing it a source Stream I/O.

Internalize from Stream also takes a Factory Finder parameter (presumably the same one that passes to the stream object, though not necessarily). When the Stream consists of multiple objects, the Internalize from Stream implementation can use this to construct the additional uninitialized objects that are necessary to internalize the entire stream.

26.1.6   Stream I/O Interface

The Stream I/O interface has many operations: one Read and one Write for each IDL data type. All the Write parameters take an instance of the IDL type they are to write. Only two read operations take parameters. More details on these operations appear in the following paragraphs.

When the streamable object's Externalize to Stream operation is invoked, it calls Write for each type it contains until all data is written.[1]

When a streamable object's Internalize from Stream operation is invoked, it calls Read for each type it contains until all of its data is internalized and suitably initialized.

---

1. Note that an object may write only some of its internal state if it is able to compute other states during an internalize form stream. In other words, it may conspire with other objects to take shortcuts during streaming.

The exceptions mentioned above are the Read Object and Read Graph (not an IDL data type). The Read Object operation takes two parameters:

1. Streamable Object
2. Factory Finder

The Streamable Object parameter provides two different uses: (1) to internalize an existing object and (2) as an indication to use the Factory Finder.

EXAMPLE 26-3. Stream I/O object interface

```
interface   StreamIO
{
    void    write_string(in string aString);
    void    write_char(in char aChar);
    void    write_octet(in octet anOctet);
    void    write_unsigned_long(in unsigned long anUnsignedLong);
    void    write_unsigned_short(in unsigned short anUnsignedShort);
    void    write_long(in long aLong);
    void    write_short(in short aShort);
    void    write_float(in float aFloat);
    void    write_double(in double aDouble);
    void    write_boolean(in boolean aBoolean);
    void    write_object(in Streamable aStreamable);
    void    write_graph(
               in CosCompoundExternalization::Node starting_node);//the parameter name
                                   // for the Node is not in the spec (book) so I
                                   // reuse the one from the read_graph operation
    string  read_string() raises (StreamDataFormatError);
    char    read_char() raises (StreamDataFormatError);
    octet   read_octet() raises (StreamDataFormatError);
    unsigned long read_unsigned_long() raises (StreamDataFormatError);
    unsigned short read_unsigned_short()
        raises (StreamDataFormatError);
    long    read_long()
        raises (StreamDataFormatError);
    short   read_short()
        raises (StreamDataFormatError);
    float   read_float()
        raises (StreamDataFormatError);
    double  read_double()
        raises (StreamDataFormatError);
    boolean     read_boolean()
        raises (StreamDataFormatError);
    Streamable  read_object(
                    in FactoryFinder    there,
                    in Streamble        aStreamable)
        raises (StreamDataFormatError);
    void    read_graph(
               in CosCompoundExternalization::Node starting_node,
               in FactoryFinder there)
        raises (StreamDataFormatError);
    };
};
```

By passing in a Streamable Object reference to the Read Object operation, the operation is useful for a Persistent Object Service (POS) protocol by supporting the Restore operation on an existing object when a transaction is aborted.

In the other case, a Null Object reference is the parameter. When the Streamable Object is null, the implementation will use the Factory Finder to create an instance for the Internalize operation.

Two additional operations are graph-related:

1. Write Graph
2. Read Graph

Both of these operations take the starting node of a graph. The details about graphs are in the following section.

26.1.7   Compound Service Interfaces

The Compound Service is for objects in the Relationship Service.

The Compound Externalization service interfaces are useful for externalizing and internalizing sets of objects that have relationships to each other as defined in the CORBAservices Relationships. Objects in such relationships are the nodes in a graph. Their relationships are the arcs. Roles are the definitions of the relationships.

The Compound Externalization service supports four sets of interfaces (see Example 26-4):

1. Node
2. Role
3. Relationship
4. Propagation Criteria Factory

Without going into all the detail, each of the first three interfaces supports a pair of operations: internalize and externalize.

The Role and Relationship interfaces also support one additional operation, Externalize Propagation, which returns a Propagation value specific to the current Role or Relationship.

The Propagation Criteria Factory interface has a single operation, Create for Externalize, which returns a Traversal Criteria. The details about Traversal Criteria are in Chapter 16.

During externalization, it is the responsibility of the Stream I/O's Write Graph operation to make sure that the externalization of the graph occurs in an orderly fashion (see Examples 26-5 and 26-6).

Stream I/O's Read Graph operation is responsible for orderly internalization of such relationships. It can participate in this because the Node interface's Internalize Node operation results in a sequence of Roles, thus defining all the relationships with which the Node participates.

EXAMPLE 26-4. Compound Externalization object interfaces

```
#include    <Graphs.idl>
#include    <Stream.idl>

module  CosCompoundExternalization
{
    interface   Node;
    interface   Role;
    interface   Relationship;
    interface   PropagationCriteriaFactory;

    struct  RelationshipHandle
    {
        Relationship    theRelationship;
        ::CosObjectIdentity::ObjectIdentifier    constantRandomId;
    };

    interface   Node : ::CosGraphs::Node, ::CosStream::Streamable
    {
        void    externalize_node(in ::CosStream::StreamIO sio);

        void    internalize_node(
                    in ::CosStream::StreamIO sio,
                    in ::CosLifeCycle::FactoryFinder there,
                    out Roles rolesOfNode)
            raises (::CosLifeCycle::NoFactory);
    };

    interface   Role : ::CosGraphs::Role
    {
        void    externalize_role(in ::CosStream::StreamIO sio);
        void    internalize_role(in ::CosStream::StreamIO sio);

        ::CosGraphs::PropagationValue    externalize_propagation(
                    in RelationshipHandle       rel,
                    in :CosRelationships::RoleName   toRoleName,
                    out boolean                 sameForAll);
    };

    interface   Relationship : ::CosRelationships::Relationship
    {
        void    externalize_relationship(in ::CosStream::StreamIO sio);
        void    internalize_relationship(
                    in ::CosStream::StreamIO sio,
                    in ::CosGraphs::NamedRoles newRoles);

        ::CosGraphs::PropagationValue    externalize_propagation(
                    in ::CosRelationships::RoleName fromRoleName,
                    in ::CosRelationships::RoleName toRoleName,
                    out boolean sameForAll);
    };

    interface   PropagationCriteriaFactory
    {
        :CosGraphs:TraversalCriteria    create_for_externalize();
    };
};
```

EXAMPLE 26-5. Externalization Containment object interfaces

```
#include     <Containment.idl>
#include     <CompoundExternalization.idl>

module CosExternalizationContainment
{
    interface   Relationship :
        ::CosCompoundExternalization::Relationship,
        ::CosContainment::Relationship
    {};

    interface   ContainsRole :
        ::CosCompoundExternalization::Role,
        ::CosContainment::ContainsRole
    {};

    interface   ContainedInRole :
        ::CosCompoundExternalization::Role,
        ::CosContainment::ContainedInRole
    {};
};
```

EXAMPLE 26-6. Externalization Reference object interfaces

```
#include     <Reference.idl>
#include     <CompoundExternalization.idl>

module CosExternalizationReference
{
    interface   Relationship :
        ::CosCompoundExternalization::Relationship,
        ::CosReference::Relationship
    {};

    interface   ReferencesRole :
        ::CosCompoundExternalization::Role,
        ::CosReference::ReferencesRole
    {};

    interface   ReferencedByRole :
        ::CosCompoundExternalization::Role
        ::CosReference::ReferencedByRole
    {};
};
```

CHAPTER 27 *CORBAfacilities*

*Mechanisms are the means whereby objects
collaborate to provide some higher-level behavior.*
—Grady Booch

CORBAfacilities, formerly known as Common Facilities, are more complex and of a larger granularity than CORBAservices. CORBAfacilities are compositions of services (facilities, if you will) that are used together in related ways toward common goals. These are frameworks that appear consistently within applications without regard to their domain.

CORBAfacilities are application frameworks.

CORBAfacilities are currently divided into two broad categories, horizontal and vertical. The horizontal facilities are application-generic and have the highest potential for reuse. The vertical facilities are more application-specific and tend to recur primarily within the application niche for which they are designed.

They are subdivided horizontally and vertically.

The horizontal facilities are part of the platform architecture and thus make recommendations by way of the Platform Technical Committee. The vertical facilities exhibit domain characteristics and, therefore, make recommendations to the Domain Technical Committee.

Both cross-sections are more concerned with and specific to application types than are CORBAservices, which are primarily concerned with objects. CORBAfacilities may often support CORBAservice interfaces. CORBAfacilities objects frequently may be bearers and audiences for various CORBAservices.

Partially because of their added complexity and partially because they build on CORBAservices, the CORBAfacilities are not as complete yet. Adoption of standard facilities is only just beginning, although a large number of what are considered to be desirable categories have been catalogued.

27.1 HORIZONTAL FACILITIES

The horizontal facilities that are identified so far are classified in four groups: user interface, information management, system management, and task management. Facilities are not limited to these four groups: they are simply the ones identified so far. Once vertical facilities start showing up in multiple vertical areas, such facilities will become horizontal.

Four groups comprise the horizontal facilities.

27.1.1   User Interface Facilities

The user interface group of horizontal facilities now includes:

- Rendering management
- Compound presentation management
- User support facilities
- Desktop management
- Scripting

User interface facilities are frameworks for desktops.

It is expected to include facilities for interface style, interface enablers (rendering, compound presentation, and user support facilities), and work management (working environment and desktop, and scripting for task and process automation).

Because the technologies for most of these are not yet adopted, the following section includes descriptions of the anticipated attributes and behavior of such components. Time will certainly revise these to some degree. Even when revised they should follow the general descriptions given here, so what is currently known is documented.

27.1.1.1 Rendering Management

Rendering provides common interfaces for input and output devices.

An object's rendition is the way it appears on some output device. Included among such devices are:

- Screens
- Printers
- Plotters
- Projectors
- Various audio devices
- Various video devices

The management facility also includes rendition of objects from input devices of various types:

- Keyboard
- Mouse
- Pointers
- Trackballs
- Scanners
- Speech recognition devices
- Video equipment

The facility includes things such as:

- Window managers
- User interface class libraries
- User interface dialogue objects
- Device abstractions

27.1.1.2   *Compound Presentation Management*

This merits a separate category in the CORBAfacilities because of its similarity to Microsoft's OLE. The specification is an extension of the OpenDoc facility for compound documents.

The compound presentation adoption is based on an extension of OpenDoc.

Compound presentation is a framework that provides support for multiple entities to share a window or other presentation forms. It is seen as a facility to manage the division of a window into distinct sections or parts, each of which may be peers or may in turn be embedded in other sections. It is explicitly seen as the display portion of a compound document architecture.

Among the issues that it needs to manage are:

* Geometry
* Event distribution
* Shared control
* Rendering

The principle classes (all in IDL) are:

* Object (`ODObject`)
  - Arbitrator
  - Binding
  - Canvas
  - Clipboard
  - Dispatcher
  - Dispatch module
  - Drag and drop
  - Facet
  - Focus module
  - Focus set
  - Info
  - Link manager
  - Link spec
  - Name space
    * Object name space
    * Value name space
  - Name space manager
  - Reference count object
    * Container
    * Document
    * Draft
    * Menu bar
    * Persistent object
      –Frame
      –Link
      –Link source
      –Part

- Shape
- Storage unit
- Transform
- Window
  - Session
  - Storage system
  - Storage unit cursor
  - Storage unit view
  - Translation
  - Undo
  - Window state

The primary support classes are:

- Object
  - Drag item iterator
  - Embedded frames iterator
  - Facet iterator
  - Focus owner iterator
  - Focus set iterator
  - Frame facet iterator
  - Link iterator
  - Link manager
  - Link source iterator
  - Name space manager
  - Object iterator
  - Platform type list
  - Platform type list iterator
  - Storage unit iterator
  - Type list
  - Type list iterator
  - Value iterator
  - Window iterator

The Compound Presentation and Compound Interchange Facility is a set of classes and not a parts editor. However, this list gives some idea of complexity and comprehensive coverage that this framework provides.

27.1.1.3   *User Support Facilities*

The importance of user support facilities shows in the desire to standardize their interfaces.

Many applications today include some specialized facilities to aid the user in the efficient and effective use of applications. Unfortunately, none appears to follow any specific standards, and they are frequently rewritten from scratch by each vendor. While this does provide some market differentiation, the CORBAfacilities predicts that standardization of such facilities interfaces is important.

The architecture currently cites two specific instances:

1. Help
2. Text checking

It also gives examples of five additional expected candidates:

1. Versioning
2. Annotations
3. Graph functions
4. Spreadsheet functions
5. Standard text

A number of characteristics are cited that are expected to be present in an adopted facility. These are cited separately for Help and Text Checking.

Help
Help is expected to have the following characteristics:

- Self-contained (stand alone)
- Operation support for access, presentation, and interchange
- Multiple presentation styles
- Standard storage format
- Multiple storage styles

Help is expected to support certain IDL operations at a minimum:

- Initialization and freeing (deallocation of consumed resources)
- Attaching and detaching to an application
- Rendering
- Querying by:
  - History
  - File name and path (possibly Help files)
  - Object name (the name of the object to which Help is attached)
- Printing (copying the rendered data to a hard-copy output service or device)

Text Checking
Text checking is expected to have the following characteristics:

- Self-contained (stand alone)
- Process support for strings and files of internationalized text
- Perform lexical checks of text (regardless of font or mark-up indicators):
  - Spelling (including hyphenations)
  - Grammar
  - Word relations (such as provided by a Thesaurus)

Text checking is expected to support certain IDL operations at a minimum:

- Initialization and freeing (deallocation of consumed resources)
- Operations on both original and changed text (for versioning support)

- Customization support for at least the lexical checks listed above
- Dictionary query and the ability to provide alternate, application-specific dictionaries

27.1.1.4   *Desktop Management*

Desktop management interfaces provide consistency in desktop visualization.

Desktop management facilities contribute to the conceptual visualization of the user's working environment. The premise is that a user-owned object may be specialized by desktop implementations. It also is fundamentally capable of being specialized further by the user, project, and enterprise, with instances of each being available.

Three categories of user-owned objects have been identified:

1. Information objects
2. Tool objects
3. Task objects

This model constitutes a similar split, as does model-view-controller or three-tier client-server architectures. In simplistic terms:

- Information objects are state (data).
- Tool objects are operations used on information.
- Tasks are the protocol descriptions of how tools operate on information: their contexts, ordering, and workflow.

Information Objects

Information objects are interfaces for managing information on the desktop.

The facilities architecture describes Information objects in terms of their interaction with tools and tasks, while only barely defining what constitutes information. It does reveal that the information may be application information or may apply to workflow, model, project, or resource information.

Additionally, such Information objects may participate in:

- *Aggregations*—structured information such as grouped in *n*-level containers
- *Versions*—to support the evolution of information
- *Configurations*—to support consistency or use

Information objects are primarily motivated by the data they contain and, as objects, support the tightly coupled operations that support their use.

Tool Objects

Tool objects operate on Information objects within or on the desktop.

Tool objects are application tools that operate on Information objects. The examples given are:

- Editors
- Simulators
- Browsers
- System management tools
- Hardware tools (printers, scanners, and so on)

Tool objects manipulate the information objects in an applied manner; in other words, as applications.

Task Objects

Task objects are the rules, or contexts, by which Tool objects operate on Information objects. Task objects are workflow instances (either macro or micro) and impose ordering on operations (what operations occur next, what came before). Therefore, tasks must be able to interpret results and infer sequencing information based on current context.

Task objects are the rules Tool objects use to manipulate Information objects.

27.1.1.5   *Desktop and System Object Collaboration*

The desktop management facility implies that component objects collaborate as a manageable entity. They also must participate as a subcomponent of an enterprise. This presumes that there is an enterprise-wide facility to organize, structure, manage, and administer such facilities. Examples of some of these are:

Facilities for user profiles, structuring, access, and concurrency and synchronization

- User profile facilities for individual management
- Organizing facilities for structuring projects or groups as formal organizational entities
- Object and resource access facilities for work-flow management or security control
- Concurrency and synchronization facilities and control for versioning, parallel operation, and simultaneous collaboration between users and objects.

27.1.1.6   *Desktop Management Operations*

The minimally interesting operations that this facility should provide are:

Management of installation, setup, and information, tool, and task objects

- Installation and setup
- Session management
- Information management
- Tool management
- Task management

27.1.2   Scripting

A scripting language is expected to support:

Desktop scripting is also a requirement.

- Functional decomposition
- ORB interfaces and services
- Visual programming

The scripting portion of the Desktop CORBAfacilities is seen as potentially tightly coupled with that used in the task management facility; in other words, they might use the same language for scripting.

The requirements as specified go on to explicitly state that the scripting language be *Turing-complete,* interpretable, and able to interoperate with a lot, if not all, of the standard services and facilities.

Scripts also may find use as agents, specifically in task management where the rules language could be a scripted agent. The agent qualities of the language also would have to support use of messaging and information exchange, both as users of and communicated entities. To paraphrase, such agents would need to use the services and be transmitted by those services. It is not a requirement that the scripts be agents, however.

27.2   INFORMATION MANAGEMENT

A facility for enterprisewide information management

This set of facilities is primarily targeted at making enterprise systems. It presumes that the enterprise is composed of heterogeneous sources of information. Its purpose is to provide the tools and facilities necessary to make all of the heterogeneous information sources play together in a useful manner. It does this up to the point of security, which it defers to other standards work.

It should manage data no matter what form it possesses.

Information in databases as well as that in documents, pictures or images, and other forms are all encompassed. The four categories composing the description of this facility are said to be topical categories as opposed to operational. However, the diagrammatic view is layered in a somewhat operational sense, as Figure 27-1 shows.

Information management is a somewhat unique set of facilities in that it is expected to be used by all of the other facilities. It is almost an object service in its availability but it is a semantically rich framework and not just an object. The complexity (its framework aspect) of information management is why it is truly a facility.

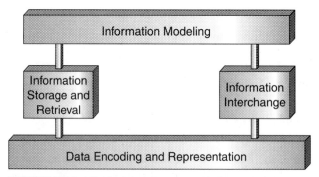

FIGURE 27-1. **The four components of information management**

27.2.1   Information Modeling Facility

Information modeling contains the structure, access, and maintenance rules. Such modeling facilities need to be able to respond to a wide variety of actual models within the enterprise, such as relational, object, hierarchic, and so on.

27.2.2   Information Storage and Retrieval Facility

Information storage and retrieval is targeted explicitly as managing storage technology products. This component (or series of such) needs to manage object-oriented, relational, networked (CODASYL), hierarchical, and other database products. This includes all of the various repositories used for a variety of purposes nowadays. Various text, document, image, and other graphics systems also require management.

Manages information in a variety of formats

This facility requires the ability to work with the various types of meta-information available with all of the above, as well as with some form of directory services, x.500 for example, in order to navigate or find such systems.

Requires navigation aids, which may be a directory service form

27.2.3   Information Interchange

Information interchange is not an individual facility, it is a category of facilities that so far has three identified members. As a whole, this category provides a commerce of information throughout the enterprise. Of necessity, it may include interchange even between dissimilar models, encodings, and media.

At least three areas require addressing.

This category is currently subdivided into three potential but primary areas to date, with more to come. Unfortunately this is the least specific area in all of facilities, and attempting to determine the precise distinction between each is left somewhat fuzzy. The first is primarily targeted as a framework for documents or complex forms of information: the Compound Interchange facility. The second is a more general-purpose or basic mechanism: a Data Interchange facility. The third proposes to enable a higher level of interchange, a semantic interchange: an Information Interchange facility.

27.2.3.1   *Compound Interchange Facility*

This facility specifically maps components through some form of persistent storage. It should include interfaces for the manipulation and interchange of data via that persistent storage.

Its presence as a separate facility is likely to permit optimization specifically in support of a Compound Document Architecture (CDA).

This is the Compound Interchange portion.

This facility description specifically mentions use with the compound presentation facility. The two together thus embody the necessary facility from which a complete CDA is composable and supportable.

This facility may address a variety of issues:

- Interaction to various presentation managers
- Immediate/interactive interchange (drag and drop, copy to a scratchpad/clipboard, or other operations on events)
- Deferred/batch interchange (bulk data transfer, disk copy, e-mail, and so on)
- Type conversion between entities conducting an interchange
- Canonical formats for interchanging data
- Something akin to a linking facility (store-and-forward, event notification of availability, and so on)
- The ability to annotate such objects

27.2.3.2   *Data Interchange Facility*

Data interchange expects more wide-ranging use.

The Data Interchange facility, on the other hand, appears to avoid the topic of persistent storage altogether. The services expected, however, are to offer a much wider range of use and a (hopefully) very lightweight implementation.

It does mention in passing that it may be used to do data exchange on behalf of compound document objects. In some sense, on that basis, it could be viewed as a linking service that complements what is expected so far from the Compound Interchange facility.

The intent is that this interchange is negotiable at runtime.

It goes on to express its potential services in terms of multiple protocols and multiple formats for the supported types of data, all of which appear to be negotiable at runtime.

The types of interchange listed are:

- Domain-specific objects, such as those generated via the externalization CORBAservice
- Structured data, such as OMG IDL defined data types (without the externalization service)
- Formatted data, including file formats, such as GIF, TIF, EPS, PDS, EDI, RTF
- Bulk data, presumably various streams
- Legacy wrapper to object, such as to a compound document object
- Legacy to legacy (both with wrappers), only the management of the interchange is under ORB control

For this to be a negotiable interchange, the facility may need to describe details about how and where to register or publish the supported protocols and formats. In theory, this would also support a means for the negotiation to make selection based on some criteria, such as optimal performance or quality of service. Such negotiation may occur or be built onto a trader service, however.

Some of the things that may be included in the technology are:

- *Methodology of interchange*—how to negotiate the necessary protocols
- *Allowable formats*—how to determine the set of formats available and how to negotiate the format to be used

- *Publication or registration of methodologies and formats*—the (meta-) protocol necessary for one object to make available its interchange mechanisms to one or more objects
- *Quality of interchange*—a way to describe the quality of the data available from an interface (quality of service, size, read-only, writeable, and other use-related factors)
- *Conversions supported*—appears to cover the non-native formats that an object understands; this is subtly different from allowable formats in that it suggests intermediate formats as opposed to direct support[1]

This facility may allow objects to pick and choose among the various data encoding and representation facilities offered.

27.2.3.3 Information Exchange Facility

The Information Exchange is described as a three-level service:

1. ORB Interoperability—infrastructure[2]
2. Object Data Interchange—service enabling technology
3. Information Exchange—semantics

Information exchanges are further classified as being mediated and nonmediated.

- Nonmediated—information exchange directly between objects
- Mediated—exchange through an intermediate object that may collate, collect, or modify data and/or operations from potentially multiple sources, in some effect creating new data

ORB Interoperability
This lowest level of service basically requires that data be described in IDL at both the sending and receiving ends. It does suggest, however, that this is a part of the ORB itself. So it is somewhat difficult if this was meant as a strong argument to others that an IIOP was highly desirable or if a framework of interfaces were needed for more complex interaction on top of the GIOP or ESIOP interfaces.

ORB interoperability is a framework to ease interoperability.

Object Data Interchange
This more elaborate middle-level service exchanges a richer set of information. The allusion is that the foregoing, lowest level of service provides only IDL descriptions minus interface types.

The object data interchange describes more interchange detail.

It suggests that it may specifically provide interfaces, with names in a context. This is referred to as a Semantic Data Service. The benefit is that one

---

1. The rationale is that the conversion software can have standard interfaces allowing wide reuse as opposed to replicating the capability everywhere in an application-specific manner as occurs now.
2. It is unclear whether this refers to the interoperability protocol, namely, GIOP, or if this something else. It appears the intention is for it to be a thin layer over one of the specified GIOPs or ESIOPs. It predates GIOP adaption.

can operate on such objects by name in context as opposed to having fore-knowledge of order within some set of objects.

Information Exchange

This highest level of service is operated within and upon by agents and mediators. The interchange at this level may include nontraditional data, presumably agents or programs.

The benefit is that it may create new data or data that is not stored somewhere within the system.[3] An example is an agent or mediator conducting a search for the requester and conjuring up new data as the result of such a search.

The Information Exchange facility is envisioned as composed of four services:

1. Content Language
2. Vocabulary
3. Communication
4. Interaction Control

Content Language Service.   This is the interpretable language used to express information, data structures, schema support, agent programs, and associated protocols, such as how to bind to, organize, and map between vocabularies, and transactions between entities. It also is an unambiguous method to utilize the vocabulary.

Vocabulary Service.   Vocabularies, which are expressed in the content language, must have a means of expressing the concepts that are desirable to communicate. Vocabularies may be specific to some domain and must support a mapping from an object's (sender or receiver) internal information to that of the vocabulary. Vocabularies may express organizations of data, such as schemas, class lattices, or first-order predicate calculus (ontilingua) constructs.

Communication Service.   The Communication service is a packaging service that bundles language with vocabularies used as well as the administration of the interchange services.

The Communication service uses the middle-layer object data interchange service to perform these services.

Interaction Control Service.   This basically controls who talks with whom as well as how. This service maps connections between objects and mediators (one-to-one, many-to-one, one-to-many). It also must determine issues of flow control, multicast, and the management of services, shutdown, recovery, cleanup, and session enablement, such as register, publish, and so on.

---

3. The word *system* may mean computer, network, or ORB.

27.2.4   Data Encoding and Representation Facility

This is the bottom layer of the information modeling facility. It is the fundamental agreement of a canonical form for data types. It also must include the methods to map between some internal form and the canonical form.

Application-level data encoding details

Encoding and representation handles issues such as preferred language sets, compression methods, lossy or lossless encodings, privacy (encryption), integrity (checksum), and other quality-of-service issues.

This is a higher-order facility than that integrated into the transport. It is an application-level service allowing or facilitating the mapping of data between objects having different notions (encodings or representations) of data that is semantically the same.

27.2.5   Time Operations Facility

The Time Operations facility is concerned with the management of time stamps, which are instances of Date Time Groups (DTG). In addition to time stamp, this facility needs to manage duration, as well as differences between two time stamps, or a start time stamp and a duration. Such differences are described as windows of time.

Time operations is a framework for time management.

27.3   SYSTEM MANAGEMENT

The system management facility is posed as an administration facility for four classes or scopes of tasks:

A framework for computer resource management and administration

1. System administration (user administration)
2. Application developer's management (developer administration)
3. System service provision (service provider administration)
4. System resource planning (enterprise administration)

Such administration encompasses tasks of control, management, monitoring, configuration, security, and policy. It needs to be concerned with physical systems management (computers, printers, modems, fax machines, terminals, routers—hardware) as well as logical entities (groups, users, processes, applications, domains—things made manifest through software).

Manages physical resources and logical entities within the enterprise

To date, 10 categories of manageable areas are listed as potential focal points for concentration:

1. Policy
2. Quality of service
3. Instrumentation
4. Data collection
5. Security
6. Collections
7. Instances

8. Scheduling
9. Customization
10. Events

Two additional areas are listed as potential future focal points:

11. Process Launch
12. Consistency

These latter two are not described. The preceding 10, however, are summarized in the following sections.

27.3.1 Policy

This facility requires mechanisms to group manageable objects under a policy. Policy controls creation, modification, and deletion of such objects. It supports activities such as default value assignment, validation checks for modifications, and the ability to define policy regions; that is, sets of policies over a group of manageable resources.

27.3.2 Quality of Service

This facility allows the selection of service level over four areas of quality:

1. Performance
2. Availability
3. Reliability
4. Recoverability

27.3.3 Instrumentation

This facility provides interfaces for the management of resource-specific data. It should provide a facility for gathering, managing, and disseminating such data. The following three examples are potential places where instrumentation management may be of interest:

- Workload
- Physical resource allocation by objects
- Responsiveness

27.3.4 Data Collection

This facility provides a mechanism to manage data collection that pertains to manageable objects. Two examples are cited:

1. Logging
2. History management

27.3.5   Security

The interfaces for this facility provide a way to manage security as an administrative task separate from whatever security is implemented.

27.3.6   Collections

This facility manages a type of object grouping, specifically those sharing two-way relations (a collection). Such operations may be applied equally to all members of the collection. It provides the ability to treat sets of objects as a whole, making it easier to query, catalog, and inform groups of objects in a single service request.

27.3.7   Instances

This facility manages collections of objects that are grouped by type. Objects sharing some common interface may also share some common policy. This allows administrators to treat multiple instances as a group.

27.3.8   Scheduling

The interfaces for this facility support the recurrence of administrative tasks. The recurrence may be triggered by regular or irregular events. A regular event may be a scheduled time. An irregular event may be an event generated by a system occurrence that occurs asynchronously.

27.3.9   Customization

This facility provides interfaces to manage the interchange of objects at runtime. Here interchange applies to the substitution of one object for another that has potentially greater capability. It is introduced to support the architecture's notion that the system is capable of switching to newer versions of objects or those with more capability without halting the entire system. If an object has no outstanding references, it is trivial. This facility is intended to support supplanting objects with outstanding references.

27.3.10   Events

This facility is intended to support all types of event management that are related to system management. It lists five possible areas to be considered:

1. Generation
2. Filtration
3. Registration
4. Aggregation
5. Forwarding

Each is specifically meant for use with management facilities.

27.4   TASK MANAGEMENT

Task management controls the workflow in the organization.

Task management is a fairly complex facility that has acquired a taxonomy of its own. The first part of this section describes the vocabulary coined by the CORBAfacilities group in order to describe the various aspects of task management. The vocabulary includes:

- Workflow definition
- Function
- Rules
- Tasks
- Information object

Tasks are blueprints or work plans.

Tasks are units of work designated for individual users or groups. They may designate single or composite operations. The operations may be serial, parallel, transient (slated only for one-time execution), or repeatable. Tasks are composed of information objects and workflow definitions. Task creation is the act of binding an information object to a workflow definition.

Information objects are targets.

An information object is the target of the tasks' operations. Such information objects may be simple (a calendar entry) or complex (multihierarchical compound documents).

Workflow is the order and control of functions.

Workflow definitions may occur in a multitude of forms. They are compositions of one or more functions and may be structured hierarchically or flat. Workflow definitions, which may contain other workflow definitions, express function-selection criteria as rules. Workflows also may derive or inherit other workflows.

Functions are atomic units that specify how they are invoked in their own execution environments. They are selected by the evaluation of conditions according to a rule. Function initiation and termination criteria may be described by a rule.

Rules express sequence and establish criteria for functions.

Rules may express sequences. Such flow sequences define the steps necessary for correct function operation. Steps may include evaluation for initiation, execution, or termination. Rules express evaluation criteria as the measure of the state of an information object.

27.4.1   Workflow

Workflow may occur ad hoc or preplanned.

The Workflow facility supports two general categories of workflow:

1. Ad hoc (transient)
2. Production based (predefined policy or procedures)

Construction may occur through scripting language or graphical interface (visual scripting), by establishing interactions between agents (predefined autonomous entities), and through other means for expressing user requests.

27.4.1.1   Ad Hoc Workflow

These are one-time or evolving task sets constructed by users or groups of users to facilitate their ability to manipulate information (knowledge work) on an as-needed basis. While such workflows may endure, they are generally constructed to solve a specific and immediate problem. Often, the original intent is not to construct a reusable entity and does not follow a predefined template or pattern.

Ad hoc workflow evolves or occurs only once.

27.4.1.2   Production-Based Workflow

These are conceived as recurring tasks or task sequences. This conception arises from fundamental policies or procedures that are in place in an organization. The field of solutions for this area is typically the domain of information systems. The operation or sequence of such operations are generally predefined by or for the organization. Key to their construction is the idea that they will be used and reused. Their operation is generally a response to a regularly scheduled time or stimuli.

Production-based workflow is a recurring task or sequence of tasks.

27.4.2   Agents

The agent facility includes two types of agents:

1. Static
2. Mobile

Static agents are generally tightly coupled to something in order to solve a specific problem. The static agent may be seen as a mobile agent that resides somewhere for an extremely long time. Mobile agents, also referred to as migrant or itinerant, are generally a form of complex messaging.

Static agents are resident, mobile agents itinerant.

Agents, in general, are semi-autonomous. They may reduce cognitive load, making tasks appear simpler. This may occur through reduction in the number of things a user must take under consideration during a task. An agent may have specialized knowledge about some category of task that enables it to perform on behalf of the user, with the intention of augmenting the user's capability.

Agents reduce cognitive load.

Agents may also support dynamic configuration or mobile computing. Such dynamism exhibits adaptive behavior by the agent in response to some stimulus or environmental initiatives.

A static agent acts as an agent engine, an execution facility in which a mobile agent actually executes. For example, mobile agents are seen to move from engine to engine. Agents may be referenced by name rather than by object reference. The possibility that agents are written in multiple languages may require support, for instance, Telescript, Java, TCL, and so on.

Agents must be concerned with:

• Marshaling and unmarshaling
• Encoding of agent containers

- Movement or migration
- Runtime registration and invocation of engines
- Runtime query for services offered and status
- Runtime security

and optionally:

- Identification and location
- Starting, stopping, and suspension
- Runtime discovery of agents and facilities, potentially by their categories

27.4.3 Rule Management

Rule management specifies and executes event-condition-action rules.

This facility manages the specification and processing of declarative event-condition-action rules. It manages acquiring, executing, and managing rules and associated facilities. It has some degree of similarity with agents in that they have a rules language and a rules engine. The language specifies the rules, and the engine executes them.

Additionally the facility needs to declare:

- How rules are used
- How they interact (between rules)
- The types of rules supported
- How they are managed and maintained
- How they are represented (for export or as notation)
- How they interact with objects

Such a facility has a widespread applicability within other facilities. It may be a subset of the agent facility or may act collaboratively in workflow facilities. They may even affect or interact closely with some services, such as object query or transaction services.

27.4.4 Automation

Automation helps manipulate large-grained routines.

This facility is targeted primarily at user-visible objects. Although not stated, similar functionality is obtained with what is known as the record/playback paradigm. However, it is not required to be only that. The automation facility is a means to automate the interaction between large-grained instances that a user would be interested in manipulating. This may occur through scripts or macros.

In order to accomplish these tasks, two interesting features are cited as requirements:

1. Encapsulation of a methods invocation as an object
2. Referencing objects through a relative specifier, as opposed to an object reference

For a coarse-grained language (a script or macro) to manipulate such objects, the objects must expose some portion of their capability. In order to manipulate or capture this capability, it must appear to be an object. Such an object, however, is a subset of the exhibiting object's behavior as occurs over a single operation or sequence of such operations. An example might be an object that increments the content of one spreadsheet cell by the value contained in another.

Automation may manifest a single operation of an object as an object.

A relative specifier is required because the automation appears strictly from the user's view. In most cases, what appears to a user as a single event is a group of objects collaborating. Such a relative specifier needs to be relative to the context as well as to the user's point of view. An example might be to delete the first word of the second paragraph on the fourth page of a report.

It may also manifest a single object as representative of a set of collaborating objects.

CHAPTER 28 *Vertical Market Facilities*

> *. . . the main effort, for now many years, has been a*
> *critical effort; the endeavor, in all branches*
> *of knowledge—theology, philosophy,*
> *history, art, science—to see the object*
> *as in itself it really is.*
> —Matthew Arnold,
> from *On Translating*
> *Homer* (1861)

Originally, the Vertical Facilities were central to CORBAfacilities with advice from Special Interest Groups (SIGs). Today, several of these SIGs are Domain (Vertical Market) Task Forces with a more specific charter.

Each Domain Task Force (DTF) represents those domain objects that are specific to a vertical market (problem domain). They are working toward establishing (and eventual selection of) common objects that are specific to their particular problem domain. These domain-specific objects are distinguished from the underlying architectural layers in that they are specific to business problem modeling and reflect the business, whereas the underlying architectures generally reflect software development (Von Neuman architectures).

28.1 THE DOMAIN TASK FORCES

The areas that are currently formal enough to be independent task forces are (see Figure 28-1):

- Business Object
- Electronic Commerce
- Financial
- Manufacturing
- Medical (Healthcare)
- Telecommunications

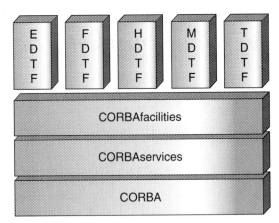

FIGURE 28-1.   Domain Task Forces

28.1.1   Business Object

The Business Object Task Force (BOTF) is almost a horizontal layer within the group of Domain Task Forces. Its focus is to develop common interfaces for general business objects. Formerly, the BOTF was known as the Business Object Management SIG (BOMSIG). It became a task force in January of 1996.

A special role befalls the Business Object Task Force (or Business Object Domain TF). They are working on problem domain objects that are potentially in use across different industries. For instance, a standard example is the Customer Object. A Customer is common across many vertical domains. It is not a CORBAfacilities issue since it is not a software framework. It is not an Object Service since it is not a secondary service that virtually all objects require. It is not specific to Financial's or Manufacturing's problem domains.

The BOTF is a repository for objects that are significant in more than one of the vertical domains (see Figure 28-2).

28.1.2   Electronic Commerce

The Electronic Commerce DTF (ECDTF) owns what are known as multimedia services. These services include content and commerce, and cover the following areas:

- Electronic content management
- Multimedia asset management
- Rights and royalties
- Electronic commerce (online retail)
- Electronic payment

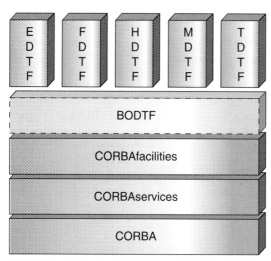

FIGURE 28-2. **OMA with Business Object**
and Domain-Specific
Task Forces

28.1.3   Financial

The CORBAfinancials Task Force (FDTF or CORBAfinancials) covers the financial services market. Some financial services are:

- Currency
- Monetary transactions
- Payroll
- Billing

The primary focus of its charter is on financial services and accounting interfaces and includes insurance and other areas. The FDTF was formerly known as the Finance SIG.

28.1.4   Manufacturing

The Manufacturing Domain Task Force (MDTF or CORBAmanufacturing) focuses on standard interfaces for all software and system aspects that are a part of the manufacturing or product life cycle. It covers but is not limited to areas such as:

- Development
- Product support
- Remanufacturing
- Recycling

28.1.5   Healthcare

The CORBAmed Task Force (HDTF or CORBAmed) concentrates on object
interfaces in the healthcare industry's domain.

28.1.6   Telecommunications

The Telecommunications Domain Task Force (TDTF or CORBAtel) centers
its efforts on identifying, specifying, and applying interfaces for the domain
of the telecommunications industry.

Glossary

Abstract Data Type An encapsulation of a data structure and the public procedures that manipulate that data structure into a single entity.

Activation The preparation of something that is to be made active on the runtime, along with the context needed for it to begin receiving requests and responding to them.

ADT See *Abstract Data Type*

Affinity A measure of interaction coupling between two communicating entities.

Affinity Analysis A means of analyzing the frequency of interaction between two or more entities.

Argument An instance of a parameter.

Attribute A characteristic of a variable that is implicitly visible and remembers procedural operations for an object.

Audience A client willing to avail itself of a service if offered.

Base Class The class that implements the base type.

Base Type The root node of type graph.

Basic Object Adapter A CORBA pseudo-object that is primarily responsible for one set of style-of-activation policies for CORBA objects.

Bearer A server offering a secondary service in addition to its primary functionality.

Behavior The semantic intent of an object contract.

Binding The time at which an association occurs between names and the aspect being bound, such as host or object code.

BOA See *Basic Object Adapter*

Business Rules A set or sequence of operations that perform meaningful services for a business.

Call Back A mechanism by which a server provides a deferred response to a client via a channel the client registers with the server.

CFA See *Common Facilities Architecture*

Class The structural description of an object that includes group management, extent, and life cycle operations for its members.

Client A requester of either services or resources, or both.

Client-implementation The functional code within a service requester.

Client-server The separation into two architectural entities—the client that makes a service request and the server that responds to it.

Client-Side Either in the client or on the request side of an operation.

COM Common Object Model.

Common Facilities CORBA object frameworks that are general, not application domain-specific, and have wide applicability to application construction.

Common Facilities Architecture The architectural model that acts as a basis and roadmap for the selection of Common Facilities.

Common Object Request Broker Architecture An architectural selection of the OMG for distributed object management and its associated services and frameworks.

Common Object Services CORBA object services that individual objects find useful in most systems.

Contract An object interface including its preconditions, postconditions, and invariants.

CORBA See *Common Object Request Broker Architecture*

COS See *Common Object Services*

Coupling An association between two entities that affects the demand on the computational environment.

DCE See *Distributed Communication Environment*

DCE CIOP See *DCE Common Inter-ORB Protocol*

DCE Common Inter-ORB Protocol The first ESIOP is the Common Inter-ORB Protocol, which is a subset of DCE.

DCOM Distributed Common Object Model

DII See *Dynamic Invocation Interface*

Distributed Communication Environment An RPC available from the Open Software Foundation.

Distributed Object Model The architecture and interaction model of objects in a distributed environment.

DOM See *Distributed Object Model*

DSI See *Dynamic Skeleton Interface*

Dynamic Binding Binding that occurs during runtime.

Dynamic Invocation Interface The dynamic counterpart of static IDL for making runtime requests on interfaces.

Dynamic Linking The runtime load and resolution of symbols for executable code.

Dynamic Skeleton Interface Runtime interpreter for skeleton code.

Dynamic Typing . The validation of structural characteristics of code at runtime.

Encapsulation An abstraction mechanism that hides data structure from public view except through manipulating procedures.

Environment Specific Inter-ORB Protocol A protocol for ORB interoperability that is useful and available in specific environments.

ESIOP See *Environment Specific Inter-ORB Protocol*

Event Service A notification service that interested objects may register for to receive notification of an event.

Exception The notification that some exceptional failure or fault condition has occurred.

Failure Model The set of all types and conditions under which a system (particularly distributed) may fail.

Filter A process that performs some fixed function on a stream from one process, passing it after processing to another process.

General Inter-ORB Protocol The protocol interface required for conformance to the requirements of CORBA interoperability.

GIOP See *General Inter-ORB Protocol*

Granularity An abstract scoping issue that is used to discuss objects and their size in terms of their functionality and the services they offer.

IDL See *Interface Definition Language*

IIOP See *Internet Inter-ORB Protocol*

Implementation The portion of a code composition that provides functionality when executed.

Inheritance The mechanism by which classes may be specialized from more general classes.

Inheritance Lattice A graph showing the inheritance relations for a family of classes.

Interface The complete protocol used by a class for all of its messaging.

Interface Definition Language The syntax and semantic specification of a language specific to defining interfaces.

Internet Inter-ORB Protocol The protocol required by the CORBA architecture for communication and operation between ORBs.

Invariants The aspects of a class that are true and never vary.

Invocation An instance of making a request.

Kind An indication of the nature of a particular quality.

Latency The roundtrip time from request to response.

Library Object Adapter   A theoretical object adapter with a style of activation that is well suited for dynamic libraries.

Life Cycle Service   An object service providing life cycle services—create, copy, move, delete—for objects.

LOA   See *Library Object Adapter*

Message Protocol   A message description.

Method   A single request or message made available by a server.

Middleware   A software layer that exists between an application and the operating system.

Narrower Type   A type in a graph that is toward the leaf-side.

OA   See *Object Adapter*

Object   An instance of a class that supports encapsulation, inheritance, and polymorphism.

Object Adapter   A component of the CORBA architecture that supports specific styles of implementation.

Object Data Management Group   A consortium of OODBMS vendors that are working toward standard CORBA interfaces for their products.

Object Linking and Embedding   A model for compound document composition.

Object Management Group   An organization that provides a forum for its members to agree on the minimal requirements for distributed objects and their associated services.

Object Reference   A runtime local (client-side) proxy of a CORBA object, which the client uses as if it were the actual object.

Object Request Broker   A proxy that decouples objects from their clients.

Objref   See *Object Reference*

ODMG   See *Object Data Management Group*

OLE   See *Object Linking and Embedding*

OMG   See *Object Management Group*

Operation   A method on a service.

ORB   See *Object Request Broker*

Parameter   The type of an argument in a signature.

Peer   A process that is generally a clone or at least equally capable of both making and servicing requests.

Persistent   Something that survives beyond a process.

Polymorphic   Something that exhibits polymorphism.

Polymorphism   The ability of an object to exhibit different behavior given the identical message.

Postconditions   Conditions that must be valid after a method is invoked.

PIDL   See *Pseudo-IDL*

Preconditions   Conditions that must be valid prior to method invocation.

Pseudo-IDL   IDL that describes something that will not be implemented in IDL.

Pseudo-object   An object whose creation does not depend on IDL.

Repository   A queryable store.

Request   A message send.

Request for Information   A request for preliminary information on a topic, which will then be used as advice to the writers of an RFP.

Request for Proposal   A solicitation for submission of technology that, minimally, meets or satisfies all of the included requirements.

Request-Response   A message send with result.

RFI   See *Request for Information*

RFP   See *Request for Proposal*

Semantics   Meaning.

Sender-Receiver   Entities involved with message-passing primitives.

Server   An entity providing a service or resource.

Server-side   Either in the server or on the response side of the message.

Service   Functionality performed on a requester's behalf

Signature   The complete description of a method that includes the message (parameter names and types) and the response (type) or the potential exceptional conditions that may be expected after invoking the method.

Skeleton   The server-side code output by the IDL compiler that has no implementation when produced.

Static Binding   The binding that occurs before runtime.

Static Linking   Linking that occurs before runtime.

Static Typing   Type checking that occurs prior to runtime.

Strong Typing   Strict typing.

Stub   The implementation code that the IDL compiler produces for the client-side of an object.

Subtype   A specialization of the current type.

Supertype   A wider type than the current type; to the root side of the type graph.

Three-tier   A client-server system (two-tier) that moves the business logic into a separate layer, or tier.

Two-tier   A client-server system in which the business logic is contained within either the client or server layers (tiers), or both.

Type   An abstraction used for composition that describes the underlying properties of an entity and, as a protection mechanism, is used to verify the expected consistency of such entities.

Type Extent   The complete set of all types.

Type Graph   A directed acyclic graph showing the relations of types to one another, where each type is a node and their immediate relation is an arc.

Up Call   The call made from the object adapter into an implementation, where Up indicates the call is directionally up the protocol stack.

Weak Typing   Type verification that is lackadaisical.

Wider Type   The immediate root-side type of the current type.

Bibliography

Agha, Gul, Peter Wegner, and Akinori Yonezawa, Eds. 1993. *Research Directions in Concurrent Object-Oriented Programming*. Cambridge, MA: MIT Press.

Ben-Natan, Ron. 1995. *CORBA: A Guide to Common Object Request Broker Architecture*. New York: McGraw-Hill.

[Booch-1994] Booch, Grady. 1994. *Object-Oriented Analysis and Design with Applications, Second Edition*. Menlo Park, CA: Benjamin/Cummings.

[Brooks-1975] Brooks, Frederick P., Jr. 1975. *The Mythical Man Month: Essays on Software Engineering*. Reading, MA: Addison-Wesley.

[Brooks-1987] Brooks, Frederick P., Jr. 1987. No silver bullets: Essence and accidents of software engineering. *IEEE Computer*, 20(4): 10-19.

Cattell, R.G.G., Ed. 1994. *Object Database Standard: ODMG — 93, Release 1.1*. San Francisco: Morgan Kaufmann.

Cattell, R.G.G. 1994. *Object Data Management: Object-Oriented and Extended Relational Database Systems*. Reading, MA: Addison-Wesley.

[Coppleston-1946] Coppleston, Frederick S.J. 1946. *A History of Philosphy, Volume I: Greece and Rome*. Westminster, MD: Newman Press.

Couch, Leon W., II. 1995. *Modern Communication Systems: Principles and Applications*. Englewood Cliffs, NJ: Prentice Hall.

Coulouris, George, Jean Dollimor, and Tim Knidberg. 1994. *Distributed Systems: Concepts and Design*. Reading, MA: Addison-Wesley.

Drucker, Peter F. 1985. *Management: Tasks, Responsibilities, Practices*. New York: Harper Colophon Books/Harper & Row.

Drucker, Peter F. 1989. *The New Realities: In Government and Politics/ In Economics and Business/ In Society and World View*. New York: Harper & Row.

Drucker, Peter F. 1992. *Managing for the Future: The 1990s and Beyond*. New York: Truman Talley Books/PLUME/Penguin.

Ellis, Margaret A., and Bjarne Stroustrup. 1990. *The Annotated C++ Reference Manual*. Reading, MA: Addison-Wesley.

Fingar, Peter, Dennis Read, and Jim Stikeleather, Eds. 1996. *Next Generation Computing: Distributed Object for Business*. New York: SIGS Books and Multimedia.

Ford, Warwick. 1994. *Computer Communications Security: Principles, Standard Protocols, and Techniques*. Englewood Cliffs, NJ: PTR Prentice Hall.

Gamma, Erich, Richard Helm, Ralph Johnson, and John Vlissides. 1995. *Design Patterns: Elements of Reusable Object-Oriented Software*. Reading, MA: Addison-Wesley.

Gorman, Michael M. 1994. *Enterprise Database in a Client-Server Environment*. New York: John Wiley & Sons.

Goscinski, Anderzej. 1991. *Distributed Operating Systems: The Logical Design*. Reading, MA: Addison-Wesley.

Graham, Ian. 1995. *Migrating to Object Technology*. Reading, MA: Addison-Wesley.

[Gregory-1987] Gregory, Richard, Ed. 1987. *The Oxford Companion to the Mind*. Oxford: Oxford University Press.

[Gries-1981] Gries, David. 1981. *The Science of Programming*. New York: Springer-Verlag.

Guttman, Michael, and Jason R. Matthews. 1995. *The Object Technology Revolution*. New York: John Wiley & Sons.

Halsall, Fred. 1996. *Data Communications, Computer Networks, and Open Systems, Fourth Edition*. Reading, MA: Addison-Wesley.

Hammer, Michael, and James Champy. 1993. *Reengineering the Corporation: A Manifesto for Business Revolution*. New York: Harper Business/HarperCollins.

Henderson-Sellers, Brian. 1996. *Object-Oriented Metrics: Measures of Complexity*. Englewood Cliffs, NJ: PTR Prentice Hall.

Hetzel, Bill. 1993. *Making Software Measurement Work: Building an Effective Measurement Program*. New York: John Wiley & Sons.

Hutt, Andrew T. F., Ed. 1994. *Object Analysis and Design: Comparison of Methods*. New York: John Wiley & Sons.

Islam, Nayeem. 1996. *Distributed Objects: Methodologies for Customizing Systems Software*. Los Alamitos, CA: IEEE Computer Society Press.

Jacobson, Ivar, Magnus Christerson, Patrik Jonsson, and Gunnar Overgaard. 1992. *Object-Oriented Software Engineering: A Use Case Driven Approach, Fourth Edition*. Reading, MA: Addison-Wesley.

Jacobson, Ivar, Maria Ericsson, and Agneta Jacobson. 1994. *The Object Advantage: Business Process Reengineering with Object Technology*. Reading, MA: Addison-Wesley.

[Khoshafian-1995] Khoshafian, Setrag, and Razmik Abnous. 1995. *Object Orientation, Second Edition*. New York: John Wiley & Sons.

Kilov, Haim, and James Ross. 1994. *Information Modeling: An Object-Oriented Approach*. Englewood Cliffs, NJ: PTR Prentice Hall.

[Lamport-1992] Lamport, Leslie. 1992. Quote from e-mail message sent by author.

Lampson, B. W., M. Paul, and H. J. Siegert, Eds. 1988. *Distributed Systems Architecture and Implementation: An Advanced Course*. New York: Springer-Verlag.

[Liskov-1988] Liskov, Barbara. 1988. Data abstraction and hierarchy. Proceedings of Object-Oriented Programming Systems, Languages, and Applications, Orlando, (October 1987). *SIGPLAN Notices* 23(5):17-34.

MacBride, Andrew R., and Joshua Susser. 1996. *Byte Guide to OpenDoc*. New York: McGraw-Hill.

Macrae, Norman. 1992. *John von Neumann*. New York: Pantheon Books/Random House.

Microsoft Corporation. 1993a. *OLE 2 Programmer's Reference, Volume 1: Working with Windows Objects*. Redmond, WA: Microsoft Press.

Microsoft Corporation. 1993b. *OLE 2 Programmer's Reference, Volume 2: Creating Programmable Applications with OLE Automation*. Redmond, WA: Microsoft Press.

Mowbray, Thomas J., and Ron Zahavi. 1995. *The Essential CORBA: Systems Integration Using Distributed Objects*. New York: John Wiley & Sons.

Mullender, Sape, Ed. 1993. *Distributed Systems, Second Edition*. Reading, MA: Addison-Wesley.

Naugle, Matthew. 1994. *Network Protocol Handbook*. New York: McGraw-Hill.

Object Management Group (OMG), Richard Mark Soley, Ed. 1992. *Object Management Architecture Guide*. OMG TC Document No. 92.11.1, Rev. 2.0, Second Edition. New York: John Wiley & Sons.

[OMG-1994a] OMG, Jon Siegel, Ed. 1994a. *Common Object Services Specification, Volume I*, by AT&T/NCR, BNR Europe, Digital, Groupe Bull, Hewlett-Packard, HyperDesk, ICL PLC, IBM, Itasca Systems, Novell, O2 Technology SA, Object Design, Objectivity, Ontos, Oracle, Persistence Software, Servio, SunSoft, Teknekron Software, Tivoli Systems, and Versant Object Technology. OMG Document No. 94-1-1, Rev. 1.0, First Edition. New York: John Wiley & Sons.

OMG. 1994b. *IDL C++ Language Mapping Specification: OMG RFP Submission by Expersoft Corporation*, by Digital, Hewlett-Packard, IONA Technologies, IBM, Novell, and SunSoft. OMG Document No. 94-8-2. New York: John Wiley & Sons.

[OMG-1995] OMG. 1995, updated March 28, 1996. *CORBAservices: Common Object Services Specification* (self-published).

OMG and X/Open. 1991. *The Common Object Request Broker: Architecture and Specification*, by Digital, Hewlett-Packard, HyperDesk, NCR, Object Design, and SunSoft. OMG Document No. 91.12.1, Rev. 1.1. New York: John Wiley & Sons.

Orfali, Robert, Dan Harkey, and Jeri Edwards. 1994. *Essential Client-server Survival Guide*. New York: Van Nostrand Reinhold.

Orfali, Robert, Dan Harkey, and Jeri Edwards. 1996. *The Essential Distributed Objects Survival Guide*. New York: John Wiley & Sons.

Otte, Randy, Paul Patrick, and Mark Roy. 1996. *Understanding CORBA: The Common Object Request Broker Architecture*. Upper Saddle River, NJ: PTR Prentice Hall.

Ozsu, M. Tamer, with Umeshwar Dayal and Patrick Valduriez. 1994. *Distributed Object Management*. San Mateo, CA: Morgan Kaufman.

Peters, Tom. 1987. *Thriving on Chaos*. New York: Harper Perennial/HarperCollins.

Putnam, Lawrence H., and Ware Meyers. 1992. *Measure for Excellence: Reliable Software on Time, Within Budget*. Englewood Cliffs, NJ: Yourdon Press Computing Series/PTR Prentice Hall.

Renaud, Paul E. 1993. *Introduction to Client-Server Systems: A Practical Guide for Systems Professionals*. New York: John Wiley & Sons.

Schwartz, Mischa. 1987. *Telecommunication Networks: Protocols, Modeling, and Analysis*. Reading, MA: Addison-Wesley.

Siegel, Jon, Ed., with Dan Frantz. 1996. *CORBA: Fundamentals and Programming*, by Digital; Hal Mirsky, Expersoft; Raghu Hudli, IBM; Peter de Jong, Alan Klein, and Brent Wilkins, Hewlett-Packard; Alex Thomas and Wilf Coles, ICL; Sean Baker, Iona Technologies; and Maurice Balick, SunSoft. New York: John Wiley & Sons.

Sims, Oliver. 1994. *Business Objects: Delivering Cooperative Objects for Client-Server.* New York: McGraw-Hill.

Spewak, Steven H., with Steven C. Hill. 1992. *Enterprise Architecture Planning: Developing a Blueprint for Data, Applications, and Technology.* New York: John Wiley & Sons.

Stallings, William. 1988. *Handbook of Computer-Communications Standards.* New York: Macmillan.

[Stevens-1971] Stevens, Wallace. 1971. *Poem from The Palm at the End of the Mind: Selected Poems and a Play.* New York: Vintage.

Sullo, Gary C. 1994. *Object Engineering: Designing Large-Scale Object-Oriented Systems.* New York: John Wiley & Sons.

Tanenbaum, Andrew S. 1996. *Computer Networks, Third Edition.* Englewood Cliffs, NJ: Prentice Hall.

[Taylor-1990] Taylor, David A. 1990/1998. *Object-Oriented Technology: A Manager's Guide, Second Edition.* Reading, MA: Addison-Wesley.

Taylor, David A. 1992. *Object-Oriented Information Systems: Planning and Implementation.* New York: John Wiley & Sons.

Taylor, David A. 1995. *Business Engineering with Object Technology.* New York: John Wiley & Sons.

Tsai, Thomas C. 1995. *A Network of Objects.* New York: Van Nostrand Reinhold.

Walton, Mary. 1988. *The Deming Management Method.* New York: Perigee Books/ Putnam.

[Yonezawa-1987] Yonezawa, A., and M. Tokoro. 1987. Object-oriented concurrent programming: An introduction, p. 13. In *Object-Oriented Concurrent Programming.* Cambridge, MA: MIT Press.

Index